AF731684

ANDAMAN & NICOBAR

DEVELOPMENT REPORT

सत्यमेव जयते

PLANNING COMMISSION

GOVERNMENT OF INDIA

Andaman and Nicobar Islands
Development Report

सत्यमेव जयते

PLANNING COMMISSION
GOVERNMENT OF INDIA
NEW DELHI

Published by

ACADEMIC FOUNDATION
NEW DELHI

First Published in 2008 by
Academic Foundation
4772-73 / 23 Bharat Ram Road, (23 Ansari Road), Darya Ganj, New Delhi - 110 002 (India).
Phones : 23245001 / 02 / 03 / 04. Fax : +91-11-23245005. E-mail : academic@vsnl.com
www.academicfoundation.com

Published under arrangement with :
Planning Commission,
Government of India,
New Delhi.

Cataloging in Publication Data--DK
Courtesy: D.K. Agencies (P) Ltd. <docinfo@dkagencies.com>

India. Planning Commission.
Andaman and Nicobar Islands development report /
Planning Commission, Government of India.
p. cm.
Includes bibliographical references (p.)
ISBN 13: 9788171886524
ISBN 10: 8171886523

1. Human services--India--Andaman and Nicobar Islands. 2. Infrastructure (Economics)--India--Andaman and Nicobar Islands. 3. Agricultural industries--India--Andaman and Nicobar Islands. 4. Andaman and Nicobar Islands (India) --Economic conditions. 5. Andaman and Nicobar Islands (India)--Economic policy. I. Title.

DDC 330.954 88 22

Designed and typeset by Italics India, New Delhi
Printed and bound in India.

Contents

The Core Committee 9
Message from Deputy Chairman, Planning Commission 11
Foreword from Member, Planning Commission 13
List of Tables and Annexures 15
Acknowledgements 19
Executive Summary 23

1. Development of Andaman Nicobar Islands: A Profile and Emerging Issues 33

Introduction
Area and Location
Climate
Demography
Natural Resources
Income Level and Growth in the UT
Infrastructure
Growth of Co-operatives
Growth of Small Scale Industrial Units (SSIs)
Growth of Registered Factories
Growth in Enterprises in Service Sector
Meagre Resources of the UT
Carrying Capacity of the UT
Emerging Issues
Directions for Development of UT

2. Financial Position and Outlook 55

Trends in Receipts and Expenditure
Structure of Expenditure
Status of Local Bodies
Resource Mobilisation
Expenditure Control
Institutional Framework
Revenue and Expenditure Projections for the Tenth Five-year Plan
Main Findings and Conclusions

...CONTD. ...

3. **Infrastructure: An Assessment** 67

Introduction
New Approaches to the Provision of Infrastructure
Roads and Bridges
Inter-island Connectivity
Civil Aviation
Urban and Rural Water Supply
Housing

4. **Shipping and Maritime Services** 75

Introduction
Present Status and Major Concerns
Development of Allied Sectors related to Maritime Transportation Services
Air Services between Mainland and ANI
Comparison of Shipping Costs per pax with Costs of Air Services
Summary of Main Proposals

5. **Human Development** 83

ANI in Human Development Map of India
Education
Health and Family Welfare
Nutrition

6. **Issues in Tribal Development** 99

Introduction
The Aborigines
The Nicobarese
Conservation and Development of Scheduled of Tribes (STs)
Health and Education
Empowerment of Tribals and Systems of Governance
Poverty Alleviation
Tribal Sub-Plans (TSP)
Some Concerns
Some Measures for Improving the Tribal Development Programmes

7. **Agriculture and Animal Husbandry** 119

AGRICULTURE
Status of Agriculture
Strategies for Improvement
Low Input—Low Volume—high Value Organic Agriculture
Specific Suggestions for Identified Crops
Post-Tsunami Scenario

ANIMAL HUSBANDRY AND DAIRY
Measures of Reclamation of Agricultural Land
Livestock: Status
Strategy for Development

8. Fisheries and Sea Food Industry 133

Strength, Weaknesses, Opportunities and Threats
Potential and Current Exploitation
Capture Fisheries
Pelagic
Demersal
Deep Sea/oceanic Fisheries
Strategy for Development
Coastal Fisheries
Upgradation/Replacement of Traditional Crafts with Motorised Boats
Construction of Mechanised Boats
Deep-Sea/oceanic Fisheries
Promotion of Private Long Liners/Purse Seiners
Commissioning of Collector Vessels
Ecolabelling
Fisheries Regulation
Infrastructure
Capacity Building
Improving the Socioeconomic Status of Fishermen and Strengthening Fishermen Co-operatives
Potential for Mariculture in ANI
Strategy for Development of Sea Food Industry
Seafood Processing
Summing Up
Recommendations

9. Small-scale, Village and Forest Based Industries 151

Organisational Set-up, Industrial Policy and Infrastructure in ANI
Contribution of Secondary Sector to GSDP
Issues
The Way Ahead
Bamboo based Industry
Handicrafts and Village Industries

10. Biodiversity Conservation and Forest Management 165

Introduction
Forest Management: An Overview
Management Units in the Current Working Plans
Future Strategies of Forest Management
Management of Mangroves
Cane and Bamboo Development
Application of GIS in Forestry Sector

11. Tourism in Andaman and Nicobar Islands 203

Introduction
Tourism Policy in ANI
Tourism Industry and Tourism Economy
Tourism in the Andaman & Nicobar Islands
Challenges for Tourism Development in ANI
Additional Issues in Tourism Development
Summary

...CONTD. ...

12. Manpower Planning and Employment 221

Employment and Population Dynamics
Trends in Employment
Trends in Labour Productivity
Issues
Measures to Improve Employment Situation
Measures to Improve Labour Productivity
Employment Generation: Some Projections

13. Disaster Management 239

Where Do We Stand?
The Coastal Regulation Zones, 1991
Disaster Management/Plan/Strategy/Mechanism in ANI
Suggestions

References 247

The Core Committee*

Dr. (Mrs.) Syeda Hameed — **Chairperson**
Member, Planning Commission

Chief Secretary — **Member**
Andaman & Nicobar Administration

Joint Secretary (State Plans) — **Member**
Planning Commission

M. Govinda Rao — **Member**
Director, NIPFP

The Study Team

National Institute of Public Finance and Policy, New Delhi (Lead Agency)
Rita Pandey
Mukesh Anand

Central Agricultural Research Institute, Port Blair
R.B. Rai, R.P. Medhi, N. Ravisankar
R. Soundarajan, S. Dam Roy, P. Krishnan, B. Ganesh Kumar

Indian Council of Forest Research and Education, Dehradun
Mudit Kumar Singh
M. Maria Dominic Savio

National Institute of Ocean Technology, Chennai
V. Sampath
M. Vijayakumaran

National Ship Design and Research Centre, Vishakhapatnam
K.V. Mohana Rao

Central Food Technological Research Institute, Mysore
V. Prakash

* Composition as on August 4, 2004.

एम. एस. आहलुवालिया
MONTEK SINGH AHLUWALIA

उपाध्यक्ष
योजना आयोग
भारत
DEPUTY CHAIRMAN
PLANNING COMMISSION
INDIA

MESSAGE

The Andaman & Nicobar Development Report is a result of the Planning Commission's initiative to sponsor State Development Reports with much of the work for preparation of the documents being done by reputed national level institutes. The endeavour is to produce quality reference documents on development profiles of individual States and UTs and the possible strategies for accelerating growth and development, and reducing poverty and inequality.

The Tsunami of December 2004 has adversely affected the livelihood of the people in Andaman and Nicobar Islands. The Report suggests a long-term plan to restore livelihoods and also highlights the critical gaps in infrastructure. The analysis and findings of the Report can provide useful inputs for policies and programmes.

I hope the publication of the Report will stimulate debate on the growth strategies appropriate for Andaman & Nicobar Islands and will assist the islands to move to a higher growth path and to achieve all round human and economic development.

Montek S Ahluwalia

(M.S. AHLUWALIA)

योजना भवन, संसद मार्ग, नई दिल्ली – 110001 दूरभाष : 23096677, 23096688 फैक्स : 23096699
Yojana Bhawan, Parliament Street, New Delhi : 110001 Phones: 23096677, 23096688 Fax : 23096699 E-mail : dch@yojana.nic.in

सत्यमेव जयते

डॉ. सईदा हमीद
Dr. Syeda Hameed

सदस्य
योजना आयोग
योजना भवन
नई दिल्ली–110 001
MEMBER
PLANNING COMMISSION
YOJANA BHAWAN
NEW DELHI-110 001

FOREWORD

In the Tenth Plan, the Planning Commission initiated the preparation of State Development Reports (SDRs) in coordination and with the support of State Governments and Union Territory Administrations. These reports are prepared by reputed national level institutions, aimed at taking stock of the affairs in important sectors, identifying critical gaps and suggesting the road ahead.

The Andaman & Nicobar Islands Development Report is a well-researched document incorporating the suggestions of planners, decision makers, NGO's and those who are concerned with achieving a better quality of life for the people of the islands. It analyses the entire range of development issues faced by our island territory in Bay of Bengal. National Institute of Public Finance and Policy (NIPFP), the lead agency for preparing the report, has coordinated the efforts of other partner agencies viz. Indian Council of Agricultural Research (ICAR), Indian Council of Forestry Research and Education (ICFRE), Dehradun, National Institute of Ocean Technology (NIOT), Chennai, National Ship Design and Research Centre (NSDRC), Vishakapatnam and Central Food Technological Research Institute (CFTRI), Mysore. The report is an outcome of a wide variety of views of experts and activists at meetings and seminars held in both Port Blair and New Delhi.

The Tsunami and earthquake on 26n December 2004 caused large-scale damage to the overall economy and infrastructure in Andaman & Nicobar Islands (ANI) and changed the development paradigm of these islands. The impact of these natural disasters and modification in development priorities have been incorporated in the report. These include several formidable challenges especially in social and economic infrastructure like health, education, issues related to tribal development, housing, ports, shipping and air connectivity.

I would like to place on record the Planning Commission's appreciation for the valuable inputs provided by Dr. M. Govind Rao, Dr. Rita Pandey and Dr. Mukesh Anand of the NIPFP; Dr. Ayyappan, Dr. R.B.Rai, Shri. R.P. Medhi, Shri N. Ravisankar, Shri R. Soundarajan, Shri S. Dam Roy, Shri P. Krishnan and Shri B. Ganesh Kumar of the ICAR; Dr. Mudit Kumar Singh and Shri M. Maria Dominic Savio of the ICFRE; Shri V. Sampath and Shri M. Vijaykumaran of the NIOT; Shri K.V.Mohan Rao of the NSDRC and Shri V. Prakash of the CFTRI.

I would like to thank Lt. Gen (Retd.) M.M. Lakhera and Prof. Ram Kapse, Lt. Governors of Andaman & Nicobar Islands, Shri Manoranjan Bhakta, Member of Parliament (ANI) and Shri Shumsher Sheriff, Shri D.S. Negi, Shri V.V. Bhat and Shri Pradeep Singh, Chief Secretaries, A & N Administration. I would also like to thank other serving and retired officials of A&N Administration

(SYEDA HAMEED)

दूरभाप : 23096570 फैक्स : 23096571
Telephone: 23096570 Fax : 23096571, E-mail: s.hameed@yojana.nic.in

List of Tables, Figures and Annexures

Tables

1.1 Population of India and Andaman Nicobar Islands 34

1.2 Population in the Age Group of 0-6 Years 34

1.3 Population, Child Population (Age Group of 0-6) and Literates by Resident and Sex (2001) 34

1.4 Population by Birth 35

1.5 Population Distribution under Various Age Group 35

1.6 Urban Population 36

1.7 Trends in Urbanisation in ANI (1951-2001) 36

1.8 District wise Population in ANI 36

1.9 Status of ANI on Selected Parameters in India (1991-2001) 37

1.10 Sex Ratio in ANI and Other UTs and States 38

1.11 Sex Ratio of Total Population and Child (0-6 age group) Population (2001) 38

1.12 Level and Growth of Incomes in India and ANI 39

1.13 Sector-wise Contribution to GSDP: Current and Constant Prices 41

2.1 Revenue Receipts and Expenditure of Andaman & Nicobar Islands 56

2.2 Tax-Wise Receipts of Andaman & Nicobar Islands: Revised Estimates 57

2.3 Item-Wise Non-tax Receipts of Andaman & Nicobar Islands: Revised Estimates 58

2.4 Expenditure of Andaman & Nicobar Islands: Actuals 59

2.5 Composition of Expenditure of Andaman & Nicobar Islands 60

2.6 Status Regarding Transfer of Function to Urban Local Bodies as per 74th Amendment of the Constitution 61

2.7 Revenue Receipts and Expenditure of Municipal Board of Andaman & Nicobar Islands 62

2.8 Revenue and Expenditure Projections of Andaman & Nicobar Islands for the Tenth Five-year Plan 64

3.1 State-wise Road Density by Area (km.) (Per '000 sq. km.) 69

3.2 State-wise Road Density by Population (km.) (Per Lakh of Population) 70

3.3 Villages Connected by Roads as on 31st March 1995 71

3.4 Per Capita Consumption of Electricity in Different States and UTs (kWh) (Arranged in Descending Order of 1999-00) 72

4.1 Vessels Operated by Department of Shipping Services in Andaman & Nicobar Islands 76

4.2 Arrival of Tourists in Andaman & Nicobar Islands....... 76

4.3 Demand for New Vessels in ANI 77

5.1 Human Development Indices 83

5.2 Literacy in Andaman & Nicobar Islands and other Union Territories and States 84

5.3 Rural Urban Literacy in Andaman & Nicobar Islands 85

5.4 Gross Enrolment Ratio 2000-2001 85

5.5 Dropout Rate in Class I-V 85

5.6 Dropout Rate in Class I-VIII 86

5.7 Dropout Rate in Class I-X 86

5.8 Adjusted Intensity of Formal Education 86

5.9 Accessibility of Schools in Rural Areas 87

5.10 Teacher-Pupil Ratio 87

5.11 Infant Mortality Rate 91

5.12 Infant Mortality Rate: Rural and Urban 92

5.13 Under Five Mortality Rate 92

5.14 Birth Rate 92

5.15 Death Rate 93

5.16 Death Rate: Rural-Urban 93

5.17 Number of Persons Reporting Ailment during Last 15 Days in Rural Area (1995-1996) 94

5.18 Number of Persons Reporting Ailment during Last 15 Days in Urban Area (1995-1996) 95

5.19 District-Wise Health Infrastructure in Andaman & Nicobar Islands 95

5.20 Beds in Hospitals 96

5.21 Share of Public Expenditure on Health in Total Public Expenditure 96

5.22 Ninth Plan Outlay and Expenditure 97

6.1 Distribution by Gender of the ST Population 105

6.2 Tribal Population in the A&NI 106

6.3 Distribution of Great Andamanese by Age and Gender (As on July 01, 2003) 106

6.4 Distribution of Onges by Age and Gender (As on July 01, 2003) 106

6.5 Distribution of Shompens by Age and Gender (As on July 01, 2003) 106

6.6 Adult Tribals Made Literate 108

6.7 Poverty in the Tribal Areas (Among the Nicobarese) 111

6.8 Ration Supply per Adult per Month 111

6.9 Year-wise Registration and Placement of Members of Scheduled Tribes 112

6.10 Tribal Sub-Plan (TSP)–I Draft Annual Plan 2003-04–Financial Outlays: Proposals for TSP 113

6.11 Statement Showing Funds Released and Unspent Balance from 1996 to 2002 114

6.12 Achievement of the Ninth Plan, Growth in the Size of the Tenth Plan 115

6.13 Structure of Outlay and Expenditure of the Total and Tribal Sub-Plan Component of the Ninth and Tenth Plans 116

7.1 Major Agricultural Crops Grown in different Islands 120

7.2 Series-wise Distribution of Soils (ha) in different Islands 121

7.3 Investment Requirements 122

7.4 Infrastructure Requirement for Spices 124

7.5 Infrastructure Requirement for Medicinal and Aromatic Plants 124

7.6 Exotic Tropical Fruit Crops with Export Potential 124

7.7 Infrastructure Requirement for Fruits 125

7.8 Infrastructure Requirement for Protected Cultivation of Vegetables 125

7.9 Infrastructure Requirement for Floriculture 125

7.10 Infrastructure Requirement for Green Orchid 126

7.11 Infrastructure Status for the Hi-tech Post-Harvest Handling in A&N Islands 126

7.12 Infrastructure for Value-added Coconut 126

7.13 Estimated Production Potential of Horticultural Crops 127

7.14 Livestock Population in Andaman & Nicobar Islands 131

7.15 Funds Requirements 132

8.1 Damage to Fishery due to Tsunami 133

8.2 Year-wise Details of Export of Fish and Fish Products (kg.) from ANI 134

8.3 Post-Harvest Infrastructure Facilities Available in ANI 134

8.4a Fishery Potential and Exploitation (Demersal) 136

8.4b Fishery Potential and Exploitation (Pelagic) 137

8.4c Fishery Potential and Exploitation (Oceanic) 138

8.5 Infrastructure Requirement for Development of Coastal Fishery 140

8.6 Infrastructure Requirement for Development of Deep-Sea/Oceanic Fisheries 140

8.7 Projection of Profit from Lobster Fattening Programme through Sea Cage Culture for Four sq. m. Area 143

8.8 Economics of Mud Crab Fattening 144

9.1a Medium Scale Industries in A&N Islands 1996-2003 152

9.1b Small Scale Industries in A&N Islands 1996-2003 153

9.2a Region-wise Small-Scale Industries in A&N Island as on 31.03.2003 153

9.2b District-wise Distribution of Small-Scale and Village Industries 2002-2003 153

9.3 Contribution of Industrial Sector to GSDP at Constant (1993-94) Prices 154

9.4 Growth of Secondary Sector (1993-94 to 1997-98) 154

9.5 Employment, Investment and Production in Small-Scale Sector in ANI 155

9.6 CAGR of Registered Factories during 1990-91 to 1995-96 156

10.1 Cane Species in the Middle Andamans 180

10.2 Estimation of Growing Stock of Cane in Middle Andaman Forest Division 181

10.3 Supply of Cane to Small-scale Industries (SSIs) and Settlers from Middle Andaman Forest 181

10.4 Cost Factors for Departmental Extraction of Cane 182

10.5 Quantity of Bamboo Collected 182

10.6 Trend in the Collection of Bamboo and its Correlation with the Population Increase 182

11.1 Distances of Some Selected National and International Locations from ANI 211

11.2 Promotional Expenditures in 1995 216

12.1 Distribution of Population (Workforce by Major Activities) as per 1991 Census 222

12.2 Employment in Organised Sector by State/Union Territory 222

12.3 Growth in Employment in Urban and Rural Areas 223

12.4A Per 1000 Distribution of Usually Working Persons in the Principal Status and Subsidiary Status Taken Together by Broad Industry Division for each State/Union Territory 225

12.4B Per 1000 Distribution of Usually Working Persons in the Principal Status and Subsidiary Status Taken Together by Broad Industry Division for each State/Union Territory 226

12.5A Per 1000 Distribution of Usually Employed by Category of Employment For Different States and Union Territories 227

12.5B Per 1000 Distribution of Usually Employed by Category of Employment for Different States and Union Territories 228

12.6A Percentage of Employed Persons who had Changed Nature of Work by State/UT, 1999-2000 229

12.6B Percentage of Employed Persons who had Changed Nature of Work by State/UT, 1999-2000 230

12.7A Labour Force Participation Rates by State/Union Territory, 1999-2000 231

12.7B Workforce Participation Rates by State/Union Territory, 1999-2000 231

12.8 Incidence of Unemployment in Urban and Rural Areas 232

12.9A Usual Principal Status Unemployment Rate among the Youth (15-29 years) for each State and Union Territory 233

12.9B Usual Principal Status Unemployment Rate among the Youth (15-29 years) for each State and Union Territory 234

12.10 Labour Productivity among Indian States and Union Territories in 2001-02 235

Figures

1.1 Trends in Per Capita GSDP 39

1.2 Trends in Per Capita Incomes: India and Andaman Nicobar Islands 39

5.1 CBSE Examination Result of A & N Islands (Pass Percentage) 88

5.2 Capital Public Expenditure on Education 89

5.3 Per Capital Public Expenditure on Health (In Rupees) 97

7.1 Land Utilisation Pattern 119

7.2 Reclamation of Agriculture Land 129

7.3 Reclamation of Agriculture Land 130

9.1 Behaviour of Marginal Productivity of Capital and Labour 154

9.2 Behaviour of Marginal Productivity of Capital and Labour 155

Annexures

1.1 State Domestic Product of ANI with 1993-94 Base 47

1.2 GSDP of ANI with 1993-94 Base, by Broad Groups of Sectors 47

1.3 NSDP of ANI with 1993-94 Base, by Broad Groups of Sectors 48

1.4 Growth Rates of Gross and Net SDP of Different States and UTs during 1993-94 to 2001-02, with Base as 1993-94 49

1.5 Employment Status in ANI 50

1.6 All-India Price Indices and Minimum Wage Rate in ANI 51

1.7 Co-operative Societies in ANI 52

1.8 Status of Industry, Commerce, and Motor Transport 53

2.1 Functions Specified for Transfer to Rural Local Bodies 66

2.2 Functions Specified for Transfer to Urban Local Bodies 66

9.1 Incentives and Supportive Measures Extended by Directorate of Industries, ANI 160

9.2 Registered Factory Sector in Andaman & Nicobar Islands 162

9.3 Status of Industrial Estates in 1999 163

9.4 Industrial Training Centres in A&N Island in the Year 1999 163

10.1 Biodiversity Conservation and Forest Management 183

13.1 Tenth Plans Schemes Towards Disaster Preparedness and Mitigation 244

13.2A Summary of Reconstruction and Rehabilitation Assistance 245

13.2B Sector-wise Summary of Reconstruction and Rehabilitation Assistance Requested by ANI 246

13.3 Measures taken by the ANI Administration to provide Immediate Relief after Tsunami 246

Pictures

10.1 Ecotourism in Andaman & Nicobar Islands 173

10.2 Coral Reef based Tourism at Jolly Buoy, Mahatma Gandhi Marine National Park 173

10.3 View of Mangrove Vegetation at Mahatma Gandhi Marine National Park 173

10.4 View of Degraded Mangrove Vegetation due to Biotic Interference 173

10.5 Artificial Regeneration of Mangrove Species in Andaman & Nicobar Islands 173

10.6 Natural Regeneration of Mangrove Species in Andaman & Nicobar Islands 173

Acknowledgements

Work on this Report was initiated at the behest of Planning Commission of India. We thank Planning Commission and Andaman & Nicobar Islands administration for entrusting the task of preparation of this Report to NIPFP as lead agency. In preparation of this Report we have received invaluable support and suggestions from people in different government departments and ministries and from various NGOs. A list of people whom we met and would like to thank is given below.

We are especially grateful to Dr. (Mrs.) Syeda Hameed, Member Planning Commission and Chairperson of the Core Committee overseeing the preparation of the Report for encouragement, advice and many constructive suggestions. We are also grateful to Dr. D.N. Tewari, former Member of the Planning Commission and former Chairman of the Core Committee for his overall guidance and extremely useful suggestions at the seminar held in January 2004 at Port Blair to discuss the draft report. Inputs received from Mrs. Adarsh Mishra, Principal Advisor to the Planning Commission, at the seminar held in September 2005 in New Delhi to discuss the draft final report and also during the course of the finalisation of the report were extremely helpful. We thank Dr. Rajan Katoch of the Planning Commission for very useful discussions and suggestions during the course of the report. Inputs received from Mr. R. Sridharan are also gratefully acknowledged. We also thank Shri Rajat Sachar of the State Plan Division of the Planning Commission for active coordination of the project and all the members of the Core Committee for their support from time to time.

We would like to express our appreciation for the cooperation extended to us by the officials of the Andaman & Nicobar Islands (ANI) Administration. In particular, we would like to thank Shri Pradeep Singh and Shri V.V. Bhat, former Chief Secretaries for their help during our visits to the Union Territory and for their insights into major aspects of the economy of the UT. Shri Dev Singh Negi, Chief Secretary, helped us with very useful information in preparation of Chapter 13 on disaster management and constructive suggestions at the seminar held in September 2005 in New Delhi. The staff of the Planning division of ANI administration deserves our special appreciation for their help in organising meetings and travel around the UT and as a resource unit for data and information in the report.

The preparation of chapters on some specific subjects in this report were commissioned to different institutions (specialising in these subjects) by the Planning Commission as follows: Chapter 4 on Shipping—National Ship Design and Research Centre, Vishakhapatnam; Chapter 7 on Agriculture—Indian Council for Agricultural Research (ICAR), New Delhi; Chapter 8 on Fisheries and Sea Food—ICAR and Department of Ocean Development, New Delhi; Chapter 10—Indian Council for Forestry Research and Education (ICFRE), Dehradun; and chapter on Science and Technology—Council for Scientific and Industrial Research (CSIR), New Delhi. On the advice of the Core Committee some changes were made in the chapter scheme of the draft final report. In doing this, material in the SDR had to be rearranged. Main changes include: background material provided by ICFRE on Bamboo Based Industry has been included in Chapter 9; background information on Science and Technology provided by CSIR has been included in Chapters 3, 5 and 9; and information on fisheries received from ICAR has been included in Chapter 8 in the report. A project team led by Dr. (Mrs.) Rita

Pandey at NIPFP prepared the remaining chapters of the report. NIPFP team also abridged and edited the chapters contributed by the above mentioned institutions to meet the requirements of the report. However, the responsibility for the contents of these chapters including the conclusions and recommendations lies with the respective institutions who have prepared these chapters. Dr. Pawan K. Aggarwal who was associated with the study in initial stage prepared drafts of Chapters 2 and 3. R. Periannan and Anurodh Sharma provided excellent secretarial assistance. Rita Wadhwa edited several chapters in the report. Dr. M. Govinda Rao, Director NIPFP and Member of the Core Committee, provided overall guidance, encouragement and advice to NIPFP team.

Hon'ble Lt. Governor, Prof. Ram Kapse

Dr. (Mrs.) Syeda Hameed, Member Planning Commission

Dr. D.N. Tewari, former Member Planning Commission

Mr. Manoranjan Bhakta, Member of Parliament, Lok Sabha

Mr. Bishnupada Ray, Former Member of Parliament, Lok Sabha and members of his think-tank Mr. Sripad Deshpande, Mr. Jaswant, Mr. Shankar Rao, Mr. A.K. Biswas, Mr. Mustafa, Mr. Ramamurthy

Mrs. Adarsh Mishra, Principal Advisor, Planning Commission

Mr. R. Sridharan

Dr. Rajan Katoch, JS (SP), Planning Commission

Mr. Dev Singh Negi, Chief Secretary

Mr. Pradeep Singh, former Chief Secretary

Mr. V.V. Bhat, former Chief Secretary

Mr. K.S. Siddhu, Chief Coordinator, Core Group, Tsunami Rehabilitation Programme, Planning Commission

Mr. Rajat Sachar, Director, Planning Commission

Mr. Anshu Prakash, DC and Secretary, Planning

Mr. S. Hemachandran, former DC and Secretary, Planning

Mr. Uddipta Ray, Secretary, Education

Mr. A. Anbarasu, Secretary, Tourism, IT, Transport, Tribal Welfare

Mr. M.M. Kutty, Secretary, Finance

Mr. S.S. Choudhary, CCF

Mr. K.K. Dahiya, CEO, *Zilla Parishad*

Mr. Ajay Chagti, ADM

Dr. (Mrs.) Namita Ali, Director, Health

Mr. R.N. Mangla, Director, Education

Mr. K. Mahesh, Director, Social Welfare

Mr. B. Mahto, Director, Animal Husbandry

Mr. Ashok Sharma, Director, Industries

Mr. M.A. Salaam, Director, Agriculture

Mr. S.A. Awaradi, Director, Tribal Welfare

Mr. Tarsem Kumar, registrar, Co-operative Societies

Mr. G. Rama Rao, labour Commissioner

Mr. K.C. Ghoshal, AC, Tribal Welfare

Mr. S.M. Dey, AC, Car Nicobar

Mr. Joshi, DC & DM, Nicobar

Mr. G.C. Khattal, CE, APWD

Mr. Manmohan Singh, SE, Electricity

Mr. Aberdeen Blair, Chieftain

Mr. Sameer Acharya, SANE

Swami Amrita Rupa Nanda, Secretary Ramakrishna Mission

Mr. Mohammad Jadwet, President Andaman Chamber of Commerce

Mr. P.R. Damodaran, Vanvasi Kalyan Ashram

Ms. Anuradha S. Chagti, Dy. Secretary, Planning

Ms. Aradhana Srivastava, NIPFP

Mr. Halder, Planning Officer

Mr. A. Selvam, Statistical Assistant, Planning

Mr. Ibrahim Ali Hussain, Vice Captain, Tribal Council

Mr. F.S. Richardson (MD, Ellon Hinengo Limited)

Mr. Akash Mahapatra, Director, Department of Information Publicity and Tourism

Mr. Jijo Thomas, Tourist Information Officer

Mr. M.K. Biswas, Assistant Secretary, Planning

Ms. Pratibha Pande, New Delhi

Dr. Sarang Kulkarni, Reef Watch Marine Conservation

Dr. Ravi Chellam, UNDP

Mr. Pankaj Sekhsaria, Kalpvriksh

Ms. Tara Gandhi, MSSRF

Dr. R. Mandal, MoEF

Ms. Ayesha Majid, Tribal Council, Nancowry

Mr. Rasheed Yosoof, Tribal Council, Nancowry

Rita Pandey
& Study Team

Executive Summary

Andaman & Nicobar Islands (ANI), a beautiful Union Territory situated in the Bay of Bengal is under the administration of the Central Government of India. The UT is bestowed with abundant marine resources and green vegetation. It has 349 islands and has a geographic area of 8,249 sq. km. of land. Of these islands only 38 have human habitation. Since prehistoric times these islands have been the homes of aboriginal tribes. The areas inhabited by tribal population are notified as tribal reserve which constitutes 34 per cent of the forest area. In 1858, the British founded a penal settlement here. These Islands were subsequently opened up for settlement for people from the mainland India, East Pakistan (now Bangladesh), Sri Lankan repatriates, and ex-servicemen.

The UT scores relatively well in terms of human development indicators, but faces problems of stagnation of per capita income and unemployment. This Report takes stock of the prevailing economic, social and ecological conditions in ANI, and assesses the main constraints to its economic progress and ecological sustainability. The Report recommends the policy and institutional changes required for achieving the objective of eco-friendly sustainable development. The key objectives of the development strategy are to create income generation opportunities by empowering the people through locally relevant education and employable skills, and building the requisite social and physical infrastructure.

Economy: The Present Challenges and New Strategy

The UT's total population is around 3.56 lakh. While nominal income of the UT has been growing at an annual rate of over 8 per cent per annum, since 1993-94 the real per capita income has stagnated. The incidence of unemployment has increased during nineties and has been more prevalent among women. Labour productivity has shown a declining trend since 1996-97. Furthermore, with more than 30 per cent population below the age of 25, the number of young people entering the workforce will increase in near future. Due to its geographical location and fragile ecosystem, the UT has certain limitations to absorb uncontrolled influx of people. It is reported, that the islands are already facing the problem of encroachment both of forest as well as revenue land.

A stagnant primary sector combined with declining industrial activity has severely limited employment opportunities outside government. Public administration has, by default, become the propelling force behind income growth. Development initiatives undertaken in ANI have often failed to produce desired results on account of lack of foresight and focused approach. The cornerstone of the development strategy pursued so far has been the direct involvement of administration in all areas of the economic activity rather than being an active facilitator. This has also had adverse implications for the financial health of the UT. Growth in revenue has decelerated and the composition of expenditure has substantially changed in favour of revenue expenditure undermining the growth potential of the UT. The expansionary impact of public expenditure in terms of income generation has been limited. This could partly be due to significant dependence of ANI on imports from outside and gaps in expenditure management.

Any developmental strategy in the UT must take into account its potential and build on its strengths: relatively high literacy rate and good health status; an abundant natural resource endowment; potential for development of tourism; and potential for exports of fishery products, medicinal plants, spices, coconut and horticulture products. The developmental strategy should, however, take note of the fact that ANI is a coastal region several miles away from mainland India; is a biodiversity hotspot with a variety of endemic species of flora and fauna; is home to ethnic communities—a large number which are dependent completely on the natural environment and resources; islands are dispersed and ecologically sensitive; and is located in a region identified under the 'seismic zone V'. Also, strategic location of the islands of this UT in terms of the defence of the country cannot be overemphasised.

Given the abundant natural resources in ANI it would be prudent that its development strategy is based on: (i) sustainable exploitation of natural resources—marine products, high value agricultural and horticulture products, and tourism; (ii) strengthening social infrastructure (in keeping with the requirements of thrust areas) like education, health, vocational training, farmers' training and extension services; (iii) developing physical infrastructure such as roads, modern communications network, efficient inter-island transport, adequate water and power supply, improved connectivity with mainland India, and neighbouring countries; and (iv) fiscal consolidation and reform.

Fiscal Consolidation and Reform

The broad contour of the fiscal reform includes healthy growth of revenues, broadening the resource base, strengthening tax administration, rationalisation of user-charges and subsidies, and ensuring expenditure efficiency and accountability.

In ANI deceleration in growth of revenue is mainly due to negative growth in receipts from two of the major revenue items, namely forestry and wildlife, and inland water transport, largely owing to the Supreme Court's ruling on conservation of forests. This, however, implies that the UT needs to look for new sources of revenue. While some additional revenue can be realised from the existing taxes such as property tax through administrative reforms, substantial revenue can be obtained by implementing sales tax in the UT. In view of the national consensus on replacing sales tax in all Indian states by a value added tax[1] (VAT), it will be prudent to introduce a simple system of VAT with a high threshold and single rate. A low rate of about four per cent would facilitate smooth introduction of the tax by minimising the potential local resistance to a new tax. Another major step in improving the finances of the UT would be to focus on production of those items that would reduce dependence on imports from outside the UT and/or provide competitive advantage in export out of the UT.

It would also be important to undertake a detailed study to identify areas where there may be clear scope for improving cost recovery in public services. However, caution needs to be exercised in assessing the potential for improving recovery rates by raising user charges, as there may be scope for reducing costs by locating and minimising sources of inefficiency including leakages in the provision of services. We should also take note of the fact that ANI is a small island economy and some subsidies may have been required to achieve some scale of operation, which in turn, may be technologically constrained. There is a possibility that presence of subsidy can lead to misuse and also attract people for settlement in these islands. There appears some evidence to suspect misuse/excess demand for some health services.[2] However, in the case of services where the introduction of service was a prime concern, the assessment of the subsidisation strategy should be viewed as a loss minimisation strategy.

Appropriate institutional arrangements would be necessary for successful implementation of these suggestions. For example, to realise the full-tax potential, it may be prudent to set up a separate tax department. A tax research unit in the tax department will also be required for formulating and evaluating tax policies and analysing implication of subsidies. Fiscal operations should be made transparent to public. There should be full disclosure of policy intentions, periodic reports on receipts and expenditure, and planning and implementation of development programmes. Computerisation and adoption of modern techniques of tax administration including self-assessment and selected audit of taxpayers would go a long way in imparting efficiency and improving revenues of the UT and the local bodies.

At the third tier of the governance, that is, at the local level, innovative techniques should be evolved in assessing property tax along with self-assessment.[3] The

1. In simple terms, VAT can be defined as a multi-point sales tax with set off for the tax paid on purchases. Accordingly, a dealer (shopkeeper) would pay sales tax on his purchases and collect sales tax on his sales, and pass on the excess collection (that is tax collected on sales minus tax paid on purchases) to the exchequer, periodically, which could either be monthly or quarterly.

2. Based on our discussions with people including government employees.

3. In assessing the property tax, some municipalities in India have shifted from rental value basis to a system based on physical characteristics of the property such as location, covered area. Feasibility of this system combined with self-assessment may be explored in the case of UT.

financial needs of the rural local bodies should be assessed normatively as advocated by the Second Finance Commission on Union Territories. And provision should be made for the necessary revenues or devolving the revenue resources to the local bodies.

Sectoral Strategies

Education, Health and Nutrition

ANI has made significant improvement in terms of creating infrastructure for delivery of school education. However, a lot remains to be done for improving the quality of education. Decentralised administration, involvement of stakeholders and NGOs, and performance measurement of schools will help bring about accountability into the performance of schools. Information on the islands' culture and ecosystem should be integrated into the syllabus of schools. This will inculcate in children an awareness of the fragility of the environment in which they live, make learning more relevant, and sensitise them to the importance of sustainable use of natural resources.

Creation of locally relevant technical and vocational skills in the labour force is crucial. Courses and curriculum of vocational and technical training schools should be reviewed in light of the identified thrust areas and to ensure that teaching modules are in tune with the market demand. Consultations with technical and vocational institutes of repute in the country will help a great deal in this effort. Specialised institutions in mainland India should also be encouraged to open outreach centres in ANI. The education department should set up a cell to monitor skills which are in demand in the market and for job opportunities.

Basic health indicators have improved significantly in ANI. A decentralised delivery of primary healthcare and meaningful participation of stakeholders and NGOs can help in further improving the quality of service. Provision of healthcare should have strong preventive focus. Traditional systems of medicines should also be encouraged. ANI has rich forest resources that have a variety of medicinal plants. Local knowledge also exists about holistic indigenous medical remedies. This should be effectively incorporated into the community health programme. Attractive packaging of these (especially for non-islanders and foreigners) has great potential for generating both employment and revenue. Alcoholism is an emerging problem. Community efforts in alcohol rehabilitation programmes are more effective than medical intervention. NGOs and community based organisations can make useful and effective contribution in addressing this problem.

Owing to a large number of cases of vitamin and iron deficiency in people, it is important to educate people about the importance of foods rich in vitamins and minerals. Initially, the administration may have to intervene to ensure that the vegetables and fruits are grown locally and made available to people at affordable prices. Vitamin and mineral rich local varieties such as bamboo shoots and *sahjan* that can be easily cultivated on the island should be popularised among islanders through media, and health and community workers. Also, a mobile hospital to provide specialised medical services in far-flung areas.

Infrastructure

Transport: Good transport system is one of the key determinants of economic development of an economy. Increase in population, changes in economic activity, lifestyle, and other demographic and social developments in ANI have resulted in an increase in demand for vehicles and also the number of trips. Condition of existing roads needs to be improved and new roads be constructed to provide better connectivity of the villages to the main roads, as also for inter-connectivity of the villages. To improve durability of roads, use of upgraded technology is essential. To facilitate smooth flow of traffic, some of the existing narrow culverts need to be replaced by suitable bridges, and some new bridges need to be constructed over some of the *nullahs*. To meet the financial needs of rural roads and bridges, the Tenth Five-year Plan provided a sum of Rs. 33 crore.

However, given the limited land area and topography of ANI, it is not feasible to rely on road expansion alone to improve the connectivity in the region. Abundant water resources in ANI offer an excellent opportunity to develop water-based transport facilities to carry people and goods between islands. This has not received the desired attention. For ships and boats being used currently, have outdated technology having adverse implications for the speed and environmental pollution.

There is a need to improve air services between ANI and the mainland. This could provide the necessary boost to trade and tourism in the UT. A plan for improving air connectivity of the UT in the medium term needs to be evolved. In this context, extending the length of airstrips at Diglipur and Campbell Bay may also be considered. For inter-island connectivity helicopter services are available in some of the islands and the existing infrastructure includes helipads at Port Blair, Rangat, Mayabunder, Diglipur, Car Nicobar, Neil Island, Havlock, Campbell Bay, and Nancowry. Expansion of helicopter services to Baratang, Long Islands, and other inhabited Islands has been under active consideration. Current level of subsidy in helicopter services is unsustainable. While fast mode of transport between the widely dispersed islands is desirable, it would be important to ensure that the inefficiencies in delivery of services are minimised.

Energy: Diesel generating sets are the major source of energy in the UT. Accordingly, the cost of production is very high in the range of Rs. 7 per unit. Dispersed habitats of varying sizes and population densities in ANI, call for a prudent energy policy, which is not dependent on only one or two conventional sources of energy but exploits a mix of energy sources in view of the local requirements and opportunities.

While islands with small population could be provided biomass based energy, islands with big population could be provided solar energy. In addition, other non-conventional energy sources such as wind, sun, biomass, sea tides should be exploited to the maximum extent. Initial studies do reveal potential of these energy sources on these islands, though further studies need to be conducted to design suitable projects and establish commercial viability of these projects. Some of the potential projects may include: OTEC Plants (10 to 50 MW) at South Andaman, Chingue Islands and Tillang Islands; Wind Farms at Car Nicobar; Solar Photo Voltaic Power Plants in the regions not covered by the conventional power supply, these could also supplement conventional power supply in other regions.

Water: Currently, about 150 lakh litre of drinking water is supplied everyday. Owing to the growth of population, demand for drinking water is expected to grow to 370 lakh litre by the year 2025 as per the available estimates. For meeting the growing demand for drinking water, the supply needs to be substantially augmented. This would require expeditious completion of the ongoing schemes, and identification of new commercially viable schemes. Such ongoing schemes include: revival of Dilthaman Tank; Nayagoan-Chakragaon Diggi Project; Chouldhan Scheme; and artificial ground water recharge schemes recommended by the Central Ground Water Board. In addition, two new schemes—raising the height of Dhanikari Dam and Indira Nullah Project may be undertaken to meet medium term requirement of the urban areas.

ANI receives good rains. In the absence of any conscious policy for rainwater harvesting, the UT has not been able to turn this huge advantage to the benefit of its people. Holistic approach on water harvesting is therefore, a must. In order to meet the long-term demand for drinking water, the feasibility studies initiated in respect of the tapping of water from the Rutland Island, and conversion of part of the sea at Flat Bay into a freshwater lake should be finalised early for seeking approval of the Ministry of Environment and Forests. The low thermal desalinisation water treatment technology successfully implemented in Lakshadweep should be replicated in ANI.

Capacity to treat raw water also needs to be augmented. The existing distribution system designed by Central Public Health & Environmental Organisation (CPHEEO) is considered to be adequate to cope with the projected water supply up to the year 2011. Additional clear water reservoirs would need to be constructed to cope with the supply load for subsequent years.

Rural Water Supply: As per census 2001, out of 502 villages only about 340 are fully covered by the public provision of water. Proper water treatment plants are available only in a few places such as Diglipur, Rangat, Mayabunder, Bakultala, Bambooflat and Kamotra. This implies that treatment plants need to be constructed to supply clean drinking water to other villages. Water should be duly treated by using locally available technology.

Housing: Studies for low cost housing, energy efficient housing, and earthquake resistant housing have already been conducted by various agencies like Laurie Bakers, Cost Fort Group, and Space Design Consultants. Their recommendations may be considered. ANI is located in a region identified under the seismic zone V, corresponding to high incidence of seismic activity. The region has one of the largest identified fault lines in the tectonic arrangement causing severe turbulence in the 10-degree channel separating the two groups of islands. Building by- laws in ANI should adequately reflect this. There is a need to popularise and promote locally available building materials in construction activity such as; timber, rocks and sandstones, cement/polymer composite sheets/ boards made from coir fibre, particle boards made from sawdust and rice husk.

Shipping and Maritime Services

The mainland-island sector is adequately served at present. However, MV *Akbar* needs to be replaced in 2006. The priority thus is to improve the inter-island sector services, especially to the southern islands. There is urgent need for improving the efficiency of services and rationalising the subsidy in shipping. The costs of air services between mainland and islands appear comparable with the costs of shipping services in this sector, if the capital, infrastructure, maintenance, and communication costs of shipping are included. In view of this, more flights may be introduced between mainland-island sector.

Considering the vital role of communications in the safety of sea operations, upgradation of shore-based facilities along the island coastline should be taken up. Because of the strategic location of the islands, the surveillance of the approaching vessels, especially in the northern and southern tip, is important. Two sub-control stations, one each at the northern and southern tip islands respectively, and a Master Control Centre at Port Blair, may be installed. A planned maintenance system in the form of a software package is a must to scientifically monitor the maintenance requirements of the vessel, thereby saving time and cost overruns usually associated with unplanned maintenance and repair. Technical capabilities of personnel need to be strengthened. Developing shipping related educational and training facilities should get top priority. A detailed feasibility study should be carried out to assess the feasibility of the proposed transshipment port at Great Nicobar Island which could be an alternative to Colombo port. An offshore bunkering facility in ANI as an extended service to the ships passing through this region once the transshipment port comes through may be considered.

Scheduled Tribes

The principal issue of concern for the tribes is 'influx' of the non-tribal. Influx leads to gradual impoverishment and reduced availability of resources but the greater damage occurs in disturbing the relatively calm social fabric.

Another important concern relates to 'medical and health' services, where specialised personnel are needed, especially for the gynaecological and orthopaedic cases. The issue of conservation and development of small and diminutive tribes may require some detailed study on aspects relating to inbreeding amongst such tribes. Transportation is also a serious concern for the tribals. Given the cost disabilities, it is imperative that the proportion allocated for the tribal sub-plans (TSPs) be revised upwards. Additionally, there is also a need to ensure that the funds allocated and expended under the TSP go on to directly benefit the tribal population. Within this broad sector, there is a more urgent need to strengthen the inter-island connectivity.

The strengthening and adaptation of the education system to their needs is another expressed concern of the tribal people. Introduction of vocational training may infuse greater efficiency in utilisation of the resources at their disposal. Their art and culture relating to painting and sculpting should be preserved and promoted. Specific efforts should also be made to conserve their traditional skills with ethno-medicine and herbal treatment.

The tribal who were mainly hunter-gatherers utilised substantial amount of available time for game hunting, collecting water, etc. for their normal sustenance. In general, they continue to have poor saving habits, perhaps because of relatively low perception of risk for sustenance and the relative abundance of resources. Given this background, (a) the supply of water, almost at the doorstep in all villages, (b) near complete electrification of the villages, (c) provision of scaled ration and clothing, etc. all without any commensurate requirement of labour, may result in inducing the tribals to lose their traditional skills and become addicted to doles. An important issue therefore relates to the gradual erosion of social mores and the menace due to introduction of foreign 'liquor'. There is thus an urgent need to reassess the existing system of doles and some approach should be adopted to foster development of the indigenous skills particularly those with potential for commercial exploitation, for example, fishing and bamboo cultivation. There is an urgency to realise the limitations of the mainstream people, to understand the needs of the tribals and they must be allowed to decide, for themselves, the pace at which they may wish to integrate with the mainstream.

Agriculture

Agricultural growth needs to be stepped up. The strategy should focus on low input-low volume high value agriculture. Food grain production should be at subsistence level; vegetables, oilseeds and perishables should be at semi-commercial level; and coconut, areca nut, medicinal plants, orchids should be at commercial level. In this context, the following measures need special attention: high quality seeds, modern production techniques, irrigation, access to credit, transport and marketing facilities, integrated pest management, and farmers' training. There is a good scope for export of high value products like coconut, spices, fruits, flowers, medicinal and aromatic plants and processed products. Organic farming should be promoted and product certification system should be developed to help farmers fetch relatively higher prices for their products. Coconut and areca nut are important crops in ANI however yield of these crops is low. Farmer's training in modern techniques of cultivation will improve the yield of these crops; and multi-tier cropping (with pepper, clove and nutmeg) will increase the value of produce per unit area. Modern methods for processing of *copra* should be used. In order to exploit the export potential, commercialisation of identified products needs to be encouraged by investing in marketing and storage facilities, promoting/developing linkages with food processing industries and creating efficient transport facilities. Agricultural extension services should be strengthened. Formation of 'organic agro-product estates' along the lines of Small Farmers Agro-Business Consortium should be considered.

Tsunami has caused severe damage to soil in ANI. Appropriate measures depending upon the extent and type of damage need to be taken to reclaim the agricultural land. In addition, a number of preventive measures will be required.

Fisheries and Sea Food Industry

With one-fourth of the total coastline of India and about 80 per cent of the total Exclusive Economic Zone, ANI has significant potential in fisheries. Present level of marine fish production is about 12 per cent of the estimated potential. Though recent earthquake followed by a tsunami has caused substantial loss (estimated at Rs. 34.37 crore) there is enormous scope for commercial exploitation of culture and deep-sea fishing. Concerted efforts would be required in realising this potential. This would include provision of pre- and post- harvest infrastructure such as boats, vessels, navigational aids; collection, handling, storage, processing, and packaging facilities; access to finance; training of fishermen; strengthening of fishermen co-operatives; transportation facilities; and aggressive marketing.

Specific recommendations include: (i) augmenting the supply of the raw material such as finfish, shellfish and seaweed through capture and culture fisheries for feeding the existing processing units and also to meet the needs of new units which should be encouraged to come up in near future; (ii) in the case of mud crab fattening, lobster fattening, and seaweed farming, people's participation should be encouraged. While technology for this could be provided by various institutions located in ANI, such as Andaman & Nicobar Centre for Ocean Science and Technology/ National Institute of Ocean Technology, Central Agricultural Research Institute and the Fisheries Department, the funding support for such activities could come either from the lead/commercial banks, National Bank for Agricultural and Rural Development (NABARD) and/or from the budgetary allocations made for fisheries related activities; (iii) introducing fishing crafts designed by CIFT; (iv) fleet of mechanised boats should be increased to 50-90 by the end of Eleventh Five-year Plan; (v) introducing integrated brackish water farming in tidal areas; (vi) introducing marine fisheries regulation act; (vii) and constructing landing centres and a major fishing harbour in Campbell Bay.

Small Scale, Village and Forest based Industries

The ecological and environmental conditions do not permit setting up of large-scale industrial units in ANI. Industrial development in ANI should focus on; fishery, agro and horticulture based fresh and processed products, cane and bamboo and related industries, and handicrafts units of small and medium scale. The encouragement to private investment in industry by ensuring the availability of basic inputs (commercialise identified products keeping in mind their commercial value and the comparative advantage of the island) and infrastructural facilities, and easing the process of various approvals is necessary. Commercialisation of identified products would imply establishing effective forward and backward linkages so as to sustain a symbiosis between industry and agriculture, encouragement to the use of modern technology and scientific techniques, investment in irrigation, development of fast means of intra-island transportation, and strengthening of farmers' training and extension services.

The UT will need to introduce relevant and quality vocational training programmes in line with industry needs. Private participation should be encouraged in this area as well.

Starting the process of reaching out to the investors besides convening meetings with them directly in order to attract investments in a viable fashion will be an important element of the industrial promotion strategy. Prospective for investment is not productive if done on a general basis. Such prospecting should be purposive after the identification of specific viable projects. It is here that besides the relevant departments of administration the Andaman & Nicobar Islands Integrated Development Corporation (ANIDCO) can make an important contribution to the development of the UT through the ongoing techno-economic studies followed by financing viable projects. It can also act as a catalyst in bringing other financing sources. Improvement in connectivity with mainland will provide greater confidence to financiers and investors. With the ongoing efforts of conducting trade pacts with neighbouring countries there would be much greater probability of full export potential being realised.

For promoting tiny sector, infrastructural support around clusters and upgradation of technology will be the starting point. Simultaneously, the government should promote links with external agents such as buyers and export traders. Such agents can provide management know-how, good quality raw material, good design, and new technologies. Government should also facilitate purposeful interaction between designers, NGOs, and craft producers.

Biodiversity Conservation and Forest Management

Future forest management strategy for the Andaman & Nicobar Islands should lay special emphasis on forest protection, conservation of biodiversity, scientific management of mangroves, cane and bamboo development, and promotion of high value, low volume ecotourism. Development of an effective communication network within the Department of Environment and Forests is essential for the conservation of biodiversity. Development of a sound database on forestry sector and implementation of the IT Plan already developed will facilitate planning and execution of development schemes as well as conservation plans. Projects on biodiversity characterisation and bio-prospecting, coral reef monitoring, mangrove conservation, and conservation and sustainable utilisation of medicinal plants should be undertaken in collaboration with institutions having expertise in these subjects. Special emphasis on environmental education through establishment of eco-clubs in schools, and creation of nature interpretation centres would be necessary to generate environmental awareness, especially amongst the young. To facilitate ecotourism in the islands, development of camping facilities, trekking routes, coral sighting trips and facilities to visit turtle nesting sites may be considered.

Joint Forest Management programmes needs to be launched on an experimental basis in selected areas. Social forestry and agroforestry should also be promoted for meeting the requirements of people in non-forest areas. Cultivation of cane and solid bamboo on private and revenue land needs to be encouraged. Agroforestry with multipurpose indigenous species including bamboo, cane, and other high value crops such as spices needs to be tried out. The ANI administration should encourage farmers to take up commercial plantation of bamboo. New technologies have been developed for making various value added products from bamboo. There is a need to commercialise these to provide a boost to the local economy.

Tourism

ANI offers good potential for tourism. The region offers spectacular nature and scenery, and opportunities for relaxation in peaceful setting. The principal challenge, facing the growth of tourism in ANI, is connectivity and the commensurate infrastructure to facilitate faster, direct and regular accessibility. However, caution needs to be exercised in that, any large-scale investment in transportation infrastructure development should be essentially backed by the priorities, needs, and demands of the resident population. In this regard, priority must be accorded to inter- and intra-island services.

The relative dearth of open land along with the need to conserve the green cover as well as the coastal zones of this fragile ecosystem, calls for greater stress on the development of water based transportation system. However given that airstrips already exist in Diglipur and Campbell Bay, these can be utilised with greater efficiency for transporting tourists from mainland to the islands.

Special effort must be made towards realistic assessment and projection of tourist traffic. This should keep in view the limited carrying capacity, short tourist amenable season and the sparse latitudinal distribution of the islands. The employment and income generating potential of tourism should also be cautiously analysed along both the quality and quantity dimensions. Caution needs to be exercised in that all tourists are not necessarily the 'high value' tourist. The availability of trained guides is a prerequisite towards promoting tourism and the existing perception on this aspect is not very encouraging. Closely linked to the perception of pristine environmental conditions is the availability of health and hygiene facilities. However, the commonly expressed view is that the islands lack in quality health facilities. Special efforts may have to be initiated to dispel such perceptions.

There is need for greater macroeconomic consistency in planning and investment including scope for private-sector participation. In the present structure, there exist multiple agencies with overlapping functions. Special drives for tourism promotion, by affiliating with the media and motion pictures association (including ecological and environmental content based television channels like, Discovery, National Geographic and History) can be very useful. Such drives may firmly place ANI in the viewers' mind-space. Increase in the level of promotional expenditures may have a salubrious effect on the quality and quantity of tourists. The commensurate eating, lodging and security needs should also be carefully assessed.

Employment Generation

Decline in growth of employment opportunities is reflected in the growing incidence of unemployment in the UT. A major concern is worsening employment scenario in rural areas—long-term shift in the structure of employment in rural areas shows that self-employment has eroded, share of regular employment has stagnated and casualisation of labour has increased. Yet another concern is low and declining productivity of industrial workers in ANI.

In the organised segment, the public sector continues to play a very dominant role, and accounts for more than 86 per cent of employment in the UT. It can not absorb more people. ANI needs a new approach to increase its employment potential—moving consciously to source jobs from non-organised sectors, particularly from rural-based farm and non-farm sectors. Fisheries, food processing, horticulture and floriculture, medicinal plants, bamboo and cane have great potential for generating employment. Tourism, handicrafts, ship repair and servicing also have good potential.

While physical remoteness and inadequate markets locally are crucial factors that have stifled the growth of potential sectors in ANI, it must be recognised that the investment plans of the UT have not given desired attention to investment on developing/improving necessary infrastructure for the development and growth in potential sectors. Such infrastructure would include efficient transport facilities, irrigation, crop (including sea food) storage, handling and processing, packaging, and marketing infrastructure. Government should make efforts to create a favourable environment for private investment to supplement its efforts. Opening up markets in the neighbouring countries by developing and opening waterways would also provide a thrust to growth in economic activity and employment.

Disaster Management

There is a need for greater emphasis on reducing risk factors by preventing/reducing the occurrences of natural phenomenon and also reducing the negative impact in the event of a natural phenomenon. This can happen when disaster prevention and mitigation is considered a high-return investment with benefits in the form of long-term cumulative cost savings.

Disaster management should be mainstreamed into development strategies/projects of all stakeholders—Central government, UT administration and local bodies, and international organisations, including the UN and international financial institutions. Programmes for disaster management should be action oriented and transparent with realistic targets and clear accountability. Measurable indicators should be developed to help the UT administration and other stakeholders assess their progress in implementation of disaster management programmes. ANI administration needs to be better equipped to undertake techno-economic and environmental appraisal of developmental projects to ensure the suitability of such projects for the UT. Ecological monitoring of various natural assets is yet another necessity. A suitable administrative arrangement for this purpose needs to be created.

Appropriate measures should be taken to induce a wider appreciation and sensitisation about the unique natural environment and ecology of the ANI and the risks associated with the unsustainable use of natural resources. In this context, it would be important to collect and institutionalise the widely dispersed traditional knowledge and customs in the islands to mitigate the risk of natural hazards; spread awareness among people about the various government programmes; and educate people about the importance of conservation and sustainable use of natural capital, and the need to adequately respond to early warning signals, and follow safety and evacuation plans. At the same time people can help put together and institutionalise the widely dispersed traditional knowledge and customs to mitigate the risk of natural hazards. Government responses based on community's own priorities, knowledge, and resources are likely to be more acceptable to people and thus more effective in reducing risk factors.

Adequate provision and maintenance of physical infrastructure such as safe shelter in the event of a natural phenomenon can be very capital intensive and can divert limited resources towards reducing perceived but infrequent risks rather than addressing more urgent social needs. Lifeline infrastructure in at-risk areas, such as health centres/hospitals, offices, emergency headquarters, schools, must be disaster-proof—serving both a protective and symbolic function. People are more likely to respond positively to evacuation plans when protective shelters are familiar structures located in familiar places.

Broader financial arrangement, in terms of social security and insurance can also be a significant institutional mechanism for relief and rehabilitation.

Chapter 1

Development of Andaman Nicobar Islands: A Profile and Emerging Issues

Introduction

Andaman & Nicobar Islands (ANI) is a Union Territory (UT) of India since 1956. It is under the administration of the Central Government of India. Presently, it does not have its own legislature. The East India Company developed Andaman Islands in the eighteenth century for providing safe harbour to its ships during the monsoons. Subsequently in 1858, the British founded a penal settlement here. In 1874, the Andaman & Nicobar Regulations placed the settlement under the Government of India with the Chief Commissioner as its judicial administrator. This pre-Independence administrative structure continued till 1982 when Lt. Governor replaced the Chief Commissioner as the administrator. Subsequently, a *Pradesh* Council with people's representatives was constituted to advise the administration. Until 31st July 1974, ANI constituted one district with its headquarters at Port Blair. On 1st August 1974, the Nicobar Islands was constituted as a separate revenue district with a Deputy Commissioner at Car Nicobar, the district headquarters.

Since prehistoric times these islands have been the home of aboriginal tribes namely; the Great Andamanese, Onges, Jarawas and *Sentinelese*, all of Negrito origin, in the Andaman group of islands, while the tribes in the Nicobar islands are Nicobarese, and the Shompens, both of Mongoloid stock. The areas inhabited by tribal population are notified as Tribal Reserve. The Tribal Reserves constitute 34 per cent of the forest area. These Islands were subsequently opened up for settlement for people from East Pakistan (now Bangladesh), Sri Lankan repatriates, and ex-servicemen.

Area and Location

ANI is a group of 349 islands and has a geographic area of 8,249 sq. km of land. Of these islands only 38 have human habitation. The UT consists of two groups of islands, *viz.*, Andaman & Nicobar, separated by 10 degree channel. There are 325 islands in Andaman group covering 6408 sq. km. area, while the Nicobar group has 24 islands covering 1,841 sq. km. These islands are situated in the Bay of Bengal between 6° and 14° North latitudes, and 92° and 94° East longitudes with 86.93 per cent recorded tropical rain forest. The northernmost point is about 901 km. away from the mouth of Hoogly River and about 190 km. from Myanmar. The southernmost island is Great Nicobar, whose southernmost tip is only 150 km. away from Sumatra, Indonesia. The capital of the ANI is Port Blair, which is 1,255 km. from Kolkata, 1,190 km. from Chennai and 1200 km. from Vishakhapatnam. There is abundance of marine wealth with 3 lakh sq. metres exclusive economic zone besides huge potential for culture fisheries. The UT is bestowed with abundant green vegetation.

Climate

The climate of these islands can generally be described as tropical, and warm. Temperature is moderate (23.5-31.2 °C) and the average humidity is high (80 per cent). The territory receives heavy rainfall in Southwest monsoon and Northeast monsoon. Annual normal rainfall varies in different parts of the territory

Demography

Settlers from the mainland dominate the population of ANI. Tribal population constitutes only 8.27 per cent of the total population. As per Census 2001, the population of the UT was 3,56,265 accounting for 0.03 per cent of the total population of India. In terms of the population this UT comes 32nd among the states

TABLE 1.1

Population of India and Andaman Nicobar Islands

Census Year	India			Andaman & Nicobar Islands		
	Population	Percentage Decadal Growth Rate	Annual Exponential Growth Rate	Population	Percentage Decadal Growth Rate	Annual Exponential Growth Rate
1951	361088090	13.31	1.25	30971	-8.28	-0.86
1961	439234771	21.64	1.96	63548	105.19	7.19
1971	548159652	24.80	2.20	115133	81.17	5.94
1981	683329097	24.66	2.22	188741	63.93	4.94
1991	843387888	23.86	2.14	280661	48.70	3.97
2001	1027015247	21.34	1.93	356265	26.94	2.39

Source: Census of India (2001). *Provisional Population Totals, Andaman & Nicobar Islands.*

TABLE 1.2

Population in the Age Group of 0-6 Years

Census Year	Population in the Age Group of 0-6 years	Percentage of the 0-6 Age Group to Total Population	Percentage Decadal Growth Rate in Population
1961	13859	21.81	
1971	23875	20.74	72.27
1981	39037	20.68	63.51
1991	46349	16.51	18.73
2001	44674	12.54	-3.61

Source: Census of India (2001). *Provisional Population Totals, Andaman & Nicobar Islands.*

and UTs in India. Though the decadal population growth in UT was higher than the all-India rates of 21.3 per cent and 23.9 per cent during the nineties and eighties respectively, there has been a continuous decline in the growth rate of population since 1971. For instance, decadal growth rates in sixties and seventies were 81.17 per cent and 63.93 per cent respectively as against 48.7 per cent during 1981-1991 and 26.94 per cent during 1991-2001 (Table 1.1). One of the main reasons behind the decline in population growth is decline in child (0-6 age group) population to -3.61 (Table 1.2) in nineties that appears to be due to low birth rate which in turn

TABLE 1.3

Population, Child Population (Age Group of 0-6) and Literates by Resident and Sex (2001)

District/Tehsil	Rural/Urban	Population		Age Group 0-6		Literates	
		Male	Female	Male	Female	Male	Female
A & N Islands	**Rural**	**128837**	**111021**	**15915**	**15535**	**94740**	**68968**
	Urban	**64148**	**52259**	**6818**	**6406**	**51796**	**37441**
Andaman District	Rural	106230	91602	13231	13004	79148	57906
	Urban	64148	52259	6818	6406	51796	37441
Diglipur Tehsil	Rural	22615	20265	3362	3219	15700	11516
	Urban	-	-	-	-	-	-
Mayabunder Tehsil	Rural	12745	11159	1625	1667	9566	7210
	Urban	-	-	-	-	-	-
Rangat Tehsil	Rural	20673	18142	2469	2437	15566	11491
	Urban	-	-	-	-	-	-
Ferragunj Tehsil	Rural	22235	19593	2393	2432	17329	13456
	Urban	3620	3170	414	380	2770	2120
Port Blair Tehsil	Rural	27962	22443	3382	3240	20987	14233
	Urban	60528	49089	6404	6026	49026	35321
Nicobar District	Rural	22607	19419	2684	2531	15592	11062
	Urban	-	-	-	-	-	-
Car Nicobar	Rural	10639	9634	1141	1061	7594	5801
	Urban	-	-	-	-	-	-
Nancowry Tehsil	Rural	11968	9785	1543	1470	7998	5261
	Urban	-	-	-	-	-	-

Source: Census of India (2001). *Provisional Population Totals, Andaman & Nicobar Islands.*

can be attributed to improvements in literacy, and life expectancy at birth, and low IMR.

Although ANI recorded a higher average annual population growth of 3.8 per cent during 1971-2001 compared to 2.1 per cent for all-India during the same period, but it is significant to note that there has been a steady decline in population growth rate in ANI since 1971 (Table 1.1). Table 1.3 gives the *tehsil*-wise population in Andaman & Nicobar Islands. The increase in population in this UT is to a large extent due to the immigration of people from mainland. While the inflow of people from other countries has declined significantly over the years, migration from mainland India still continues (Table 1.4). Of the Indian born population in ANI, one-third constitutes from the mainland. Among the population born abroad a majority are from Bangladesh. The migrant Indians are however from Tamil Nadu, Bihar, Andhra Pradesh, Kerala and West Bengal. Main occupations of the people include agriculture, animal husbandry, fishing, forestry and plantations, construction, transport, trade and commerce. Small-scale handicrafts also provide some employment avenues.

Age structure of population is an important aspect of demography of a region. An economy with a larger share of population in economically productive age group has high potential for growth. So far as the age structure of population in ANI is concerned two points are worth noting from Table 1.5. One, percentage share of 50+ age group and 15-19 age group has increased and that of 0-14 age group has declined during the eighties.

TABLE 1.4

Population by Birth

(Per Cent)

Census Year	*Born in India*	*Born Abroad*	*Unclassified*	*Born in Andaman and Nicobar Islands*	*Born in Other States of India*
1951	89.65	10.35	-	69.59	30.41
1961	83.43	16.57	-	59.53	40.47
1971	87.46	12.47	0.07	57.44	42.56
1981	91.53	8.46	0.01	64.95	35.05
1991	94.53	5.40	0.07	64.40	35.60

Source: Census of India, various issues.

Two, although percentage share of population in 0-14 age group has declined when compared with 1981 census figures, in absolute terms it accounted for 36 per cent of the total population in 1991 implying that a larger and larger number of young people will continue to enter the workforce. These people will also have to provide for an increasing number of elderly people.

According to 2001 census, the percentage of urban population in ANI is higher (32.67 per cent) than the national average (27.78 per cent) (Table 1.6). This, to a large extent, is due to the extension of the boundary of Port Blair town and due to the inclusion of 2 census towns, *viz.*, Garacharma and Bambooflat in the urban area. Himachal Pradesh has the lowest (9.79) percentage of urban population and Delhi (93.01 per

TABLE 1.5

Population Distribution under Various Age Group

Census/Age Group	*1971*		*1981*		*1991*	
	Population	*Percentage*	*Population*	*Percentage*	*Population*	*Percentage*
0-14	43706	37.96	74871	39.67	101630	36.21
15-19	8679	7.54	16325	8.65	28219	10.05
20-24	13222	11.48	19223	10.18	27762	9.89
25-29	14100	12.25	20191	10.70	29243	10.42
30-39	18589	16.15	27328	14.48	41038	14.62
40-49	9644	8.38	17253	9.14	27202	9.61
50-59	4162	3.61	7878	4.17	14371	5.12
60+	3031	2.63	5439	2.88	9546	3.40
Age not stated	-	-	233	0.12	1650	0.59
Total	**115133**	**100**	**188741**	**100**	**280661**	**100**

Source: Census of India, various issues.

TABLE 1.6

Urban Population

(Per Cent of Total Population)

Censu Year	Andaman and Nicobar	Chandigarh	Dadra and Nagar Haveli	Daman and Diu	Delhi	Lakshadeep	Pondicherry	Goa	Himachal Pradesh	Mizoram	India
1951	22.15	-	-	38.02	82.4	-	-	12.96	6.45	3.54	17.29
1961	22.15	82.80	-	36.36	88.75	-	24.11	14.80	6.34	5.36	17.97
1971	22.77	90.55	-	37.56	89.70	-	42.04	25.56	6.99	11.36	19.91
1981	26.30	93.63	6.67	36.75	92.73	46.28	52.28	32.03	7.61	24.67	23.34
1991	26.70	89.69	8.47	46.80	89.93	56.31	64.00	41.01	8.69	46.10	25.71
2001	32.67	89.78	22.89	36.26	93.01	44.47	66.57	49.70	9.79	49.50	27.78

Source: Census of India, various issues.

TABLE 1.7

Trends in Urbanisation in ANI (1951-2001)*

Census Year	Total Population	Annual Exponential Growth Rate for Total Population	Total Number of Towns	Total Urban Population	Present Urban Population	Decennial Growth of Urban Population		Annual Exponential Growth Rate for Urban Population
						Numbers	Per Cent	
1951	30971	-	1	7789	25.15	-	-	-
1961	63548	7.19	1	14075	22.15	6286	80.7	5.92
1971	115133	6.94	1	26218	22.77	12143	86.27	6.22
1981	188741	4.94	1	49634	26.3	23416	89.31	6.38
1991	280661	3.97	1	74955	26.71	25321	51.02	4.12
2001	356265	2.39	3	116407	32.67	41452	55.3	4.4

Note: * Prior to 1951, there was no urban area in this UT.

Source: Census of India (2001). *Provisional Population Totals*, Andaman & Nicobar Islands.

cent) recorded the highest. There was no urban area in this UT up to 1941. During 1951 census, Port Blair town was first declared as urban area which had a population at 7,789 accounting for 25.15 per cent of total population of this UT. The urbanisation trend in ANI is presented in Table 1.7. Population of Port Blair City is 1,01,186 as per 2001 census.

ANI consists of two districts, *viz.*, Andaman district and Nicobar district. While the Andaman district is divided into 5 *tehsils*, the Nicobar has two *tehsils*. 88.2 per cent population of the UT lives in Andaman district of which 37 per cent live in urban areas. Nicobar district does not have any urban areas. During the nineties decadal population growth rate in Andaman district was 30.4 per cent (55.3 per cent urban and 18.8 per cent rural) against 7.2 per cent population growth in Nicobar district (Table 1.8). The population density in A & N islands has increased from 34 per sq. km. in 1991 to 43 per sq. km. in 2001. The sparseness of this UT is reflected in its low population density *vis-à-vis* the all-India density of 324 in 2001. This UT ranked third, from the bottom, among all States and UTs in terms of population density (Table 1.9).

TABLE 1.8

District wise Population in ANI

Census	Andaman and Nicobar Islands	Andaman District	Percentage of District Population to Total Population	Nicobar District	Percentage of District Population to Total Population
1951	30971	18962	61.23	12009	38.77
1961	63548	48985	77.08	14563	22.92
1971	115133	93468	81.20	21665	18.80
1981	188741	158287	83.87	30454	16.13
1991	280661	241453	86.03	39208	13.97
2001	356265	314239	88.2	42026	11.8

Source: Census of India, various issues.

TABLE 1.9

Status of ANI on Selected Parameters in India (1991-2001)

States/Uts	*Area (Sq. km)*	*Population#*	*Density# (Person Per sq. km)*	*Urban# Population (Per cent)*	*Literate# (Per cent)*	*Per Capita Income## (Rupees)*
India	3287263	1027015247	324	27.78	65.38	10087
States						
Andhra Pradesh	275045	75727541	275	28.08	61.11	9,318
Arunachal Pradesh	83,743	1091117	13	20.41	54.74	9170
Assam	78,438	26638407	340	12.72	64.28	5978
Bihar	94,163	82878798	880	10.47	47.53	3768
Chhattisgarh	135191	20795956	154	20.08	65.18	*
Goa	3,702	1343998	363	47.77	82.32	*
Gujarat	196024	50596992	258	37.35	69.97	13434
Haryana	44,212	21082989	477	29	68.59	13709
Himachal Pradesh	55,673	6077248	109	9.79	77.13	9177
Jammu & Kashmir	222236	10069917	99	24.88	54.46	7435
Jharkhand	79,714	26909428	338	22.25	54.13	*
Karnataka	191791	52733958	275	33.98	67.04	10928
Kerala	38,863	31838619	819	25.97	90.92	9678
Madhya Pradesh	308000	60385118	196	26.67	64.11	*
Maharashtra	307713	96752247	314	42.4	77.27	15410
Manipur	22327	2388634	107	23.88	68.87	7213
Meghalaya	22429	2306069	103	19.63	63.31	7826
Mizoram	20987	891058	42	49.5	88.49	*
Nagaland	16579	1988636	120	17.74	67.11	*
Orissa	155707	36706920	236	14.97	63.61	5411
Punjab	50362	24289296	482	33.95	69.95	14678
Rajasthan	342239	56473122	165	23.38	61.03	8272
Sikkim	7096	540493	76	11.1	69.98	9818
Tamil Nadu	130058	62110839	478	43.86	73.47	12504
Tripura	10491	3191168	304	17.02	73.66	6604
Uttar Pradesh	53483	166052859	689	20.78	57.36	6373
Uttaranchal	238566	8479562	159	25.59	72.28	*
West Bengal	88752	80221171	904	28.03	69.22	9425
Union Territories						
A & N Islands	**8249**	**356265**	**43**	**32.67**	**81.18**	*
Chandigarh	114	900914	7903	89.78	81.76	*
Dadra & Nagar Haveli	491	220451	449	22.89	60.03	*
Daman & Diu	112	158059	1411	36.26	81.09	*
Delhi	1483	13782976	9294	93.01	81.82	*
Lakshadweep	32	60595	1894	44.47	87.52	*
Pondicherry	480	973829	2029	66.57	81.49	*

Source: #–Census of India (2001). *Provisional Population Totals*, Paper 1 of 2001, DCO, Andaman & Nicobar Islands.

##–Department of Planning, Economic and Statistical Organisation (2002). *Statistical Abstract of Haryana*, Government of Haryana.

*–Ministry of Information and Broadcasting (2002). India 2002, A Reference Annual, Publication Division, Government of India, New Delhi.

TABLE 1.10

Sex Ratio in ANI and Other UTs and States

Census	*Andaman and Nicobar Islands*	*Chandigarh*	*Dadra and Nagar Haveli*	*Daman and Diu*	*Delhi*	*Lakshadweep*	*Pondicherry*	*Kerala*	*Uttar Pradesh*	*Punjab*	*India*
1951	625	781	946	1125	768	1043	1030	1028	910	844	946
1961	617	652	963	1169	785	1020	1013	1022	909	854	941
1971	644	749	1007	1099	801	978	989	1016	879	865	930
1981	760	769	974	1062	808	975	985	1032	885	879	934
1991	818	790	952	969	827	943	979	1036	879	882	927
2001	846	773	811	709	821	947	1001	1058	898	874	933

Source: Census of India, various issues.

Sex ratio is one of the reliable indicators of the status of women in a society. High mortality rate among females, infanticide and foeticide affect the sex ratio adversely. Sex ratio in ANI though improved from 818 females per 1000 males in 1991 to 846 in 2001 it is low when compared with Kerala at 1058 and all-India at 933 (Table 1.10). However, sex ratio of 0–6 age group population in ANI was higher at 965 compared to 933 for all-India in 2001. What is worrisome is a decline in sex ratio of age 0–6 population from 973 in ANI in 1991 to 965 in 2001. Sex ratio in Nicobar district was higher at 859 *vis-à-vis* 844 in Andaman district. Amongst the 5 *tehsils* in Andaman, Diglipur *tehsil* has the highest sex ratio at 896 and Port Blair *tehsil* has lowest at 808. Rural areas in this UT have recorded a higher sex ratio at 862 (all ages) and 976 (0-6 age group) as against urban areas where sex ratio is at 815 (all ages) and 940 (0–6 age group) (Table 1.11). Decline in sex ratio in this age group has been observed in a number of states, during nineties, excepting Tripura, Mizoram, Kerala, Andhra Pradesh, Uttaranchal and Lakshadweep. To what extent this can be attributed to availability of means for sex determination needs to be investigated.

TABLE 1.11

Sex Ratio of Total Population and Child (0-6 age group) Population (2001)

UT/Dist./Tehsil	*Sex Ratio of Total Population*			*Sex Ratio of Child Population*		
	Rural	*Urban*	*Total*	*Rural*	*Urban*	*Total*
A & N Islands Total	**862**	**815**	**846**	**976**	**940**	**965**
Andaman District	862	815	844	983	940	968
Diglipur *Tehsil*	896	-	896	957	-	957
Mayabunder *Tehsil*	876	-	876	1026	-	1026
Rangat *Tehsil*	878	-	878	987	-	987
Ferrargani *Tehsil*	881	876	880	1016	918	1002
Port Blair *Tehsil*	803	811	808	961	941	948
Nicobar District	859	-	859	943	-	943
Car Nicobar *Tehsil*	906	-	906	930	-	930
Nancowry *Tehsil*	818	-	818	953	-	953

Source: Census of India (2001). *Provisional Population Totals, Andaman and Nicobar Islands.*

Natural Resources

According to the Forest Survey of India (2005), the ANI has about 87 per cent of the total geographical area as forest area and only about 50,000 ha is available for cultivation and allied activities distributed in various islands. At present the major crops being grown are paddy, coconut, areca nut, vegetables and fruits.

The soils of ANI have developed under dominant influence of vegetation and climate over diverse parental material. Soil cover is rather thin, varying from 2m to 5m. It is mostly alluvial on hilltops while diluvial in ridges and valleys. The coastal flats have an admixture of sand, silty clay and diluvial material with fine fragments of coral lime. The soil is, in general, mild to moderately acidic with humus on top. The water holding capacity of soil ranges between 100-200 mm/m.

Andaman & Nicobar Islands have an aggregate coastline of 1,912 km., which is about one-fourth of the total coastline of India. The continental shelf area is very limited with an estimated area of 16,000 sq. km. and the sea is very deep within a few kilometres from the shore. The Exclusive Economic Zone (EEZ) around the islands encompasses around 0.6 million sq. km. which is 30 per cent of the EEZ of India. This provides a great opportunity for fisheries and to exploit other marine resources. More than 2.4 lakh tonnes of pelagic, demersal and oceanic fishery resources are estimated to be available for exploitation but at present, only around 10 per cent of the estimated potential is being harvested.

Forests in ANI can be broadly categorised as evergreen forests, semi-evergreen forests, deciduous forests, littoral forests, mangrove forest, swamp forests, cane brakes and bamboo brakes. Islands have also been endowed with a variety of plants and animals which makes them an internationally acknowledged hotspot for biodiversity.

Income Level and Growth in the UT

A large coastline and rich natural resources in relation to the population in Andaman & Nicobar Islands has resulted in reasonably high per capita Gross State Domestic Product (GSDP). In 2001-02, per capita GSDP in the UT at Rs. 15,703 was higher than the all-India average of Rs. 12,203 by about 28 per cent (Table 1.12). In keeping with the overall trend in the country, the economic activity in the UT was dominated by the services sector with its contribution estimated at 47.5 per cent in 2001-02. The contribution of the primary sector was about 30 per cent whereas the manufacturing sector contributed just about 20 per cent of the GSDP in the UT. There is hardly any manufacturing activity in the UT and for whatever little there is, it is in wood processing and with the present restrictions on the exploitation of forests, the activity has naturally stagnated.

A worrisome feature of the income trends in the UT is the virtual stagnation of per capita income. The per capita GSDP in current prices has shown a steady increase until 1997-98, and after a marginal decline in the next year continued to increase thereafter. However, at constant (1993-94) prices, the per capita GSDP in the UT, after peaking at Rs. 18,058 in 1997-98, declined to Rs. 16,229 in 1998-99 and stabilised around Rs. 15,500 thereafter (Annexure 1.1, Figure 1.1). This is in contrast to the steadily increasing trend in per capita GDP in the country. Thus, the difference between per capita GSDP in the UT and the average per capita GDP in the country has continuously narrowed over the years. In 1981-82, per capita GSDP in the UT was more than double the per capita GDP in the country. By 2001-02, the difference has considerably narrowed and the per capita GSDP in the UT was higher than the country average by just about 20 per cent (Annexure 1.1, Figure 1.2).

TABLE 1.12

Level and Growth of Incomes in India and ANI

Year	Per Capita GSDP Andaman and Nicobar	Per Capita GDP-India	Time Period	Growth Rate: Per Capita GSDP Andaman and Nicobar	Growth Rate: Per Capita GDP India
1981-82	12901	6143	1981-1991	0.98	3.35
1991-92	14708	8199	1991-2002	0.01	4.23
1995-96	18862	9697	1993-2002	-0.94	4.20
2001-02	15703	12203	1981-2002	1.84	3.61

Source: Computed.

FIGURE 1.1

Trends in Per Capita GSDP

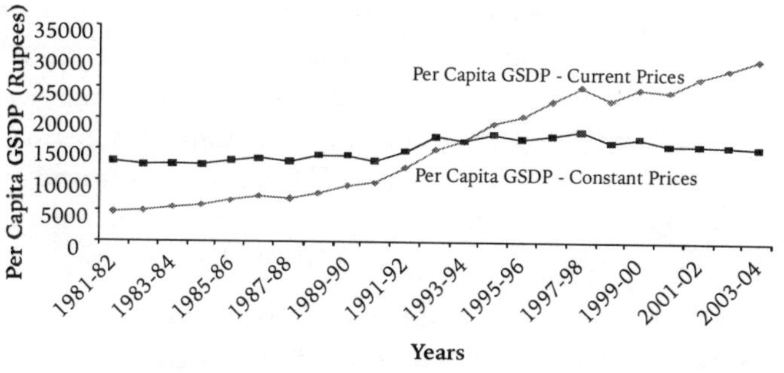

FIGURE 1.2

Trends in Per Capita Incomes: India and Andaman Nicobar Islands

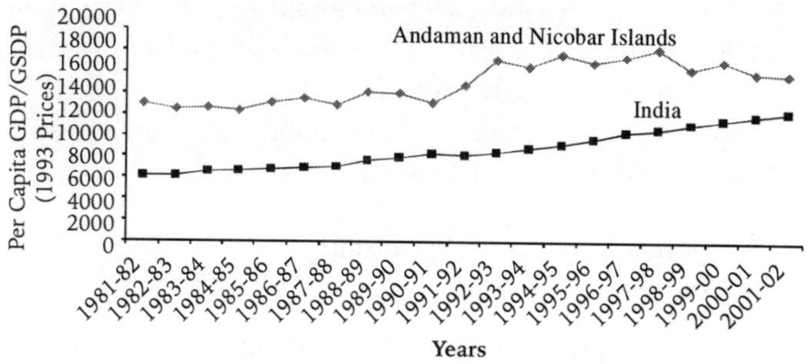

Thus, the growth performance of UT, however, is a matter of concern. Post-economic reforms, while the growth of Indian economy has accelerated, the growth of GSDP in the UT has shown a significant deceleration, particularly after 1993-94. As shown in Annexure 1.1, the average annual growth of GSDP at current prices decelerated from 12.9 per cent during the period, 1981-82 to 1990-91, to 8.8 per cent during 1993-94 to 2001-02 (column 2). In constant (1993-94) prices, the GSDP growth declined from 5.6 per cent during 1981-82 to 1990-91 to 2.4 per cent during 1993-1994 to 2001-02 (column 6). Similar trend is seen in the growth performance of Net State Domestic Product (NSDP) as well.

The trend in the level of living is better understood when we examine the estimates of per capita GSDP in constant prices. Table 1.12 presents the growth rates of GSDP in the UT and per capita GDP (factor cost) in India (for details, see Annexure 1.1). It is seen that during the decade, 1981-1991, the per capita GSDP in the UT exceeded the growth rate of population by one percentage point and thus it grew by one per cent per year on average. However, during the decade of the 1990s, the per capita GSDP in the UT had been stagnant. During the entire period, the per capita GSDP growth was significantly lower than the average per capita GDP growth in the country and the difference in the growth rate has increased sharply during the 1990s. The seriousness of the issue becomes clear when we consider the sub-period 1993-2002. During this period, the per capita GSDP in the UT actually showed a declining trend in contrast to the 4.2 per cent annual growth in average per capita GDP in the country.

The low and declining growth performance of the economy and the declining level of per capita income in the UT underline the challenges faced in arresting the trend and reorient the economy to achieve the target set for the Tenth Five-year Plan. In order to take the economy on the sustainable path of accelerated development during the next decade, it is important to initiate both policy and institutional changes. The objective of this State Development Report is to take stock of the prevailing economic scenario, identify opportunities, challenges and risks in the path of economic progress, and indicate policy and institutional changes required for achieving the objective.

Contribution of Primary, Secondary, and Tertiary Sectors

The composition of GSDP and NSDP in terms of the three broad sectors, i.e., primary, secondary, and tertiary in the UT, at both current and constant (1993-1994) prices is presented in Annexures 1.2 and 1.3. Notably, over the years, in keeping with the national trend, while the contribution of the primary and secondary sector has shown a declining trend, the share of the tertiary sector has shown a sharp increase. The primary sector share was about 45 per cent of total GSDP at both current and constant prices. Over the years the share declined steadily to 35 per cent in current prices and 30 per cent in constant prices. Similarly, the secondary sector share in current prices has declined from about 26 per cent in 1981-82 to about 19 per cent in 2001-02 though in constant prices the decline was marginal from about 25 per cent to 22 per cent during the two decades. In contrast, the share of tertiary sector in constant prices remained steady at about 30 per cent until 1990-91 but thereafter increased steadily to 47.5 per cent in 2001-02. A marked increase in the share of the tertiary sector was particularly noted after 1997-98 following the pay revision of government employees.

The contribution of the three sectors to increase in incomes is summarised in Table 1.13. Since 1995-96, the increase in GSDP at constant prices was entirely in the tertiary sector. In fact, even in absolute terms, incomes in both primary and secondary sectors declined in 2001-02 over 1996-97. The tertiary sector increase was over 210 per cent so that it could offset the declines in the other two sectors and increase the total GDP marginally. At current prices, the contribution of tertiary sector to the growth of GSDP since 1996-97 was about 70 per cent. These estimates show that not only there has been a deceleration in the growth of GSDP in the UT, but also that whatever marginal increase in incomes is observed is due mainly to the pay revisions of the organised sector employees. The increase in the material output during the last few years has been negligible.

From Annexure 1.3, it may be noted that the contribution of the primary, secondary, and tertiary sectors to the NSDP of the UT is similar to that observed in the case of GSDP. During 1981-82 to 2001-2002, the contribution of tertiary sector to the NSDP at current prices increased from less than 32.27 per cent to above 45 per cent (column 4), and that to the NSDP at 1993-94 prices increased from about 18 per cent to above 39 per cent (column 8). Correspondingly, the contribution of primary sector to the NSDP at current prices declined from about 44 per cent in 1981-82 to below 31 per cent in 1999-2000 (column 2), and that to the NSDP at 1993-94 prices declined from about 45 per

TABLE 1.13

Sector-wise Contribution to GSDP: Current and Constant Prices

(Per Cent)

	GSDP—Current Prices				*GSDP—Constant (1993) Prices*			
	Primary	*Secondary*	*Tertiary*	*Total*	*Primary*	*Secondary*	*Tertiary*	*Total*
1. Composition								
1981-82	45.05	25.78	29.17	100.0	44.23	24.67	31.09	100.00
1985-86	45.90	24.86	29.23	100.0	45.58	23.27	31.15	100.00
1990-91	44.31	22.78	32.91	100.0	47.94	22.42	29.64	100.00
1995-96	40.03	23.45	36.53	100.0	38.76	23.64	37.60	100.00
2000-01	33.84	19.30	46.86	100.0	30.22	22.40	47.38	100.00
2001-02	35.42	18.85	45.73	100.0	30.08	22.44	47.48	100.00
2. Contribution to Growth								
1980-91	43.94	21.28	34.78	100.00	55.12	18.05	26.84	100.00
1991-96	39.43	26.02	34.56	100.00	24.47	31.85	43.68	100.00
1996-2002	31.59	-0.81	69.23	100.00	-60.46	-49.19	209.66	100.00

Source: Computed.

cent in 1981-82 to about 28 per cent in 1999-2000 (column 6), although some increase in the contribution is noted in the subsequent two years following sharp decline in the contribution of tertiary sector due to negative contribution of transport during this period. The contribution of secondary sector to the NSDP at current prices declined from above 23 per cent in 1981-82 to below 18 per cent in 2001-02 (column 3), and that to the NSDP at 1993-94 prices declined from above 22 per cent in 1981-82 to about 21 per cent in 2001-02 (column 7).

The above discussion seems to suggest relatively lesser exploitation of growth potential of primary and secondary sectors.

The ecology of the UT is congenial for substantial exploitation of the primary sector, particularly agriculture and fishery. A planned exploitation of agriculture and fishery could provide the necessary boost to manufacturing and self-employment.

Invariably, the growth of an economy is accompanied by relatively higher contribution from the secondary sector, particularly manufacturing and construction. Given the high freight charges from and to the mainland, it would be prudent to focus on production of those products that would reduce dependence on import from outside the UT and/or provide competitive advantage in export out of the UT. For the purpose of export, goods of low volume but high value based on locally available inputs should be identified, and production of these goods encouraged. If the economy has to benefit from these developments, development of adequate infrastructure is necessary. In achieving this goal, governmental effort could be supplemented by private effort through joint ventures or by providing limited financial incentives to potential private entrepreneurs.

Relative Status of the UT

Given its peculiar geographical location and structure, ANI is not strictly comparable with states and other UTs in India. Although smallest among the states and UTs in terms of population, it belongs to the category of high per capita income states and UTs. A comparison of the UT is made with states and other UTs subject to these caveats. For this purpose, growth rates of GSDP and NSDP of different states along with those for all-states and all-India, at current and 1993-94 prices, are estimated for the period 1993-94 to 2001-02, and reported in Annexure I.4.

From Annexure I.4, it may be noted that, during 1993-94 to 2001-02, ANI performed poorly as compared to all-India level, all-states level, and most states and UTs. For, GSDP at current prices grew at the rate of 8.8 per cent in ANI while it grew at the rate of 13.1 per cent at all-India level, 12.1 per cent at the all-state level, and in the range of 10.0 to 19.9 per cent in most states and other UTs (column 3). GSDP at 1993-94 prices grew at the rate of about 2.4 per cent in the UT while it grew at the rate of about 6.2 per cent at all-India level, about 5.4 per cent at the all-state level, and in the range of 4.2 to 12.2 per cent in most states and other UTs (column 4). Similarly, NSDP at current prices grew at the rate of 8.6 per cent in the UT while it grew at the rate of 13.2 per cent at all-India level,

12.1 per cent at the all-state level, and in the range of 10.1 to 21.1 per cent in most states and other UTs (column 5). NSDP at 1993-94 prices grew at the rate of about 2.2 per cent in the UT while it grew at the rate of about 6.1 per cent at all-India level, about 5.2 per cent at the all-state level, and in the range of 3.2 to 13.0 per cent in most states and other UTs (column 6).

The foregoing discussion indicates that the performance of the UT in the recent period has been poor and is far from being consistent with the growth target set for the country in the Tenth Five-year Plan. There is, therefore, a need to identify factors responsible for poor growth of the UT, and overcome impediments. In this context, other than revamping the primary and secondary sectors as discussed above, it may be useful to review the status of infrastructure development in the UT that is considered to be a driving force for growth of any economy.

Unemployment and Productivity of Labour

Growth in employment is a desirable outcome of development process, and captures the economic attainment and hence the level of well-being of the people. In ANI minimum wage rate as well as unemployment seems to have increased over time. Some of the relevant information relating to unemployment in the UT is furnished in Annexure I.5. From this table, it may be noted that the number of placements by the employment exchange followed a declining trend from 636 in 1991-92 to 324 in 1998-99 (column 4). Unemployment as percentage of population has increased from 5.7 in 1991-92 to 7.7 in 1998-99 (column 6). This trend is likely to have continued in the subsequent period implying still higher unemployment. There is no indication of increase in avenues of employment, during the period under consideration.

Between 1983 and 1993-94 employment in ANI grew at 6.1 per cent, which was third highest in the country and substantially higher than the national average of 2.1 per cent. Furthermore, during this period growth in female employment was more than three times than that of male employment and growth in employment in rural areas was substantially higher than in urban areas. During 1993-94 to 1999-2000, growth in employment decelerated sharply to -0.7 per cent against the all-India average of 1.6 per cent.[1] This can be attributed mainly to the decline in growth of employment in rural areas for both males and females, and for females in urban areas.

In the organised segment, although the public sector continues to play a very dominant role, and accounts for more than 86 per cent of employment in the UT, the number of government employees has remained stagnant around 33,500 during the nineties (column 11). Although the private sector did make some contribution to employment, there is a need to create more jobs. Labour productivity in the UT appears to have declined as against the rise at all-India level and in most states and UTs. A comparison of labour productivity in various states and UTs, in terms of per worker value of output and per worker net value added shows that the per worker value of output in the UT declined from Rs. 1.87 lakh in 1996-97 to Rs. 1.28 lakh in 2001-02 whereas it registered a rise at all-India level from Rs. 7.78 lakh in 1996-97 to Rs. 11.88 lakh in 2001-02. Similarly, per worker net value added in the UT declined from Rs. 0.58 lakh in 1996-97 to Rs. 0.19 lakh in 2001-2002, whereas it registered a rise at all-India level from Rs. 1.62 lakh in 1996-97 to Rs. 1.83 lakh in 2001-02.

It is important to note that in a scenario of declining labour productivity, minimum wage rate in the UT has been substantially raised over time from Rs. 27 in 1992-93 to Rs. 100 in 2002-03 (column 5 in Annexure I.6). It may also be noted from this table that the raise in the minimum wage rate has been of the order of 35 to 43 per cent whereas the increase in consumer price index (CPI) during the corresponding periods has been only 12 to 25 per cent in CPI of industrial workers (column 8), 15 to 24 per cent in CPI of urban non-manual workers (column 9), and 6 to 22 per cent in CPI of agricultural labourers (column 10). The raise in minimum wage combined with the declining labour productivity might have had an adverse impact on employment in the UT.

Infrastructure

The UT is faced with various infrastructural bottlenecks, such as:

- high cost of electricity, and low utilisation of hydropower potential;
- poor connectivity to the mainland as well as rest of the world;
- absence of international airport and shipyard;
- poor intra-island connectivity;
- poor inter-island transmission facilities;

1. This can partly be attributed to closure of wood-based industries.

- poor facilities for storage, marketing and transport of crops/goods; and
- poor facilities related to tourism.

Most of the above-mentioned infrastructural bottlenecks affect adversely the export and tourism potential of the UT. Specifically, high cost of electricity and freight charges could be considered as factors detrimental to exploitation of export potential of the UT, while poor connectivity and underdevelopment of other tourism services could hinder the tourism potential of the UT. Upgradation of infrastructure would go a long way in the development of the UT.

Growth of Co-operatives

Activity of co-operatives has increased during 1991-92 to 2002-03. While the number of co-operatives has more than doubled, their membership and share capital increased to about one and one-half times (Annexure 1.7). Average working capital of co-operatives increased from less than Rs. 6 lakh in 1991-92 to above Rs. 20 lakh in 2001-02. The increase in the activity of co-operatives is seen in both the districts of the UT, i.e., Andaman group of Islands (AI) and Nicobar group of Islands (NI). The growth in terms of number of co-operatives has been faster in the former while that in terms of average size of co-operatives has been faster in the latter. During 1991-92 to 2002-03, the number of co-operatives more than doubled in AI (from 380 to 861), and only marginally increased in NI (from 62 to 73). On the other hand, working capital of co-operatives increased by little less than threefold in AI as compared to more than tenfold in NI, between 1991-92 and 1998-99.

Growth of Small Scale Industrial Units (SSIs)

The SSIs have played an active role in the development of the UT and their contribution seems to have increased over time (Annexure 1.8). The number of SSIs increased from 944 in 1991-92 to 1316 in 1998-99 (column 5). Growth in SSIs was skewed in favour of AI. For, the number of SSIs in NI remained stagnant at 34 (column 4), and in AI, it increased from 910 in 1991-92 to 1282 in 1998-99 (column 3). The number of SSIs availing of loans and the amount of loan sanctioned per such unit has also registered an increase from less than one-half lakh in 1991-92 to more than one lakh in 1998-99. These developments can be interpreted as initial steps towards progress. Government policies that will facilitate faster growth of these units, such as support for export and organised domestic marketing, as discussed earlier, can go a long way in providing boost to the growth of the UT.

Growth of Registered Factories

During 1991-92 to 2001-02, the growth of registered factories is found tardy. There has been only marginal increase in the number of working factories, from 45 in 1991-92 to 48 in 2001-02 (column 6 in Annexure 1.8). In fact, the average number of workers employed in a registered factory declined from 5,314 in 1991-92 to 4,993 in 2001-02 (column 7). To an extent decline in the average number of workers employed in a registered factory is because of reduced activity rather than on account of technical progress, it is a sign of stagnation or recession.

Growth in Enterprises in Service Sector

Growth of Theatres and Restaurants

Theatres and restaurants have stimulated the growth of the UT. The number of units as well as employment provided by these units has increased over time (Annexure 1.8). While the number of units increased from 65 in 1991-92 to 267 in 2001-02 (column 10), employment provided increased from 538 persons in 1991-92 to 1175 persons in 2001-02 (column 11).

Growth of Shops

Like the theatres and restaurants, establishment of shops have also stimulated the growth of the UT. The number of shops as well as employment provided by these shops has increased over time. The number of shops increased from 1,012 in 1991-92 to 1,413 in 2001-02, though there has been some fluctuation in the intermediate period (column 8 in Annexure I.8). Employment provided by these shops more than doubled from 2,158 persons in 1991-92 to 4,328 persons in 1998-99 (column 9 in Annexure 1.8).

Growth of Transport Services

The number of buses owned by private agencies has increased from 33 in 1994-95 to 160 in 2001-02 while the number of government buses on the roads has declined from 110 in 1991-92 to 55 in 2001-02 (columns 12 and 13 in Annexure 1.8). This suggests substantial increase in the role of the private sector in providing transport services in the UT.

Education and Health Status

The importance of education in fostering economic growth, social well-being and social stability is well recognised. Education not only has a direct role in human resource development but it is an instrument to facilitate other developmental aims.

Literacy rate for the UT has improved substantially between 1981 and points in 1981 to less than 11 percentage points in 2001 which is remarkable. Similarly, the rural-urban disparity in literacy rate has also declined from 11 percentage points in 1991 to about 8 percentage points in 2001.

In spite of poor connectivity, both within and across the islands significant improvement has been made in creating infrastructure for elementary education. The number of primary and middle schools increased from 22 to 208 and 2 to 55, respectively, during 1951-52 to 2001-2002. However, retention rate of students is poor and surely not commensurate with the high per capita expenditure on primary education relative to all-India average. Further, performance of students measured in terms of percentage of students passed in grades X and XII, especially in grade X has been poor.

Vocational and technical training schools have relatively good teacher student ratio, indicating adequate provision of such institutions in relation to the current demand. There is, however, a need to periodically monitor skills which are in demand in the market and constantly feed this information to the vocational and technical institutes. This would help them in reviewing the courses offered, from time to time, to ensure that the courses and teaching modules are in tune with the market demand.

In ANI, health indicators have improved significantly over the years. Better health and medical facilities have resulted in a decline in Infant Mortality Rate (IMR) from 95 per 1000 in 1981 to 21.21 per 1000 in 2001, against the all-India rate of 71 per 1000 in 2001. The birth rate in ANI is much below the national average and one of the lowest in country after Goa. It has declined from 20.0 in 1991 to 19.1 in 2000 and to 16.08 in 2001 against the all-India average of 29.5 and 25.8 respectively during the same period. It is significant to note that the birth rate in rural areas of ANI is marginally lower (19) than birth rate in urban area (19.3). One reason could be consistent decline in IMR and improvement in literacy rate.

Death rate in ANI has shown a continuous decline from 8.4 in 1981 to 2.82 in 2001, which is one of the lowest in the country. Death rate is favourable for females *vis-à-vis* males. The maternal mortality rate in ANI was below 0.5 per 100 live births in 2001; a result of improved natal care. For instance, institutional delivery rate was impressive 82 per cent in 2001, second highest in the country after Daman and Diu. Under the National Family Welfare Programme the ANI has achieved couple protection rate of 58.16 per cent. Performance of ANI in Immunisation of children against identified preventable diseases is impressive with 95.97 per cent children covered under various antigens.

Population coverage of health care facilities in ANI is impressive. Presently the UT has 19 PHC, 4 CHC, and 104 sub-centres. In addition to this, there are two district hospitals, one referral hospital, one *ayurvedic* dispensary, eight homeopathic dispensary and five urban health centres. On an average, one sub-centre covered 3,423 people; one PHC and CHC each covered 18,736 and 89,000 people respectively, which was better than the national average of 4,579, 27,364 and 2,00,014 respectively, during the year 1999. Availability of health infrastructure is relatively better (in terms of the number of sub-centres, PHCs and CHCs) in Nicobar district which is a predominantly rural area. In 2001, doctor-population and nurse-population ratios were 1:2800 and 1:1140, respectively.

Medical services are almost free for everyone in the state and food and medicines are distributed at no cost to all in-patients in hospitals and primary health centres. The state also pays for secondary and tertiary health care treatment outside the state. Per capita public expenditure on health in ANI is one of the highest in the country.

Meagre Resources of the UT

The financial position of the UT is precarious. The revenue raised by the UT accounts for less than 10 per cent of the expenditure of the UT. Taxes contribute a meagre amount, and most of the public utilities provided by the UT are highly subsidised leading to an insignificant recovery of costs incurred. The UT needs to make efforts to visibly improve revenue realisation in a phased manner.

Carrying Capacity of the UT

Due to its geographical location and fragile ecosystem, the UT has certain limitations to absorb uncontrolled influx of people. These islands are already facing the problem of encroachment both of forest as well as revenue land. Security considerations also demand curb on uncontrolled movement of population to these islands. However, controlling the influx of population is a complex issue which involves political, legal and administrative considerations. At the behest of Islands Development Authority (IDA), Ministry of Home Affairs (MHA) had set up a sub-group to look into this and suggest measures to put a curb on uncontrolled influx of population. The sub-group in its report suggested a two-pronged strategy; first, aimed at neutralising the motivating factors which lead to influx (*viz.* impression regarding availability of land, job opportunities, and better economic conditions, etc.); and second, to make ingress of unwanted people into the islands difficult. The supreme count of India in its order of 17th May 2002, also observed that ANI is located in an eco-fragile area therefore special measures are required to preserve its eco-diversity. In this context, it directed the UT administration to issue identity cards to islanders to facilitate a check on influx of people into the islands. The court also directed the UT administration to take several other measures to stop destruction of natural forests and other resources in ANI. Some progress has been made on this by the UT administration. The draft regulations for controlling migration submitted by the ANI administration are being examined by the MHA from the constitutional angle and also in light of the decision to open up the islands for tourism.

Emerging Issues

- Less than satisfactory growth:
  - The growth not commensurate with the target set for the country in the Five-year Plan.
  - Poor relative growth of the UT.
- Declining contribution of primary and secondary sectors:
  - Less than full exploitation of agricultural crops and fisheries.
  - Stagnating industrial growth.
- Declining labour productivity.
- Rising unemployment.
- Limited carrying capacity of the UT.
- Less than full exploitation of potential areas:
  - High value crops (spices, fruits, medicinal plants, horticulture).
  - Fisheries and other marine resources.
- Inadequate quality infrastructure:
  - High cost of electricity.
  - Poor post-harvest facilities.
  - Absence of international airport and shipyard.
  - Inadequate development of places of tourist attraction.
- Less than full decentralisation to the ground level.
- Lesser involvement of private sector in potential growth areas.
- Meagre resource mobilisation:
  - Absence of major source of tax revenue (sales tax).
  - Poor recovery of costs from public utilities.

Directions for Development of UT

It will be useful to follow the following development strategies:

- In principle, policy of liberalisation should be followed. However, in the short and medium term emphasis should be on production for local consumption; and as far as possible, local production should be based on high intensity of locally available inputs.
- Greater role of government as facilitator:
  - Infrastructure development.
  - Schemes for greater involvement of private sector in development.
- Focus should be on sustainable growth based on its natural resources and on a participatory basis. The following sectors offer scope for development:
  - High value agriculture.
  - Fishery and other marine resources.
  - Horticulture, spices, medicinal plants.
- Creation of technical and vocational skills in the labour force is crucial. Government should support and encourage technical and vocational schools in the private sector with strong linkages with industry, fishery, and agriculture.
- Pruning of subsidies.
- People's participation at the grass-roots-level that

is devolution of functions and commensurate tax powers to the third tier of the government.

- Good governance with transparent tax policies and administrative procedures, and appropriate incentives to reward good performance. It is critical to develop institutional mechanism particularly to bring accountability into the system.

ANNEXURE 1.1

State Domestic Product of ANI with 1993-94 Base

Year	At Factor Cost & At Current Prices				At Factor Cost & At 1993-94 Prices				
	GSDP (Rs. Lakh)	NSDP (Rs. Lakh)	PC-GSDP (Rs.)	PC-NSDP (Rs.)	GSDP (Rs. Lakh)	NSDP (Rs. Lakh)	PC-GSDP (Rs.)	PC-NSDP (Rs.)	Population
1	2	3	4	5	6	7	8	9	10
1981-82	9003	9362	4770	4960	24349	23367	12901	12381	188741
1982-83	10069	10300	5085	5202	24567	23004	12408	11618	198000
1983-84	11673	11998	5620	5777	26167	25079	12599	12075	207700
1984-85	13117	13348	6020	6126	26981	26058	12382	11959	217900
1985-86	15145	15150	6637	6639	29812	27594	13064	12092	228200
1986-87	17406	17079	7286	7149	32077	29332	13427	12278	238900
1987-88	17669	16890	7076	6764	32183	29330	12889	11746	249700
1988-89	20733	19920	7956	7644	36692	33225	14080	12749	260600
1989-90	24648	24511	9072	9021	37835	34206	13925	12590	271700
1990-91	27009	26198	9540	9254	36920	33151	13041	11710	283100
1991-92	34591	32797	12073	11448	42139	36971	14708	12904	286500
1992-93	44705	41037	15035	13802	50992	47025	17149	15815	297338
1993-94	50869	46816	16508	15192	50869	46816	16508	15192	308153
1994-95	61282	56457	19200	17688	56071	51679	17567	16191	319175
1995-96	67497	61489	20422	18604	55729	50745	16862	15354	330510
1996-97	78683	72012	22964	21017	59629	54463	17403	15896	342630
1997-98	89689	81280	25219	22855	64223	58147	18058	16350	355640
1998-99	84934	75569	23045	20504	59815	53444	16229	14501	368563
1999-00	94794	81935	24890	21513	64791	57568	17012	15115	380857
2000-01	95726	87187	24517	22330	61801	56169	15828	14386	390452
2001-02	106856	97324	26671	24292	62911	57178	15703	14272	400642
2002-03	116263	105524	28063	25470	64446	58414	15555	14099	414299
2003-04	126499	114414	29527	26706	66018	59676	15410	13929	428421
Growth Rate (%)									
1981-91	12.93	11.99			5.65	4.81			4.62
1993-02	8.80	8.43			2.44	2.16			3.41

Notes: 1. GSDP and NSDP for the years 2002-03 and 2003-04 are estimated by applying the growth rate during 1993-94 to 2002, to the base 2001-02.
2. Population figure for a year is as on 1st October of the year (1992-93 to 2001-02)

ANNEXURE 1.2

GSDP of ANI with 1993-94 Base, by Broad Groups of Sectors

(Per Cent)

Year	At Current Prices				At 1993-94 Prices			
	Primary	Secondary	Tertiary	Total (2-4)	Primary	Secondary	Tertiary	Total (6-8)
1	2	3	4	5	6	7	8	9
1981-82	45.05	25.78	29.17	100.00	44.23	24.67	31.09	100.00
1982-83	46.15	23.16	30.68	100.00	44.44	22.22	33.34	100.00
1983-84	46.16	23.94	29.91	100.00	45.47	22.46	32.07	100.00
1984-85	45.06	23.84	31.10	100.00	43.74	22.44	33.82	100.00
1985-86	45.90	24.86	29.23	100.00	45.58	23.27	31.15	100.00
1986-87	45.34	22.85	31.82	100.00	45.20	21.26	33.54	100.00

...Contd. ...

...Contd. ...

Year	At Current Prices				At 1993-94 Prices			
	Primary	Secondary	Tertiary	Total (2-4)	Primary	Secondary	Tertiary	Total (6-8)
1	2	3	4	5	6	7	8	9
1987-88	46.12	20.93	32.95	100.00	48.22	19.76	32.02	100.00
1988-89	42.61	23.70	33.69	100.00	48.21	20.54	31.25	100.00
1989-90	42.61	22.57	34.82	100.00	45.69	21.84	32.48	100.00
1990-91	44.31	22.78	32.91	100.00	47.94	22.42	29.64	100.00
1991-92	40.60	21.00	38.40	100.00	43.37	21.00	35.64	100.00
1992-93	34.13	23.06	42.81	100.00	40.25	20.25	39.49	100.00
1993-94	42.34	19.87	37.80	100.00	42.34	19.87	37.80	100.00
1994-95	38.82	24.54	36.64	100.00	38.47	24.53	37.00	100.00
1995-96	40.03	23.45	36.53	100.00	38.76	23.64	37.60	100.00
1996-97	36.79	25.89	37.32	100.00	35.07	26.39	38.55	100.00
1997-98	34.34	25.62	40.05	100.00	30.21	27.54	42.26	100.00
1998-99	35.68	18.45	45.87	100.00	32.60	19.98	47.42	100.00
1999-00	31.38	20.27	48.35	100.00	28.94	22.53	48.53	100.00
2000-01	33.84	19.30	46.86	100.00	30.22	22.40	47.38	100.00
2001-02	35.42	18.85	45.73	100.00	30.08	22.44	47.48	100.00

Notes: 1. Primary sector comprises agriculture, forestry and logging, fishery, and mining and quarrying.
2. Secondary sector comprises manufacturing, construction, and electricity, gas and water supply.
3. Tertiary sector comprises transport, storage and communication, and trade, hotels and restaurants.
4. Others sector comprises banking and insurance, real estate and dwellings, public administration, and other services.

Sources: 1. This table is based on information compiled/obtained from:
2. Andaman & Nicobar Administration, *Report on Estimation of State Domestic Product, Andaman & Nicobar Islands: 1980-81 to 1996-97*, Port Blair.
3. Central Statistical Organisation, File downloaded from the internet for the period 1993-94 to 1998-99 with base 1993-94.

ANNEXURE 1.3

NSDP of ANI with 1993-94 Base, by Broad Groups of Sectors

Year	At Current Prices				At 1993-94 Prices			
	Primary	Secondary	Tertiary	Total (2-4)	Primary	Secondary	Tertiary	Total (6-8)
1	2	3	4	5	6	7	8	9
1981-82	44.28	23.45	32.27	100.00	45.43	22.54	32.03	100.00
1982-83	45.90	20.82	33.28	100.00	46.44	18.41	35.14	100.00
1983-84	45.65	21.96	32.39	100.00	46.48	20.34	33.18	100.00
1984-85	44.90	21.70	33.40	100.00	46.77	18.67	34.56	100.00
1985-86	46.22	22.92	30.87	100.00	48.14	19.15	32.71	100.00
1986-87	45.90	21.36	32.75	100.00	47.97	16.34	35.69	100.00
1987-88	47.02	19.82	33.16	100.00	51.31	14.99	33.70	100.00
1988-89	43.53	22.52	33.95	100.00	51.07	16.59	32.34	100.00
1989-90	42.39	20.88	36.74	100.00	48.10	17.46	34.44	100.00
1990-91	41.92	20.84	37.23	100.00	49.65	16.80	33.55	100.00
1991-92	39.16	19.60	41.24	100.00	45.89	16.04	38.06	100.00
1992-93	33.64	22.80	43.56	100.00	40.92	20.01	39.07	100.00
1993-94	42.93	19.18	37.90	100.00	42.93	19.18	37.90	100.00
1994-95	39.08	24.18	36.73	100.00	38.74	24.16	37.10	100.00
1995-96	40.30	22.84	36.87	100.00	38.99	23.01	38.00	100.00
1996-97	36.67	25.69	37.64	100.00	34.89	26.18	38.93	100.00
1997-98	34.06	25.55	40.39	100.00	29.68	27.52	42.81	100.00

...Contd. ...

...Contd. ...

Year	At Current Prices				At 1993-94 Prices			
	Primary	Secondary	Tertiary	Total (2-4)	Primary	Secondary	Tertiary	Total (6-8)
1	2	3	4	5	6	7	8	9
1998-99	35.58	17.54	46.88	100.00	32.42	19.07	48.50	100.00
1999-00	30.81	19.61	49.58	100.00	28.45	21.92	49.64	100.00
2000-01	35.45	17.87	46.68	100.00	31.54	21.11	47.35	100.00
2001-02	37.11	17.45	45.44	100.00	31.40	21.15	47.45	100.00

Notes and *Sources*: Same as for Annexure 1.2.

ANNEXURE 1.4

Growth Rates of Gross and Net SDP of Different States and UTs during 1993-94 to 2001-02, with Base as 1993-94

(Per Cent)

S. No.	State/ Union Territory	GSDP at Current Prices	GSDP at 1993-94 Prices	NSDP at Current Prices	NSDP at 1993-94 Prices	Population 1997-98
1	2	3	4	5	6	7
All States						
1.	Andhra Pradesh	12.49	5.54	12.65	5.52	1.27
2.	Arunachal Pradesh	10.65	3.55	10.48	3.28	2.11
3.	Assam	10.04	2.08	10.26	1.95	1.51
4.	Bihar	10.93	4.20	10.86	4.08	2.67
5.	Chhattisgarh	9.75	3.29	9.09	2.82	1.59
6.	Goa	16.10	8.95	16.97	9.36	0.68
7.	Gujarat	10.85	5.44	10.14	4.52	1.59
8.	Haryana	13.06	5.79	13.07	5.57	2.43
9.	Himachal Pradesh	14.59	6.74	14.67	6.43	1.75
10.	Jammu & Kashmir	12.85	4.45	12.97	4.24	2.45
11.	Jharkhand	7.82	3.32	8.42	3.72	1.78
12.	Karnataka	14.02	8.18	14.05	8.13	1.48
13.	Kerala	13.81	5.31	13.87	5.11	1.06
14.	Madhya Pradesh	10.31	4.62	10.16	4.43	2.15
15.	Maharashtra	11.13	5.02	11.40	4.84	2.08
16.	Manipur	14.76	7.72	15.22	8.10	2.23
17.	Meghalaya	13.47	6.90	13.98	7.34	2.57
18.	Mizoram	13.74	NA	14.28	NA	2.46
19.	Nagaland	9.48	3.12	9.52	3.19	5.22
20.	Orissa	11.00	4.47	11.02	4.49	1.42
21.	Punjab	12.21	5.20	12.17	4.93	1.91
22.	Rajasthan	12.77	6.52	12.82	6.49	2.55
23.	Sikkim	13.72	7.83	14.13	7.61	2.49
24.	Tamil Nadu	12.75	6.03	12.73	5.79	0.99
25.	Tripura	16.16	7.87	16.66	8.16	1.14
26.	Uttar Pradesh	11.59	4.18	11.63	3.99	2.21
27.	West Bengal	14.55	7.05	14.83	7.12	1.53
28.	All-States	12.07	5.41	12.13	5.24	1.86
B. Union Territories						
29.	**Andaman & Nicobar Islands**	**8.80**	**2.44**	**8.55**	**2.20**	**3.41**
30.	Chandigarh	15.80	9.15	15.58	9.23	3.60
31.	Delhi	15.09	8.28	15.43	8.36	3.68
32.	Pondicherry	19.87	12.20	21.11	12.98	1.89
33.	All-India	13.12	6.19	13.21	6.10	1.93

ANNEXURE 1.5

Employment Status in ANI

Year	*Applicants Registered with Employment Exchange*					*Government Employees at the End of the Year*				
	Total Live Registrations	*New Registrations*	*Placements Made*	*Population*	*(2) As Per Cent of (5)*	*Group A*	*Group B*	*Group C*	*Group D*	*Total*
1	*2*	*3*	*4*	*5*	*6*	*7*	*8*	*9*	*10*	*11*
1991-92	17010	3718	636	297000	5.73	287	380	11205	21586	33458
1992-93	20899	3418	575	307900	6.79	299	382	11165	22038	33884
1993-94	18170	4305	573	308153	5.90	306	423	11424	21453	33606
1994-95	21921	4312	457	319175	6.87	316	411	11435	22803	34965
1995-96	25556	3635	607	330510	7.73	340	441	12095	24038	36914
1996-97	23186	4234	201	342630	6.77	344	460	12164	21853	34821
1997-98	25203	3696	427	355640	7.09	362	472	12632	20513	33979
1998-99	28271	3700	324	368563	7.67	367	484	12673	20039	33563
1999-00				380857						
2000-01				390452						
2001-02				400642						
2002-03				411098						
2003-04				421827						

Source: Directorate of Economic and Statistics, *Andaman & Nicobar Islands Basic Statistics, 1996-97 to 1998-99* (Tables 13.1, 13.2, 13.4 and 13.6), and for earlier years, Andaman & Nicobar Administration, Port Blair.

ANNEXURE 1.6

All-India Price Indices and Minimum Wage Rate in ANI

Year	All-India Consumer Price Index (CPI)			Andaman & Nicobar Islands			Percentage Increase in all-India CPI with Reference to Wage Revision in ANI			Minimum Per Day Wage in Select Regions			
				Minimum wage									
	Industrial Workers	Urban Non-Manual Employees Base: 1984-85=100	Agricultural Labourers (Base: 1986-87=100	Rate Per Day (Rs.)	Since	Percentage Increase Over the Previous Rate	Industrial Workers	Urban Non-Manual Employees	Agricultural Labourers	Tamil Nadu	West Bengal	New Delhi	Puduicherry
1	2	3	4	5	6	7	8	9	10	11	12	13	14
1991-92	219	183	167										
1992-93	240	202	188	27	13.08.1992								
1993-94	258	216	195										
1994-95	279	232	210	37	23.09.1994	37.04	16.25	14.85	11.90				
1995-96	313	259	234										
1996-97	342	283	256	50	07.02.1997	35.14	22.58	21.98	21.62				
1997-98	366	302	267										
1998-99	414	340	296										
1999-00	428	352	298	70	22.02.2000	40.00	25.15	24.38	16.41	104	81	103	50
2000-01	444	371	305										
2001-02	463	390	309										
2002-03	480	404	317	100		42.86	12.24	14.81	6.33				
2003-04													

Note: All-India indices for the year 2002-03 are based on average of eight months: April through November.

Sources: 1. Government of India, *Economic Survey 2002-03*.

2. Administration Andaman & Nicobar Islands.

ANNEXURE 1.7

Co-operative Societies in ANI

Year	All Co-operative Societies at the Year End					Co-operative Societies at the Year End in									
						Andaman Islands					Nicobar Islands				
	No. of Societies	Member-ship	Share Capital (Rs. Lakh)	Reserve Fund (Rs. Lakh)	Working Capital (Rs. Lakh)	No. of Societies	Member-ship	Share Capital (Rs. Lakh)	Reserve Fund (Rs. Lakh)	Working Capital (Rs. Lakh)	No. of Societies	Member-ship	Share Capital (Rs. Lakh)	Reserve Fund (Rs. Lakh)	Working Capital (Rs. Lakh)
1	2	3	4	5	6	7	8	9	10	11	12	13	14	15	16
1991-92	442	51756	198	299	2590	380	47857	160	266	2475	62	3899	38	33	116
1992-93	427	52018	192	299	2598	363	47525	102	267	2480	64	4439	90	33	119
1993-94	440	52063	193	675	1419	376	47570	103	582	3459	64	4493	90	93	560
1994-95	458	61255	274	957	5736	392	56147				66	5108			
1995-96	469	61454	275	1049	7929	404	56373				65	5081			
1996-97	500	61864	277	1028	9476	434	56772	176	650	8000	66	5092	101	378	1476
1997-98	564	62774	281	1099	9536	497	57655	180	1026	8374	67	5119	101	72	1162
1998-99	600	63236	288	1239	8127	533	57999	185	1166	6966	67	5237	103	72	1162
1999-00															
2000-01															
2001-02	818	65899	310	2532	17685										
2002-03	934	72495	340			861					73				
2003-04															

Source: *Andaman & Nicobar Islands Basic Statistics*, 2001-02, 1996-97 to 1998-99 (Tables 11.1 to 11.4), and for earlier years, Directorate of Economic and Statistics, Andaman & Nicobar Administration, Port Blair.

ANNEXURE 1.8

Status of Industry, Commerce, and Motor Transport

Year	*Industry*						*Commerce*				*Motor Transport*		
		Small Scale Industrial Units			*Registered Factories*		*Shops etc.*		*Theatres and Restaurants*		*State Transport*		
	Large/ Medium Scale Industrial Units	*Andaman Islands*	*Nicobar Islands*	*Total*	*Working Factoris*	*Average Workers Employed Daily*	*Units*	*Employment*	*Units*	*Employment*	*No. of Buses Owned*	*No. of Buses on Road*	*Buses Owned by Private Agencies*
1	*2*	*3*	*4*	*5*	*6*	*7*	*8*	*9*	*10*	*11*	*12*	*13*	*14*
1991-92	5	910	34	944	45	5314	1012	2158	65	538	178	110	
1992-93	5	975	34	1009	45	5314	868	2500	105	550	145	101	
1993-94	5	1032	34	1066	43	5116	892	3040	105	550	162	108	
1994-95	5	1086	33	1119	43	5116	922	3240	110	590	162	103	33
1995-96	5	1143	32	1175	46	6478	943	3305	128	680	164	103	46
1996-97	5	1185	31	1216	46	6475	943	3925	128	680	163	88	61
1997-98	5	1232	34	1266	46	5383	998	4002	148	790	164	83	73
1998-99	5	1282	34	1316	46	5365	1050	4328	170	920	160	69	113
1999-00													
2000-01													
2001-02	2			1400	48	4993	1413		267	1175	179	55	160
2002-03													
2003-04													

Source: *Andaman & Nicobar Islands Basic Statistics*, 2001-02, 1996-97 to 1998-99 (Tables 4.1, 16.1 to 16.4, 23.4), and for earlier years, Directorate of Economic and Statistics, Andaman & Nicobar Administration, Port Blair.

Chapter 2

Financial Position and Outlook

Finances are one of the most important aspects and requirements for the development of an economy. In this chapter, we examine the trends in financial position of ANI, assess its strengths and weaknesses, and make suggestions for improvement.

The ANI is classified as a "Union Territory". It falls in the category of a UT without a legislature. Since it comprises a small territory, and a corresponding small population, and has special locational characteristics one can understand that the ANI cannot be made easily self-reliant financially. Further, it is not entirely appropriate to compare it with other states and UTs in India. In what follows we review and analyse:

(i) the trends in revenues and expenditures;

(ii) the composition of revenue receipts and expenditures;

(iii) the composition and buoyancy of tax and non-tax revenues; and

(iv) the status of local bodies.

On the basis of the results of our analysis, suggestions are made for reforms.

Trends in Receipts and Expenditure

The revenue generated by the UT accounted for less than 10 per cent of its expenditure and 7.5 per cent of GSDP in 2002-03, though in some years the former was higher it never exceeded 18 per cent. From Table 2.1, it may be noted that the revenue to expenditure ratio increased from 9.7 per cent in 1991-92 to 17.3 per cent in 1995-96 but declined gradually to 9.9 in 2002-03 (column 7), implying a gradual deterioration of fiscal health of the UT. This is corroborated by the observed growth rates of revenue and expenditure. The former grew at the rate of 8.2 per cent per annum while the latter grew at 11.3 per cent between 1991-92 and 2003-04 (Table 2.1, columns 2 and 6). Also, expenditure buoyancy was 1.02 as against revenue buoyancy of 0.87 implying more than proportional increase in expenditure and less than proportional increase in revenue following an increase in GSDP. These indicate that fiscal health of the UT may thus deteriorate unless additional revenues are mobilised and rise in expenditure growth is curtailed.

Tax Revenues

Tax revenue made only a meagre contribution to the total revenues of the UT in spite of an increase in its share in total revenues from 3.9 per cent in 1991-92 to 14.2 per cent in 2003-04 (Table 2.1, column 5). The rate of growth of tax revenue was substantially higher at 19.8 per cent as compared to growth of non-tax revenue at 7.2 per cent (columns 3 and 4). The buoyancy of tax revenue was also higher at 1.88 as against 0.78 for non-tax revenues. Maintaining the same degree of buoyancy, however, would entail better enforcement in addition to widening of the existing base. In the UT, the tax to GSDP ratio has stabilised around 1 per cent (column 11), whereas the tax to GSDP ratio at the all-states level is above 5 per cent.

Sales tax has been a major source of revenue for most states and UTs accounting for more than 60 per cent of their tax revenue, but remains unutilised in ANI. An analysis of the taxes levied by the UT reveals that between 1991-92 and 2003-04 land revenue, stamps and registration fees, and state excise collections grew at rates above 19 per cent, and taxes on vehicles grew at about 13 per cent per annum (columns 3 to 6, Table 2.2). These grew much faster than GSDP yielding high buoyancy of above 1.7, except for taxes on vehicles at about 1.2. However, maintaining this rate of tax revenue growth may not be easy. The growth of tax

TABLE 2.1

Revenue Receipts and Expenditure of Andaman & Nicobar Islands

Year	*Revenue Receipts (RE)*					*Receipts as Percentage of Expenditure*				*Receipts as % Age of GSDP*	
	Total Revenue (Rs. Crore)	*Tax Revenue (Rs. Crore)*	*Non-tax Revenue (Rs. Crore)*	*Percentage Share of Taxes*	*Total Expenditure (Rs. Crore)*	*Total Revenue*	*Tax Revenue*	*Non-tax Revenue*	*GSDP (Rs. Crore)*	*Tax*	*Non-tax*
1	2	3	4	5	6	7	8	9	10	11	12
1991-92	30.70	1.21	29.49	3.94	317.25	9.68	0.38	9.30	346	0.35	8.53
1992-93	42.01	1.68	40.33	4.00	312.06	13.46	0.54	12.92	447	0.38	9.02
1993-94	49.50	3.72	45.78	7.52	318.50	15.54	1.17	14.37	509	0.73	9.00
1994-95	61.49	4.74	56.75	7.71	380.00	16.18	1.25	14.93	613	0.77	9.26
1995-96	75.33	6.83	68.50	9.07	434.94	17.32	1.57	15.75	675	1.01	10.15
1996-97	76.80	3.65	73.15	4.75	458.80	16.74	0.80	15.94	787	0.46	9.30
1997-98	89.42	8.65	80.77	9.67	517.61	16.69	1.62	15.08	897	0.96	9.01
1998-99	89.84	9.27	80.57	10.32	648.66	13.85	1.43	12.42	849	1.09	9.49
1999-00	91.30	9.98	81.32	10.93	758.88	12.09	1.32	10.77	948	1.05	8.58
2000-01	93.78	10.76	83.02	11.47	819.32	11.58	1.33	10.25	957	1.12	8.67
2001-02	92.85	11.67	81.18	12.57	809.81	11.42	1.44	9.99	1069	1.09	7.60
2002-03	87.74	12.60	75.14	14.36	885.17	9.91	1.42	8.49	1163	1.08	6.46
2003-04 (BE)	89.14	12.66	76.48	14.20	992.23	8.98	1.28	7.71	1265	1.00	6.05
Period: 1991-92 to 2003-04											
GR	8.23	19.80	7.23	10.69	11.34	-2.77	7.62	-3.68	10.17		
Buoyancy	0.87	1.88	0.78	1.01	1.02	-0.15	0.86	-0.24			
Period: 1997-98 to 2003-04											
GR	-0.14	7.07	-1.08	7.22	9.88	-8.82	-2.23	-9.68	6.56		
Buoyancy	-0.05	0.96	-0.19	1.01	1.24	-1.26	-0.25	-1.40			

Notes: RE: Revised Estimates; GR: Growth Rate

Sources: 1. Columns 2 to 4 from *Detailed Demand for Grants* (Vol. 2), Ministry of Home Affairs, Union Government of India, for different years.
2. Columns 6 to 9 from *Expenditure Budget of Union Government of India*, Vol. 1, Annexure 3, for different years.

revenue has already decelerated to 7.1 per cent per annum between 1997-98 and 2003-04.

Contribution of Non-Tax Revenues

The ratio of non-tax receipts to GSDP of the UT has declined from about 10 per cent in 1995-96 to about 6 per cent in 2003-04 (column 12, Table 2.1). The revenue receipts from two major sources, namely, forestry and wildlife and inland water transport registered negative growth in the last two years. Revenue receipts from forestry and wildlife declined from Rs. 3150 lakh in 1996-97 to Rs. 1600 lakh in 2001-02 and to Rs. 650 lakh in 2003-04 (Table 2.3, column 10). Similarly, revenue receipts from inland water transport declined from Rs. 970 lakh in 1996-97 to Rs. 500 lakh in 2001-02 and further to Rs. 50 lakh in 2003-04.[1] The Supreme Court's ruling banning felling of trees and maintaining the forest in their original form has had an adverse impact on the timber-based industry, in turn affecting the revenue receipts from forestry and wildlife with which it has a backward linkage, as well as inland water transport with which it has a forward linkage.

There are, however, other items that have registered impressive growth rate exceeding 15 per cent per annum. These are tourism (37 per cent), fishery (27 per cent), ports and light houses (23 per cent), shipping (20 per cent) and administrative services (16 per cent). Their contribution to the total non-tax receipts is however low, as these items had narrow bases to begin with. Maintaining this growth rate of revenue may therefore be difficult. The growth of non-tax revenue has already turned negative (-1.1 per cent) during 1997-98 to 2003-04.

1. The items for which the revenue receipts did not exceed Rs. 20 lakh in 2003-04 are clubbed in the category "others".

TABLE 2.2

Tax-Wise Receipts of Andaman & Nicobar Islands: Revised Estimates

(Rs. Lakh)

Year	*Tax Receipts*						
	All Taxes	*Land Revenue*	*Stamps and Registration*	*State Excise*	*Taxes on Vehicles*	*Other Taxes and Duties on Good and Services*	*GSDP at Current Prices*
1	*2*	*3*	*4*	*5*	*6*	*7*	*8*
Symbol	*AT*	*LR*	*S&R*	*SE*	*TOV*	*OT*	*GSDP*
1991-92	121	7	12	90	8	4	34591
1992-93	168	7	14	134	9	4	44705
1993-94	372	12	14	331	10	5	50869
1994-95	474	40	19	400	10	5	61282
1995-96	683	55	28	582	12	6	67497
1996-97	365	66	29	250	14	6	78683
1997-98	865	73	35	730	19	8	89689
1998-99	**927**	**64**	**39**	**797**	**19**	**7**	84934
1999-00	**998**	**57**	**44**	**870**	**20**	**7**	94794
2000-01	1076	50	50	950	20	6	95726
2001-02	1167	67	70	1000	26	4	106856
2002-03	1260	84	90	1050	32	4	116263
2003-04(BE)	1266	90	90	1050	32	4	126499
GR: 1997-98 to 2000-01	**7.55**	**-11.85**	**12.62**	**9.18**	**1.72**	**-9.14**	
Period: 1991-92 to 2003-04							
GR	**19.80**	**21.43**	**19.20**	**20.55**	**12.77**	**0.02**	**10.17**
Buoyancy	**1.88**	**2.16**	**1.71**	**1.94**	**1.17**	**0.12**	

Note: Figures in bold are estimates. GR: Growth Rate.

Source: Government of India, *Detailed Demand for Grants* (Vol. 2) of Ministry of Home Affairs (Union Territories without Legislature) for different years.

Structure of Expenditure

During 1991-92 to 2003-04, total expenditure grew at about 11.3 per cent per annum as against 10.2 per cent per annum growth in GSDP. However, for the period 1997-98 to 2003-04, expenditure grew at about 9.9 per cent per annum as against 6.6 per cent per annum growth in GSDP (columns 10 and 11, Table 2.4). The deceleration in expenditure growth in the recent period occurred largely due to lower growth in capital expenditure (vehicle of growth of an economy). During this period, while revenue expenditure grew at about 14.3 per cent per annum the growth of capital expenditure turned negative (-0.6 per cent per annum). Consequently, the share of capital expenditure has also declined from above 44 per cent in 1991-92 to less than 21 per cent in 2003-04 (column 12 in Table 2.5), with deleterious effect on the GSDP growth of the UT.

Between 1991-92 and 2003-04, total non-plan expenditure grew at above 12.3 per cent per annum as against 10.3 per cent per annum growth in plan expenditure. However, during 1997-98 to 2003-04, non-plan expenditure grew faster at above 12.7 per cent per annum, while the growth of plan expenditure declined to 6.7 per cent per annum (columns 4 and 7 in Table 2.4). The share of plan expenditure, thus, declined from about 48.5 per cent per annum in 1991-92 to about 41.3 per cent per annum in 2003-04 (column 2 in Table 2.5).

Within the plan expenditure, capital expenditure fell more sharply and registered a negative growth of -0.4 per cent per annum. Consequently, the share of capital expenditure in total plan expenditure declined from above 90 per cent in 1991-92 to below 50 per cent in 2003-04 (column 6 in Table 2.5).

The above trends in expenditure do not augur well for the growth of the ANI. If the UT is to be put on a faster growth path, capital expenditure needs to be augmented simultaneously with containment of revenue

TABLE 2.3

Item-Wise Non-tax Receipts of Andaman & Nicobar Islands: Revised Estimates

(Rs. lakh)

Year	*Total Non-Tax Receipts*	*Police*	*Stationary and Printing*	*Public Works*	*Other Administrative Services*	*Water Supply and Sanitation*	*Crop Husbandry*	*Fisheries*	*Forestry and Wildlife*	*Power Projects*	*Village and Small Industries*	*Ports and Light Houses*	*Shipping*	*Road Transport*	*Inland Water Transport*	*Tourism*	*Others*	*SDP at Current Prices*
1	*2*	*3*	*4*	*5*	*6*	*7*	*8*	*9*	*10*	*11*	*12*	*13*	*14*	*15*	*16*	*17*	*18*	*19*
Symbol	*TNTR*	*Police*	*S&P*	*PW*	*OADM*	*WS&S*	*CH*	*Fishery*	*F&W*	*PP*	*V&SSI*	*P&LH*	*SHIP*	*Roads*	*IWT*	*Tourism*	*Others*	*GSDP*
1991-92	2949.00	6.00	13.00	0.00	14.00	26.00	28.00	2.50	1817.00	300.00	9.00	60.00	110.00	133.00	370.00	2.00	67.50	34591
1992-93	4033.00	11.00	20.00	25.00	22.00	45.00	40.00	6.00	2000.00	400.00	15.00	156.00	450.00	250.00	516.00	5.00	87.00	44705
1993-94	4578.00	25.00	22.00	22.00	22.00	70.00	42.00	7.00	2100.00	455.00	20.00	240.00	700.00	275.00	500.00	6.00	92.00	50869
1994-95	5675.20	14.00	22.00	38.00	23.00	70.00	45.00	7.00	2650.00	600.00	29.00	480.00	750.00	342.00	500.00	18.00	116.20	61282
1995-96	6850.49	16.00	23.00	72.00	26.00	30.00	35.00	8.49	3000.00	850.00	20.00	500.00	860.00	391.00	924.00	30.00	85.00	67497
1996-97	7315.00	18.00	24.00	50.00	28.00	38.00	42.00	12.00	3150.00	950.00	29.00	565.00	910.00	410.00	970.00	33.00	115.00	78683
1997-98	8076.50	26.00	24.00	99.00	35.00	77.00	54.00	35.00	2800.00	1620.00	25.00	620.00	1200.00	470.00	850.00	55.00	111.50	89689
1998-99	**8056.83**	**27.27**	**26.42**	**99.33**	**39.42**	**61.90**	**52.63**	**36.59**	**2659.76**	**1708.42**	**24.31**	**684.27**	**1398.64**	**381.83**	**712.20**	**57.24**	**110.92**	84934
1999-00	**8132.46**	**28.60**	**29.07**	**99.67**	**44.40**	**49.76**	**51.30**	**38.26**	**2526.54**	**1801.67**	**23.65**	**755.21**	**1630.16**	**310.19**	**596.74**	**59.57**	**111.32**	94794
2000-01	8302.00	30.00	32.00	100.00	50.00	40.00	50.00	40.00	2400.00	1900.00	23.00	833.50	1900.00	252.00	500.00	62.00	112.50	95726
2001-02	8118.00	40.00	40.00	100.00	113.00	62.00	50.00	40.00	1600.00	2250.00	24.00	1233.00	1800.00	170.00	400.00	90.00	130.00	106856
2002-03	7514.70	40.00	55.00	300.00	82.70	80.00	40.00	40.00	650.00	2500.00	35.00	1254.00	1950.00	226.00	37.00	120.00	139.00	116263
2003-04 (BE)	7648.60	40.00	60.00	350.00	82.60	100.00	50.00	45.00	650.00	2500.00	35.00	1278.00	1950.00	230.00	50.00	120.00	142.00	126499
GR:1997-98 to 2000-01	**0.92**	**4.89**	**10.06**	**0.34**	**12.62**	**-19.61**	**-2.53**	**4.55**	**-5.01**	**5.46**	**-2.74**	**10.37**	**16.55**	**-18.76**	**-16.21**	**4.07**	**0.30**	**2.20**
Period: 1991-92 to 2003-04																		
GR	**7.14**	**13.83**	**10.59**	**24.66**	**16.35**	**5.82**	**3.06**	**26.76**	**-7.24**	**20.42**	**7.16**	**23.21**	**19.79**	**-0.33**	**-13.91**	**36.72**	**4.84**	**10.17**
Buoyancy	**0.78**	**1.32**	**0.96**	**2.46**	**1.44**	**0.59**	**0.35**	**2.42**	**-0.54**	**1.88**	**0.78**	**2.22**	**1.94**	**0.19**	**-1.11**	**3.29**	**0.49**	**1.00**

Note: Government of India, *Detailed Demand for Grants* (Vol. 2), Ministry of Home Affairs (Union Territories without Legislature) for different years

Source: Figures in bold are estimates. GR: Growth rate.

TABLE 2.4

Expenditure of Andaman & Nicobar Islands: Actuals

(Rs. Crore)

Year	*Plan Expenditure*			*Non-plan Expenditure*			*Total Expenditure*			
	Revenue	*Capital*	*Total*	*Revenue*	*Capital*	*Total*	*Revenue*	*Capital*	*Total*	*GSDP (Rs. Crore)*
1	*2*	*3*	*4*	*5*	*6*	*7*	*8*	*9*	*10*	*11*
1988-89(RE)			66.00			80.76			146.76	207
1989-90(RE)			63.47			110.58			174.05	246
1990-91(RE)			97.00			126.38			223.38	270
1991-92(RE)	15.37	138.63	154.00	162.13	1.12	163.25	177.50	139.75	317.25	346
1992-93(RE)	23.19	131.81	155.00	155.90	1.16	157.06	179.09	132.97	312.06	447
1993-94(RE)	24.93	131.57	156.50	160.83	1.17	162.00	185.76	132.74	318.50	509
1994-95(RE)	32.70	167.30	200.00	178.79	1.21	180.00	211.49	168.51	380.00	613
1995-96(RE)	62.48	153.44	215.92	217.81	1.21	219.02	280.29	154.65	434.94	675
1996-97(RE)	64.38	157.92	222.30	235.29	1.21	236.50	299.67	159.13	458.80	787
1997-98	77.91	175.51	253.42	260.30	3.89	264.19	338.21	179.40	517.61	897
1998-99	103.92	216.08	320.00	327.24	1.42	328.66	431.16	217.50	648.66	849
1999-00	103.37	294.90	398.27	357.42	3.19	360.61	460.79	298.09	758.88	948
2000-01	104.54	308.44	412.98	403.69	2.65	406.34	508.23	311.09	819.32	957
2001-02	181.78	183.95	365.73	442.71	1.37	444.08	624.49	185.32	809.81	1069
2002-03(RE)	196.89	205.17	402.06	481.64	1.47	483.11	678.53	206.64	885.17	1163
2003-04(BE)	205.49	204.51	410.00	580.32	1.91	582.23	785.81	206.42	992.23	1265
Period: 1991-92 to 2003-04										
GR	24.01	5.27	10.27	12.30	5.34	12.26	14.36	5.27	11.34	10.17
Buoyancy	2.15	0.50	0.94	1.09	0.58	1.09	1.28	0.50	1.02	
Period: 1997-98 to 2003-04										
GR	18.50	-0.42	6.70	12.88	-9.87	12.71	14.29	-0.56	9.88	6.56
Buoyancy	2.46	-0.35	0.75	1.67	-1.12	1.65	1.87	-0.36	1.24	

Notes: Expenditure Budget of Union Government of India, Vol. 1, Statement 2, for different years.

Source: RE: Revised Estimates; BE: Budget Estimates.

expenditure. Further, the UT should also raise its revenues through improved taxation, and allocating the additional revenue for expenditure on developmental activities.

Status of Local Bodies

Until the 73rd and 74th amendment of the Constitution in 1992, local bodies did not have any statutory power for taxation. The rural local bodies as per the 73rd amendment and the urban local bodies as

per the 74th amendment of the Constitution are now statutory bodies, and are required to be empowered to raise their own resources commensurate with the specified functions to be assigned to them. As per the Constitution, 29 functions are specified for transfer to rural local bodies (Annexure 2.1), and 18 functions are specified for transfer to urban local bodies (Annexure 2.2). The own resources of the local bodies need to be supplemented with transfers/grants from the respective states and/or central government. Each state is supposed to constitute a State Finance Commission periodically, for making recommendations on devolution of functions and revenues to the local bodies.

The Second Finance Commission on UTs without legislature (covering Andaman & Nicobar Islands) has submitted its report recently. The thrust of the report is on:

- Devolution of all identified functions to the local bodies along with taxing powers.
- Consolidation of financial position of local bodies commensurate to the devolution of functions.

TABLE 2.5

Composition of Expenditure of Andaman & Nicobar Islands

(Per Cent)

Year	*Total Expenditure*			*Plan Expenditure*			*Non-plan Expenditure*			*Total Expenditure*		
	Plan	*Non-plan*	*Total*	*Revenue*	*Capital*	*Total*	*Revenue*	*Capital*	*Total*	*Revenue*	*Capital*	*Total*
1	*2*	*3*	*4*	*5*	*6*	*7*	*8*	*9*	*10*	*11*	*12*	*13*
1988-89(RE)	44.97	55.03	100									
1989-90(RE)	36.47	63.53	100									
1990-91(RE)	43.42	56.58	100									
1991-92(RE)	48.54	51.46	100	9.98	90.02	100	99.31	0.69	100	55.95	44.05	100
1992-93(RE)	49.67	50.33	100	14.96	85.04	100	99.26	0.74	100	57.39	42.61	100
1993-94(RE)	49.14	50.86	100	15.93	84.07	100	99.28	0.72	100	58.32	41.68	100
1994-95(RE)	52.63	47.37	100	16.35	83.65	100	99.33	0.67	100	55.66	44.34	100
1995-96(RE)	49.64	50.36	100	28.94	71.06	100	99.45	0.55	100	64.44	35.56	100
1996-97(RE)	48.45	51.55	100	28.96	71.04	100	99.49	0.51	100	65.32	34.68	100
1997-98	48.96	51.04	100	30.74	69.26	100	98.53	1.47	100	65.34	34.66	100
1998-99	49.33	50.67	100	32.48	67.53	100	99.57	0.43	100	66.47	33.53	100
1999-00	52.48	47.52	100	25.95	74.05	100	99.12	0.88	100	60.72	39.28	100
2000-01	50.41	49.59	100	25.31	74.69	100	99.35	0.65	100	62.03	37.97	100
2001-02	45.16	54.84	100	49.70	50.30	100	99.69	0.31	100	77.12	22.88	100
2002-03(RE)	45.42	54.58	100	48.97	51.03	100	99.70	0.30	100	76.66	23.34	100
2003-04(BE)	41.32	58.68	100	50.12	49.88	100	99.67	0.33	100	79.20	20.80	100

Notes: Computed on the basis of data compiled from *Expenditure Budget of Union Government of India*, Vol. 1, Statement 2, for different years.

Source: RE: Revised Estimates; BE: Budget Estimates.

- Normative assessment of fiscal needs of local bodies.
- Higher own tax revenues: Taxes that according to the Commission are suitable for assigning to local bodies include property tax, profession tax, octroi, ferry tax, hoarding tax, toll tax on bridges and roads.
- Autonomy of local bodies in determining tax bases and rates, subject to floor rates.

The UT has already transferred 8 of the 18 functions to the lone urban local body (Port Blair Municipal Corporation) and 6 of the 29 subjects to rural local bodies (Panchayati Raj Institutions). Transfer of other functions is being undertaken in phases for a smooth transition. The UT is, however, not alone in transferring less than the mandated number of functions to the local bodies. For example, with regard to urban local bodies, the number of functions transferred is 8 in Andhra Pradesh and Punjab, 9 in Rajasthan, and 11 in Maharashtra, although there also are states where most of the functions have been transferred, like 16 in Madhya Pradesh, 17 in Haryana and West Bengal and all 18 in Kerala and Tamil Nadu. These details along with information on transfer of functions effected in select states are presented in Table 2.6.

Functions requiring greater degree of skill and planning like, urban planning including town planning, regulation of land use and construction of buildings, planning for economic and social development, and slum improvement and upgradation, have been transferred by only half of the states selected.

The local bodies have been mandated, not to run deficit budgets. Their resources include their own revenues and the grants and transfers from the other tiers of the government. Unlike the case of the UT, resources raised by local bodies remain at their discretion. This retains the incentive for raising own resources, though generally these may fall short of the required resources because of mismatch of revenue powers and functions assigned to them. The financial position of the PBMC in Table 2.7 throws some light on the mismatch.

The own revenues of the municipality cover a significant part of its expenditure. The revenue to

TABLE 2.6

Status Regarding Transfer of Function to Urban Local Bodies as per 74th Amendment of the Constitution

Sl. No.	12th Schedule Items	No. of Function Transferred	Function Number 1	2	3	4	5	6	7	8	9	10	11	12	13	14	15	16	17	18
1.	**Andaman & Nicobar Islands**	**8**																		
2.	Andhra Pradesh	8	N	N	N	Y	N	Y	N	Y	Y	N	N	Y	N	Y	N	Y	N	Y
3.	Gujarat	14	N	N	Y	Y	Y	Y	Y	Y	Y	N	N	Y	Y	Y	Y	Y	Y	Y
4.	Haryana	17	Y	Y	Y	Y	Y	Y	Y	Y	Y	Y	Y	Y	Y	Y	Y	Y	Y	N
5.	Karnataka	16	Y	Y	N	Y	Y	Y	N	Y	Y	Y	Y	Y	Y	Y	Y	Y	Y	Y
6.	Kerala	18	Y	Y	Y	Y	Y	Y	Y	Y	Y	Y	Y	Y	Y	Y	Y	Y	Y	Y
7.	Madhya Pradesh	16	Y	Y	Y	Y	Y	Y	Y	Y	Y	N	Y	Y	N	Y	Y	Y	Y	Y
8.	Maharashtra	11	N	N	N	Y	Y	Y	Y	N	N	N	Y	N	Y	Y	Y	Y	Y	Y
9.	Punjab	8	Y	Y	Y	Y	Y	Y	Y	Y	Y	Y	Y	Y	Y	Y	Y	Y	Y	Y
10.	Rajasthan	9	N	N	N	Y	Y	Y	Y	N	N	N	N	N	N	Y	Y	Y	Y	Y
11.	Tamil Nadu	18	Y	Y	Y	Y	Y	Y	Y	Y	Y	Y	Y	Y	Y	Y	Y	Y	Y	Y
12.	Uttar Pradesh	14	N	N	N	Y	Y	Y	N	Y	Y	Y	Y	Y	Y	Y	Y	Y	Y	Y
13.	West Bengal	17	Y	Y	N	Y	Y	Y	Y	Y	Y	Y	Y	Y	Y	Y	Y	Y	Y	Y
14.	No. of States/UTs that transferred the function		7	7	6	12	11	12	9	10	10	7	9	10	9	12	11	12	11	11

Notes: Y—Yes, assigned to Municipalities; N—No, not assigned.

List of functions assignable to urban local bodies (12th Schedule)

1. Urban planning including town planning.
2. Regulation of land use and construction of buildings.
3. Planning for economic and social development.
4. Roads and bridges.
5. Water supply for domestic, industrial and commercial purposes.
6. Public health, sanitation, conservancy and solid waste management.
7. Fire services.
8. Urban forestry, protection of the environment and promotion of ecological aspects.
9. Safeguarding the interests of the weaker sections of the society including, the handicapped and the mentally retarded.
10. Slum improvement and upgradation.
11. Urban poverty alleviation.
12. Provision of urban amenities and facilities such as parks, gardens, playgrounds.
13. Promotion of cultural, educational and aesthetic aspects.
14. Burials and burial grounds, cremation grounds, and electric crematorium.
15. Cattle pounds, prevention of cruelty to animals.
16. Vital statistics including registration of births and deaths.
17. Public amenities including street lighting, bus stops, public conveniences.
18. Regulation of slaughter houses and tanneries.

Source: Compiled from various documents.

TABLE 2.7

Revenue Receipts and Expenditure of Municipal Board of Andaman & Nicobar Islands

Year	*Revenue (Rs. Lakh)*							*Expenditure (Rs. Lakh)*	*Revenue as Percentage of Expenditure*	*Octroi as Percentage of*	
	Total	*Entertainment Tax*	*Octroi*	*Property Tax*	*Water Charges*	*Conservancy Fee*	*Others*			*Revenue*	*Expenditure*
1	*2*	*3*	*4*	*5*	*6*	*7*	*8*	*9*	*10*	*11*	*12*
1991-92	322.36	0.76	216.74					377.41	85.41	67.24	57.43
1992-93	338.08	1.41	222.87					446.26	75.76	65.92	49.94
1993-94	404.75	0.70	291.59					576.41	70.22	72.04	50.59
1994-95	570.00	1.32	422.00					631.72	90.23	74.04	66.80
1995-96	588.32	1.18	418.51					945.82	62.20	71.14	44.25
1996-97	704.76	1.05	522.81					1049.40	67.16	74.18	49.82
1997-98	907.78	0.00	674.02					979.14	92.71	74.25	68.84
1998-99	1124.84	0.00	822.39					1162.55	96.76	73.11	70.74
1999-00											
2000-01											
2001-02	1679.23	0.51	1420.03	33.65	164.61	16.17	44.25	1487.17	112.91	84.56	95.48
2002-03											
2003-04											
GR: 91-99 (%)	20.10	5.03	21.87					18.14			

Sources: 1. *Andaman & Nicobar Islands Basic Statistics*, 1996-97 to 1998-99, and for earlier years, Directorate of Economic and Statistics, Andaman & Nicobar Administration, Port Blair

2. *Andaman & Nicobar Islands at a Glance, 2002*, Directorate of Economics and Statistics, Andaman & Nicobar Islands, Port Blair

expenditure ratio was above 70 per cent in the early 1990s. The ratio has since improved, and in fact, exceeded 100 per cent in 2001-02 implying a revenue surplus scenario (column 10). This occurred, because the revenues of the municipality have grown faster (at 20.1 per cent) than the expenditure (at 18.1 per cent). The impressive growth of revenue is attributable to the healthy growth of octroi[2] that grew at the rate of 21.9 per cent (column 4) and its share in revenue has accordingly increased from 67.2 per cent in 1991-92 to 84.6 per cent in 2001-02 (column 11).

It may, however, be noted that the dependence of the municipality on octroi has increased over time. Revenue from octroi accounted for about 57 per cent of the expenditure in 1991-92 and about 95 per cent of the expenditure in 2001-02 (column 12 in Table 2.7). In view of certain inherent weaknesses of octroi most of the states that levied octroi have already abolished it. Alternatives to octroi need to be explored to phase it out in ANI, in the medium term.

Resource Mobilisation

The potential of the UT in realising higher tax revenue as well as non-tax revenue should be fully exploited. Tax revenue can be mobilised through appropriate tax reforms and non-tax revenue can be mobilised through higher cost recovery in public services.

Reform of the Tax System

As discussed earlier, tax revenues can be raised significantly through suitable tax reforms as the tax to GSDP ratio in the UT, which is around one per cent, is substantially lower than the all-state ratio of above five per cent. While some additional revenue can be realised from the existing taxes such as entertainment tax and property tax through administrative reforms, substantial revenue can be obtained by implementing sales tax that has hitherto not been introduced in the UT. In view of the national consensus, on replacing sales tax in all Indian states, by a value added tax

2. Octroi is a levy charged on entry of goods into an urban (such as a municipality) jurisdiction, on the basis of value or quantity of goods. In the case of Andaman and Nicobar Islands, it is levied on entry of goods into jurisdiction of Port Blair Municipal Corporation (PBMC).

(VAT),[3] it will be prudent to introduce a simple system of VAT with a high threshold and single rate. A low rate of about four per cent would facilitate smooth introduction of the tax by minimising the potential local resistance to a new tax. This stand-alone system of VAT in the UT would not interfere with the design characteristics adopted in the other states and UTs because of the specific geographical location of the UT.

Computerisation and adoption of modern techniques of tax administration including self-assessment and selected audit of taxpayers would go a long way in imparting efficiency, minimising scope for taxpayer harassment, and generating substantial revenues for the UT and the local bodies. At the third tier of the government, that is, at the local level, innovative techniques should be evolved in assessing property tax along with self-assessment.[4]

Improved Recovery of Costs of Public Services

Own revenues contribute less than 10 per cent of the expenditure. This contribution must improve if the UT has to move on a sustainable growth trajectory, consistent with the growth targets set for the Tenth Five-Year Plan. Thus, it would be important to undertake a detailed study to identify areas where there may be clear scope for improving cost recovery.

However, caution needs to be exercised in assessing the potential for improving recovery rates by raising user charges, as there may be scope for reducing costs by locating and minimising sources of inefficiency including leakages in the provision of services. Further, some subsidies may have been required to achieve some scale of operation, which in turn, may be technologically constrained.[5]

Expenditure Control

Expenditure in the UT can be controlled mainly through reduction or elimination of subsidies and partial or full participation of the private sector in service delivery. In selective activities such as building and operation of roads and bridges, and development of select islands for promoting tourism, private sector participation (PSP) can result in substantial expenditure compression. Further, PSP opens doors to modern technology, and results in cost-effective service delivery besides improvement in quality of services.

There is a possibility that presence of subsidy can lead to misuse—but then this would be true for any universal subsidy programme. There appears some evidence to suspect misuse/excess demand for some health services.[6] In the case of services where the introduction of service was a prime concern, the assessment of the subsidisation strategy should be viewed as a revenue maximisation strategy or a loss minimisation strategy.

There is also a tendency to create new employment in the public sector, which results in surplus staff in government departments. This causes a burden on scarce public resources and harbours inefficiency. Identifying and retrenching excess staff at a later date places a heavy burden on the exchequer as this is evident from the voluntary retirement schemes introduced recently in many public sector banks. Efforts should be made for greater private sector participation and employment to provide expenditure efficiency.

Institutional Framework

To implement the suggestions emerging from the discussions in the earlier sections, appropriate institutions for training, planning, developing modern tax designs, developing modern techniques of tax administration, etc. need to be put in place. Some of these tasks could be assigned to specialised institutions, and for execution of these functions, capacities may be developed in the government departments with involvement of private institutions and/or specialised professionals.

So far the UT has managed without a separate tax department. It will, however, be in the interest of the UT to set up a separate tax department to focus

---

3. In simple terms, VAT can be defined as a multi-point sales tax with set off for the tax paid on purchases. Accordingly, a dealer (shopkeeper) would pay sales tax on his purchases and collect sales tax on his sales, and pass on the excess collection (that is tax collected on sales minus tax paid on purchases) to the exchequer, periodically, which could either be monthly or quarterly.

4. In assessing the property tax, some municipalities have shifted from rental value basis to a system based on physical characteristics of the property such as location, covered area. Feasibility of this system combined with self-assessment may be explored in the case of UT.

5. Quite often the technological indivisibility of operating a service may lead to excess capacity building in the short run. The preliminary sunk cost of provisioning may inhibit any subsequent attempt to take advantage of the later technological improvements (either in the form of divisibility of operations or in the form of upgradation of the scale of operations). This then reflects as poor planning, which unless undertaken meticulously may have severe long-term implications.

6. This came out during our discussions with local people, including government employees.

attention on issues in taxation. A tax research unit in the tax department will also be required for formulating and evaluating tax policies and analysing the implications of subsidies.

Revenue and Expenditure Projections for the Tenth Five-year Plan

Revenue and expenditure projections are obtained by taking 2002-03 as the base year, and using buoyancy coefficients with reference to GSDP for the period 1991-1992 to 2003-04. GSDP is taken to grow at an increasing rate over the Tenth FYP period, that is, during 2002-03 to 2006-07. The growth rate of GSDP during 2003-04, 2004-05, 2005-06 and 2006-07 is taken to be 8.8, 9.0, 9.5 and 10.0 per cent, respectively. If 'b' is the buoyancy coefficient of revenue or expenditure and 'r' is the growth rate of GSDP in a year, then the revenue or expenditure, as the case may be, would grow at the rate of 'br' per cent. Projections of total revenue are obtained by adding the projections of tax and non-tax revenues. Similarly, projections of total expenditure are obtained by adding projections of revenue expenditure, capital expenditure and loans and advances.

From Table 2.8, it would be seen that in the business-as-usual case the gap between revenue and expenditure would widen over time because the expenditure buoyancy is greater than revenue buoyancy (columns 2 and 5). The expenditure level that was about 10 times the revenue in 2002-03 increases to 11 times in 2006-07. This trend of increase in revenue-expenditure gap can be reversed through an improvement in revenue buoyancy and expenditure control. Given the limited scope for expenditure control through reduction or elimination of subsidies in the short-run, greater emphasis has to be laid on improving revenue buoyancy.

TABLE 2.8

Revenue and Expenditure Projections of Andaman & Nicobar Islands for the Tenth Five-year Plan

Year	*Revenue Receipts (RE)*			*Expenditure (RE)*						
	Total Revenue (Rs. Crore)	*Tax Revenue (Rs. Crore)*	*Non-tax Revenue (Rs. Crore)*	*Total (Rs. Crore)*	*Revenue Expenditure (Rs. Crore)*	*Capital Expenditure (Rs. Crore)*	*Loans & Advances (Rs. Crore)*	*GSDP at Current Prices (Rs. Crore)*	*Yearly Growth Rate of GSDP (Percent)*	*Revenue of the Municipality from Octroi (Rs. Crore)*
1	*2*	*3*	*4*	*5*	*6*	*7*	*8*	*9*	*10*	*11*
1991-92	30.70	1.21	29.49	317.25	177.50	139.32	0.43	346		2.17
1992-93	42.01	1.68	40.33	312.06	179.09	132.39	0.58	447	29.24	2.23
1993-94	49.50	3.72	45.78	318.50	185.76	132.08	0.66	509	13.79	2.92
1994-95	61.49	4.74	56.75	380.00	211.49	164.98	3.53	613	20.47	4.22
1995-96	75.33	6.83	68.50	434.94	280.29	151.35	3.30	675	10.14	4.19
1996-97	76.80	3.65	73.15	458.80	299.67	158.61	0.52	787	16.57	5.23
1997-98	89.42	8.65	80.77	535.60	357.80	177.10	0.70	897	13.99	6.74
1998-99	89.84	9.27	80.57	648.66	431.16	216.86	0.64	849	-5.30	8.22
1999-00	91.30	9.98	81.32	755.00	458.93	295.28	0.79	948	11.61	9.87
2000-01	93.78	10.76	83.02	809.56	498.39	310.26	0.91	957	0.98	11.84
2001-02	92.85	11.67	81.18	813.00	625.66	186.31	1.03	1069	11.63	14.20
2002-03	87.74	12.60	75.14	885.17	678.53	205.03	1.61	1163	8.80	16.36
2003-04(BE)	89.14	12.66	76.48	992.23	785.81	203.39	3.03	1265	8.80	
GR	8.23	19.80	7.23	11.32	14.33	5.29	6.75	10.17		21.64
Buoyancy	0.87	1.88	0.78	1.02	1.28	0.50	0.70			1.73
Projections with Buoyancy and Base Year 2002-03										
2002-03	87.74	12.60	75.14	885.17	678.53	205.03	1.61	1163	8.80	16.36
2003-04	95.01	14.68	80.32	970.74	755.03	214.01	1.71	1265	8.80	18.86
2004-05	103.16	17.17	85.99	1067.45	842.04	223.59	1.82	1379	9.00	21.79
2005-06	112.63	20.23	92.40	1180.57	944.48	234.16	1.94	1510	9.50	25.37
2006-07	123.68	24.04	99.65	1313.30	1065.42	245.81	2.08	1661	10.00	29.76

Notes: RE: Revised Estimates; UTs.: Union Territories

Sources: Same as in Table 2.1

Note also that the PBMC's revenue from octroi is projected to grow from Rs. 16.36 crore in 2002-03 to Rs. 29.76 crore in 2006-07. The municipality would require compensation of that order, if octroi were to be abolished.

Forest conservation in ANI provides spillover benefits to the rest of the country and also the world in terms of carbon sequestration to mitigate climate change problems, and the protection of biodiversity. There are now some institutional arrangements to capture these benefits in the form of financial flows. An example is the instrument of clean development mechanism (CDM) under Kyoto Protocol for Climate Change. This however needs to be explored further. Given that there is a trade-off between commercial and conservation benefits of forests, from even the national perspective ANI should explore the possibility of resource transfers from the central government for the spillover benefits generated from the forest conservation.

Main Findings and Conclusions

The revenue raised by the UT accounts for less than 10 per cent of its expenditure. Taxes make a meagre contribution to the total revenue of the UT. The tax to GSDP ratio in the UT is around 1 per cent, whereas the tax to GSDP ratio at the all-states level is above 5 per cent.

The UT has the potential for raising substantial additional tax revenue by introducing sales tax. The same should be introduced in the form of a VAT with high threshold and single low rate (say 4 per cent). Growth of the currently levied taxes has been encouraging, but maintaining this growth would require greater emphasis on enforcement.

In the recent past, the contribution of non-tax revenue to the receipts of the UT has declined. The ratio of non-tax receipts to GSDP of the UT has declined from about 10 per cent in 1995-96 to about 6 per cent in 2003-04, and the growth of non-tax revenue has turned negative (-1.1 per cent) during 1997-98 to 2003-04.

The receipts from two of the major revenue items, namely forestry and wildlife, and inland water transport registered negative growth, along with sharp dip in receipts in the last two years, largely owing to the Supreme Court's ruling on conservation of forests.

The composition of expenditure has substantially changed in favour of revenue expenditure, undermining the growth potential of the UT. The share of capital expenditure has declined from above 44 per cent in 1991-92 to less than 21 per cent in 2003-04. If the UT is to be put on faster growth trajectory, capital expenditure needs to be augmented simultaneously with containing of revenue expenditure.

The UT has made significant progress in transferring functions to local bodies as per the 73rd and 74th amendments to the Constitution. It has adopted the strategy of transfer of functions in stages, for smooth transition. The UT has already transferred 8 of the 18 functions to the lone urban local body, PBMC, and 6 of the 29 subjects to PRIs. The transfer of the remaining functions should be taken up earnestly along with the transfer of funds and functionaries.

The financial health of the PBMC appears satisfying as it is managing its expenditure mainly from its own resources. The problem however is in its heavy dependence on octroi that has the potential to adversely affect the growth of the UT because it acts as a barrier to free trade. The scenario with revenue loss arising from abolishing octroi could be dealt with by a suitable mix of compensation by the UT and/or the central government, adequate upward revision of user charges for the services provided by the municipality, and private sector participation in provision/delivery of services.

The financial needs of the rural local bodies should be assessed normatively as advocated by the Second Finance Commission on Union Territories. And provision should be made for the necessary revenues or revenue resources to the local bodies.

Expenditure control should be exercised by all possible means such as reduction or elimination of subsidies, private sector participation in service delivery, and rationalising the strategy of employment generation in the public sector.

Appropriate institutional arrangements would be necessary for implementing the emerging suggestions. For example, to realise the full tax potential, it may be prudent to set up a separate tax department. A tax research unit in the tax department will also be required for formulating and evaluating tax policies and analysing implication of subsidies.

ANNEXURE 2.1

Functions Specified for Transfer to Rural Local Bodies

1. Agriculture, including agricultural extension.
2. Land improvement, implementation of land reforms, land consolidation and soil conservation.
3. Minor irrigation, water management and watershed development.
4. Animal husbandry, dairying and poultry.
5. Fisheries.
6. Social forestry and farm forestry.
7. Minor forest produce.
8. Small-scale industries, including food processing industries.
9. Khadi, village and cottage industries.
10. Rural housing.
11. Drinking water.
12. Fuel and fodder.
13. Roads, culverts, bridges, ferries, waterways, and other means of communication.
14. Rural electrification, including distribution of electricity.
15. Non-conventional energy sources.
16. Poverty alleviation programme.
17. Education, including primary and secondary schools.
18. Technical training and vocational education.
19. Adult and non-formal education.
20. Libraries.
21. Cultural activities.
22. Markets and fairs.
23. Health and sanitation, including hospitals, primary health centres and dispensaries.
24. Family welfare.
25. Women and child development.
26. Social welfare, including welfare of the handicapped, and the mentally retarded.
27. Welfare of the weaker sections, and in particular, of the scheduled castes and the scheduled tribes.
28. Public distribution system.
29. Maintenance of community assets.

ANNEXURE 2.2

Functions Specified for Transfer to Urban Local Bodies

1. Urban planning, including town planning.
2. Regulation of land use and construction of buildings.
3. Planning for economic and social development.
4. Roads and bridges.
5. Water supply for domestic, industrial and commercial purposes.
6. Public health, sanitation, conservancy and solid waste management.
7. Fire services.
8. Urban forestry, protection of the environment and promotion of ecological aspects.
9. Safeguarding the interests of the weaker sections of the society including the handicapped and the mentally retarded.
10. Slum improvement and upgradation.
11. Urban poverty alleviation.
12. Provision of urban amenities and facilities such as parks, gardens, playgrounds.
13. Promotion of cultural, educational and aesthetic aspects.
14. Burials and burial grounds, cremation grounds, and electric crematorium.
15. Cattle ponds, prevention of cruelty to animals.
16. Vital statistics including registration of births and deaths.
17. Public amenities including street lighting, bus stops, public conveniences.
18. Regulation of slaughter houses and tanneries.

Chapter 3

Infrastructure: An Assessment

Introduction

The availability of adequate infrastructure facilities is vital for accelerating the growth of a region. This chapter analyses the status of infrastructure development in ANI, and highlights the infrastructure requirements to stimulate economic development and improve the quality of life of people.

Plan of this chapter is as follows: next section discusses new approaches to the provision of infrastructure services and draws broad policy guidelines for application in ANI. Section 3.3 is focused on roads as means of connectivity, while Section 3.4 looks at aviation. Section 3.5 examines the status of energy. Sections 3.6 and 3.7 cover water supply, and housing, respectively. The status of and requirements for infrastructure in respect of shipping, agriculture, fishery, and tourism is discussed in chapters 4, 7, 8 and 11, respectively.

New Approaches to the Provision of Infrastructure

Infrastructure services are characterised by the existence of positive externalities implying that recovery of full cost through user charges may not be appropriate. Further, the provision of these services usually involves high upfront costs and long payback periods.

Infrastructure services, because of the externalities, economies of scale, and lumpy investments are predominantly provided by the public sector. However, in the recent years, attempts have been made to commercialise infrastructure services because public provision of these services is found to be less than satisfactory as it lacks both efficiency and quality.

With the globalisation of economies all over the world, the need to provide efficient infrastructure services at competitive prices has been felt. The potential benefits of commercialisation of infrastructure services have provided the necessary motivation for exploring new approaches for provision of such services, which were traditionally considered to be purely in the domain of public sector. The new approaches are perceived to promote efficiency as well as quality, resulting in cost-effectiveness.

There is substantial change in general environment in the recent years that makes it feasible to adopt new approaches in providing infrastructure services. Some of the notable features of the changed environment are:

- Technological changes have overcome the limitations of traditional mechanisms of providing infrastructure services.
- Capacity of the private sector to raise resources globally.
- Success of joint ventures in the provision of infrastructure services.
- Scope of bundling or unbundling certain infrastructure services such as solid waste management into collection, transportation and disposal functions, for partial privatisation.
- Increased acceptance of dual policy of decontrolling and regulating production and/or supply/distribution of infrastructure services.

The new approaches to the provision of infrastructure services are based on identification of services that can be provided on commercial basis, bundling or unbundling of services to induce the private sector, and appropriate regulation and monitoring. The possible new approaches include the following:

- Private provision of services subject to regulation. For example, transport facilities in specified areas, and solid waste management. Private sector can be induced to provide these facilities on low-density routes by bundling low-density routes with high-density routes subject to the regulation that trips on the high-density road will be a specified multiple of trips on the low-density road.
- Outsourcing the services of private sector, such as in production and/or distribution of electricity, collection and/or transport of solid waste, and treatment and bulk supply of water. The other functions can remain with the public sector such as retail distribution and pricing of water.
- Build-operate-transfer (BOT) or build-own-operate-transfer (BOOT): Under a BOT project, the private entrepreneur makes investment in the project, operates the facility for a specified period with a user charge, and finally transfers the facility to the government, e.g. construction of roads, and bridges.

Roads and Bridges

Roads and bridges facilitate transportation of goods and passengers, and provide linkages between centres of production and distribution. Generally, there are three categories of roads that is national highways, state roads, and municipal/rural roads. A national highway facilitates inter-state traffic, as the UT of ANI is located in the Bay of Bengal far away from the mainland; there is no land connection feasible with the mainland. The roads in the UT are divided into three categories *viz.*, trunk roads (inter-island roads), urban roads (primarily roads within the Port Blair township), and rural roads (roads linking villages to a trunk road, or inter-village roads). As per the 73rd and 74th amendments of the Constitution, the rural and urban roads are to be looked after by the Panchayati Raj Institutions (PRIs) and Port Blair Municipal Corporation (PBMC), respectively. The responsibility of the upkeep of the trunk roads rests with the administration of UT.

There are three trunk roads *viz.*, Andaman Trunk Road (ATR, 333 km.), Little Andaman Trunk Road (LATR, 24 km.), and Great Nicobar Trunk Road (GNTR, 93 km.) having an average width of 3.6 m. The urban roads of varied lane width in the city of Port Blair add up to about 117 km., and rural roads measure about 722 km. (including interior village roads extending to 122 km.).

Due to substantial forest area (over 85 per cent) in the UT, the road density (by area) cannot be easily compared with that of other states and UTs. Road density (by area) in the UT has been low, just next to Jammu and Kashmir, Lakshadweep and Daman and Diu. In 1990-91, it was 109 km. per 1000 sq. km. as against 609 km. per 1000 sq. km. at all-India level. In spite of substantial improvement in road density in the UT during 1990-91 to 1996-97, its relative position remained unchanged (Table 3.1). One of the primary reasons for this is the huge forest area of the UT. The relative position of the UT in terms of road density with reference to population (km. per lakh of population) is however, better (Table 3.2). Road density by population in the UT is higher than that at the all-India level, reflecting low population density.

Condition of many existing roads is poor having an adverse impact on the speed of road traffic and life of vehicles. Widening the existing roads and construction of new roads in urban as well as rural areas is desirable to cope with the ever increasing traffic, but priority should be given to replacing narrow culverts by bridges, and repairing and maintaining in good condition the existing roads and bridges.

Rural road network connects all the villages with population exceeding 1000, while only 52 per cent of the villages with population below 1000. This scenario is better than that of in many states and at the all-India level (Table 3.3). However, the condition of the existing roads is less than satisfactory. All weather connectivity for many villages is limited, with poor connectivity farmers get lower price for their produce while urban consumer pays higher price. Condition of existing roads needs to be improved and new roads be constructed to provide better connectivity of the villages to the main roads, as also for inter-connectivity of the villages. To improve durability of roads, use of upgraded technology is essential. To facilitate smooth flow of traffic, some of the existing narrow culverts need to be replaced by suitable bridges, and some new bridges need to be constructed over some of the *nullahs*. To meet the financial needs of rural roads and bridges, the Tenth FY P provided a sum of Rs. 33 crore.

Inter-island Connectivity

Good transport system is one of the key determinants of economic development of an economy. Increase in population, changes in economic activity, lifestyle, and other demographic and social developments in ANI have resulted in an increase in

TABLE 3.1

State-wise Road Density by Area (km.) (Per '000 sq. km.)

(Arranged in Descending Order of 1996-97)

Sl. No.	States/Union Territories	1971-72	1981-82	1990-91	1991-92	1992-93	1993-94	1994-95	1995-96	1996-97
1	2	3	4	2	3	4	5	6	7	8
1.	Delhi	7984	10527	14061	14227	15285	16441	16562	17961	17961
2.	Chandigarh	710	1250	14000	14000	14545	14773	14836	15664	15936
3.	Pondicherry	3508	4286	5146	11201	4707	4814	4771	4782	4908
4.	Kerala	3106	2751	3488	3567	3472	3554	3585	3650	3749
5.	Goa	1581	2141	1988	1945	1965	1969	1974	2015	2314
6.	Orissa	366	772	1258	1260	1366	1371	1348	1363	1687
7.	Tamil Nadu	714	1020	1512	1523	1533	1560	1572	1582	1588
8.	Tripura	386	759	1341	1342	1397	1399	1402	1404	1404
9.	Punjab	594	916	1077	1078	1128	1132	1133	1155	1278
10.	Maharashtra	316	586	721	730	729	731	731	1168	1176
11.	Nagaland	284	379	890	901	480	775	777	828	1107
12.	Dadra & Nagar Haveli	460	492	642	642	727	729	1039	1057	1088
13.	Assam	383	760	836	836	853	410	868	872	872
14.	Uttar Pradesh	382	520	682	692	655	668	679	806	868
15.	Karnataka	525	557	686	701	727	728	729	744	751
16.	Andhra Pradesh	264	468	486	493	590	603	625	628	647
17.	Haryana	307	542	599	601	609	607	615	631	637
18.	Himachal Pradesh	215	369	451	459	503	519	538	532	542
19.	Bihar	670	481	4912	492	505	505	505	492	508
20.	Manipur	392	239	298	314	314	315	472	482	490
21.	Gujarat	221	375	413	419	428	436	437	443	464
22.	Madhya Pradesh	162	242	316	321	465	469	476	449	451
23.	Rajasthan	146	212	358	363	368	372	380	393	379
24.	Meghalaya	303	233	289	291	328	334	344	375	378
25.	Sikkim	329	156	225	227	241	251	257	258	258
26.	Mizoram	43	119	177	179	268	296	312	328	229
27.	West Bengal	599	642	695	700	674	196	770	874	196
28.	Arunachal Pradesh	125	152	128	131	135	138	142	122	168
29.	**Andaman & Nicobar Islands**	**82**	**83**	**109**	**110**	**105**	**105**	**106**	**148**	**160**
30.	Jammu & Kashmir	40	53	59	56	56	56	57	95	97
31.	Lakshadweep	N.A	N.A	N.A	N.A	N.A	N.A	N.A	N.A	33
32.	Daman & Diu	N.A	N.A	N.A	N.A	N.A	N.A	N.A	N.A	26
33.	India			609	615	643	652	661	720	750

Sources: 1. Centre for Monitoring Indian Economy, *Infrastructure*, January 2001.
2. Ministry of Surface Transport (various issues). *Basic Road Statistics*.

demand for vehicles and also the number of trips. However, given the limited land area and topography of ANI, it is not feasible to rely on road expansion alone to improve the connectivity in the region. Abundant water resources in ANI offer an excellent opportunity to develop water-based transport facilities to carry people and goods between islands. This has not received the desired attention.

Inter-island connectivity in ANI is poor in terms of both the frequency of service and the speed of vehicles. Further, obsolete technology and poor maintenance of boats and ferries can be a serious threat to marine life.

TABLE 3.2

State-wise Road Density by Population (km.)
(Per Lakh of Population)

(Arranged in Descending Order of 1995)

Sl. No.	*States/ Union Territories*	*1981*	*1988*	*1995*
1	*2*	*3*	*4*	*5*
1.	Arunachal Pradesh	2089.49	1130.80	1317.80
2.	Nagaland	754.98	1024.70	1073.30
3.	Mizoram	231.35	666.70	939.60
4.	Orissa	454.00	741.30	666.30
5.	Goa	697.69	578.80	608.60
6.	Himachal Pradesh	464.32	523.80	586.80
7.	Manipur	406.35	462.70	585.00
8.	Tripura	380.10	544.60	544.70
9.	Dadra & Nagar Haveli	209.62	310.00	503.00
10.	Kerala	410.00	425.60	480.40
11.	Sikkim	335.00	488.10	456.00
12.	Meghalaya	358.96	478.50	428.90
13.	Tamil Nadu	256.62	345.10	367.80
14.	Pondicherry	351.49	447.30	336.00
15.	Madhya Pradesh	200.00	241.10	319.30
16.	Karnataka	296.72	340.30	312.00
17.	Assam	235.50	323.10	305.30
18.	Rajasthan	187.00	310.20	296.30
19.	**Andaman & Nicobar Islands**	**351.60**	**363.70**	**290.80**
20.	Maharashtra	171.22	330.00	285.50
21.	Punjab	275.40	303.10	282.40
22.	Chandigarh	28.67	319.30	272.00
23.	Gujarat	171.22	219.50	263.40
24.	Andhra Pradesh	219.73	256.80	258.70
25.	Delhi	221.60	306.00	242.20
26.	Haryana	178.82	200.90	166.60
27.	Jammu & Kashmir	194.73	219.80	163.50
28.	Uttar Pradesh	136.05	165.90	154.10
29.	Bihar	119.73	121.30	101.80
30.	West Bengal	104.29	105.60	90.70
31.	Daman & Diu	NA	NA	NA
32.	Lakshawadeep	NA	NA	NA
33.	India	216.80		258.20

Source: Ministry of Surface Transport (various issues). *Basic Road Statistics*.

Faster vehicles will not only improve the attendance of the employees in various offices/establishments, schools and health centres but will also provide necessary boost to the trade and tourism industry in ANI. Chapter 4 deals with these issues in detail.

Civil Aviation

Air connectivity is vital for the growth of an economy. To develop tourism, it is requisite. In ANI, the airport at Port Blair is the only airport open to civilians. It can support only small aircraft like Boeing 737. Work to extend the runway from 6,000 ft. to 11,000 ft. is in progress and would facilitate landing of aircraft with more carrying capacity.

At present, direct flights to Port Blair are available only from three destinations *viz*., Chennai, Kolkata, and Vishakhapatnam. Direct flights from other major cities such as Bangalore, Delhi, Hyderabad and Mumbai would substantially improve connectivity of these islands to the mainland through sharp reduction in travel cost and removal of inconvenience of overnight stay at Kolkata, Chennai or Vishakhapatnam. Further, if Port Blair is declared as an international airport and direct flights are permitted from neighbouring countries, then travel costs from international destinations such as Thailand, Indonesia, and Myanmar will be substantially reduced, and in fact, would be less than the cost of travel to the mainland. This could provide the necessary boost to trade and tourism in the UT. A plan for improving air connectivity of the UT in the medium term needs to be evolved. In this context, extending the length of airstrips at Diglipur and Campbell Bay may also be considered.

Helicopter services are available in some of the islands in the UT. The existing infrastructure includes helipads at Port Blair, Rangat, Mayabunder, Diglipur, Car Nicobar, Neil Island, Havlock, Campbell Bay, and Nancowry. Expansion of helicopter services to Baratang, Long Islands, and other inhabited Islands has been under active consideration. While fast mode of transport between the widely dispersed islands is desirable, it would be important to ensure that the inefficiencies are minimised. Currently, helicopter services are heavily subsidised. The extent of subsidy is 90 per cent for the local people and 75 per cent for others. Any expansion of helicopter services should be self-financing, and the current level of subsidy should be reviewed. The high cost of helicopter services and hence high subsidy could partly be the result of operational inefficiency. The feasibility of reducing these costs needs to be explored.

Energy

Diesel generating (DG) sets is the major source of energy in the UT. Accordingly, the cost of production is very high in the range of Rs. 7 per unit. Out of the total installed capacity of 65 MW, 59 MW is based on DG sets, indicating that about 90 per cent of the electricity requirement is met from DG sets. This includes 20 MW capacity in the private sector that is

TABLE 3.3

Villages Connected by Roads as on 31st March 1995

Sl. No.	States/Union Territories	With Population < 1000*		With Population 1000-1500		With Population > 1500	
		Villages Connected	As % of Total Villages	Villages Connected	As % of Total Villages	Villages Connected	As % of Total Villages
1	2	3	4	5	6	7	8
1.	Andhra Pradesh	4554	32.79	2234	59.30	9361	96.51
2.	Arunachal Pradesh	638	20.09	40	81.63	31	96.88
3.	Assam	12058	64.22	1907	100.00	1812	100.00
4.	Bihar	14757	27.72	3250	53.24	5809	70.60
5.	Delhi	54	100.00	37	100.00	123	100.00
6.	Goa	172	100.00	100	100.00	101	80.16
7.	Gujarat	8022	81.74	3207	98.71	5033	99.64
8.	Haryana	3229	98.60	1159	99.91	2309	99.96
9.	Himachal Pradesh	7133	43.63	249	94.68	189	96.43
10.	Jammu & Kashmir	2880	57.18	503	82.32	526	92.77
11.	Karnataka	6454	34.64	2584	74.66	4251	86.14
12.	Kerala	6	100.00	10	100.00	1252	100.00
13.	Madhya Pradesh	14065	22.13	2935	66.30	2745	94.33
14.	Maharashtra	6447	25.73	4862	94.54	6165	99.68
15.	Manipur	708	40.23	101	91.82	165	98.80
16.	Meghalaya	2372	49.49	64	100.00	45	100.00
17.	Mizoram	295	74.68	286	100.00	56	100.00
18.	Nagaland	768	87.37	131	99.24	108	100.00
19.	Orissa	12228	29.73	3062	86.89	2645	99.85
20.	Punjab	8779	99.29	1657	100.00	1689	100.00
21.	Rajasthan	6863	24.87	1890	78.52	3270	99.09
22.	Sikkim	256	69.00	42	87.50	22	104.76
23.	Tamil Nadu	12066	60.73	2436	105.27	3916	99.95
24.	Tripura	3330	79.61	215	91.49	300	100.00
25.	Uttar Pradesh	32106	35.57	7430	65.20	10586	97.13
26.	West Bengal	11351	41.06	3572	64.95	3073	62.36
27.	**Andaman & Nicobar Islands**	**223**	**48.48**	**16**	**100.00**	**15**	**100.00**
28.	Chandigarh			3	100.00	13	100.00
29.	Dadra & Nagar Haveli	30	88.24	13	100.00	25	100.00
30.	Daman & Diu	11	100.00	5	100.00	10	100.00
31.	Pondicherry	207	100.00	31	100.00	53	100.00
32.	India	172062	37.45	44031	75.88	65698	91.73

Note:* Data pertains to 31st March 1994.

Source: CMIE, 2001.

sold to ANI administration. The only hydro-power plant in North Andaman has the installed capacity of 5.25 MW. Further, the distribution process of electricity is not trouble free. Distribution lines cannot be laid in some of the tribal reserves, because of the Supreme Court's rulings. Honourable Supreme Court's judgement should be honoured; however, the ANI administration should make an appeal to seek clearance from the court. Other measures should also be used to reduce soaring transmission and distribution losses.

Per capita consumption of electricity in the UT has substantially increased during the nineties. In fact, it almost doubled during 1989-90 to 1996-97. Yet, it remains less than that in many states and is far below the national average. During 1999-2000, the per capita electricity consumption in the UT

TABLE 3.4

Per Capita Consumption of Electricity in Different States and UTs (kWh) (Arranged in Descending Order of 1999-00)

Sl. No.	*State/UT*	*1970-71*	*1974-75*	*1980-81*	*1989-90*	*1996-97*	*1999-00*
1.	Daman & Diu		130.8	276.4	440.1	2346.7	3927.4
2.	Dadra & Nagar Haveli	13.5	14.8	56.3	878.8	2298.8	3882.8
3.	Pondicherry	175.8	214.4	263.7	592.4	1034.5	931.9
4.	Chandigarh	280.2	363.7	309.0	686.2	794.4	823.8
5.	Punjab	156.2	154.2	303.6	620.5	789.9	921.1
6.	Goa	96.9	157.5	250.8	411.2	719.9	712.5
7	Gujarat	124.4	165.0	238.8	436.8	685.7	834.7
8.	Delhi	250.6	299.2	403.8	673.6	589.7	653.2
9.	Maharashtra	151.7	172.6	244.5	393.6	557.0	520.5
10.	Haryana	88.8	115.1	209.5	367.4	508.3	530.8
11.	Tamil Nadu	124.9	126.4	186.0	295.0	469.4	484.1
12.	Orissa	72.9	69.2	114.0	249.2	446.7	354.6
13.	Madhya Pradesh	45.2	61.3	100.3	217.4	368.4	351.7
14.	Karnataka	101.5	119.3	146.0	272.8	338.3	380.1
15.	Andhra Pradesh	50.4	55.4	101.8	233.5	331.7	391.1
16.	Rajasthan	36.8	55.9	99.4	191.6	294.4	334.5
17.	Himachal Pradesh	34.1	58.8	66.4	191.9	278.5	339.1
18.	Kerala	71.4	79.4	112.0	171.0	235.8	261.8
19.	Lakshadweep		11.2	26.8	143.6	234.2	217.9
20.	Jammu & Kashmir	36.8	52.7	74.8	176.4	223.7	267.9
21.	**Andaman & Nicobar Islands**	**26.1**	**27.2**	**42.3**	**109.7**	**210.0**	**222.4**
22.	West Bengal	107.3	106.1	117.0	136.2	196.6	204.4
23.	Uttar Pradesh	48.5	50.0	83.1	157.4	194.3	175.8
24.	Sikkim			37.2	103.3	182.4	192.4
25.	Bihar	45.9	48.0	74.1	109.9	145.1	140.8
26.	Meghalaya		31.3	31.0	106.4	134.5	160.3
27.	Manipur	4.7	7.7	7.9	79.5	127.9	69.5
28.	Mizoram		4.3	5.6	65.0	107.6	120.7
29.	Assam	20.0	24.0	33.5	92.7	88.0	95.5
30.	Nagaland	7.8	27.2	34.2	58.6	80.8	84.7
31.	Arunachal Pradesh		3.4	14.6	56.6	80.4	68.6
32.	Tripura	4.5	6.0	14.5	45.0		95.5
33.	India	79.8	174.9	120.5	236	334	354.7

Source: Planning Commission (2002). *Five Year Plan (2002-2007)*, Vol. 3, Government of India, New Delhi, p. 85.

was 222 units as against 355 at the all-India level (Table 3.4).

According to the estimates of demand for electricity made by the Central Electricity Authority (CEA), the peak demand during the years 2015-16, 2021-22 and 2026-27 will be 111 MW, 226 MW and 323 MW, respectively. This would require an installed capacity of about 158 MW in 2015-16, 323 MW in 2021-22 and 461 MW in 2026-27. This would entail a heavy subsidy in the electricity consumption in the UT unless a substantial reduction is brought about in its cost of generation. This calls for careful planning for adopting alternative low-cost means of generation of electricity such as hydro-power generation and natural gas based power plants. Feasibility studies would need to be conducted to explore the possibility of adopting these alternative means of electricity generation.

Dispersed habitats of varying sizes and population densities in ANI, call for a prudent energy policy, which is not dependent on only one or two conventional sources of energy but exploits a mix of energy sources in line with the local requirements and opportunities. Bamboo is a precious resource with huge potential for generation of income. Technology has been developed to use the tops of bamboo to produce energy. This should be explored further by undertaking a pilot project. While islands with small population could be provided biomass based energy, islands with big population could be provided solar energy. In addition to the above-mentioned energy sources, other non-conventional energy sources such as wind, sun, biomass, sea tides should be exploited to the maximum extent. These will facilitate environment friendly provision of electrical power, and might work out to be cost-effective. Initial studies do reveal potential of these energy sources on these islands, though further studies need to be conducted to design suitable projects and establish commercial viability of these projects. The potential projects may include:

OTEC Plants

IIT Chennai identified South Andaman, Chingue Islands and Tillang Islands as appropriate Islands for setting up OTEC plants in the range of 10 to 50 MW.

Wind Farms

Initial enquiries seem to reveal the possibility of establishing wind farms at Car Nicobar to meet its energy requirements.

Solar Photo Voltaic (SPV) Power Plants

These could be used specifically in the regions not covered by the conventional power supply. Also, these could supplement conventional power supply in other regions.

Solar Thermal Energy Plants

The feasibility of solar thermal energy based plants for refrigeration, air-conditioning, water heating and hot air drying should be explored.

Geothermal Energy or Methane based Power Plants

The feasibility of utilising available geothermal energy at Barren Islands and methane in the mud volcanoes at Baratang Islands for power generation needs to be explored.

Tidal difference Power Stations

An earlier study of the CEA revealed the feasibility of such plants in South Andaman and Middle Andaman. The commercial viability of such projects should be explored.

Power shortages and poor quality of power cause consumer dissatisfaction. This coupled with high power tariff not only makes the industries uncompetitive but also acts as a huge disincentive to potential entrepreneurs. ANI cannot afford to be in this situation any more.

Urban and Rural Water Supply

Owing to the ever rising demand for water because of population pressure and other reasons, raw water resources, water treatment capacities, and water distribution systems need to be augmented. This would require substantial improvement in the existing infrastructure and development of new infrastructure in the urban as well as rural areas.

Urban Water Supply

PBMC supplies water in the urban areas falling in its jurisdiction. These are Port Blair, Garacharma, Bamboo Flat, Mannie Bay, School Line and Austinabad. Currently, about 150 lakh litre of drinking water is supplied to these areas, everyday. Owing to the growth of population, demand for drinking water is expected to grow to 370 lakh litre by the year 2025 as per the estimates made by the UT. For meeting the growing demand for drinking water, the supply needs to be substantially augmented. This would require expeditious completion of the ongoing schemes, and identification of new commercially viable schemes. The following ongoing schemes should be expeditiously completed:

- Revival of Dilthaman tank.
- Nayagoan-Chakragaon Diggi project.
- Chouldhan scheme.
- Artificial ground water recharge schemes recommended by the Central Ground Water Board (CGWB).

In addition, the following two new schemes may be exploited to meet medium term requirement of the urban areas:

- Raising the height of Dhanikari Dam.[1]
- Indira Nullah Project.

ANI receives good rains. In the absence of any conscious policy for rainwater harvesting, the UT has not been able to turn this huge advantage to the

1. Feasibility study for increasing the height of *Dhanikari* Dam is under way.

benefit of its people. Holistic approach on water harvesting is therefore, a must.

In order to meet long-term demand for drinking water, the feasibility studies initiated in respect of tapping the water from Rutland Island and conversion of part of the sea at Flat Bay into a freshwater lake should be finalised early for seeking approval of the Ministry of Environment and Forests (MoEF)

Accordingly, capacity to treat raw water also needs to be augmented. Capacities of the existing treatment plants may be expanded and new treatment plants constructed at suitable places. Water treatment using locally available technology should, however, get priority.

The Low Thermal Desalination Water Treatment technology successfully implemented in Lakshadweep should be replicated in ANI.

The existing distribution system designed by CPHEEO is considered to be adequate to cope with the projected water supply up to the year 2011. Additional clear water reservoirs would need to be constructed to cope with the supply load for subsequent years.

Rural Water Supply

As per Census 2001, out of 502 villages only about 340 are fully covered by the public provision of water. Proper water treatment plants are available only in a few villages such as Diglipur, Rangat, Mayabunder, Bakultala, Bambooflat and Kamotra. This implies that treatment plants need to be constructed to supply pure drinking water to other villages. Water should be duly treated by using locally available technology.

Housing

Studies for low cost housing, energy efficient housing, and earthquake resistant housing have already been conducted by various agencies like Laurie Bakers, Cost Fort Group, and Space Design Consultants. Their recommendations may be considered. ANI is located in a region identified under the seismic zone V, corresponding to high incidence of seismic activity. The region has one of the largest identified fault lines in the tectonic arrangement causing severe turbulence in the 10-degree channel separating the two groups of islands. Building by-laws in ANI should adequately reflect this. There is a need to popularise and promote locally available building materials in construction activity in ANI. The following materials could be gainfully utilised in construction of housing and other buildings:

- Different species of timber.
- Rocks and sand stones.
- Cement/polymer composite sheets/boards made from coir fibre.
- Particle boards made from sawdust, and rice husk.

Chapter 4

Shipping and Maritime Services

Introduction

Sea transportation has an important role to play in the economic development of ANI. Provision of adequate and good quality services is therefore crucial. This chapter discusses the following aspects of sea transportation in ANI:

- Shipping supply and demand scenarios during Tenth FYP and beyond based on the estimates of the traffic for passenger transportation and cargo movement between mainland—island, inter-island and foreshore sectors.
- Direct and indirect employment in ports, shipping, construction, repairs and services.
- Development of harbours and jetties.
- Development of other infrastructure including communication, bunkering, tourism, security and safety of ports; and environmental issues.

Present Status and Major Concerns

The maritime transportation sector comprises shipping services for transportation of people and materials and the infrastructure to facilitate the shipping services. While the Directorate of Shipping Services looks after procurement, manning, maintenance and operation of the vessels owned by the Administration, the Port Management Board is responsible for administering and creating the infrastructure facilities which include ports, communication, radars, jetties, etc. Formulation and implementation of the programmes for providing ports and harbour structures including allied facilities in the islands, is however undertaken by the Andaman Lakshadweep Harbour Works (ALHW).

There are 23 notified Ports, which are strategically located between Latitude 6° 40' and 13° 50' North, and Longitude 92° 10' and 94° 20' East. Of these, Port Blair, located at a distance of around 700 nautical miles from the mainland, is designated as an Intermediate Port and is the main port of call for both mainland to island as well as inter-island shipping services. Other important destinations on the inter-island routes are Diglipur, Mayabunder, Rangat, Hut Bay (in Little Andaman), Mus (in Car Nicobar), Malacca (in Car Nicobar), Nancowry, and Campbell Bay (in Great Nicobar), which are accorded the status of minor port. Three prominent International Shipping Routes (ISR) pass between these islands at Coco/Preparis Channel in the North, 10-degree channel in the middle, and 6-degree channel in the South, underscoring the strategic significance of the island territory.

Supply and Demand for Maritime Transport Services in ANI

The Directorate of Shipping Services, which is responsible for manning, maintenance and operation of the 80 vessels in the fleet operates in the four sectors namely, Mainland-Island Sector (M-I), Inter-Island Sector(I-I), Foreshore Sector (F-S) and the Harbour Ferry Services (HFS) (Table 4.1).

Mainland-island (M-I) Service

The ANI is connected to Mainland of India by sea from Calcutta, Chennai and Vishakhapatnam. All passenger services to Mainland are from Port Blair only. At present five vessels are operating in this sector. They operate from Port Blair and only occasionally one vessel is diverted for sailing *via* Car Nicobar. Main features of M-I service are:

TABLE 4.1

Vessels Operated by Department of Shipping Services in Andaman & Nicobar Islands

Sl. No.	*Type of Vessel*	*Total (No.)*
1.	Mainland-Island Pax-cum Cargo	05
2.	Inter-Island Pax Vessel	09
3.	Foreshore Vessels	22
4.	Harbour Ferry	31
5.	Water Barge	03
6.	VIP Vessel	04
7	Ambulance	01
8	Mooring Vessel	03
9.	Oil Tanker	01
10.	Tug	01
	Total	**80**

Source: Complied by Author.

- the average capacity utilisation of these vessels during the last three years was about 64.66 per cent in case of passenger traffic and 9.32 per cent for the cargo;
- cargo loading/unloading time is substantial and it adversely affects the turnaround time of the vessels;
- Port Blair has no cargo loading/unloading facility in the passenger embarkation jetties.

Currently, the average frequency of the vessel from mainland to Port Blair is two trips a month per vessel. In this context, the following is suggested:

TABLE 4.2

Arrival of Tourists in Andaman & Nicobar Islands

Sl. No.	*Year*	*Domestic*	*Foreign*	*Total*
1.	1995	64490	3849	68339
2.	1996	67958	5796	73754
3.	1997	73558	4724	78282
4.	1998	74732	4915	79647
5.	1999	77448	6036	83484
6.	2000	81432	4684	86116
7.	2001	85866	5249	91115
8.	2002	90629	4707	95336
9.	2003	93899	4281	98180
10.	2004	105004	4578	109582
11.	2005	110254	4807	115061
12.	2010	137818	6009	143826
13.	2015	172272	7511	179783
14.	2020	215340	9388	224729
15.	2025	269175	11736	280911

Source: As in Table 4.1.

- Acquisition of faster vessels: Currently, speed of the vessel is about 15 knots and journey time is approximately 10 days including the time spent by the vessel at port. A service speed of 20 knots is advisable for these vessels to limit the turnaround time to less than 10 days. This will result in an increase in frequency to three trips a month which can be increased further to four trips per month if the port time at each end is reduced.
- Improve jetty facilities: Present infrastructure needs to be upgraded for fast embarkation/disembarkation of passengers.
- Removal of cargo hold in fully passenger ship will result in increase in passenger amenities.
- Better manoeuvrability for vessels or quick berthing with little or no tug assistance.
- Better accommodation facilities in view of expected increase in tourist flow.

Inter-island Service (I-I)

Inter-island services serve the ports through open sea. There are about 10 routes in this sector of which 3 are in the Northern group of islands and 7 in the southern group. Currently, there are nine vessels operating in this sector. Two vessels of higher capacity (400 passengers) are under construction. Three vessels will be out of service by 2007 resulting in a reduction of Pax. capacity of 800. The present capacity in terms passengers is 1500 and for cargo it is 1160 tonnes.

Foreshore (F-I) Service

Foreshore services connect Port Blair with ports at Neil, Havelock, Baratang, Long islands, Kadamtala and Rangat on eight routes. Presently, 22 vessels are operating on these routes with a capacity of 1,747 passengers and 250-tonnes cargo. The estimated demand for new vessels in various sectors up to 2025 is presented in Table 4.3.

Shipbuilding and Repairs in ANI

Shipbuilding

There is no shipbuilding activity in ANI except building of small crafts and fibre boat vessels in the private yards.

Ship Repairs

For proper maintenance and repair of vessels it is necessary to have adequate repair facilities. The existing marine dry dock in ANI can handle vessels of up to 85

TABLE 4.3

Demand for New Vessels in ANI

Plan	Year	*Requirement of New Vessels*								
		M-I Sector			*I-I Sector*			*Foreshore*		
		Qty	*Capacity*	*Class*	*Qty*	*Capacity*	*Class*	*Qty*	*Capacity*	*Class*
Xth Plan	2002-03									
	2003-04									
	2004-05		2	400 Pax	Class V					
			1	500 Pax	Class V					
	2005-06									
	2006-07		1	500 Pax	Class V					
	2007-08	1	1000 Pax	Class V						
Post Xth Plan Period	2008-09									
	2009-10	1	500 Pax	Class V						
	2010-11				1	500 Pax	Class V			
	2011-12	1	1000 Pax	Class V						
	2012-13							2	100 Pax	Class VI
	2013-14	1	1000 Pax	Class V	1	500 Pax	Class V	2	100 Pax	Class VI
	2014-15				1	500 Pax	Class V	1	100 Pax	Class VI
	2015-16	1	1000 Pax	Class V				1	100 Pax	Class VI
	2016-17							1	100 Pax	Class VI
	2017-18									
	2018-19							2	100 Pax	Class VI
	2019-20							2	100 Pax	Class VI
	2020-21	1	1000 Pax	Class V		6	100 Pax	Class VI		
						2	100 Pax	Class VI		
	2021-22	1	1000 Pax	Class V	1	500 Pax	Class V	6	100 Pax	Class VI
	2022-23							2	100 Pax	Class VI
	2023-24									
	2024-25	1	1000 Pax	Class V	1	500 Pax	Class V			

Source: As in Table 4.1.

mt. only. Repairs carried out at the mainland yards take very long affecting the fleet utilisation adversely. A dry dock facility for repairing larger vessels may be considered in the private or joint sector in ANI.

Development of Harbours and Jetties

The Port Management Board and the ALHW are successfully meeting the current demand for infrastructure for smooth functioning of maritime transportation services in the Islands. Any future expansion in shipping services would require adequate expansion and upgradation of supporting infrastructure.

Post-Tsunami Developments in Shipping and Other Maritime Infrastructure

Tsunami has caused extensive damage to ports, harbours and allied facilities in these islands. Six projects have been identified for taking up on turnkey basis. These are: development of Katchal harbour for berthing of M-I ships, development of a new jetty at Teressa for berthing of I-I ships (these projects require immediate initiation for development), preparation of a DPR for transshipment port, construction of breakwaters at Mus, and Malacca Additional Dry Dock for M-I vessels.

It is imperative to have a comprehensive master plan for development of ports and harbours taking into consideration rehabilitation and reconstruction of the damaged port infrastructure and the need for modernisation and creation of additional facilities.

Development of Allied Sectors related to Maritime Transportation Services

Employment

The maritime and shipping sector in Andaman & Nicobar Islands plays an important role in providing employment.

Direct Employment

Direct employment is provided as follows:

a.	Afloat Establishment	-	849
b.	Dockyard	-	162
c.	Dockyard Industrial Employees	-	459
d.	Port Management Board	-	519
	Total		1989

Indirect Employment

Indirect employment is expected to be eight to ten times of the direct employment, though there are no official estimates available.

Manpower and Training Requirement

There is a shortage of trained staff. The need for upgradation of technical skills through systematic training in maritime practices is a necessity. ANI administration should make an assessment of the training needs of the existing staff. It also needs to be assessed whether training facilities available in ANI are adequate. In the light of this assessment, training facilities should strengthened and/or enhanced. Staff may also be sent for training to institutions in mainland.

Environmental Management

Developmental activities including shipping services may have adverse impact on the natural environment of the Islands. In order to safeguard against this, environmental impact assessments must be carried out for various activities including construction of ports and harbours, dredging and disposal of dredged material and ship discharges.

Maritime Communication, Safety and Traffic Management

Safety of operations being paramount in any policy consideration, planning for sea transportation in ANI must adequately reflect the same. The ANI presently has 8 coastal stations along its coastline. All these stations are equipped with MF/HF for communication with ships. In addition to these, the territory has 8 VHF stations, and installation of 11 additional VHF stations is presently under way. Considering their strategic importance, 2 MF coast stations, 1 at Port Blair and the other at Nancowry, may be considered for upgradation along with DSC watch keeping.

Vessel Traffic Management System (VTMS)

VTMS has an important role in surveillance of vessels, especially in the Northern and Southern tip islands. Two sub-control stations, one each at the Northern and Southern tip islands respectively, and a Master Control Centre at Port Blair, may be considered for installation. The proposed system will have high performance radars integrated with state-of-the-art computer systems. It will also provide safety and meteorological information to ships in the VTMS coverage area. The system may be integrated with the port's Management Information System (MIS).

Development of Management Information System

Senior officials at various levels are required to take timely decisions on different issues, particularly those related to key organisational processes. To make the present system more efficient an integrated MIS needs to be developed.

Planned Maintenance System for Ships

Maintenance of on-board equipment is a continuous requirement throughout the economic life of a vessel. In order that maintenance activity is carried out on a regular basis, there is a need for a software, which would enable the operators and the managers to plan and schedule the tasks without overlooking any item. A planned maintenance system (PMS) may be considered for development in the form of a software package.

System for Monitoring Dry-dock Repairs

All the vessels required to be docked for maintenance and repair. Material management, procurement, storage, and dispersal of material for ship repairs are major tasks which are being done manually at present. A computerised system will impart efficiency to this important activity.

Development of Activities Related to Maritime Sector

The issue of developing Great Nicobar Islands has been debated for many years including the development of a transshipment port in the Southern Islands. Recently, it has been decided to undertake a detailed feasibility study for establishing such a project and accordingly in a recent meeting of the Island Development Authority, Rs. 150 lakh has been allocated for conducting such a study in Tenth Five-year Plan.

Transshipment Port at Great Nicobar

Presently, the containers to various port in Indian sub-continent are trans-shipped from Dubai, Colombo and Singapore. The advantage of Colombo and Singapore for container traffic is their geographic locations being adjacent to the equatorial shipping line stretching from Gulf/Red Sea to the South East China Sea. The Great Nicobar Island enjoys the same geographical advantage being close to this equatorial shipping line used by large container carriers.

The Great Nicobar Island is located centrally between Singapore/Colombo and just north of sea traffic to Southeast Asia and beyond. This is an extremely busy route. Deviation time (from International Shipping Lanes) in the table below shows the geographical advantages of the Great Nicobar Islands.

	Deviation Hours
To Colombo	8
Tuticorin	20
Mumbai	31
Cochin	18
Chennai	35
Chittagong	100
Great Nicobar	2

The advantages of setting up a transshipment port at Great Nicobar Islands can be summarised as follows:

- Proposed transshipment port at Great Nicobar Islands will be an alternative to Colombo. International ships are looking for alternate to Colombo because of high insurance premiums on ships visiting Sri Lankan port at present.
- Conservative estimates indicate that 10 per cent of the total Indian import cargo and substantial cargo for Bangladesh, Myanmar and Thailand will be transshipped from Great Nicobar Islands Port.
- Indian coastal shipping would get a boost.
- It will help overall development of ANI.

Setting up an Oil Refinery

Setting up of an oil refinery with an exclusive berth at the location of transshipment port or at any other place in Southern Group of Islands could be considered since deep-water shelter basin is available.

Bunkering Facility in ANI

The project would be feasible if the prices of supplies made at this port are internationally competitive.

Ship Repair Facility

If the proposals for setting up of transshipment port at ANI comes through, then dry docks/Syncrolifts integrated with shore based ships repair facilities can also be developed in conjunction with the transshipment port at the same location to provide repairs facilities to Indian and foreign vessels.

Need for Declaration of SEZ

The present regulations in respect of environment protection, coastal zone management, forestry, and issues in security of the region do not permit large-scale investments. The Government of India and the ANI Administration may identify and declare a suitable area/region as a Special Economic Zone. The incentives and facilities available under Special Economic Zone could be made available to the promoters of such projects to ensure large investment flows.

Air Services between Mainland and ANI

A high level Task Force has been set up to study and suggest ways of reducing shipping expenditure. Introducing air services between the mainland-island sector is seen as an option.

Introduction of air services between mainland India and ANI has been under discussion for a long time. Various options available for promoting air travel by either acquisition (purchase) of new air crafts or by taking these on lease for operating dedicated air services between Mainland and Port Blair have been analysed in this section.

Air Services based on Present Expenditure and Operations

Based on the existing expenditure and operations by the Indian Airlines, the direct and indirect costs have been analysed. It is observed that per passenger direct costs work out to 68 per cent and indirect costs 32 per cent of the total cost of Rs. 6,989. In case of a Boeing (B737) the cost per passenger is lower at Rs. 6,611. The direct costs account for 74 per cent and indirect costs account for 26 per cent of the total cost per passenger.

Operation of Air Services under Different Options

Taking average occupancy at 80 per cent the following three options have been worked out.

Option–1. Acquisition of aircraft by the ANI administration: The new aircraft—A320 type—costs about Rs. 250 crores, which includes spares and components and ground equipment and machinery. Assuming a 20 year lifespan, the cost per passenger works out to Rs. 7,119. If depreciation and interest on capital cost are excluded, the cost per passenger works out to Rs. 5,095.

Option–2. Operating air services by leasing an aircraft: Based on the assumptions as above, the cost per passenger works to Rs. 6,041. If interest on capital is excluded, the cost per passenger works out to Rs. 5,845.

Option–3. Operating air services by chartering an aircraft: Based on the assumptions and a chartering rate of Rs. 3,30,000 per hour, the cost per passenger works out to Rs. 7,050. If the chartering rate is assumed at Rs. 2,50,000 per hour instead of Rs. 3,30,000, then cost per passenger works to Rs. 5,450.

Comparison of Shipping Costs per pax with Costs of Air Services

Shipping costs per passenger: Taking into account of the total operating expenditure[1] on 51 voyages (on M.V. *Swarajdweep*, as a standard since the vessel is new) and the total accommodation units 85,272 available on the vessel, expenditure per accommodation works to Rs. 2,053. If depreciation cost of the vessel is not taken into account the expenditure works out to Rs. 1,073. The costs do not take into account capital costs of buying ships, and development of land-based infrastructure like jetties, navigational equipment, establishment.

The cost of travel by air (per passenger) between Mainland-Islands is comparable with the cost per passenger by ship if capital costs of buying ships/aircrafts and development of land-based infrastructure are included.

Summary of Main Proposals

Shipping Services

- There is no alternative to shipping to serve transportation requirements in Andaman & Nicobar Islands in the Inter-Island and Foreshore sectors.
- Five vessels are operated in the M-I sector at present. The acquisition process for new vessels has been initiated for the replacement of MV *Akbar* by 2006. MV *Nancowry* would also need to be replaced in the next FYP.
- The I-I Sector services, especially to the Southern Islands, need to be improved on a priority basis.
- For smooth and efficient functioning of shipping services the following may be considered:
  - A techno-economic analysis of shipping operations may be carried out with expert professional support at regular intervals (quarterly/half yearly).
  - Management Information System is a must to efficiently monitor, plan and execute the operations.
  - Modernisation of the marine dockyard and provision of modern repair equipment are needed in order to augment repair facilities. At least two dry docks may be promoted in the private sector (one each in the Northern and Southern Group of Islands) by the A&N Administration to meet the demand for annual survey and repairs of the fleet.

Air Services

- The costs of air services in the M-I sector are comparable with the tariff of shipping services, if both capital and operation costs of shipping are included. In view of this, government may consider augmenting air services in M-I sector.

Maritime related Activities

- In view of the vital role of communications in safety of sea operations, upgradation of shore based facilities along the island coastline as per GMDSS rules applicable for coast stations needs immediate attention.
- Because of the strategic location of the islands surveillance of vessels, especially in the Northern and Southern tip islands, is necessary. Two sub-control stations, one each at the Northern and Southern tip islands respectively, and a Master Control Centre at Port Blair, may be considered for installation.
- A PMS may be considered for development in the form of a software package to scientifically monitor the maintenance activities of the vessel, thereby saving time and cost overruns usually associated with unplanned maintenance/ repair.
- Maritime education and training facilities need to be strengthened.

Development of a Transshipment Port

In view of the geographical advantages of Great Nicobar Islands development of a transhipment port may be considered. Conservative estimates indicate that 10 per cent of the total Indian import cargo and most of the cargo for Bangladesh, Myanmar and Thailand can be transshipped from Great Nicobar Islands Port.

1. Three year average (2002-03 to 2004-05).

However, there is a need to carry out a detailed study to establish its business as well as environmental feasibility.

Crude Oil Refinery/Offshore Bunkering Facility

Setting up of an oil refinery with an exclusive berth at the location of transshipment port or at any other place in Southern Group of Islands may be considered. Similarly, an offshore bunkering facility may also be considered.

It is important to note that establishment of a transshipment port and crude oil refinery with bunkering facilities in the islands may have serious environmental implications for the marine life and lives of primitive tribal population. The tectonic activity in the region has also cast doubts on the appropriateness of projects of this kind in ANI. The feasibility reports of these projects should clearly bring out the potential damage to the environment by these projects in order to facilitate a careful and well-considered decision on them.

Post-Tsunami Developments in Shipping and Other Maritime Infrastructure

Tsunami has caused extensive damage to shipping. Six projects have been identified for execution on turnkey basis. These are: development of Katchal harbour for berthing of M-I ships, development of a new jetty at Teressa for berthing of I-I ships (these projects require immediate initiation for development), preparation of a DPR for transshipment port, construction of breakwaters at Mus and Malacca and additional dry dock for M-I vessels.

Besides, a comprehensive master plan for development of ports and harbours is required. The plan should take into consideration rehabilitation and reconstruction of the damaged port infrastructure, and modernisation and creation of additional facilities.

Chapter 5

Human Development

The level of a society's income alone no longer measures its development, as this measure does not reflect the true level of human development. Human development refers to the enlargement of choices available to people as the result of economic development. UNDP in its *Human Development Report* identifies these choices as those that are related to lead a long and healthy life, and acquire knowledge and access to resources to lead a decent standard of living. This chapter looks at the status of human development in ANI, initially in the background of relative ranking of human development indices developed by the Planning Commission, Government of India and then in terms of the indicators of attainment of education and health both in relative and absolute terms.

ANI in Human Development Map of India

National Human Development Report 2001 (Planning Commission, 2002) has constructed three core indices of human development, namely, Human Development Index (HDI), Gender Disparity Index (GDI), and Human Poverty Index (HPI). The HPI includes indicators that reflect the development of society as a whole. The HDI captures the deprivation in important aspects of human development. The GDI has been estimated to reflect the relative attainments of females compared to that of males for a common set of variables. These indices have been constructed for all states and UTs in India and they have been ranked on the basis of these indices. These indices facilitate inter-regional and inter-temporal comparisons of human development. The value of the three indices—GDI, HDI and HPI and the rankings based on them for ANI and some other states and UTs are presented in Table 5.1. It is seen from Table 5.1 that the ANI has shown substantial improvement throughout the eighties in all the three indices and its relative ranking among various states and UTs in India on the basis of these indices. Performance of ANI in respect of GDI is commendable. It has improved from an index value of 0.645 in 1981 to 0.857 in 1991, which is the highest in the country. This implies that on an average the attainments of women on the human development indicators were more than 85 per cent those of men. Further, HDI in ANI has improved both

TABLE 5.1

Human Development Indices

Index	*ANI*		*Lakshadweep*		*Delhi*		*Kerala*		*Goa*		*Pondicherry*		*All-India*	
	1981	*1991*	*1981*	*1991*	*1981*	*1991*	*1981*	*1991*	*1981*	*1991*	*1981*	*1991*	*1981*	*1991*
GDI	21 (0.645)	1 (0.857)	8 (0.688)	24 (0.680)	22 (0.595)	10 (0.69)	1 (0.872)	2 (0.825)	2 (0.785)	13 (0.775)	13 (0.753)	5 (0.793)	(0.623)	(0.676)
HDI	11 (0.394)	5 (0.574)	7 (0.434)	10 (0.532)	3 (0.495)	2 (0.62)	2 (0.500)	3 (0.591)	5 (0.445)	4 (0.575)	12 (0.386)	6 (0.571)	(0.302)	(0.381)
HPI	11 (38.58)	9 (27.09)	3 (26.82)	2 (15.88)	2 (19.27)	3 (17.0)	6 (32.12)	5 (19.93)	5 (29.25)	18 (37.71)	9 (35.79)	6 (24.16)	(47.33)	(39.36)

Note: Figures in parentheses are index values.

Source: Planning Commission (2002). *National Human Development Report 2001*, Government of India, New Delhi.

in rural, as well as in urban areas in the eighties. What is more, relative HDI ranking of rural areas in ANI has increased from 12 in 1981 to 5 in 1991, while for urban areas it has declined from 2 in 1981 to 4 in 1991, implying that regional disparity has narrowed down. Similarly, improvement in HDI in rural areas has been more than that in urban areas of ANI.

Education

The importance of education in fostering economic growth, social well-being and social stability is well recognised in the literature. Education has not only a direct role in human resource development but also a critical facilitative role in almost all developmental aims. Improved educational attainment has significant linkages with many other indicators of social well-being.

Trends

Literacy Rate

Inter-temporal and Inter-regional Performance: Literacy rate for the UT has improved substantially between 1981 and 2001). The ANI now ranks 8th in literacy among various states and UTs in the country (Table 5.2). The gap between male and female literacy rate has narrowed from 17 percentage points in 1981 to less than 11 percentage points in 2001 which is remarkable. Similarly, the rural-urban disparity in literacy rate has also declined from 11 percentage points in 1991 to about 8 percentage points in 2001 (Table 5.3).

Elementary and Secondary Education

Apart from the literacy rate there are other indicators that explain the educational attainment of a society. The enrolment ratio, dropout rate, teacher-pupil ratio, and intensity of formal education are some of these.

Enrolment Ratio

Gross enrolment (GE) in elementary schools (primary and middle) recorded impressive increase between 1981 and 2001 with 88.99 per cent GE in the age group of 6-14 years as against 81.58 per cent for all-India in 2001-2002 (Table 5.4). The UT performed well in terms of regional as well as gender equity in school enrolment.

Net Enrolment (NE) at primary level, obtained by subtracting the number of underage and overage children enrolled, was only 63.8 (29,331 children) as against 71 per cent at all-India level in 1997-98 implying that at least 36.2 per cent (16,669 children) children in the 6-10 age group remained out of school in the year 2000. However, a door-to-door family survey conducted in 2002 in ANI, reported the out-of-school children in the 6-14 age group at only 2,373, indicating that the number of out of school children in the 6-10 age group has declined significantly between 2000 and 2002.

Dropout Rates

Dropout rate is the percentage of students dropping out of class in a given year. Regarding the status of

TABLE 5.2

Literacy in Andaman & Nicobar Islands and other Union Territories and States

States/UTs	*1981*			*1991*			*2001*		
	Males	*Females*	*Persons*	*Males*	*Females*	*Persons*	*Males*	*Females*	*Persons*
Andaman & Nicobar Islands	**70.29**	**53.2**	**63.19**	**78.99**	**65.46**	**73.02**	**86.07**	**75.29**	**81.18**
Chandigarh	78.89	69.31	74.81	82.04	72.34	77.81	85.65	76.65	81.76
Dadra & Nagar Haveli	44.64	20.37	32.7	53.56	26.98	40.71	73.32	42.99	60.03
Delhi	79.28	62.6	71.94	82.01	66.99	75.29	87.37	75	81.82
Daman & Diu	74.5	46.7	59.9	82.66	59.4	71.2	88.4	70.37	81.09
Lakshadweep	81.24	55.32	68.42	90.18	72.89	81.78	93.15	81.56	87.52
Pondicherry	77.09	53.03	65.14	83.68	65.63	74.74	88.89	74.13	81.99
Kerala	87.73	75.65	81.56	93.62	86.13	89.81	94.2	87.86	90.92
Bihar	40.6	16.52	32.05	52.49	22.89	38.48	60.32	33.57	47.53
All-India	56.38	29.76	43.57	64.13	39.29	52.21	75.64	54.03	65.2

Source: Planning Commission, *National Human Development Report 2001*, Government of India, New Delhi, p.186.

TABLE 5.3

Rural Urban Literacy in Andaman & Nicobar Islands

Category	*1981*			*1991*			*2001*		
	Males	*Females*	*Persons*	*Males*	*Females*	*Persons*	*Males*	*Females*	*Persons*
Rural	65.79	47.59	58.12	75.99	61.99	69.73	83.9	72.23	78.55
Urban	81.86	68.98	76.71	86.59	75.08	81.69	90.35	81.65	86.48
Total	70.29	53.2	63.19	78.99	65.46	73.02	86.07	75.29	81.18

Source: Planning Commission, *National Human Development Report 2001*, Government of India, New Delhi, pp.187-188.

TABLE 5.4

Gross Enrolment Ratio 2000-2001

States/UTs	*Classes I-V(6-11 Years)*			*Classes VI-VIII(11-14 Years)*			*Classes I-VIII(1-14 Years)*		
	Boys	*Girls*	*Total*	*Boys*	*Girls*	*Total*	*Boys*	*Girls*	*Total*
Andaman & Nicobar Islands	**87.83**	**91.07**	**89.34**	**89.61**	**87.01**	**88.36**	**88.46**	**89.59**	**88.99**
Chandigarh	65.17	65.55	65.35	68.21	73.43	70.59	66.28	68.32	67.23
Dadra & Nagar Haveli	144.22	102.74	122.58	88.42	55.88	72.15	124.52	87.12	105.29
Daman & Diu	105.05	94.25	99.65	98.80	67.22	81.26	102.97	83.85	93.03
Delhi	60.12	62.55	61.30	52.78	53.75	53.24	57.46	59.5	58.44
Lakshadweep	106.98	92.90	99.94	129.30	109.35	119.33	114.42	98.38	106.4
Pondicherry	86.56	74.55	80.37	95.43	86.15	90.73	89.76	78.64	84.06
Kerala	87.71	86.54	87.14	99.80	94.76	97.33	92.32	89.68	91.03
Bihar	98.24	60.49	79.87	40.71	20.72	31.29	75.92	45.62	61.35
All-India	104.91	83.92	95.66	66.68	49.94	58.64	90.26	72.36	81.58

Source: Government of India, *Economic Survey 2002-2003*.

dropout rate in ANI the following observations have been made (Tables 5.5 to 5.7):

- school drop out rate in A&N Islands has declined significantly over the past two decades and is significantly lower than all-India average;
- dropout rate is relatively higher in higher classes;
- the gap between the drop out rates for boys and girls has reduced over the years; and
- though the dropout rate has declined over the years, it is still higher than the Tenth Plan target of bringing it down to 10 per cent.

Intensity of Formal Education

The school enrolment rates do not accurately capture the spread of education because these do not take into account the high dropout rates and poor attendance, etc. In view of this concern, NHDR 2001

TABLE 5.5

Dropout Rate in Class I-V

States/Uts	*1981-82*			*1998-99 (Provisional)*		
	Boys	*Girls*	*Children*	*Boys*	*Girls*	*Children*
Andaman & Nicobar Islands	**33.1**	**40.6**	**36.5**	**21.3**	**21.05**	**21.19**
Chandigarh	25.4	31.9	23.3	-4.93	-4.14	-4.56
Dadra & Nagar Haveli	69.1	73.3	70.1	30.66	44.39	36.46
Daman & Diu	20.6	28.6	24.4	2.05	-0.32	0.96
Delhi	18.1	26.8	22.1	18.89	27.56	23.13
Lakshadweep	9.3	16.7	7.9	-0.57	6.64	2.89
Pondicherry	0	6.2	6.2	-3.37	-2.15	-2.78
Kerala	9.4	10.7	10.1	-11.06	-6.83	-9.00
Bihar	67.8	73.7	69.6	58.28	62.00	59.65
All-India	51.1	57.3	53.5	38.23	41.34	39.58

Source: Planning Commission, *National Human Development Report 2001*, Government of India, New Delhi, p.206.

TABLE 5.6

Dropout Rate in Class I-VIII

States/UTs	*1981-82*			*1998-99 (Provisional)*		
	Boys	*Girls*	*Children*	*Boys*	*Girls*	*Children*
Andaman & Nicobar Islands	**39.1**	**47.9**	**43.0**	**23.24**	**28.10**	**25.61**
Chandigarh	13.5	26.9	19.5	55.10	-3.26	1.40
Dadra & Nagar Haveli	85.8	87.5	86.4	57.34	63.09	59.79
Daman & Diu	41.2	52.7	48.2	-6.50	6.82	-0.17
Delhi	31.7	35.3	29.6	19.9	9.13	14.49
Lakshadweep	34.9	67.1	50.7	19.46	24.69	21.86
Pondicherry	29.3	49.1	38.3	-2.11	-2.05	-2.08
Kerala	22.3	23.6	23.0	-5.48	-3.46	-4.49
Bihar	77.7	87.0	80.4	75.39	80.12	77.06
All-India	68.5	77.7	72.1	54.40	60.09	56.82

Source: Planning Commission, *National Human Development Report 2001*, Government of India, New Delhi, p.207.

TABLE 5.7

Dropout Rate in Class I-X

States/UTs	*1981-82*			*1998-99 (Provisional)*		
	Boys	*Girls*	*Children*	*Boys*	*Girls*	*Children*
Andaman & Nicobar Islands	**65.48**	**73.24**	**69.32**	**47.85**	**44.63**	**46.32**
Chandigarh	50.68	63.73	56.48	13.17	7.83	10.61
Dadra & Nagar Haveli	95.05	94.70	94.92	76.58	79	77.65
Daman & Diu	78.27	79.85	78.99	47.34	46.33	46.88
Delhi	24.58	37.95	30.86	-40.92	-68.2	-54.13
Lakshadweep	58.66	69.69	63.50	56.43	54.89	55.69
Pondicherry	63.83	70.38	66.74	37.71	35.73	36.78
Kerala	46.69	43.33	45.07	30.02	19.16	24.70
Bihar	84.95	92.23	86.92	81.40	87.26	83.47
All-India	79.44	86.81	82.33	65.44	70.22	67.44

Source: Planning Commission, *National Human Development Report 2001*, Government of India, New Delhi, p.208.

constructed an indicator of intensity of formal education in constructing this indicator, a weighted average of the share of class-wise enrolment in the total enrolment in classes I-XII is taken, with weights increasing over successive classes from I-XII. This is then adjusted by the gross enrolment ratio for the population of children in the age group of 6-18 years, to correct for the children in the school going age group who are not enrolled. This is called adjusted intensity of formal education. A higher value implies a higher level of enrolment in higher classes, i.e., retention of children in schools for a longer duration without dropping out, and also a larger proportion of children, of school going age group, enrolled in school. In A&N Islands it has increased from 2.54 in 1978 to 4.35 in 1993 against the all-India average of 2.04 and 2.7 respectively during these years (Table 5.8). During this period the gender gap and rural urban disparity has also declined in this union territory. This is an achievement worth taking note of.

TABLE 5.8

Adjusted Intensity of Formal Education

States/UTs	*1978*			*1993*		
	Boys	*Girls*	*Children*	*Boys*	*Girls*	*Children*
Andaman & Nicobar Islands	**2.86**	**2.21**	**2.54**	**4.44**	**4.25**	**4.35**
Chandigarh	2.80	2.59	2.70	4.24	4.65	4.43
Dadra & Nagar Haveli	2.36	1.15	1.74	3.33	2.12	2.74
Daman & Diu	3.59	2.77	3.14	4.47	3.88	4.19
Delhi	4.30	3.56	3.95	4.39	4.56	4.47
Lakshadweep	4.65	3.19	4.11	5.35	4.25	4.81
Pondicherry	3.52	3.21	3.39	5.14	4.54	4.84
Kerala	3.92	3.67	3.79	3.99	3.90	3.94
Bihar	1.98	0.65	1.34	2.17	1.14	1.69
All-India	2.61	1.42	2.04	3.10	2.26	2.70

Source: Planning Commission, *National Human Development Report 2001*, Government of India, New Delhi, pp.211-212.

Availability and Accessibility to Schools

In spite of poor connectivity both within and across islands in ANI, significant improvement has been made in developing infrastructure for elementary education. Although performance of ANI in terms of equity in creating educational infrastructure across the two districts, and also across the urban and rural areas appears satisfactory, disparity in number of schools per thousand population across *tehsils* needs to be explored further in the light of population density, local terrain, and transport facilities. Available data in respect of location of schools, in terms of distance from house, in rural areas shows poor performance of this UT (Table 5.9). For instance, population with primary and upper primary schools within 1 km. radius was lower than all-India average in 1993. Performance of UT in this respect could not be examined in recent years owing to lack of data.

Teacher-Pupil Ratio

Teacher-Pupil ratio (TPR) is the number of students per teacher. This ratio was favourable in ANI at all levels

TABLE 5.9

Accessibility of Schools in Rural Areas

States/UTs	1978				1993			
	Population with Primary School		*Population with Upper Primary School*		*Population with Primary School*		*Population with Upper Primary School*	
	Within Habitation	*Within 0.5 k.m*	*Within Habitation*	*Within 0.5 k.m*	*Within Habitation*	*Within 0.5 k.m*	*Within Habitation*	*Within 0.5 k.m*
Andaman & Nicobar Islands	**70.49**	**71.59**	**33.38**	**37.40**	**70.45**	**74.02**	**44.37**	**52.59**
Chandigarh	89.42	97.95	61.42	75.57	89.86	90.44	47.15	63.33
Dadra & Nagar Haveli	45.43	71.74	11.24	31.55	40.05	66.75	10.07	49.91
Daman & Diu	6.82	71.17	20.62	41.32	72.25	90.52	63.67	95.3
Delhi	85.29	99.09	55.66	86.78	81.93	88.57	58.31	87.1
Lakshadweep	100.00	100.00	99.64	99.64	86.32	94.49	73.29	73.29
Pondicherry	87.72	93.70	53.19	75.50	74.75	91.56	43.73	72.85
Kerala	83.35	85.81	59.44	70.15	76.67	84.07	50.54	67.51
Bihar	77.98	87.44	23.14	44.14	77.19	77.51	27.13	56.52
All-India	78.53	85.13	33.47	46.57	77.81	85.50	37.73	56.91

Source: Planning Commission, *National Human Development Report 2001*, Government of India, New Delhi, p.214.

of school when compared with all-India average and some other states (Table 5.10). The performance of Nicobar district (rural area) was better *vis-à-vis* urban Andaman district (predominantly urban) in respect of TPR.

TPR at pre-primary level was, however, poor at 1:50 in this UT. Studies have shown that most of the social, emotional, and basic skill development in children takes place at the pre-primary and primary level, which is achieved with greater teacher-pupil interaction, and attention of teachers. Thus, TPR at pre-primary level should be improved.

The teacher-pupil ratio was 18 for secondary and 16 for senior secondary schools. Such a favourable TPR partly attributable to low population density and delivery of education in five different languages, calls for re-examining the current policy of not allowing school admission to the unsuccessful students in Board exams of X and XII.

TABLE 5.10

Teacher-Pupil Ratio

States/UTs	1982-83			1992-93			1997-98		
	Primary	*Upper Primary*	*Secondary*	*Primary*	*Upper Primary*	*Secondary*	*Primary*	*Upper Primary*	*Secondary*
Andaman & Nicobar Islands	**22**	**21**	**24**	**21**	**21**	**22**	**21**	**20**	**22**
Chandigarh	20	31	24	24	21	31	42	29	28
Dadra & Nagar Haveli	45	33	20	40	30	24	39	39	25
Daman & Diu	29	28	29	35		19	45	38	13
Delhi	36	26	25	31	20	21	39	30	28
Lakshadweep	33	30	19	26	25	16	33	18	15
Pondicherry	26	29	25	27	28	31	27	24	27
Kerala	33	31	30	32	31	30	30	29	29
Bihar	41	35	33	52	43	37	62	49	42
All-India	40	34	29	45	43	29	42	37	29

Source: Planning Commission, *National Human Development Report 2001*, Government of India, New Delhi, p.215.

Performance in Examinations

Information on examination results of the students reveals a dismal performance for class X with pass percentage at 39.80 for secondary schools in 2001-02 (Figure 5.1). Educational achievements in class XII were better relatively with pass percentage of 71.35 in 2001-02. One worrisome feature of secondary education is that the students failing in class 10 are not given opportunity to attend school even though the examination board allows them to take exams in failed subjects. This policy seems unfair and needs to be reviewed.

FIGURE 5.1

CBSE Examination Result of A & N Islands (Pass Percentage)

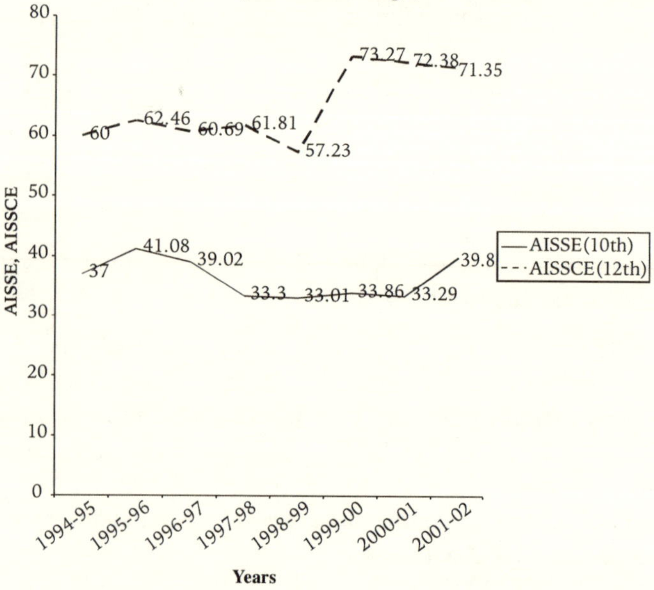

In addition, an Adult Education Programme is being implemented through 81 Jana Shiksha Nilayam and 68 non-formal educational centres. Computer education has been introduced in 16 schools through private sector participation. There are 34 schools run by private management, however, in view of the better performance of and demand for private schools private participation in provision of education should be encouraged.

Higher Education

There are two degree colleges in this UT; Jawaharlal Nehru Rajkeeya Mahavidyalaya (JNRM) at Port Blair and Mahatma Gandhi Government College (MGGC) at Mayabunder. JNRM offers B.A., B.Sc., B.Com., M.A. and M.Sc. in various subjects and has a TPR of 1:26.2. No gender disparity is seen in enrolment. The pass percentage at post graduation level was relatively better (79.35) than that for graduation level (38.06) during 1998-99. Performance of girls was better than boys in all the courses.

The MGGC at Mayabunder offers only B.A. and has a TPR of 1:10. Pass percentage was poor at 39.56 per cent during the year 1998-99. The pass percentage in case of girls was 49.35, which is significantly higher than that for boys (32.38 per cent). The education department also provides fellowships for higher studies, M.Phil., Ph.D. and other courses, in various universities in the mainland. In addition, there is one teachers' training institute and a B.Ed. In both the colleges, enrolment of girls was far higher than boys. There is no private participation in provision of higher education in ANI.

Vocational and Technical Education

In order to impart vocational and technical training, an industrial training institute (ITI), and two polytechnics are functioning in the UT. Dr. B.R. Ambedkar Government Polytechnic at Port Blair with a TPR of 6.13 offers courses in civil engineering, mechanical engineering, and computer applications. The pass percentage was around 60 per cent in 1998-99. The second government polytechnic with a staff of 11 teachers offers courses in electronics, fisheries engineering, fishing boat skipper, hotel reception and bookkeeping, housekeeping, and cookery. The enrolment in this polytechnic was low in spite of the fact that it offered courses, which may also be useful for self-employment. Low enrolment could be attributed to poor quality of education, lack of employment opportunities, lack of supporting environment for self-employment and preference for employment in government sector. No evaluation reports were available, however, to verify this conjuncture.

The ITI at Dollyganj, offers training courses for draughtsman, surveyor, fitter, electrician, automobile mechanic, welder and those associated with information technology and electronic system maintenance. It also provides training in stenography, exclusive for women. A total of 1,306 students have enrolled up to 2001 in this institute. Of these, 883 (67.6 per cent) had passed. Sixty per cent (527) of those passed out got employment in trades related to their training, 73 in other trades, and 26 per cent remained unemployed. Of those employed, about 65 per cent got placement in the government, 21.8 per cent joined the private sector organisations, and the remaining 13.5 per cent were self-employed. Apart from this, the education department also awards scholarships for study in mainland for various courses like medical science, engineering, veterinary science, agricultural science, hotel management, and other professional and technical courses. There is no private participation in technical and vocational education.

Public Expenditure on Education

Public expenditure on education is one of the determining factors of educational attainment of a region. As noted earlier, the ANI administration is the major provider of educational facilities, and contribution by the private sector is small.

A substantially high share of elementary education in total expenditure on education indicates UTs commitment to universalisation of education. The per capita public expenditure on education in ANI is one of the highest in the country and is rising (Figure 5.2). It may be noted, that the per capita expenditure figures in respect of ANI do not include expenditure on art and culture, and sports unlike in the case of expenditure figures for other states. On making an adjustment for this, per capita expenditure in ANI would be even higher. High per capita expenditure can partly be explained by different terrain, poor transport facilities, low population density, and delivery of education in five different languages. Since many of these factors are given and there is little that could be done about them, the administration should focus on improving the productivity of expenditure on education.

FIGURE 5.2

Capital Public Expenditure on Education

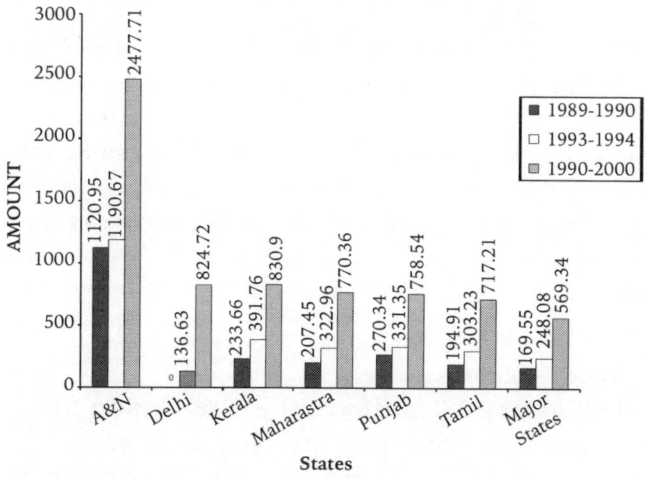

Delivery of Education

The whole territory is divided into seven educational zones: South Andaman, Wimberlygunj, Rangat, Diglipur, and Mayabunder in Andaman district and Car Nicobar and Nancowry in Nicobar district. Education is provided in five languages, *viz.*, English, Hindi, Tamil, Telugu, and Bengali. The Director of Education with the assistance of three Assistant Directors of Education heads the education administration in the UT at school level. Sarva Shiksha Abhiyan (SSA) is a new intervention for spread of elementary education. The SSA is aimed at providing useful and relevant elementary education to all children in the age group of 6-14 years by 2010 and to bridge the social and gender gaps with the active participation of the community in the management of schools. Necessary preparations for implementation and monitoring of SSA are in progress in UT. The following special schemes are in operation:

Centrally Sponsored Schemes

- free higher education to tribal girls students as special central assistance at Banasthali Vidyapith, Rajasthan;
- free uniform to tribal students;
- free material for sports and games in tribal areas;
- mid-day meal to tribal students of classes I–VIII;
- free notebooks and textbooks to tribal students; and
- free coaching classes for tribal students.

UT Sponsored Schemes

- free textbooks and uniforms to all tribal students and those belonging to BPL families;
- travel concession for students attending schools beyond 4 km of the residence;
- hostel stipend to the hostelers;
- attendance scholarship to all tribal students;
- mid-day meal to primary and middle school children;
- students of tribal and rural area are provided with free boarding and lodging facilities for studies in Port Blair; and
- reservation of seats for higher courses in mainland.

In addition, the departments of Social Welfare, Tribal Welfare, and Women Development and Child Welfare implement specific schemes and contribute in provision of education in ANI.

Challenges

The Tenth Five-year Plan, with a view to improving the access, usefulness, and quality of education has emphasised on reducing the gender and regional disparities, adoption of state specific strategies for delivery of education, increased private participation in management of institutions, use of information technology, and revision of curricula with emphasis on vocationalisation and employment creation in secondary and higher education. In ANI while significant steps have been taken in improving the access to education, and minimising regional and gender disparities, enhancement in the quality of education and its usefulness in the local context has not received the desired attention. The retention rate of students remains poor, performance of students measured in terms of percentage of students passed at all levels, especially in grade X, also remains poor, the curriculum is yet to be reviewed. The specific challenges therefore are:

- tackling low net enrolment ratio and high dropout rates, and improving accessibility of schools in rural areas;
- reviewing curricula at all levels for providing useful and locally relevant education of high quality. Introducing locally relevant vocational courses and lower level math and science courses at secondary level;
- improving infrastructure for quality education by convergence of multiple schemes with overlapping objectives leading to creation of thin infrastructure, leakage, and poor monitoring and quality control; and
- strengthening vocational and technical training and making it responsive to changing local needs.

Strategy

Studies conducted in India reveal that the main reasons for school dropout include the need for children to work, their lack of interest in studies, lack of visible learning outcomes in literacy and other skills, and lack of functional utility of education in the medium term. As child labour is not a major issue in ANI, improvement in quality and functional utility of education needs to be focused upon. In this context, the following measures are suggested.

In order to create demand for education, it is important to ensure conducive school environment which has adequate enabling infrastructure and motivated, committed and enthusiastic teachers (the principal instrument of education), useful and relevant curriculum, and active community participation. Information on islands' culture, and the ecosystem could effectively be integrated into the syllabus from primary school. This will inculcate in children an awareness of the fragility of the environment in which they live, as well as make learning more relevant. To motivate the teachers, regular orientation in teaching methods, training and short-term exchange programmes should be implemented. Interaction of the officials in Directorate of Education with the management of renowned schools in mainland and other experts would facilitate in bringing about appropriate changes in the existing programmes for the training of teachers.

Good infrastructure is a necessity in raising the learning achievements. Thus, there is a need to establish convergence between various departments to check creation of duplicate and thin infrastructure. An extensive review of the purpose and coverage of various schemes and their relevance in the present context should be undertaken periodically. This would help in strengthening the existing infrastructure and will make monitoring feasible for quality control.

There is a need to investigate the alternatives available for improving the quality of service delivery, to get more value for every rupee of government expenditure. While the government should retain the overall responsibility to ensure universal access to education; to achieve the improvement in quality of education, involvement and participation of local bodies, voluntary organisations and local communities should be made more systematic and formal to benefit from their active and meaningful contribution. The SSA prescribes that Village Education Committee (VEC) would have a key role in implementation of SSA. It appears that VECs either do not exist or are not effective. There is a need to constitute VECs and strengthen them to benefit from their contribution. This would help to make the delivery system more efficient and responsive to the changing local needs, bring about accountability into the performance of teachers and schools, and bring about convergence of services.

In this context, there is a role for performance indicators as well. Performance measurement should include both comparisons across schools and comparison of school with its own past. While the former can provide inputs on the attainable levels for the school, the latter can provide evidence of change in the performance over time. Some suggested indicators are; enrolment rates, retention rate from one class to the next, percentage of students passing class X and

XII exams, percentage of students passing class X and XII exams in first division, expenditure on teaching aids per student, expenditure on teachers training and orientation, and expenditure on counselling of students to help chart their future. Rewards and penalties for good and poor performance respectively, will provide incentives for schools to improve.

Courses and curriculum of vocational and technical training should also be reviewed from time to time to ensure that teaching modules are in tune with the industry demand. Courses in information technology, electronic system maintenance and other fast developing fields need a special mention here. To improve demand for technical and vocational training centres and enhance performance of students in these schools, some basic courses of one or two semesters may be imparted before teaching those courses that may be highly technical and require sound grounding in science and maths. The education department should also set up a cell to monitor skills which are in demand in the market, and job opportunities.

A conservative policy of emphasising on general skills like science, social science and math in secondary education seems more appropriate. This system would not only provide students a strong grounding to enrol for extensive vocational training but would also provide flexibility enough to fit into a variety of occupations or go for higher studies in various fields. There is, however, scope for introducing certain vocational courses at secondary level that do not require strong mathematical and scientific skills. Similarly, the UT should consider introducing lower level courses say 'level B' in math and science at secondary school level for those pursuing/want to pursue vocational courses.

Creation of technical and vocational skills in the labour force is crucial. Employment based training has an advantage over the same routine type of training. Potential employers know more about the demand for labour than the formal school system does, and they are better placed to follow technological developments in a variety of occupations. Government should support and encourage technical and vocational schools in the private sector with strong linkages with industry. This does not imply that the public vocational and technical schools should be closed down. Private schools would play a complementary role. People will enrol in them voluntarily, pay for their courses, and thereby help to ensure the relevance of what those schools offer. If students pay the cost of education, they are likely to make better choices on whether to enrol and what to study. For the talented poor, selective scholarships and loans can be provided. Government vocational schools typically financed by the taxpayer generally provide inadequate alternative. Government schools would compete with private schools and some may be closed down if their enrolment rates drop below pre-specified levels.

Institutions such as Indian Institute of Technology and Manipal Academy should be encouraged to set up technical training centres in ANI. Selective scholarships can be provided for economically disadvantaged sections.

Health and Family Welfare

A society with healthy people has a greater potential to develop. Healthy life is not only an indicator of personal well-being of a person, but also facilitates all other objectives of life. A person with better health has greater opportunity to pursue his goals and can devote more time, money, and other resources towards productive uses.

Trends

Infant Mortality Rate (IMR)

In ANI there has been significant improvement in health indicators over the years. For instance, the IMR was 21.21 per thousand in 2001, against the national average of 71 per thousand in 2001 (Table 5.11). However greater effort is required for improving IMR in rural areas (Table 5.12). Child Mortality Rate (less than

TABLE 5.11

Infant Mortality Rate

UTs/States	*1981*			*1991*			*2001*
	Male	*Female*	*Person*	*Male*	*Female*	*Person*	*Person*
Andaman & Nicobar	**114**	**76**	**95**	**71**	**61**	**69**	**21.21***
Chandigarh	141	96	118	50	47	48	30
Dadra & Nagar Haveli	149	82	117	84	73	81	61
Daman & Diu	87	93	90	61	50	56	NA
Delhi	108	92	100	55	51	54	51
Lakshadweep	170	88	132	100	78	91	32
Pondicherry	100	68	84	32	35	34	21
Kerala	61	48	54	45	41	42	16
Maharashtra	131	106	119	72	76	74	49
Punjab	138	114	127	81	53	74	54
Tamil Nadu	114	93	104	55	51	54	53
All-India	122	108	115	74	79	77	71

Sources: For year 1981 and 1991: Planning Commission, *National Human Development Report 2001*, Government of India, New Delhi, p.226.

For year 2001: Government of India, *Economic Survey 2002-2003*.

*: in Status Paper on Health Services in A & N Islands.

TABLE 5.12

Infant Mortality Rate: Rural and Urban

UTs/States	1981			1991			2000		
	Rural	Urban	Total	Rural	Urban	Total	Rural	Urban	Total
Andaman & Nicobar Islands	**106**	**40**	**95**	**72**	**53**	**69**	**27**	**10**	**23**
Chandigarh	161	114	118	49	49	48	28	26	28
Dadra & Nagar Haveli	114	156	117	81	81	81	62	14	58
Daman & Diu	85	92	90	61	38	56	38	57	48
Delhi	106	100	100	88	50	54	32	32	32
Lakshadweep	142	114	132	101	76	91	25	29	27
Pondicherry	96	74	84	35	33	34	33	15	23
Kerala	56	49	54	45	42	42	14	14	14
Maharashtra	131	67	119	85	47	74	57	33	48
Punjab	135	104	127	81	56	74	56	38	52
Tamil Nadu	116	78	104	62	40	54	57	38	51
All-India	123	67	115	84	51	77	74	43	68

Source: Planning Commission, *National Human Development Report 2001*, Government of India, New Delhi, p.227.

five year) has also improved over the years though still remains higher when compared with Chandigarh, Pondicherry, Delhi, Kerala, and Daman and Diu, however, there is no significant gender disparity in child mortality rate (Table 5.13).

Birth Rate and Death Rate

Birth rate in ANI is much below the national average and one of the lowest in country after Goa. It is significant to note that the birth rate in rural areas of ANI is marginally lower (19) than birth rate in urban areas (19.3). This could be partly due to consistent decline in IMR and improvement in the literacy rate (Table 5.14). Death rate in ANI has shown a continuous decline and is one of the lowest in the country (Table 5.15). Death rate is favourable for females *vis-à-vis* males but is higher in rural areas than in urban areas (Table 5.16).

TABLE 5.13

Under Five Mortality Rate

UTs/States	1981			1991		
	Male	Female	Person	Male	Female	Person
Andaman & Nicobar Islands	**117**	**110**	**113**	**89**	**85**	**88**
Chandigarh	72	74	73	70	69	71
Dadra & Nagar Haveli	154	138	146	96	85	91
Daman & Diu	83	80	81	79	71	72
Delhi	93	99	96	74	66	70
Lakshadweep	201	175	189	139	142	140
Pondicherry	117	113	115	67	65	66
Kerala	85	76	80	60	61	60
Maharashtra	146	144	145	89	93	91
Punjab	104	118	111	97	82	92
All-India	147	157	152	91	101	94

Source: Planning Commission, *National Human Development Report 2001*, Government of India, New Delhi, p.228.

TABLE 5.14

Birth Rate

UTs/States	1991	1995	2000
Andaman & Nicobar Island	**20.0**	**18.7**	**19.1 (16.08*)**
Chandigarh	13.9	19.5	-
Dadra & Nagar Haveli	31.1	29.7	-
Daman & Diu	27.9	21.8	-
Delhi	24.7	23.3	-
Lakshadweep	27.1	25.5	-
Pondicherry	19.2	20.1	-
Kerala	18.3	18.0	17.9
Maharashtra	26.2	24.5	21.0
Punjab	27.7	24.6	21.6
Tamil Nadu	20.8	20.3	19.3
All-India	29.5	28.3	25.8

Source: For Year 1991 and 1995: Census of India, *State Profile 1991*.
For Year 2000: Government of India, *Economic Survey 2002-03*.
*: The figure is for 2001 as given in Status paper on health services in Andaman & Nicobar Islands.

TABLE 5.15

Death Rate

UTs/States	*1981*			*1991*			*1997*		
	Male	*Female*	*Person*	*Male*	*Female*	*Person*	*Male*	*Female*	*Person*
Andaman & Nicobar Islands*	-	-	**8.4**	**7**	**4.4**	**5.8**	**6**	**4.1**	**5.1**
Chandigarh	-	-	2.4	4.5	4.7	4.6	4.5	3.9	4.2
Dadra & Nagar Haveli	-	-	-	12	10.9	11.5	9.7	6.7	8.2
Daman & Diu	-	-	10.2	10.2	7.8	9	6.8	5.1	5.9
Delhi	-	-	7.1	6.5	6.1	6.3	5.8	5	5.4
Lakshadweep	-	-		5.3	4.1	4.7	6.4	6.1	6.2
Pondicherry	-	-	7.3	7.5	5.7	6.6	9.3	6.7	8
Kerala	7.8	5.5	6.6	6.9	5.2	6	7.6	4.9	6.2
Maharashtra	9.7	9.4	9.6	8.5	7.9	8.2	7.9	6.7	7.3
Punjab	10.1	8.7	9.4	8.7	6.8	7.8	8	6.8	7.4
Tamil Nadu	12.1	11.6	11.8	9.7	8	8.8	8.8	7.2	8
All-India	12.4	12.7	12.5	10	9.7	9.8	9.2	8.6	8.9

Note: *The death rate for ANI in 2001 is 2.82 (Status Paper on Health Services in Andaman & Nicobar Islands).

Source: Planning Commission, *National Human Development Report 2001*, Government of India, New Delhi, p.236.

TABLE 5.16

Death Rate: Rural-Urban

UTs/States		*1981*			*1991*			*2001*		
		Male	*Female*	*Person*	*Male*	*Female*	*Person*	*Male*	*Female*	*Person*
Andaman & Nicobar Islands	**Rural**	-	-	**9.2**	**7.9**	**4.8**	**6.4**	**6.6**	**4.5**	**5.6**
	Urban	-	-	**2.4**	**4.4**	**3.2**	**3.9**	**4.4**	**2.7**	**3.6**
All-India	Rural	13.4	13.9	13.7	10.7	10.5	10.6	9.8	9.4	9.6
	Urban	8.0	7.6	7.8	7.5	6.7	7.1	7.0	6.0	6.5
Kerala	Rural	7.9	5.6	6.7	7.2	5.2	6.2	7.6	5.0	6.3
	Urban	7.1	4.5	5.8	5.6	4.9	5.3	7.8	4.5	6.1

Source: Planning Commission, *National Human Development Report 2001*, Government of India, New Delhi, pp.237-238.

Maternal Mortality Rate

The maternal mortality rate in ANI was below 0.5 per 100 live births in 2001; implying excellent natal care. Institutional delivery rate was impressive 82 per cent in 2001, second highest in the country after Daman and Diu. Institutional delivery rate in rural area is lower than in urban areas. Thus, there is a need to identify factors why rural women shy away from delivery in hospitals and take appropriate measures to overcome these.

Couple Protection Rate and Vaccination of Children

Though ANI has achieved couple protection rate of 58.16 per cent in 2001 against the national average of 48.2 per cent in 1998-99, examples to follow in this respect would be Kerala, West Bengal, Himachal Pradesh and Delhi. Performance of ANI in immunisation of children against identified preventable diseases was impressive with 95.97 per cent children covered under various antigens in 2001, as against the all-India average of 42 per cent in 1998-99.

Major Diseases

The information on morbidity pattern of a population is essential for efficient provision of public health services. The main diseases prevalent in ANI are:

- Acute Respiratory Infection.

- Pyrexia of unknown origin (viral fever).
- Gastro-Intestinal Disorder.
- Nutritional diseases which include Anaemia and Vitamin Deficiency.
- Malaria.

Persons Reporting Ailment and Persons Hospitalised

The UT does not maintain data on morbidity patterns. However, analysis of NSSO data on morbidity (July 1995-June 1996) shows that while overall morbidity is lower in ANI than national average and also from that of many other states and union territories, morbidity in case of males was higher than females in ANI though at national level the morbidity was higher for females than their male counterparts (Tables 5.17 and 5.18).

Studies show that in many cases women in India, do not report to doctors because of some social taboos or because they may feel that the health of their male counterpart is more important and thus do not pay adequate attention to their own health. This, however, needs to be investigated further in order to find out whether morbidity cases go unreported among females/males or traditional systems of medicine are being used by people.

The rural urban disparity in morbidity level is high in ANI. During the reference year, 15 people per thousand population reported ailment in urban areas against 27 in rural areas. National average for morbidity in urban and rural areas was 54 and 55 per thousand population respectively (Tables 5.17 and 5.18).

Information on the number of persons hospitalised indicates level of morbidity, access to and quality of health care facilities, and awareness to avail health services. Therefore, a small number of hospitalisation cases does not necessarily imply a low morbidity level though it is indicative of a broad relative picture. NSSO survey (1995-96) shows that in contrast with the all-India picture, while morbidity in rural areas is lower *vis-à-vis* urban areas, number of persons hospitalised was more in rural areas than in urban areas in ANI implying availability of health care facilities in rural areas and also awareness among people.

Apart from these general health conditions there are some psychosocial problems in this territory. The suicide rate has been on increase. A total of 137 and 126 suicide cases respectively have been reported in 2000-01 and 2001-02. Alcoholism is another problem and is rising. Fifty seven cases of alcoholism were treated in 2001 and 85 cases in 2002 by the district hospital in Port Blair.

TABLE 5.17

Number of Persons Reporting Ailment during Last 15 Days in Rural Area (1995-1996)

(Persons per Thousand Population)

UTs/States	*Acute Ailment*			*Chronic Ailment*			*Any Ailment*		
	Male	*Female*	*Person*	*Male*	*Female*	*Person*	*Male*	*Female*	*Person*
Andaman & Nicobar Islands	**26**	**23**	**25**	**4**	**1**	**2**	**30**	**24**	**27**
Chandigarh	130	144	135	10	29	18	140	173	153
Dadra & Nagar Haveli	47	50	48	-	19	9	47	69	57
Daman & Diu	10	30	20	25	21	23	35	51	43
Delhi	22	22	22	1	-	0	23	22	23
Lakshadweep	45	22	34	24	29	26	63	51	57
Pondicherry	70	103	87	8	-	4	78	103	91
Kerala	80	79	80	36	40	38	116	119	118
Maharashtra	37	38	37	14	15	15	51	52	52
Punjab	55	57	56	15	25	20	71	81	76
Tamil Nadu	36	42	39	16	10	13	52	53	52
All-India	41	44	42	13	14	13	54	57	55

Source: Planning Commission, *National Human Development Report 2001*, Government of India, New Delhi, p.255.

TABLE 5.18

Number of Persons Reporting Ailment during Last 15 Days in Urban Area (1995-1996)

(Persons per Thousand Population)

UTs/States	*Acute Ailment*			*Chronic Ailment*			*Any Ailment*		
	Male	*Female*	*Person*	*Male*	*Female*	*Person*	*Male*	*Female*	*Person*
Andaman & Nicobar Islands	**16**	**11**	**14**	**2**	**0**	**1**	**18**	**11**	**15**
Chandigarh	76	96	85	50	45	48	127	141	133
Dadra & Nagar Haveli	56	54	55	3	-	2	59	54	57
Daman & Diu	28	39	34	12	6	9	41	44	43
Delhi	34	28	31	12	12	12	46	40	43
Lakshadweep	46	47	46	4	-	2	50	57	48
Pondicherry	43	71	57	18	1	10	62	72	67
Kerala	63	59	61	25	28	27	88	88	88
Maharashtra	33	38	35	13	13	13	45	51	48
Punjab	67	52	60	17	34	25	84	86	85
Tamil Nadu	38	51	44	13	16	14	50	66	58
All-India	39	43	41	13	15	14	51	58	54

Source: Planning Commission, *National Human Development Report 2001*, Government of India, New Delhi, p.256.

Healthcare and Family Welfare Facilities

Population covered by Healthcare Infrastructure

Population coverage of healthcare facilities in ANI is impressive. Provision of health infrastructure is presented in Table 5.19.

Presently the UT has 19 PHC, 4 CHC, and 104 sub-centres. In addition to this, there are 2 district hospitals, 1 referral hospital, 1 ayurvedic dispensary, 8 homeopathic dispensaries and 5 urban health centres. On an average, one sub-centre covered 3,423 people; one PHC and CHC each covered 18,736 and 89,000 people respectively, which was above national average of 4,579, 27,364 and 21,4000 respectively, during the year 1999. Availability of health infrastructure is relatively better (in terms of the number of sub-centres, PHCs and CHCs) per thousand population in Nicobar district which is a predominantly rural area. In 2001, the doctor-population and nurse-population ratios were 1:2800 and 1:1140 respectively in ANI.

TABLE 5.19

District-Wise Health Infrastructure in Andaman & Nicobar Islands

Hospital	*Andaman District*	*Nicobar District*	*Total*
Sub Centre	73	31	104
Primary Health Centre	15	4	19
Community Health Centre	3	1	4
District Hospital	1	1	2
Homeo Dispensary	5	3	8
Ayurvedic Dispensary	1	0	1
Urban Health Centre	5	0	5
Referral Hospital	1	0	1
Total	104	40	144

Source: Status Paper on Health Services in Andaman & Nicobar Islands.

Provision of hospital beds in ANI has an urban bias. This is mainly because of 412 bedded G.B. Pant referral hospital in Port Blair (Table 5.20). G.B. Pant hospital in Port Blair is reported to be equipped to handle sophisticated treatments including open-heart surgery. Under a Consultancy Services scheme, specialised doctors from Chennai visit the ANI from time to time and provide consultancy and operation services. A tele-medicine service between the G.B. Pant Hospital and Sri Ramachandra Medical College, Chennai is in operation to facilitate medical consultation with specialist doctors through teleconferencing and video-conferencing. This facility is expected to result in capacity building of in-house doctors and other support staff thereby, leading to reduction in both public and private expenditure incurred when chronic/critical patients are referred to hospitals in mainland. ANI implements a scheme under which emergency patients in far-flung areas are evacuated either by diverting sailing of the ship or by helicopter for treatment in hospitals. With the continuous improvement in

TABLE 5.20

Beds in Hospitals

Hospital	*Andaman District*	*Nicobar District*	*Urban Area*	*Rural Area*	*Total*
Referral Hospital	412	-	412	-	412
District Hospital	42	112	-	154	154
Community Health Centre	158	43	-	201	201
Primary Health Centre	155	45	-	200	200
Total	767	200	412	555	967

Source: Status Paper on Health Services in Andaman & Nicobar Islands.

healthcare facilities in CHCs, PHCs and district hospitals and increase in the number of health centres, the number of patients evacuated in a year has steadily declined from 35 patients in 1993 to 2 in 2001.

Tribal areas are reported to be well covered with primary health infrastructure. In addition, with a view to encourage tribal population to contribute their traditional knowledge in healthcare, a scheme is being implemented which combines indigenous tribal medicines with that of homeopathic and ayurvedic medicines. With a view to improve the access and utilisation of health services by tribal population, ANI is implementing one more scheme in collaboration with WHO. The unique feature of the scheme is involvement of health workers from tribal community in delivering health services. There are various national programmes to control diseases such AIDS, TB, cancer, malaria, leprosy and blindness.

Family Welfare

To promote small family, improve literacy, discourage early marriage, and to provide social security to women in old age, the ANI is implementing a scheme called "Planned Families by 2000 AD", since 1996. Girls between the age group of 13-21 who are permanent residents of these islands or residing in this UT for more than 10 years are eligible for registration under the scheme. Achievements under the scheme were the following:

- During 1995-96–June 2001 a total of 19,633 girls registered under the programme;
- 3,452 girls received incentives on passing 10th standard;
- 1,360 cases of delayed marriage received incentives; and
- 5,160 women received incentives for adopting small family norms.

Year-wise data on the achievements under this scheme is not available, therefore no analysis of the trends in achievements since the inception of the programme could be made.

Public Expenditure on Health and Family Welfare

Medical services are almost free for everyone in the state and food and medicines are distributed at no cost to all in-patients in hospitals and primary health centres. The state also pays for secondary and tertiary healthcare treatment outside the UT.

The share of expenditure on health to total expenditure in this UT was close to average expenditure of 14 major states in India during 1999-2000 but was lower than Kerala and Tamil Nadu (Table 5.21). Per capita public expenditure on health in ANI is, however, highest in the country. Between 1989-90 and 1993-94, it increased by 22.55 per cent registering a 4.5 per cent growth per annum. Growth in per capita expenditure on health was even higher between 1993-94 and 1999-2000. Per capita expenditure increased to Rs. 920.31 in 1999-2000 which was little over six times higher than the average for 14 major Indian states, and about four times higher than per capita public health expenditure in Kerala, that has

TABLE 5.21

Share of Public Expenditure on Health in Total Public Expenditure

(in Percentage)

Year	*A&N Islands*	*Delhi*	*Kerala*	*Maharashtra*	*Punjab*	*Tamil Nadu*	*Major States*
1989-1990	4.93	-	6.66	4.66	5.59	5.78	5.40
1993-1994	4.88	8.70	5.81	4.51	4.48	5.60	5.16
1999-2000	5.15	7.51	5.51	3.64	4.66	5.54	4.80
2000-2001	4.81	-	-	-	-	-	-

Note: Calculated from various issues of RBI State Finance for other states and Delhi. A&N Island's figure is calculated from Budget documents of the UTs.

shown better performance than the ANI in terms of many health indicators (Figure 5.3). Though difficult terrain and poor connectivity in ANI also contribute to higher per capita costs but such high magnitudes of per capita expenditure suggest presence of inefficiencies in the provision and delivery of service.

FIGURE 5.3

Per Capital Public Expenditure on Health (In Rupees)

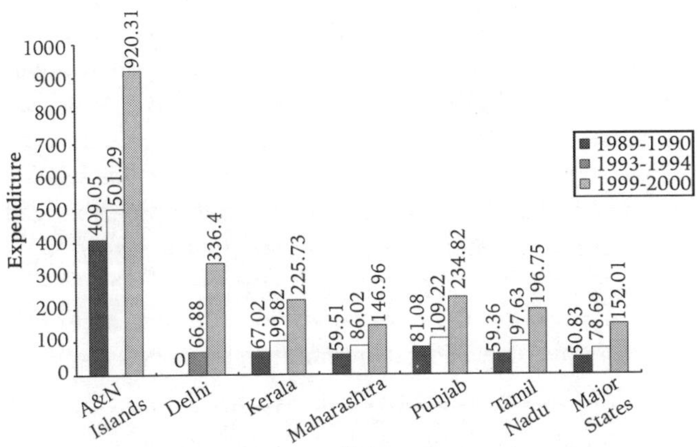

A total of Rs. 10033.20 lakh was spent during Ninth Five-year Plan (1997-2002), out of which Rs. 6562.94 lakh was revenue expenditure and Rs. 3481.88 lakh capital expenditure. G.B. Pant Hospital at Port Blair has a major share in the revenue expenditure for the Health and Family Welfare Department. Scheme-wise outlay and expenditure on health services are displayed in Table 5.22.

Challenges

In ANI, efficiency of use of funds can increase through greater involvement of stakeholder fraternity. The administration should aim to create space for the private sector (especially in tertiary care), for the community-centred actions, and for the meaningful participation of NGOs. The UT should move from providing all health services free to everyone by introducing a reasonable level of user charge. A beginning can be made by levying user charge on curative services. The poor and vulnerable sections should, however, be protected through direct targeting. A mobile hospital (hospital ship) to provide specialised medical services in far-flung areas.

Traditional systems of medicines such as naturopathy, ayurveda, homeopathy should also be encouraged. ANI has rich forest resources that house a variety of medicinal plants. Local knowledge also exists about holistic indigenous medical remedies. This should be effectively incorporated into the community health programme for effective and low cost solution to many health problems. Attractive packaging of these (especially for non-islanders and foreigners) has great potential for generating both employment and revenue.

Strategy

While the existence of the public sector in health ensures that there is more widespread potential access to the service, often there are complaints of poor quality of service being provided by the public sector. It is, therefore, useful to involve voluntary organisations and communities in the provision of those public health services that have a large service content. A strategy should be worked out to also involve local bodies in the medium term. Involvement of local level governments, voluntary organisations, and communities can help in improving the accountability of the public health providers, improve inter-sectoral coordination and bring about convergence of services.

TABLE 5.22

Ninth Plan Outlay and Expenditure

(Rs. In Lakh)

Name of the Scheme	*Ninth Plan Outlay*			*Ninth Plan Expenditure*		
	Revenue	*Capital*	*Total*	*Revenue*	*Capital*	*Total*
1. Primary Health Centre	846.00	2784.00	3630.00	2019.07	2281.60	4328.60
2. Strengthening of District Hospital	199.00	521.00	720.00	992.98	255.29	1176.68
3. Upgradation of G.B.P. Hospital	481.00	895.00	1376.00	1643.89	528.27	2236.47
4. Strengthening of Directorate	132.00	383.00	515.00	279.00	123.62	400.32
5. Planned Family by 2000 AD	1500.00	-	1500.00	1368.00	0	1368.00
6. ACA to PMGY	-	-	-	330.00	293.10	523.13
Total	3158.00	4583.00	7741.00	6632.94	3481.88	10033.2

Source: Compiled from various Plan documents.

State-provided healthcare should have strong preventive focus, i.e., providing healthier environment (sanitation, clean water, garbage disposal, clean surroundings), complete immunisation coverage, couple protection, prenatal, childbirth and postpartum, child nutrition, control of killer disease.

Decision making in resource allocation should be oriented towards improved service delivery. A selective beginning with a few schemes, such as, preventive health should be made. In this context, performance measurement and monitoring is important. Given the targets specified in terms of the quality, quantity and cost of service, a set of indicators would emerge. The need to specify the targets appropriately is therefore important.[1]

Performance measurement can be of two kinds: a survey of patients, and monitoring of some predetermined set of indices. Some suggested indicators for hospitals and PHCs, etc. are:

- Number of in-patients per doctor, per nurse and per bed.
- Number of out-patients per doctor and other staff.
- Ratio of non-wage expenditure to total expenditure.
- Ratio of own resources to total expenditure.
- Proportion of children given vaccinations.
- Proportion of underweight children and children with nutritional deficiencies.
- Number of people reporting waterborne and airborne diseases.
- Number of people reporting contagious diseases.

The information on these indicators should be collected for all constituent members and disseminated widely. While a policy should be evolved to link the resource allocation to the performance in these indicators in the medium term, the availability of information itself could be instrumental in bringing about corrective action in the short run.

As technology in healthcare develops, there may be a mismatch between infrastructure and skills of personnel. Continuing medical education for orientation and skill up-gradation is therefore essential. Training of health workers should be done periodically such that all health personnel have the necessary knowledge, attitude, skills, and programme and people orientation to effectively take care of health problems and improve the quality of service to people.

An appropriate and speedy grievance cell should be set up to improve accountability of health centres/ institutions.

Health services represent the field of joint operation, that is, health services provided by the government can be complemented by those available in the private sector. Private entrepreneurs, NGOs, self-help groups and charitable institutions can be provided certain incentives for making an entry into the market, which currently provides virtually free services.

NGOs in the area of health can be encouraged in various aspects of health at the grass-roots level through logistical and technical support. They along with PRIs can help raise people's awareness in identifying their own health problems and solving them with local knowledge and resources. A large proportion of health problems can be prevented if people have the requisite knowledge. Preventive health care programmes can be run by NGOs, PRIs, community-based organisations, using mediums such as radio, television, community gatherings.

Alcoholism is an emerging problem. Community efforts in alcohol rehabilitation programmes are more effective than medical intervention. Many of the rural people rely on more holistic indigenous medical remedies and local herbs for prevention and treatment. This could be effectively incorporated into the community health programme as they provide effective and low-cost solutions to many health problems.

Nutrition

In view of the fact that the problem of malnutrition is serious in India and that it leads to serious health problems such as chronic energy deficiency, anaemia, vitamin deficiency, obesity, the Tenth FYP emphasises on a paradigm shift in the policies to strengthen the nutrition security of India.

In ANI, a large number of cases of vitamin and iron deficiency are reported. It is therefore important that the people should be educated about the importance of foods rich in vitamins and minerals for good health besides the potential natural sources of vitamins and minerals. Initially, the government may have to intervene to ensure that the vegetables and fruits are grown locally and made available to people at affordable prices. Vitamin and mineral rich local varieties such as bamboo shoots and *sahjan* that can be easily cultivated on the island should be popularised among islanders through media, and health and community workers.

1. This section draws heavily from *Report of the Public Expenditure Reforms Commission*, Punjab, 2002.

Chapter 6

Issues in Tribal Development[1]

Introduction[2]

In the verdant greens of the Andaman & Nicobar Islands dwell some of the oldest surviving tribes of the world. The Andaman archipelago is home to four negrito tribes—the Great Andamanese, the *Jarawa*, the *Onge* and the *Sentinelese*. Recent studies conducted by the Centre for Cellular and Molecular Biology, Hyderabad show that these tribes settled in the islands some 60,000 years ago. They are the last of the First People. At least two of these four tribes—the *Jarawa* and the *Sentinelese*—continue to be hunter-gatherers and are among the most isolated communities in the world. Yet their numbers are fast dwindling. Ad hoc and often imposed contact with the outside world has introduced them to diseases and to addictive substances. It has also led to a depletion of their resource base, challenging their very existence.

The Nicobar group of islands are home to two tribes of Indo-Mongloid origins. The Shompens who live along the coasts and deep inside the forests of Greater Nicobar are hunter-gatherers. The Nicobarese are presently the largest tribal group inhabiting these islands. Unlike the other tribal groups, Nicobarese have much greater contact with the outside world. This is the only tribal group of the islands whose population has shown a consistent growth.

As the circumstances of each of these tribal groups vary significantly, they require a different set of interventions and non-interventions by the government. Before going into general issues like education, food security, poverty and Tribal Sub-Plan, this chapter will first recount the condition of each of the tribes.

The Aborigines

The Great Andamanese

The Great Andamanese, consisting of 10 territorial and linguistic groups, were at one time the largest tribe inhabiting the archipelago. It is believed that prior to the Penal Settlement of 1858, between 5000-8000 Great Andamanese lived in different parts of the Great Andaman Islands. These tribes fiercely resisted British incursions into their territory and suffered heavy casualties in the process. Subsequently, they made peace with the British and were introduced to addictive substances like opium, tobacco and alcohol. Contact with the outside world brought with it diseases and by the beginning of the twentieth century the Great Andamanese population had dwindled to 625. Their numbers further came down to 19 by 1961. Inebriated and shorn of all vitality, the remaining members of a once proud tribe are scattered across North Andamans and in Port Blair. Many had married non-autochthons or are the creation of mixed marriages. To protect them the Government brought them together and resettled them in Strait Island. Currently, there are around 52 people who claim to be of Andamanese descent. In 1970, when the meagre remnants of the Andamanese population were resettled in Strait Island, it was in tangible ways a rehabilitation, providing the small group with some access to a means for survival which had been appropriated from them. After treating them for various addictions (mostly opium), and other chronic ailments like tuberculosis or syphilis, it was erroneously assumed that by providing a stable resource

1. Development pertains to changes over time, affected without any explicit exercise of force or coercion, other than that envisaged under common law, by 'enrichment of the available set of choices' and the 'expansion of the capability to exercise those choices'.

2. This Chapter draws heavily from the reports of different Expert Committees on the *Jarawa*, in particular the recent report of the Sub-Group of Experts formed by the National Advisory Council. The chapter has also been enriched by invaluable inputs from Dr. Sita Venkateshwar (re Great Andamanese) and Ayesha Majid (re Nicobarese).

base, the Andamanese would shortly revert to their former hunting-gathering-fishing mode of existence. This was not to be. Years of disease, dependency and bungled administrative practices had destroyed not just the genetic purity of the tribe, but its very vitality.

Today, three generations can be observed among this autochthonous tribe. The oldest generation comprises of three elderly women who are distinctly 'Andamanese' in their physical appearance. They moved from North Andaman to Port Blair and have retained the habits of work and activity as in the past and form the backbone of this community.

The next generation, comprising people in their thirties and forties, grew up under the auspices of the welfare system. Assured of a daily supply of food without any individual effort, they lack the skills, typical of an 'Andamanese'. Though they went to school in Port Blair, most dropped out within a few years. Thus, they possess neither their cultural knowledge nor the wherewithal to interact with mainstream society on an equal footing. Their ambiguity of identity is compounded by ambiguity in physical appearance. This generation is heavily into drinking and many couples have strained relationships. Several individuals are currently employed by the Andaman administration.

Youth and children make up the third generation of Andamanese. Boys are introduced to alcohol either by their fathers or by the welfare staff, and girls have only to attain puberty to be seduced (sometimes with their parents' consent). Seven Andamanese children are currently studying in a school in Port Blair and one in a school in New Delhi.

Most of the generation of parents, especially the women, are articulate and are capable of assuming prominent roles as spokespersons for the indigenous groups in the islands. Of all the Andaman tribes, the Great Andamanese alone are literate and politically aware. It is important that they should be encouraged to assume wider engagement with their political situation. Children should be supported and educated so that they are able to take on meaningful jobs and roles and at the same time, the pride of the Great Andamanese in themselves and in their traditional systems needs to be revived.

There is a possibility that some Great Andamanese men are sterile either as a consequence of hereditary syphilis or other genetic anomalies. This is a matter of concern and should be handled sensitively after consultation with the community. Any course of treatment to address this possibility should target the male teenagers and children, provided there is consensus among the tribe members.

Young Great Andamanese today are choosing to marry non-Andamanese men or women. This is partly because the young boys and girls that remain today are related to one another and their traditional rules forbid consanguineous marriages. Moreover, given the extent of their interaction with the wider population, attraction to non-autochthons is only natural. The present laws, however, make it very difficult for the tribal youth to marry outsiders. Currently, one young married couple is unable to live together because the non-Andamanese young man is not permitted to stay overnight on Strait Island. He is not even allowed to live with his Great Andamanese wife at Adi Basera in Port Blair. Given the socialisation of the Great Andamanese and precarious situation of the tribe, such laws need to reviewed carefully and in consultation with the community. The tribe should be empowered to think for itself and allowed to take decisions regarding their matters.

The Jarawa

The *Jarawa* are among the few classic communities of foragers left in the world. They live in the 1028 sq. km. of dense evergreen forests which have been reserved for them. This Negrito group has attracted more attention than the other primitive tribes of Andamans primarily, because their fate has become inextricably linked with the Andaman Trunk Road (ATR); a swathe of concrete that tears through the evergreen forests that are 'home' to the *Jarawa*. A swathe which the settlers call their lifeline.

Till as late as 1997, the *Jarawa* lived in isolation and were 'hostile' towards outsiders who made incursions into their territory. The jungles of Middle and South Andaman, where the *Jarawa* live, have borne witness to many fierce fights between the *Jarawa* and the *'Eenen'* (outsider in *Jarawa* language)—be they the British, the poachers or the people engaged in construction of the ATR. Despite attacks from the 'developed' and 'civilised' world the *Jarawa* have held on to their territory and to their traditional lifestyle. Their numbers have however dwindled significantly. There are just 306 *Jarawa* that remain today. Unlike the Great Andamanese, this community has never mingled with or married non-autochthons or even autochthons from other tribes.

As the issue of the *Jarawa* and the ATR has tremendous socioeconomic and political implications, many committees have deliberated on it. In fact, the *Jarawa* has perhaps been given greater thought than all the other tribes put together. Yet the results have been far from satisfactory.

In a bid to engage with the *Jarawa*, contact missions were regularly sent with bananas, coconuts, etc. to the *Jarawa* area. Since 1974, some semblance of 'friendly' contact was even established but it was limited to government officials carrying bundles of new and alien foodstuff and other materials to *Jarawa* territory. While this did have some impact on the food habits of the *Jarawa*, the effect was minimal. Then in 1997, a young *Jarawa* boy called Enmei was found lying injured in the forest. He was treated at a hospital in Kadamtala and sent back to the forest. This, according to many marked a turning point in the *Jarawa*'s relationship with the outside world. They started visiting neighbouring villages and jetties in small groups in broad daylight.

The *Jarawa* have no concept of personal property and during these visits freely took from the settlers and their houses whatever intrigued them. These were primarily food items. Similarly when young *Jarawa* boys and girls saw vehicles on the ATR, they stopped them to ask for chips, *idlis*, biscuits, etc.—everything which was new. This led the villagers and outsiders to erroneously assume that there was food scarcity within the *Jarawa* Reserve. The government and people alike started pumping the *Jarawa* with Eenen food without giving any thought to the impact on their metabolic processes. Plantations were started in *Jarawa* areas.

All this had an adverse impact on the autochthons. While the older generation, after displaying some initial curiosity, reverted back to its original hunter-gatherer lifestyle, the younger people began to show a fascination for *eenen* articles and practices. They began to camp alongside the ATR to stop vehicles and get tobacco and junk food. This affected their hunting activities. It also initiated *Jarawa* Tourism and exposed the autochthons to voyeurism and addictions. Today, tobacco and alcohol addiction, encouraged by poachers and settlers, is widespread among the *Jarawa*. It is being used to exploit the tribe and force them into an unequal barter system. Outside influence has also strained the social fabric of the tribe. In recent years, a group of young *Jarawa* girls and orphans has broken away from the tribe and taken up residence near the settler villages. This group is extremely vulnerable and there have been reports of their exploitation.

The *Jarawa* have by and large expressed no desire to give up their traditional lifestyle. However, the impact of unregulated and unequal contact on their life is clearly visible. They have started using aluminium utensils, to cook food. Plastic and cement bags are used to store food and water. The *Jarawa* have started using discarded and new clothes given to them by outsiders. This has made them more prone to disease and increased phenomenally the incidence of skin infections. What is however more worrying is the impact this introduction of clothes can have on the *Jarawa* society which has hitherto been unaware of concepts like obscenity.

The two biggest threats to the survival of the *Jarawa* come from poaching and continued use of ATR. The Supreme Court in 2002, ordered that the portion of the ATR passing through the *Jarawa* Reserve should be closed. But this is yet to happen. Meanwhile, the *Jarawa* continue to be victims of ad hoc decisions and top-down interventions which are not guided by any systematic or thorough research. Of late, the Home Ministry has come up with a *Jarawa* policy which calls for immediate removal of all encroachments from within the Reserve and for minimum and regulated intervention. Two recent expert groups have also recommended that no attempt should be made to mainstream the *Jarawa* against their "conscious will".

The Onge

In a small island in the Andaman Sea live a hundred *Onge*. Till the late 1950s, these negritos were the sole inhabitants of Little Andaman. Though the British controlled the island after the 1890s, contact with the tribe was minimal and the *Onge* continued their traditional lives undisturbed. In 1957, the entire island was declared as a tribal reserve. Within less than a decade, however, a plan was drawn up to clear 40 per cent of the islands' forests to accommodate 12,000 settler families who would carry out red oil and timber plantations. Though the plan was never fully implemented, large sections of the Reserve were denotified and the *Onge* were squeezed out of some of their preferred habitations like Hut Bay. The final blow came in 1980, when these autochthons were bundled together and settled in two sites—Dugong Creek and South Bay. Post-tsunami, the habitation at South Bay has been destroyed and all the *Onge* have moved to Dugong Creek. A tribe which numbered 672 at the beginning of the twentieth century today has less than 100 members. Meanwhile, the number of settlers on the island has gone up from a few hundreds in 1960s to 12,000 in 1991.

The tale of the *Onge* is a classic example of good intentions gone awry. After resettling them in Dugong and South Bay, they were given rice, *dal* oil, biscuits—foods which were completely alien to a people who lived by collecting tubers and honey and by hunting wild boars and turtles. Traditionally, the *Onge* lived in huts. These huts had raised wooden platforms which served as beds. In a bid to make life 'more convenient' for the *Onge*, the administration made for them wooden houses on stilts with asbestos roofing. All these measures made the *Onge* lazy and dole dependent. They began to look towards the administration for everything.

Meanwhile, poachers and settlers alike lured them into a barter system wherein they traded precious commodities like ambergris, turtle eggs, wild boar and honey for alcohol and tobacco. The administration tried introducing them to coconut plantations, cattle rearing and pig breeding but the community rejected these measures. The school opened in Dugong Creek has not met with much success either. *Onge* of all ages, father and son, mother and daughter sit in a classroom and learn the Hindi alphabet. Not surprisingly, they have shown no interest and made little progress. They have however learnt Hindi film songs, which they prefer over their traditional numbers now.

Like in the case of the other Andaman tribes which have come into frequent outside contact, the *Onge* have fallen prey to many diseases. They have become addicted to various substances and have lost pride in their traditions and themselves. Shorn of vitality, they act as menial labour for the settlers and wait for VIP visits so that they receive 'gifts'.

One reason behind the stagnation of the *Onge* population is their traditional practice that any person—man or women—who loses his/her spouse can remarry a young *Onge*. The youth cannot refuse, irrespective of the difference in age. Frequently, young men and women are married to elderly people limiting their reproductive activities. If the tribe has to survive, it needs to be counselled against this.

Unlike the *Jarawa*, the *Onge* have come to a point where a policy of minimum intervention will not suffice. What is needed is a well thought out strategy to invigorate the tribe. Large-scale de-addiction drives supplemented by sensitive counselling need to be carried out. The dole system should be stopped immediately and the Tribal Reserve should be zealously guarded. The *Onge* should be empowered to guard the Reserve themselves. Education, if it has to be provided, should be relevant to their lifestyle and in their language.

The Sentinelese

The *Sentinelese* who inhabit the North Sentinel Islands are without doubt the most isolated community in the world. For thousands of years they have lived on their island without any kind of contact with the outside world. This group has often been termed hostile because they have reacted violently against anyone and everyone who has ventured into their territory. Poachers and government officials who have tried to establish contact with them or reach their shores have been greeted with a storm of deadly arrows.

Due to this reason knowledge about this autochthonous group is very limited. Little is known of their origins, their lifestyle, their language or even their numbers. Estimates vary between 100 and 300. It is believed that the *Sentinelese* belonged to the *Onge-Jarawa* family of tribes. At some point they either got stuck in or moved to the North Sentinel Islands. The treacherous seas and coral reefs surrounding the island ensured that they were cut off from the outside world.

Since 1967, Government of India has been sending contact parties on friendly missions to the North Sentinel Islands. As in the case of the *Jarawa*, these parties are loaded with gifts which they leave on the shores as a goodwill gesture. Though it is believed that the *Sentinelese* have become less aggressive and more open to gifts since the 1990s, they have never shown any inclination to interact with outsiders, let alone allow others to stay or explore their island. This wish of the tribe should be respected and exercises to draw them out should be suspended. We have already witnessed the harmful impact of contact on fragile communities. This experience should not be repeated with the *Sentinelese*.

It is quite possible that the tribe and its survival is threatened by poachers. Recently, the dead bodies of two men, believed to be poachers were seen lying on the shores of the Sentinel Islands. This reflects the need for stringent patrolling of the seas surrounding the island to ensure that no dent is made into the resource base of the autochthons. Such patrolling should however be done from a distance and care should be taken to ensure that the tribe does not feel threatened by it.

The Shompen

The term *Shompen* is a modified version of "Sumhalf", meaning "interior forest people" in Nicobari language. The *Shompen* are the first inhabitants of the Nicobar Islands. It is believed that they came from Sumatra and settled in their present abode, over 10,000 years ago.

A nomadic tribe of hunter-gatherers, the *Shompen* live in small bands of 25-30 people in the tropical evergreen forests of Great Nicobar. They build their huts on a raised platform, close to origin of streams so that drinking water is readily available. Streams are also used for navigation. The *Shompen* practice arboriculture and raise pandanus, colocasia, lemon, banana, chilli, tobacco, betel and coconuts. Pandanus, pigs, monitor lizard and megapod bird and its eggs are their staple foods.

Till 1969, the Great Nicobar islands were the exclusive domain of the *Shompen* and the Nicobarese. Subsequently, the government began to settle ex-servicemen on the island. As the number of settlers on the island increased and roads were built, incursions of outsiders into *Shompen* territory went up considerably. The *Shompen* began to abandon some of their traditional housing colonies. The food resources in their areas got depleted due to hunting by farmers and settlers. Further, as documented by Awaradi in his Master Plan, bands of *Shompen* who came into frequent contact with the outside world experienced high morbidity and mortality, and in some cases were completely annihilated. Diseases like dysentery and influenza wiped out scores of people. Malaria which was hitherto unknown among the *Shompen* began to show up among those tribals who interacted frequently with the Nicobarese. It is estimated that the number of *Shompen* had dwindled to 300 by 2001.[3] This is however, at best an estimate, because the *Shompen* are an extremely reclusive tribe and till date no proper enumeration of the bands which live inside the forests has been carried out.

In 1984, a *Shompen* Hut Complex was built along the East-West road to provide health, education, nutrition and other services to this tribe. It was however, found that the *Shompen* did not visit this complex frequently. They expressed little faith in our health system and little interest in our education system despite the monetary incentive.

The *Shompen* are themselves great practitioners of ethno-medicine. However, very little research has been carried out on this enigmatic tribe and this knowledge has not been documented. To empower the *Shompen*, it is vital for a group of sensitive researchers to document their traditional wisdom and to propagate its use for ensuring good health for these autochthons. A survey carried out by a team of doctors from AIIMS in 1988 found that malnutrition levels—especially protein carbohydrate deficiency—among the *Shompen* were high and fungal infections common due to poor sanitation and hygiene practices. It is time that a thorough medical study be carried out to determine the nutritional and health status of this tribe. However, the answer should not be to distribute doles. This will rob the tribe of its pride. Lack of mobility and inactivity might also hinder their metabolic processes. Instead the resources within the *Shompen* Reserve should be carefully guarded to ensure food security. The community could be counselled by a team of sensitive doctors and anthropologists on good health and nutritional practices, if necessary.

The Nicobarese

The Nicobarese are presently the largest tribal group of the Andaman & Nicobar Islands. They number around 30,000 today; a phenomenal increase from 1883 when there were less than 6000 Nicobarese. They are scattered across various islands in the Nicobar group and in some habitations on Little Andaman island. The Nicobarese are of mongoloid origin with their language rooted in the Austro-Asiatic family. It is believed that they came to these islands after the *Shompen*. Through the centuries they have had an uneasy barter system with them. As the Nicobar islands lie on an important trade route, the Nicobarese have had much contact with the outside world. They have been controlled by different groups of people including the French, Portuguese and the Danes. In 1869, the Nicobars came under British control. During World War II the Japanese took over the islands and subjected its people to much cruelty. Through all this, the Nicobarese retained much of their traditional lifestyle. Then in the beginning of the twentieth century, a young missionary called Bishop Richardson brought Christianity to the island. The religion spread rapidly and with it, education.

Though all the original inhabitants of Nicobar, barring the Shompens, are generally called Nicobarese, there exist marked differences between groups inhabiting different islands. The languages, practices and beliefs of the Nicobarese in Car Nicobar is, for instance, very different from those of the Nicobarese from the Central Group *viz.,* Nancowry Katchall, Kamorta, etc. While Car Nicobar is strictly patriarchal, the central group of islands have shades of a matriarchal society. In fact, the chief captains of Nancowry have often been women.

The Nicobarese, especially those living in Car Nicobar, have traditionally lived in extended families called *tuhets.* All assets are owned jointly by the *tuhet*

3. Estimates vary. Some people claim that there are just 150 Shompen left.

and all members including orphans, widows, etc. are looked after. Traditionally, villages were built around *tuhets* and the *tuhet* heads became village captains. Even today, in the Nicobar group of islands, the word of the Village Captain and the Tribal Council—an apex body comprising all Village Captains of an island—holds a lot of authority. It is they who arbitrate disputes, decide what developmental works should be carried out for the island and how much land should be given to whom. Of late, however, there have been some rumblings against the *diktat* of the Council.

Trade in coconuts has been the mainstay of the Nicobarese economy. For centuries, coconuts have been the barter product (like a currency) in the trade with passing vessels. However, since the 1950s, coconuts have been dried into *copra*, and marketed either through local co-operatives or sold to private traders in exchange for money or simply in lieu of rice, sugar, cloth and other necessities. Some islands are endowed with areca-palms, whose nuts also comprise a portion of the export. Apart from this market economy, the Nicobarese engage in several subsistence activities such as fishing, pig rearing, and maintaining food gardens.

Traditionally, the life and economy of the Nicobarese have been centred along the coasts. Inter-island and even inter-village communication is via boats. As the Nicobar group of islands were very close to the epicentre of the 2004 tsunami, loss to life and property was great. The tragedy was aggravated by the fact that these islands are virtually flat and there was no high ground to which the people could run. All boats that were used to move from one place to another and to go fishing were lost. Water sources were affected and wells were filled with sand and saline water. Large parts of the coasts and beaches were lost to sea. The coastline was deformed making navigation difficult. The corals and the mangrove ecosystem that provided marine food were heavily disturbed. The shock of the tsunami, the loss of a large number of people, among whom many were elders, made the Nicobarese society vulnerable to conflicts and indecisiveness. There were reports of excessive drinking. Since the tsunami, the Government has been providing relief and rehabilitation to the Nicobarese. People are presently living in temporary tin shelters whose condition is fast deteriorating. Permanent shelters are expected to come up by 2007. Meanwhile, 'free rations' comprising a range of food products such as rice, lentils, sugar, tea, spices, potatoes, onions, etc. are being distributed. Though a Cash for Work programme has been launched it hasn't proved to be very successful. Boats are being distributed by government and NGOs alike but this distribution is random and people in interior villages and islands continue to face many hardships.

The Nicobarese, like most of the tribes of ANI do not wish to leave their lands or their cultural identity. They want to 'develop', but develop at their own pace and in their own place. In fact, post-tsunami, most Nicobarese expressed a strong desire to return to their islands even when the government was hesistant to let them do so for fear of another tsunami. Thus, for the well-being of the Nicobarese, development options and economic opportunities must be brought to the islands.

One way to ensure appropriate development is to diversify the economy and provide opportunities. The Industries Department may reach out to Nicobarese to encourage their self-employment by providing loans and subsidies for the establishment of small-scale industries. Common facilities like cold storage, ice-plant, drying fish platform, etc. should be set up for promotion of fishing as a commercial activity. Subsidised seeds/saplings of coconuts, fruits and vegetables should be offered to the tribals. At the same time, the quality of education offered is extremely important. The Nicobarese have demonstrated an eagerness to send their children to school. They are also asking for quota in educational institutions in Port Blair. Meanwhile, it is important that the education imparted to the Nicobarese children assimilates their history, their traditions, their beliefs, their songs, their dances and their artistic skills. This is necessary to instil a sense of pride in the children.

Influx of illegal immigrants has been a pressing concern for the Nicobarese. Though entry into the entire Nicobar group of islands is strictly regulated under Protection of Aboriginal Tribes Regulation of 1956, illegal setters abound. In fact, most petty shops on the islands are run by illegal immigrants in connivance with some locals. These traders also act as impromptu moneylenders and many tribals are in their debt. Post-tsunami the demand for the ouster of these illegal immigrants has gained ground. The Nicobarese want their ownership rights over land to be recognised and protected. For some time now, there has also been a strong demand for the recognition of the Tribal Council as a legal entity. The Tribal Councils have, on their part, been arguing for inclusion under the Sixth Schedule of the Constitution to strengthen their traditional rights and self-governance system.

Conservation and Development of Scheduled of Tribes (STs)

Population Growth and Distribution

In 1991, 36 of the 572 islands (consisting both of islands and rock formations) of the archipelago were inhabited.[4] Of these 36, 24 fall within the Andaman group and 12 within the Nicobar group of islands with a total of 547 inhabited villages.

The percentage of ST population to total population on the ANIs, according to the census report of 1991, was 9.54 per cent. While the proportion of STs in the rural areas was 12.77 per cent, it was 0.67 per cent in the urban areas.[5] Table 6.1 reveals that in the decade between 1981 and 1991, the overall ST population of the ANIs grew by 19.72 per cent at the rate of 1.82 per cent per annum. Moreover, the female population among the STs grew faster (at 1.91 per cent per annum) than the male population (at 1.73 per cent per annum) resulting in an improvement in the gender ratio (number of females per 1000 males) from 930 in 1981 to 947 in 1991 and to 948 in 2001. While these statistics appear encouraging, a detailed break-up of the ST population over the different tribes reveals a worrisome situation. It reveals that the growth in ST population has only been on account of the Nicobarese.

Table 6.2 tracks the change in the population of the different tribes of the ANIs. It reveals that the population of all the primitive tribes continued to decline monotonically in the five decades between 1901 and 1951. These tribes were diminutive even in 1901, but their population fell to less than 100 each, by the year 1951. It is only in the decades that followed that some measures have been adopted towards their protection and conservation. The rehabilitation process the Great Andamanese (on the Strait Island) has helped reverse the decline in population in the last two decades but even today all the primitive tribal groups of ANI taken together are less than 800 in number.

TABLE 6.1

Distribution by Gender of the ST Population

Year	*Male*	*Female*	*Total*
1981	11586	10775	22361
1991	13750	13020	26770
2001	15127	14342	29469

Source: Census of India.

Meanwhile, the demographic changes that took place between 1991 and 2001 carry potently ominous signals. During this decade, the total population of the ANIs grew at an average rate of 2.41 per cent per annum against an annual average of 0.965 per cent for the STs on ANIs (registering a mere 10.08 per cent growth over the 1991 population). As a consequence, according to the Census of 2001, the proportion of ST population on the ANIs was drastically reduced to a mere 8.27 per cent (the all-India proportion of ST population stands at 8.20 per cent).

Issues in Population Stabilisation

The population decadence among the tribes continues to be threatening primarily due to episodes of diseases (often resulting in epidemic proportions) following contact with outsiders. Effective measures are therefore needed to: prevent invasion of foreign diseases;[6] and prevent reappearance of epidemic diseases

Besides this, the extremely small size of the tribes also raises questions about their ability to procreate and survive. Tables 6.3 to 6.5 focus on the population characteristics of some of the tribes. The principal determinant affecting the population stabilisation measure generally is the sex ratio (number of females per 1000 males) in the reproductive age group (considered here to be the 15–45 years age group). By this measure the ratio for both the *Onges* and the *Shompens* at 810 and 754 respectively and is a cause for concern. By and large, the sex ratio in the 0-15 years age group for all the tribes is very low and this could have serious implications.

The proportion of youth (considered here to be those in the 15–45 years age group) in the total population also has a great impact on population stabilisation. At present the *Shompens* have the highest proportion of young—53 per cent as compared to 45 and 39 per cent respectively for the *Great Andamanes* and the *Onges*. This appears to be a healthy sign. This advantage may however be nullified by certain tribal customs which give elderly men and women the right to marry young girls and boys.

Finally, the biggest threat to the survival of the primitive tribes is the constant erosion of their abode

4. This does not include Ross island, which is completely under the occupation of the defence authorities and Chatham which is connected by a bridge with Port Blair.

5. No scheduled castes (SC) are listed in the ANIs.

6. Diseases like measles, diarrhoea, malaria, tuberculosis and influenza had attained epidemic proportions and were the main causes of near annihilation of the tribals.

TABLE 6.2

Tribal Population in the A&NI

Tribe ⇩	*Island Group/ Island*	*Census Year*										
		1901	*1911*	*1921*	*1931*	*1941*	*1951*	*1961*	*1971*	*1981*	*1991*	*2001*
	Andaman Islands											
Great Andamanese	Strait Island	625	455	209	90		23	19	24	26		
Onges	Little Andamans	(672)	(631)	(346)	(250)		(150)	129	112	97		
Sentinelese	North Sentinel	(117)	(117)	(117)	(50)			(50)	(82)	NE		
Jarawas	W. Coast of S. and M. Andamans	(468)	(114)	(114)	(70)		(50)	(500)	(275)	31		
	Nicobar Islands											
Nicobarese	12 Nicobar Islands	5962	7991	8248	9589	12252	11902	13903	17874	21984		
Shompens	Great Nicobar	(348)	(375)	(375)	(200)		(20)	71	92	223		
Total							12145	14762	18102	22361	26770	29469

Notes: In the above table, data upto the year 1971 has been reproduced from the Census report for the year 1971 and the figures relating to 1981 and 1991 have been reported from the Basic Statistics (1996-97 to 1998-99). Figures in brackets are guess-estimates and NE stands for 'not enumerated'. Unfortunately, the break-up by tribes is not available in the Census Report of 1991. Moreover, the total population of the tribes is presented in the Census Reports with some reliability only from 1951 onwards. There are some variations in data for some of the years between what is reported in the Census Report of 1971 and the figures in the Master Plan prepared by S.A. Awaradi. This is especially the case in respect of the population of the primitive tribe of the Great Andamanese (for the years 1901, 1911 and 1921) and the Shompens (for the years 1921 and 1931).[31]

Source: Census Report of 1971, 2001, *Basic Statistics*.

TABLE 6.3

Distribution of *Great Andamanese* by Age and Gender (As on July 01, 2003)

Age Group	*Male*	*Female*	*Total*
0 - 15	12	9	21
15 - 45	10	11	21
45+	2	3	5
Total	24	23	47

Note: *Great Andamanese* rehabilitated on the Strait Islands.

Source: Author's Own, Directorate of Tribal Welfare (DoTW).

TABLE 6.4

Distribution of *Onges* by Age and Gender (As on July 01, 2003)

Age Group	*Male*	*Female*	*Total*
0 - 15	26	14	40
15 - 45	21	17	38
45+	10	9	19
Total	57	40	97

Note: *Onges* rehabilitated on the Dugong Creek and South Bay.

Source: Same as Table 6.3.

by outside forces. These tribes are mainly hunter-gatherers and any reduction in their resource base will have a direct impact of their food security and survival. In view of this, the Andaman administration has recently increased the area of the *Jarawa* Tribal Reserve. It is vital to check all encroachments and poaching activities within the tribal reserves.

TABLE 6.5

Distribution of *Shompens* by Age and Gender (As on July 01, 2003)

Age Group	*Male*	*Female*	*Total*
0 - 15	69	50	119
15 - 45	118	89	207
45+	53	9	62
Total	240	148	388

Notes: *Shompens* enumerated are distributed over 28 km. Camp, 24 km. Camp, 37 km. Camp, Alexandria River Camp, Dogmar River Camp, Galathia, Hin-Pou Chi, Lawful Bay, Pullobhabi, In-Hig Loil, and Chingen

Source: Same as Table 6.3.

31. Noticeably, the Master Plan does not report the population data for the year 1941 and the strength of the *Nicobarese* is reported as 8032 in the year 1921.

Acculturation

A tribe refers to people who are at a distinct techno-economic stage *vis-à-vis* the neighbouring reference community (often the dominant community). Large tribal communities may still possess the resilience to weather the tribulation of social change, concomitant to the shrinking world, but the 'little' and 'primitive'[7] communities which are normally a close part of the ecosystem, suffer heavy casualties due to outside contact.[8]

While dealing with these primitive tribal groups, the dilemma over acculturation is paramount. Should we bring the foragers into the fold of mainstream society and introduce them to all the facets of development? And if yes, at what pace? It is unfair to keep the *'junglees'* in the jungle as museum pieces while we enjoy the fruits of civilisation. Access to food, clothing, education, etc. are their constitutional rights. All that is needed is a little handholding to enable the tribes to make the transition to our world.

The other side of the argument is equally strong. Who are we to say that people should lead a particular kind of life or that one kind of life is superior to another? The primitive tribal groups of Andamans have lived in virtual isolation for between 30,000 to 60,000 years. They are among the oldest surviving people on planet earth. Can we now teach them a different way of life and ask them to abandon practices which have kept them alive all these years? Experience has shown that unregulated outside contact introduces these tribes to various addictive substances and new ailments, leading to huge loss of life. It robs them of self-respect and vitality and reduces them to mere menials in our 'mainstream' society. Given the precarious position of these tribes and their small numbers, is this a risk which can be taken? Is this what we want to reduce these proud tribes to?

Health and Education

Health Services

Over the last century we have seen a phenomenal increase in the morbidity and mortality of the primitive tribal groups as a result of contact with the outside world. Epidemics like influenza, dysentery, pneumonia which are easily treatable and manageable among the 'mainstream' population have wiped out many autochthons. Diseases to which they were not very susceptible (e.g., Shompens to malaria) have suddenly started appearing. Unfortunately, there has been no sustained or thorough research on this subject and often the unsuspecting Primitive Tribal Groups (PTGs) have been subjected to medication without studying the impact of these drugs on their immune systems. Measures like spraying DDT in tribal areas to control malaria have been initiated without considering the contamination this would cause to the water bodies from which the tribals drink. Similarly, introduction of new foods and food elements (e.g., salt in the case of the *Jarawa*) have been carried out without any thought to the possible impact on their metabolic processes. All this reflects the need for a detailed and well thought out health policy and treatment regimen for the different tribal groups.

It is important to remember that all these tribes have their own ethno-medicine which they have used effectively over the years. While it is true that these medicines might not prove effective for new ailments to which the tribes are exposed, their efficacy in treating common ailments should not be underestimated. It is vital to document the ethno-medicine and the traditional knowledge of herbs which these primitive groups possess.

Given the susceptibility of the tribes to diseases due to outside contact and their discomfort in the world outside their Reserves, *in situ* treatment should be provided to the extent possible by a team of sensitive and sensitised doctors. Use of ethno-medicine should be encouraged. When modern medicines are being used, their likely impact should first be studied and any possible side effects should be explained to the patients and their families. If there is a need to move the tribals to a health facility, care should be taken to protect them from curious onlookers and to provide an environment conducive to their lifestyle. Tribes like the *Jarawa* are given rice and *daal* at government hospitals and forced to wear clothes. This has been criticised by experts who feel these steps will adversely affect their health.

With the Great Andamanese, the *Onge* and to a certain extent with the *Shompen*, the administration faces yet another problem. These tribes have experienced a change in lifestyle. Their nomadic movement and hence activity levels have reduced, food habits have changed and some have even started using clothes. But they are yet to learn the proper health and hygiene practices that should accompany these changes.

7. Small tribal groups are communities with a population less than 15,000 and the diminutive tribes are those with population less than 1,000.

8. The urban communities in contrast form a remote part of the ecosystem.

Here it must also be acknowledged that lack of information is a major constraint in providing effective healthcare to the tribals. For example, the tribals normally do not utilise the formal system for delivery during births, which makes it extremely difficult to collate reliable data on infant and maternal mortality and the reasons behind them.

The health needs of the Nicobarese are very different from the other primitive tribes. They need access to proper healthcare facilities within their own islands due to their remoteness. Dedicated hospital ships for a group of inhabited islands will also help to prevent mortality and ensure timely treatment.

One of the principal difficulties encountered by the administration in improving the health facilities is the reluctance of health 'specialists' to undertake postings in the region.[9] In certain cases, sanctioned posts are lying vacant and even if the health infrastructure (including medicines and machines) has improved, lack of critical personnel is inhibiting.[10] This problem is, however, manifest across several departments and services. It probably calls for a serious re-examination of the personnel policy with a view to facilitate and incentivise without compromising on their performance and efficiency. Further, the lack of supporting infrastructure, including transportation requirements and the high rate of breakdown, leads to high maintenance costs of maintenance and hinders the timeliness of service delivery.

Education

While the literacy rate for the overall population of the ANI in 1991 was 73.02 per cent, for the STs it stood at 47.02 per cent (literacy rate among ST girls was 40.71 per cent). The dropout rate for boys was 26.43 per cent and that for girls 26.41 per cent. According to the census of 2001, the literacy rate for the STs has improved significantly to 58.09 per cent. As many as 51.79 per cent of the ST girls are now literate. Here it must be pointed out that the achievement in education has only been with the *Nicobarese*. The relevance of the education system to the *Onge* and *Shompen* and the advisability of bundling them in classrooms to teach them Hindi needs to be seriously reviewed. If any education has to be provided, it should be in their natural surroundings and in their own language. The content should focus on their history, culture, traditions and on skills which are relevant to their lifestyle. Even for the Nicobarese, stress should be on providing vocational training to enable the tribe to utilise locally available resources productively. For the *Jarawa* and the *Sentinelese* of course, our formal system of education holds no value or relevance.

TABLE 6.6

Adult Tribals Made Literate

Year	*Male*	*Female*	*Total*
1994-95	200	300	500
1995-96	230	270	500
1996-97	198	302	500
1997-98	239	259	498
1998-99	102	111	213

Source: A&N Administration, *Basic Statistics*, 1996-97 to 1998-99, Table 12.47.

Education Infrastructure

As far as infrastructure for schooling is concerned, there are 59 schools in the tribal areas of which 32 are primary level, 10 middle level, 10 secondary level, 5 senior secondary level and 2 *Ashram* schools. There are 4 hostels, 1 at Dollygunj, 2 in Teressa (1 for boys and 1 for girls) and 1 at Champion. However, some anecdotal observations on the prevalent education system appear to be distressing. For example, while the schools in the tribal areas have been upgraded, science has not been promoted along with the promotion of the English as the medium of instruction.[11] This despite the fact that Science is considered one of the priority concerns of the tribals (see later in section on Poverty Alleviation), the prevalent practice of 'compulsory passing' up to the eighth standard compromises on the quality of the curriculum. This results in a drastic increase in the percentage of failures (up to 50 per cent) in standard IX and, only about 20 per cent make it through to standard X while less than 5 per cent enrol at the higher secondary level. This presents a grim situation for the students. The prevalent system

9. Discussion with officials revealed, that nearly 53 vacancies exist, in the 'specialist' category. Again, even if there is need for five staff nurses, none are willing to go to Teressa and somehow only 3 posts could be filled-in as leave vacancies.

10. There are 70 family planning centres (FPCs), 3 primary health centres (PHCs), 32 sub-centres, 3 Homeo dispensaries and 1 district hospital in the tribal areas.

11. The *Nicobarese* use the Roman script themselves and it is widely believed that promotion of English would help instil greater confidence.

including the choice of curriculum, the medium of instruction and lack of quality (or in many cases, any) teachers leaves the students and the tribals disillusioned with the system. The failure to adapt their curriculum to the immediate needs results in the often ill-founded perception that the tribals are slow in absorbing their lessons.[12] However, this should not be used as an excuse to further dilute the minimum qualification requirements for recruitment into services. In the present situation, the need is not only to provide adequate number of quality teachers, but also to adapt the curriculum in a comprehensive manner. There should be special thrust on channelising them towards vocational training to enhance the productivity of the locally available resources. Given the relative lack of a literary environment at home, class-room teaching may also need to be strongly supplemented with specialised coaching amenable to the local environment and culture.

Empowerment of Tribals and Systems of Governance

Our primitive tribes are generally quite ignorant about our formal system of administration. The Nicobarese understand our setup but have their own governance structures. They do not follow the *panchayat* system. Instead they are guided by Tribal Councils which comprise of Village Captains. For example, in Car Nicobar, the tribal council is reconstituted annually and consists of (as its members) the first captains of the 15 villages. The premier of this council is the chieftain. Each village elects representatives designated as the first, second, third, fourth and fifth captains. Even women have been participating in the elections and now in one of the villages there is a first lady captain. The election at each level is by a system of secret ballot.

In most cases, arbitrage or administration of justice is carried out by the captain. For the rest, decisions are taken by the tribal council. The prevalent system is reasonably adept at solving intra-community disputes, but the tribals as a group are not equipped to combat the onslaught of poachers and encroachers. In several cases it is also commonly held that the laws, rules and regulations bear more heavily upon the tribals while the poachers and encroachers continue to circumvent the law.

The system as a whole had (perhaps) been working reasonably satisfactorily for all these years but the onslaught of encroachment has disturbed the delicate balance. Therefore the prevalent systems need to be strengthened and supplemented with the powers of the administrative apparatus. For this purpose, draft guidelines are being framed after discussion and deliberations (to assimilate views and feedback) for duediligence. Sincere efforts are under way to promote and strengthen the system of self-governance among the Nicobarese, and prevent any aggravation in the extant situation by introducing an alien system. The one main problem, however, is the unwillingness of government functionaries to be posted in the remote islands and villages. Even the people who take up postings are often unfamiliar with the tribe and its culture and there is a communication gap between the administrator and the administrated. This needs to change. All officials being posted in tribal areas should be sensitised to the community, its lifestyle and beliefs, so that they can work together.

The situation of the primitive tribes is very different. They have their own structures for dispute resolution. Any attempt to drag them into our administrative or legal systems will be disastrous. It will wreck the social fabric of these tribes and force them into a system which has no relevance to their lifestyle. Even when there are cases of infringement of rights of the tribals by non-tribals, the autochthons should not be forced to appear in courts, etc. The Andaman Adim Janjati Vikas Samiti (AAJVS) workers or the administration should be allowed to collect their statements within their natural surroundings and to dispose on their behalf. For these tribes, our primary focus should be on empowerment.

Tribes like the *Jarawa* and *Shompen* lead a nomadic lifestyle and depend on the resources available within their Reserve. There have, however, been increasing instances of poaching and encroachment within their Reserves. In fact, even the 'hostile' *Sentinelese* have not been able to escape the poachers. The poachers lure the innocent autochthons with addictive substances and exploit their resources. This must be immediately stopped. The tribes must be empowered to themselves patrol and protect their Reserves, with adequate assistance from the state apparatus. Such an experiment has been tried in Baratang and proved to be highly successful. At the same time, thorough patrolling of the seas surrounding the Reserve should be carried out and stringent punishment awarded to poachers. A livelihood survey of villages surrounding the Reserves should be carried out and livelihood security ensured to discourage poaching.

12. Most often it is the case that the populace fails to pickup or imbibe what they do not find to be relevant.

Alcoholism is a major problem amongst all the tribes and massive de-addiction drives supplemented by counselling should be carried out at least for the Great Andamanese, the *Onge* and the *Shompen*. These communities should be taken off the dole system and encouraged to learn their traditional skills. The Great Andamanese have long been exposed to the ways of our society. As they have not reverted back to their original lifestyle and have demonstrated a willingness to mix with non-autochthons, artificial barriers should not be imposed on them. They should be allowed to take decisions about their own future. For this, a process of discussion needs to be initiated within the community. Should they decide to intermix with other groups, their decision should be respected and they should be empowered through counselling, training and affirmative action to ensure that they are not reduced to menial workers in mainstream society.

The moot question in empowerment of tribals is to ensure that the system of equity and justice really works and this should be considered at three levels namely, at the level of the nation, the institutions, and the community.[13] In this context the extant role of the AAJVS also needs to be reviewed. In the medium term, the role of AAJVS may evolve along the line of activities envisioned for the Tribal Co-operative Marketing Development Federation of India Limited (TRIFED) and National Scheduled Tribes Development Corporation (NSTDC). The role of other co-operatives in fostering livelihood opportunities and commercial skills should be studied in greater detail, so as to prevent exploitation and potentially iniquitous concentration of benefits.

Poverty Alleviation

Our concept of poverty is alien to the autochthons who live amidst such natural bounty. They are in a different stage of economy. The resources for food are locally available in plenty and the concept of poverty based on calorific requirements is irrelevant. The poverty of capacity and capabilities in utilising modern tools and amenities has no simple analogy in the case of tribals, who until a few years ago lead a nomadic life.[14] The concept of money is also unknown to the tribes barring the Nicobarese and the Great Andamanese.

The spurt in encroachment, over the years, in the tribal areas and rampant poaching has however, gradually impoverished the tribes of their otherwise abundant resources. By their own standards the tribes are much poorer today—poorer because they have been gradually robbed of their only resource, their forests.

Traditionally, the tribals have always been the landowners, even though their rights may not have been formally recognised. The first blow to this traditional belief came with the reservation of forests in the name of scientific management by colonial rulers.[15] Consequently, the tribals were forced to encroach upon what was traditionally their own.[16] From owners they were reduced to illegal settlers without any resource base. This has, in fact, been the fate of tribals all over the country. The Andaman tribes have been luckier because a large part of their traditional domain was marked as Reserve for them. But over the years, this area has been squeezed to make way for settlers and developmental and infrastructure projects. This has not just reduced their resource base but has also given outsiders an opportunity to meddle with their affairs. The single most important poverty alleviation or prevention strategy for these primitive tribes then would be to ensure their rights over their land and resources.

For the Nicobarese and Great Andamanese however, other amenities need to be provided. In recent years,

13. Three typical situations may be encountered:
    - ignoring the provisions of law and constitutional obligations;
    - inequitous actions by officials not in consonance with the spirit of the law, and
    - patently illegal actions by the government.

14. Several schemes for welfare of the tribals are now in operation. For example, under the Prime Minister's Gramodaya Yojana (PMGY), in Car Nicobar, *pucca* houses were to be provided to the tribals, but given the volume of funds available, each of the families has been provided with tin-roofs (@ of Rs. 22,000 per family) for the present. Sometimes the inability to identify the desired beneficiaries results in thin spreading of available funds across the entire group resulting in unproductive expenditures. Moreover tin-roofs do not appear to be the best available option for the A&NIs.

    The chieftain of Car Nicobar however acknowledged that the schemes like Jawahar Rozgar Yojana and Indira Awaas Yojana have brought significant improvement in living standards.

    On the basis of the BPL cards issued by the Civil Supplies department, there are 1405 ST families BPL in 1999. Of these 990 are in Car Nicobar and 415 in Nancowry group of islands. There are 2359 ST families under the Antyodaya Anna Yojana, on the basis of the number of cards issued by the Civil Supplies department, of which 257 are on the Nancowry group of islands. There are 35 ST beneficiaries under the Annapurna Yojana.

    While there is no denying that the injection of public resources has yielded some benefits, several questions remain concerning their utilisation efficiency. Thus, there is a need to re-assess these schemes, if only to identify the appropriate skills and technology that are best suited for the islands and its culture.

15. But probably with an eye on its exploitation for the purpose of revenue.

16. Quite often having in his lot nothing but some unagreeable fallouts.

with the effort of the administration, most households and villages have been electrified (out of the 192 tribal villages, 171 have been electrified with an installed capacity of 7.3 MW). Piped water is supplied to the *Nicobarese* in Car Nicobar and is also made available to the Andaman tribals wherever they are rehabilitated or their settlements established. Table 6.7 gives some details of the people below poverty line (BPL), as identified by the administration, in the Nicobar district. All tribals in the Andaman district are considered BPL.

TABLE 6.7

Poverty in the Tribal Areas (Among the Nicobarese)

Island	*Number of Villages*	*Number of Families*	*Number of Members*
Car Nicobar	15	373	15790
Chowra	5	195	1454
Teressa	11	286	1357
Bambooka	1	12	50
Katchal	16	339	2119
Nancowry group	16	153	842
Trinket	1	41	229
Kamorta	16	124	718
Pillomillow	1	36	186
Kondul	1	21	114
Pullobhabi	2	70	362
Campbell Bay (*Gram Panchayat*)	1	138	672
Govindanagar	1	124	498
Laxminagar	5	126	499
Total	92	2038	24890

Notes: Non-tribal area.

Source: DoTW, A&N Administration.

Food Security

The *Great Andamanese*, the *Onge* and the *Jarawa* are provided ration as per Table 6.8 by the AAJVS.[17] However, those who are provided with employment opportunities are taken off this free ration system. Table 6.9 gives details of the placement of members of the STs in government offices.

TABLE 6.8

Ration Supply per Adult per Month

Item	*Quantity*
Rice	9 kgs.
Atta	5 kgs.
Sugar	500 gms.
Milk	500 gms.
Tea	500 gms.
Oil	500 gms.
Dalda	500 gms.
Dal	500 gms.
Salt	500 gms.
Haldi Powder	100 gms.
Chilly Powder	100 gms.
Dhaniya Powder	100 gms.
Bathing Soap	2 Nos.
Washing Soap	2 Nos.
Match Box	2 Nos.
Candle (M)	1 pkt.
Jaggery	400 gms.
Onion	500 gms.
Cerelac*	400 gms. (2 pkts.)
Amul Spray*	2 kgs.

Notes: * per child per month upto the age of 13 years but perhaps this should read 13 months

Source: Same as Table 6.7.

In this context, it must be mentioned that it has been a conscious policy of the administration to provide employment to the STs even when their productivity and output may be lower than other workers, and even if there is higher degree of absenteeism. This is not merely to serve as reservation policy for the STs but also to inculcate the culture of organised work. Effort should be made to implement the national policy on positive discrimination and affirmative action in its true letter and spirit (but only with regards to the Great Andamanese and Nicobarese),

The policy of the administration towards food security, however, needs to be reassessed. Making the tribals dole dependent will have disastrous consequences, as has already been observed among the *Onge* and Great Andamanese. The tribals have traditionally been self-sufficient and till date there has been no evidence to show food scarcity among groups like the *Jarawa*. Why then are they being given alien foodstuff as doles? Even if there was to be a danger of starvation of hunger, then the effort should be to protect and supplement the existing resource base of the tribes. As has been mentioned earlier, the biggest threat to the food security of the primitive tribes comes from the poachers.

The tsunami of December 26, 2004 has rendered several sources of potable water on the Nicobar islands nfit for human consumption. This calls for urgent action.

17. The AAJVS is an autonomous co-operative society. The ration as presented in the table pertains to an adult person per month while for a child the ration is one-half of that for an adult.

TABLE 6.9

Year-wise Registration and Placement of Members of Scheduled Tribes

Year	*Port Blair*		*Car Nicobar*		*Campbell Bay*
	Registered	*Placement*	*Registered*	*Placement*	*Registered*
1994-95	27	54	93	19	2
1995-96	51	33	214		95
1996-97	40	18	76		48
1997-98	24	31	137		
1998-99	58	15	146		

Source: *Basic Statistics*, 1996-97 to 1998-99, Table 13.5.

Tribal Sub-Plans (TSP)[18]

The desired progress for development of STs has suffered on account of certain aberrations, not so much in the size of the effort but in its quality and content, and involves some very basic issues. A crucial point about the constitutional safeguards for the scheduled castes (SCs) and STs is that they act as supplemental provisions to the basic egalitarian structure in the constitution.[19] Any weakness in that basic structure, during the operational phase, adversely affects the entire scheme for welfare and advancement of the SCs and STs.[20]

Members of the STs have been located on the margin both in terms of the geographical regions of their habitations as well as the traditional socioeconomic structure. They are at a different stage of the so-called economic development with plentiful resources at their command. So our major concern has been to ensure that: the tribal people do not lose command over their resources in the process of change and development; and while the tribal people are enabled to take full advantage of new advances in knowledge, the best in their tradition is not lost.

Objectives and Approach for TSPs

The TSPs are formulated under the five-year plans and implemented for the welfare of scheduled tribes. The TSP in most areas has an overall two-fold thrust: firstly, the socioeconomic development of the tribal areas as a whole; and secondly, that of the tribal families. While the diagnosis of the problems relating to acculturation, conservation, and development of the STs is well articulated, the programme formulation has largely continued to follow a schematic approach. Such an approach encapsulates certain presumptions about the laws of distribution as well as the diffusion of benefits. The formalisation of the process of planning and implementation thus, introduces dissonance between plan objectives and programmes. This occurs because while the stronger sections (in the society) are adept in dealing with the formal systems, it quite often proves to be detrimental for the weaker sections.

A comprehensive plan was prepared for the development of tribal areas at the national level in the Second Five-year Plan (FYP). Tribal Development Blocks (TDBs) were formed and later reviewed on the eve of the Fifth FYP. The area approach especially focusing on the TSP was further strengthened in the Fifth FYP. The TSP is generally divided into a number of integrated development projects (ITDP) and each project covers one or more TDBs. Thus, in the whole scheme of things the TSP is a macro-unit, while the TDB is a micro unit and the ITDP is a meso-unit.

Apportioning of Funds to be Placed under the TSP

The working group on Development and Welfare of the Scheduled Tribes during the Eighth Five-year Plan recommended that the quantum of funds to be earmarked under the TSP of the state/union territory (UT)[21] should be calculated on the basis of the sum total of the following:

1) A base percentage of the total state/UT plan equal to the percentage of the ST population in the state/UT to the total state/UT population.

2) A compensatory percentage of the total state plan to take care of the relative disparity between the population of the STs and the size of the tribal sub-plan area. This compensatory percentage should be subject to a minimum of 3 per cent of the state/UT plan.

---

18. The analysis of the Tribal Sub-Plan in this chapter draws heavily from the Report of the Commissioner for Scheduled Castes and Scheduled Tribes, Government of India especially the 28th Report, (see GoI, 1983 and 1990).

19. However, what was supposed to be supplemental by way of special provisions in the Constitution has been most often construed as substantive.

20. Because supplementary safeguards cannot make good the initial handicap, besides countering the adverse process intrinsic to the system as also the general slide back which members of the SCs and STs may experience as members of the larger community of weaker sections, their position will be like that of a person who tries to climb up a downward moving escalator and is required to make increasing effort even to maintain his position and not go down.

21. Though the UT has two districts, for planning purpose both are accounted for and taken as single district.

Ministry of Welfare, Government of India (GoI), provides funds for family beneficiary oriented programmes for welfare of STs under the special central assistance (SCA).

Flow of funds from central sector and centrally sponsored schemes (CSSs) for the welfare of STs.

Items under a, b and c above are added to allocate the funds under the respective sectors like health, agriculture, power, transport, tribal welfare.

Analysis of TSPs in Ninth and Tenth FYP in ANIs

Keeping the basic premises (discussed above) as a continuing theme in the Tenth FYP, as many as 22 sectors are covered in the tribal sub plan of the ANIs to achieve the goal of tribal development, both with regard to the areas as well as with regard to the tribal families. A provision of Rs. 36,509.35 lakh (Table 6.10), constituting about 14.70 per cent of the total UT plan outlay of Rs. 2,48,300.00 lakh, for the ANI, has been proposed for the TSP component of the Tenth FYP (2002-2007) and a provision of Rs. 6425.40 lakh constituting 15.67 per cent of the total annual plan outlay of the UT of Rs. 41,000 lakh is proposed for the Annual TSP 2003-04.

In addition to the above, an outlay of Rs. 533.00 lakh for the Tenth FY TSP (2002-2007) and Rs. 74 lakh for the Annual TSP (2003-04) are proposed from the SCA of the GoI. Similarly, an outlay of Rs. 475.00 lakh for the Tenth FYP TSP (2002-2007) and Rs. 225.00 lakh for the Annual plan 2003-04 are proposed out of the SCA of the GoI for implementation of welfare programmes for the primitive tribes. Often, however, the implementation of the TSPs leaves much to be desired. In fact, some of the basic premises of the new strategy remain to be operationalised. For example, as in several other states, quite often a substantial part of the SCA remains unutilised.

TABLE 6.10

Tribal Sub-Plan (TSP)–I Draft Annual Plan 2003-04–Financial Outlays: Proposals for TSP

(Rupees in Lakhs)

Sector / Item	*Ninth Plan 1997-02 at 1996-97 Prices*				*Proposals for Tenth Plan at 2001-02 Prices*		*Annual Plan 2002-03*	
	Approved Outlay		*Approved Expenditure*					
	Total Outlay	*Flow to TSP*	*Total Expenditure*	*Flow to TSP*	*Total Outlay*	*Flow to TSP*	*Total Expenditure*	*Flow to TSP*
(1)	(2)	(3)	(4)	(5)	(6)	(7)	(8)	(9)
Agriculture & Allied Activities	13789.00	1157.62	10032.99	965.82	17777.00	2567.01	2871.00	383.76
ITDP	5750.00	0.00	6495.37	0.00	14781.00	0.00	2805.00	0.00
Irrigation and Flood Control	1000.00	0.00	1222.51	0.00	2757.00	0.00	390.00	0.00
Energy	15150.00	2058.64	14153.68	1975.30	21046.00	3802.5.0	3475.00	558.05
Village and Small-Scale Industries	3800.00	169.21	5595.99	121.30	3746.00	89.45	800.00	21.45
Transport	55036.00	12206.62	75463.66	12801.19	97819.00	22055.08	15361.00	2181.83
Science and Technology	500.00	0.00	130.34	0.00	212.00	0.00	35.00	0.00
General Economic Services	4000.00	269.95	4956.36	298.14	6098.00	248.43	1132.00	45.49
Social Services	48127.00	4100.63	51418.32	4160.34	76586.00	7746.88	12823.00	1192.02
General Education	21700.00	1835.09	18288.60	1367.29	28344.00	2625.35	4650.00	426.36
Medical and Public Health	7741.00	1346.00	10076.04	1612.84	11400.00	3190.00	2050.00	385.00
Water Supply and Sanitation	6000.00	300.00	9301.65	473.05	15256.00	485.00	2575.00	135.00
Housing	5700.00	300.00	6844.57	362.85.00	7868.00	700.00	1465.00	100.00
General Services	6348.00	0.00	5272.40	0.00	7478.00	0.00	1308.00	0.00
Grand Total	**153500.00**	**19962.67**	**174741.60**	**20322.09**	**248300.00**	**36509.35**	**41000.00**	**4382.60**

Source: Annexure VIII-A, *Tenth Five Year Tribal Sub-Plan, 2002-2007.*

The total UT outlay for the Tenth FYP has been increased by 61.76 per cent over that of the Ninth Plan. However, this masks a crucial factor: while the values for the Ninth Plan are reported at 1996-97 prices, those for the Tenth plan are reported at 2001-02 prices. As a consequence, the real increase in the outlay would be significantly lower. The outlay for the TSP component for the Tenth FYP has been raised by nearly 83 per cent over that for the Ninth Plan. As a result, the TSP component for the Tenth FYP forms 14.7 per cent of the total outlay as compared to the corresponding figure of 13 per cent in the Ninth Plan.

The final outcome in the Ninth Plan was, however, significantly different from the approved outlays. While, the total approved expenditure overshot the approved outlay by about 13.84 per cent, the realised expenditure for the TSP component stood at 11.63 per cent of the total realised expenditure. This falls below the sum of the proportion of the ST population (9.54 per cent according to the 1991 Census) and the minimum 3 per cent (compensatory) additional allocation suggested by the working group on Development and Welfare of the Scheduled Tribes during the Eighth FYP.[22] The achievement in the first year (2002-03) of the Tenth FYP is not encouraging either, whereby the component of expenditure on TSP has declined to 10.69 per cent of the total annual expenditure (Table 6.12).

The largest component of the approved expenditure under the TSP component of the Ninth FYP is formed by the 'transportation' sector followed by the 'social service' sector and the 'power' sector. Within the 'social services' sector, the approved outlay on 'general education' was the highest, followed by 'medical and public health'. However, in the approved expenditure for the Ninth Plan 'medical and public health' forms the largest among the 'social services' sector and the third largest among all expenditure sectors.

The outlay for the 'transportation' sector[23] in the TSP component of the Ninth and Tenth FYP constitutes more than 60 per cent of the total outlay for the TSP. In comparison, the 'social services' sector constitutes around 21 per cent followed by the 'power' sector at around 10 per cent of the total outlay for the TSP (Table 6.13). The difference between the allocation for the respective sectors in the total expenditure is, however, not as steep as that for the TSP. Although on the face of it the structure appears to be perverse, it is quite likely that given the highly dispersed population, especially of the tribals, transportation is likely to take up the largest share of expenditure.[24]

As a proportion of approved outlay for the TSP component of the Ninth FYP, the overall expenditure achievement is 101.8 per cent. However, the 'general education' sector (within the broad category of the

TABLE 6.11

Statement Showing Funds Released and Unspent Balance from 1996 to 2002

(Rupees in Lakhs)

Scheme	*96-97*	*97-98*	*98-99*	*99-00*	*00-01*	*01-02*	*Total*
Welfare Programme of *Shompen*	3.25	3.66	8.19	8.79	5.61	9.84	39.34
Welfare Programme of *Onge*	22.11	27.21	24.82	14.27	29.76	28.45	146.62
Welfare Programme of *Great Andamanese*	3.78	5.80	8.22	6.68	11.91	6.86	43.25
Welfare Programme of *Jarawa* and *Sentinelese*	7.00	5.46	7.02	35.66	49.83	32.35	137.32
Strengthening & Maintenance of AAJVS	33.87	16.83	25.98	27.78	23.90	23.54	151.90
Total expenditure incurred	70.01	58.96	74.23	93.18	121.01	101.04	518.43
Grant-in-aid released	65.59	58.93	97.29	62.35	107.40	18.40	509.96
Unspent balance	0.00	0.00	23.06	0.00	0.00	24.28	47.34
Expenditure as percentage of grant-in-aid	106.87	75.84	67.01	69.47	146.86	79.49	86.57

Source: Author's Own, DoTW.

22. One may argue that the realised TSP expenditure is higher than the current (2001) population proportion of STs at 8.27 per cent plus the minimum 3 per cent compensatory allocation. However, this is not an appropriate benchmark for comparison, as the plans were formulated based on the 1991 population proportions. Moreover, if the non-tribal population continues to grow at a rate faster than that for the STs, then they would get completely marginalised. In order to provide them with effective protection, a strategy analogous to that adopted for fixing the number (and proportion) of representatives in Parliament from the States, may be adopted. This was adopted to avoid penalising the States that encouraged effective population control programmes. There is no reason why the STs of the ANIs should not be adequately rewarded, for (voluntarily) adopting population and resource conscious practices.

23. As also the approved expenditure in the Ninth Plan.

24. This also closely resembles the top-priority felt by the tribals.

TABLE 6.12

Achievement of the Ninth Plan, Growth in the Size of the Tenth Plan

(Per Cent)

Sector/Item	*Ninth Plan 1997-02*			*Proposals for Tenth Plan*	*Annual Plan 2002-03*	*Growth of Xth Plan Over the IXth Plan*	
	Approved Outlay	*Approved Expenditure*					
	Flow to TSP	*Total Outlay*	*Flow to TSP*	*Flow to TSP*	*Flow to TSP*	*Total Outlay*	*Flow to TSP*
(1) *	(2) = (3) / (2)	(3) = (4) / (2)	(4) = (5) / (4)	(5) = (7) / (6)	(6) = (9) / (8)	(7) = (6) / (2)	(8) = (7) / (3)
Agriculture & Allied Activities	8.40	72.76	9.63	14.44	13.37	128.92	221.75
ITDP	0.00	112.96	0.00	0.00	0.00	257.06	0.00
Irrigation and Flood Control	0.00	122.25	0.00	0.00	0.00	275.70	0.00
Energy	13.59	93.42	13.96	18.07	16.06	138.92	184.71
Village and Small-Scale Industries	4.45	147.26	2.17	2.39	2.68	98.58	52.86
Transport	22.18	137.12	16.96	22.55	14.20	177.74	180.68
Science and Technology	0.00	26.07	0.00	0.00	0.00	42.40	0.00
General Economic Services	6.75	123.91	6.02	4.07	4.02	152.45	0.00
Social services	8.52	106.84	8.09	10.12	9.30	159.13	188.92
General Education	8.46	84.28	7.48	9.26	9.17	130.62	143.06
Medical and Public Health	17.39	130.16	16.01	27.98	18.78	147.27	237.00
Water Supply and Sanitation	5.00	155.03	5.09	3.18	5.24	254.27	161.67
Housing	5.26	120.08	5.30	8.90	6.83	138.04	233.33
General Services	0.00	83.06	0.00	0.00	0.00	117.80	0.00
Grand Total	**13.00**	**113.84**	**11.63**	**14.70**	**10.69**	**161.76**	**182.89**

Notes: Derived from Table 6.10 above.

*: Numbers in parentheses after the equal to sign refer to the column numbers in Table 6.10.

'service' sector) and the 'village and small-scale industries' sector have had significantly lower expenditure (and consequently achievement)—less than 75 and 72 per cent respectively of their approved outlays. While the corresponding outlay in the Tenth FYP (as compared to the Ninth Plan) has been raised in the 'general education' sector, it has been cut drastically in the 'village and small-scale industries' sector. The allocation for the 'medical and public health' sector as well as the 'housing' sector under the 'social services' group has also been increased substantially.

In terms of physical achievement, the general conclusion for the TSP component of the Ninth FYP appears to be one of underperformance, especially in the categories of 'animal husbandry' and 'education'.[25] The appearance of 'others' category, as distinct from the STs under the targets set for educational infrastructure under the TSP, seems incongruous with the objective of the TSP. In several cases, the targets (and also achievement) of this 'others' group are significantly larger than that for the STs.

Limitations in Analysis of Plans

Most of the analysis on expenditure effectiveness is discussed in the form of the structure across various functional classifications. This approach consists merely of a positive analysis and is rarely capable of providing any normative suggestions to improve the efficiency of expenditure allocation and service delivery unless accompanied by a comparison with the structure in some identified best practice schemes.

However, the wide divergence in the basic/fundamental conditions that distinguish and necessitate the formulation of TSPs also inhibits an easy

25. It must be noted that not all sectors are amenable to clear definition of physical targets. There is thus some need to define physical targets in terms of the various steps and measures in the process of delivery of service.

TABLE 6.13

Structure of Outlay and Expenditure of the Total and Tribal Sub-Plan Component of the Ninth and Tenth Plans

(Per Cent)

Sector/Item	*Ninth Plan 1997-02*				*Proposals for Tenth Plan 2002-07*		*Annual Plan 2002-03*	
	Approved Outlay		*Approved Expenditure*					
	Total Outlay	*Flow to TSP*	*Total Expenditure*	*Flow to TSP*	*Total Outlay*	*Flow to TSP*	*Total Expenditure*	*Flow to TSP*
(1)	(2)	(3)	(4)	(5)	(6)	(7)	(8)	(9)
Agriculture & Allied Activities	8.98	5.80	5.74	4.75	7.16	7.03	7.00	8.76
ITDP	3.75	0.00	3.72	0.00	5.95	0.00	6.84	0.00
Irrigation and Flood Control	0.65	0.00	0.70	0.00	1.11	0.00	0.95	0.00
Energy	9.87	10.31	8.10	9.72	8.48	10.42	8.48	12.73
Village and Small-Scale Industries	2.48	0.85	3.20	0.60	1.51	0.25	1.95	0.49
Transport	35.85	61.15	43.19	62.99	39.40	60.41	37.47	49.78
Science and Technology	0.33	0.00	0.07	0.00	0.09	0.00	0.09	0.00
General Economic Services	2.61	1.35	2.84	1.47	2.46	0.68	2.76	1.04
Social Services	31.35	20.54	29.43	20.47	30.84	21.22	31.28	27.20
General Education	14.14	9.19	10.47	6.73	11.42	7.19	11.34	9.73
Medical and Public Health	5.04	6.74	5.77	7.94	4.59	8.74	5.00	8.78
Water Supply and Sanitation	3.91	1.50	5.32	2.33	6.14	1.33	6.28	3.08
Housing	3.71	1.50	3.92	1.79	3.17	1.92	3.57	2.28
General Services	4.14	0.00	3.02	0.00	3.01	0.00	3.19	0.00
Grand Total	100.00	100.00	100.00	100.00	100.00	100.00	100.00	100.00

Source: Author's Own.

identification of the relevant best practices. In such a situation the analysis of the expenditure structure is supplemented with some comparison of the respective physical achievements. Even this analysis quite often remains unsatisfactory or incomplete in the absence of a primary survey to affirm whether the efforts of the provider (that is the administrative machinery), and the analysis restricted to the officially recorded statistics get translated into the benefits for the recipients and whether the extant system admits having significant leakages that result in loss of efficiency.

A primary survey thus, in most cases, is an indispensable tool to suggest measures to improve efficiency of expenditure as well as to identify the relatively long-term implications of specific programmes and schemes initiated in a particular year.

Some Concerns[26]

The principal concern of the tribes—both the autochthons and the Nicobarese—is the 'influx' of non-tribals. Influx not only leads to gradual impoverishment and reduced availability of resources, it also disturbs the social fabric of tribal societies.[27]

There have also been increasing reports of the exploitation—economic as well as sexual—of the autochthonous tribes. These complaints needs to be immediately investigated and strict punishment meted out to the perpetrators of such crimes. An important concern relates to inadequacy of quality 'medical and health' services in the tribal areas, especially the unavailability of specialised lady personnel for gynaecological and orthopaedic cases.

Transportation and inter-island connectivity are serious concerns for the Nicobarese, and to a certain extent, for the Great Andamanese. There is an urgent need to increase the connectivity between different islands in the Nicobar group and between Nicobar and Port Blair. This will not only increase the access of the tribes to health, education and livelihood resources, it may also help the tribals develop stronger relations

26. This is based on informal discussions with the Tribal Council in Nancowry and with the tribal chieftain (Mr. Aberdeen Blair), and the officials of the administration in the office of the Development Commissioner at Car Nicobar. While these constitute the broad concerns, the approach and prioritisation of the redressal mechanism may need to be tailored specifically for the individual tribes.

27. Estimates suggest that there may be approximately 1000 such people already in Car Nicobar, mainly exploiting wood and fishing resources. Although it is conceded that the non-tribals cannot establish a foothold unless there is some tacit understanding with someone amongst the tribals.

within themselves.[28] The strengthening and adaptation of the 'education' system to their needs is also an expressed concern of the Nicobarese. Introduction of vocational training to enhance utilisation efficiency of the resources at their disposal may be salubrious in addressing this concern. The gradual erosion of social mores and the menace created by the introduction of foreign 'liquor' need to be checked.[29]

Most importantly, we need to stop looking down on the tribes or treating them as exhibits in a curiosity shop. They must be allowed to decide for themselves, if they wish to integrate with the mainstream, and if so, at what pace.

Some Measures for Improving the Tribal Development Programmes

Given the cost disabilities that are prevalent in the tribal areas, and more so in the case of the ANI with sparsely and highly dispersed population in far-flung, remote and inaccessible areas, it is imperative that a larger apportionment be allocated for the TSPs. Additionally, there is need to ensure that the funds allocated and expended under the TSP go on to directly benefit the tribals. Towards this end, a system should be designed that empowers the tribals to effectively participate in the formulation of the plans without further alienation. This can be achieved only if their existing system of governance is strengthened and supplemented by the provisions under the 73rd Constitutional amendment. Here it must be stated that this is not possible/relevant for the *Jarawa* and the *Sentinelese*. Similarly, neither do the *Onge* and the *Shompen* understand our governance systems, nor have they expressed any desire to be a part of it. Thus, intervention in their cases should be limited to providing health services, food security and security from poachers and outsiders. All these interventions should be carried out after in-depth research by experts and money should be made available for this purpose.

There is immediate need to stop treating the tribals as showcase items by minimising interference and direct intervention of any kind. Utmost care has to be exercised in avoiding abrupt changes by adopting and evolving some approach for fringe-area development. Most tribal areas have extensive natural resources with comparatively sparse populations. The mainstream economy, on the other hand, has a large labour surplus. In the present situation, there is substantial encroachment and influx by the mainstream people intending to dispossess the autochthons. The ongoing debate to reformulate the National Policy on Tribals and garner a clear mandate for an appropriate Scheduled Tribes (Recognition of Forest Rights) Bill is an essential step to restore and retain their command over their resources.

The tribals who were mainly hunter-gatherers used substantial amount of available time for game hunting, collecting water, etc. for their normal sustenance. In general, they continue to have poor saving habits, perhaps because of relatively low perception of risk for sustenance and the relative abundance of resources. Given this background, (a) the supply of water, almost at the doorstep in all villages, (b) near complete electrification of the villages, (c) provision of scaled ration and clothing, etc. all without any requirement of physical labour, may result in inducing the tribals to lose their traditional skills and become addicted to doles.[30] There is thus, an urgent need to re-assess the existing system of doles and to promote indigenous skills, particularly those for fishing and bamboo cultivation.

In the field of education, there is some need to adapt the existing system to local needs and to supplement class-room teaching with specialised coaching. In sports, the local skills relating to archery, javelin throwing, swimming, canoeing, and athletics can be promoted. Additionally, efforts should also be made to preserve and promote their art and culture in painting and sculpting. The tribals may be reluctant to utilise the formal system even when there exists an urgent need for specialised treatment. It may be desirable to appoint and train personnel with due recognition for gender sensitivity of the extant social customs. Special effort should also be made to archive and conserve their traditional skills with ethno-medicine and herbal treatment.

Finally, it is imperative for policy framers and administrators alike to realise that the primitive tribes

28. This is probably also the prime requirement for growth and promotion of tourism.

29. The locally prepared brew perhaps is less harmful to the physiology. Even young children engaged in labour work appear to have been exposed to liquor by outsiders. There is thus, some urgency to set up a de-addiction center for both alcohol and drug abuse.

30. There are already some incidents when the tribals have been found to spend substantially large proportion of their surplus money on liquor (even if liquor is prohibited in tribal areas).

of Andaman & Nicobar Islands are unique. To simply categorise them as Scheduled Tribes and subject this to general and ad hoc policy decisions will take away the oldest surviving inhabitants of this world.

Chapter 7

Agriculture and Animal Husbandry

Over the years, the share of the primary sector in ANI has declined steadily from about 45 per cent of GSDP at both current and constant prices in 1980-81 to 35 per cent in current prices and 30 per cent in constant prices in 2001-02. In spite of this change, which is mainly due to decline in growth of agricultural yield, primary sector continues to be the main source of employment, i.e., about 40 per cent of the workforce in 1991 Census was dependent on agriculture and allied activities. Thus, sustainable growth of this sector should form an important agenda in future policy for the development of ANI. This chapter reviews the status of agriculture, and animal husbandry and dairy in ANI, identifies factors inhibiting the growth of these activities, and suggests measures for improvement.

FIGURE 7.1

Land Utilisation Pattern

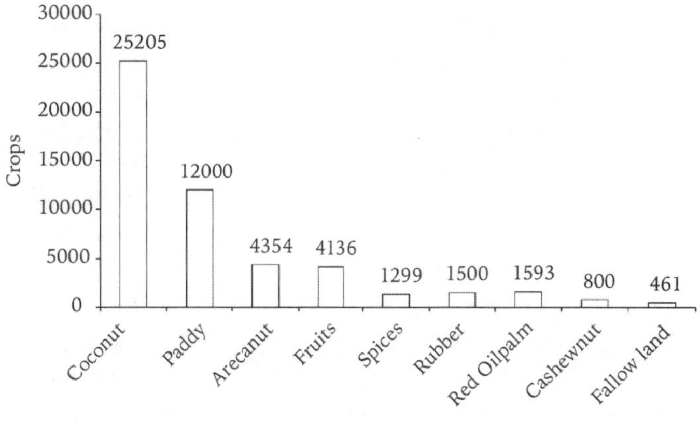

AGRICULTURE

Status of Agriculture

History of agriculture on the islands is less than a century old. In the early period of the twentieth century about 9,064 ha was under agriculture. It gradually increased following the rehabilitation of convicts and other migrants. However, it was during 7th FYP that the actual development in agriculture started. Presently, about 50,000 ha land area is under cultivation and allied activities. The major crops grown are paddy, coconut,[1] areca nut, vegetables, and fruits (Figure 7.1). Besides this, red oil palm, rubber, spices and cashew plantations also occupy sizeable land area (Table 7.1).

The number of marginal and small landholdings was 2,428 and 2,424 having 0.38 and 1.42 ha respectively, of the operational area. Andaman district has greater number of operational holdings as well as area compared to Nicobar district.

The soils in ANI can be classified into four depth classes (Table 7.2). Seventy five per cent of the total area has sandy clay to clay loam, while the remaining area is sandy to clayey. The coastal plains and some of the hills have deep soils more than 100 cm depth. The soils on tableland and hills are moderately deep (50-100 cm). The slopes and foothills are deeply eroded and are shallow (25-50 cm) or very shallow (<25 cm). The water holding capacity of soil also varies greatly (100-200 mm/m). The organic carbon content in soils is usually more than 0.5 per cent (medium to high). However, some parts of south and middle Andaman have low organic carbon status mainly because of severe erosion of the surface soils. The pH ranges from 4.5 to over 8.5. According to a survey 5,930 ha are saline acid soils of *dhanikhari* series. The coastal saline acidic soils

1. A large area is under coconut and paddy.

TABLE 7.1

Major Agricultural Crops Grown in different Islands

Sl. No.	*Name of the islands*	*Main crops*
Andaman district		
1.	Nancondum island	Coconut
2.	East island	Coconut, areca nut
3.	North andaman island	Paddy, pulses, oilseeds, vegetables, coconut, areca nut, fruits, spices
4.	Smith island	Paddy, coconut, areca nut, fruits
5.	Stewart island	Coconut
6.	Curlew island	Nil
7.	Aves island	Coconut
8.	Interview island	Coconut, areca nut
9.	Middle Andaman island	Paddy, pulses, oilseeds, vegetables, coconut, areca nut, fruits
10.	Porlob island	Coconut
11.	Long island	Paddy, vegetables, coconut, areca nut
12.	North passage island	Coconut, areca nut
13.	Strait islands	Vegetables, coconut, fruits
14.	Baratang island	Paddy, vegetables, coconut, horticultural crops, spices
15.	Peel island	Nil
16.	Havelock island	Paddy, pulses, oilseeds, vegetables, coconut, areca nut, fruits, root crops
17.	John lawrence island	Nil
18.	Neil island	Paddy, pulses, oilseeds, vegetables, coconut, areca nut, fruits, root crops
19.	South Andaman	Paddy, pulses, oilseeds, vegetables, coconut, areca nut, fruits, spices, sugarcane.
20.	Rutland island	Paddy, vegetables, coconut, areca nut, ginger, sugarcane
21.	North sentinel island	Nil
22.	Little Andaman	Paddy, pulses, oilseeds, red oil palm, vegetables, coconut, areca nut, fruits
23.	Flat bay island	Vegetables, coconut, areca nut, horticultural crops, spices
24.	Viper island	Coconut
25.	Chatham island	Not available
Nicobar district		
1.	Car Nicobar island	Coconut, areca nut, fruits, tuber crops, vegetables
2.	Chowra island	Coconut, tuber crops
3.	Teressa island	Coconut, areca nut, cashew, fruits, tuber crops
4.	Bompuka island	Coconut, tuber crops
5.	Katchal island	Paddy, red oil palm, vegetables, coconut, areca nut, rubber, spices
6.	Nancowry island	Coconut, areca nut, fruits, tuber crops
7.	Kamorta island	Coconut, areca nut, cashewnut, banana
8.	Trinket island	Coconut
9.	Little Nicobar island	Coconut, areca nut, colocasia, dioscoria
10.	Pulomilo island	Coconut, colocasia
11.	Kondul island	Dioscoria
12.	Great Nicobar island	Paddy, vegetables, coconut, areca nut, fruits
13.	Tillangchong island	Nil

generally extend 1-2 km inland, but at certain places brackish soil conditions persist 4-5 km inland.

Paddy is the main field crop. The production of pulses and oilseeds is insignificant. Similarly, sugarcane (except in Diglipur area), and maize cultivation is also scanty. The main problem is lack of irrigation. Due to high input cost, low productivity, inclement weather, and lack of competitive prices, farmers are reluctant to diversify.

TABLE 7.2

Series-wise Distribution of Soils (ha) in different Islands

Order	*Suborder*	*Great Group*	*Series*	*South Andaman*	*Middle Andaman*	*North Andaman*	*Little Andaman*	*Great Nicobar*	*Total*
Entisol	Fluvents	Tropofluvents	Schooline	2523	3950	3596	998	2477	13544
	Orthents	Troporthents	Garacharma	10915	11497	-	-	-	22412
	Aquents[a]	Fluventic sulfaquents[a]	Dhanikhari[a]	4933	564	183	-	-	5680
	Psamments	Fluventic quartipsamments	Rangachang	1724	-	-	2230	857	4811
Inceptisols	Aquepts	Umbric fluventic haplaquepts	Tushnabad	2936	-	-	-	-	2936
	Ochrepts	Typic dystrochrepts	Pahargaon	2338	8340	2771	-	1196	14645
	Ochrepts	Fluventic dystrochrepts	Wandoor	11733	-	7790	-	-	19523
Alfisols	Ustalfs	Haplustalfs	L. Andaman	-	-	450	4445	-	4895
			Total area	37102	24351	14790	7673	4530	88446

Note: Total area includes revenue forests, area under non-agricultural use, barren and uncultivated land, land under trees, groves and hills, permanent pastures and grazing land, cultivable wastes, fallow land, and net area sown; [a]acid saline and acid sulphate soils

C-14-8 variety of paddy that requires less care and matures in about 5 months is more suited for ANI. The double cropping introduced earlier was not very successful due to heavy rains in September (harvesting time of first crop). Grain storage facilities are not available and insect infestation lowers the germination considerably. Protected cultivation is yet to be adopted. Plant protection measures are also not easily available. In recent years, Trichogramma production and release technology has been adopted by the Department of Agriculture.

The coconut cultivation with areca nut is the backbone of agricultural activities in ANI. Nicobar Islands are largely dependent on coconut although paddy and other cereals are grown in small quantities in Great Nicobar. Andaman district cultivates all crops besides plantation. Neil, Havelock, and Little Andaman islands grow vegetables and are popularly called vegetable islands. Vegetables are grown in some parts of South Andaman and North Andaman also.

Strategies for Improvement

The ANI should focus on crops/crop varieties in which islands have distinct advantages. In this context, the following suggestions are made:

Paddy

More than 5,000 families are involved in cultivation of paddy. Two crops; one of medium duration and one of super short duration will help increase farmers' income in the existing rain-fed paddy cultivation. Saline resistant variety like BTS-24, 28 may be used for problem soils.

ANI receives up to 3000 mm of average annual rainfall which leads to inundation of water in the low-lying areas where no other crop can be grown. This land can be used gainfully for growing paddy. However, paddy can be maintained at subsistence level by adopting land configuration methods in a phased manner.

Farm Mechanisation

The level of mechanisation is poor and utilisation of available resources is inadequate. There is a lack of good repair shops for repair of agricultural implements. Threshing of even major crops like paddy is done manually. Therefore, there is an urgent need to enhance the level of farm mechanisation and to develop ancillary units requisite for the island.

Pulse, Oilseeds, and Cereals

The crop rotation is not being practised properly leaving the resources underutilised. Either two rice crops or one rice crop followed by suitable pulses, oilseed, and cereals like maize can be a better substitute on residual soil moisture in December supported by irrigation through watershed management.

Integrated Cropping System

In order to increase per unit area production, multiple and integrated cropping system approach is suggested. Double rice cropping in low-lying areas using one medium duration variety followed by super short duration rice varieties; saline resistant variety like BTS-24; and rotational cropping *viz.*, rice-vegetables/ rice-maize rice-oilseeds or pulses should be adopted.

Watershed Management and Irrigation

Poor irrigation measures are one of the major limiting factors in the islands. It is disturbing to note that less than 30 per cent of allocated funds for minor irrigation under the Plan was utilised for development of minor irrigation. Lack of ground water, except in Calicut belt of South Andaman, is yet another constraint. During monsoon, high rainfall results in a surplus of 1530 mm of rainwater which if managed properly can be used during the dry period. Watershed management using low cost technologies should be top priority. Soil mulching with crop residues, irrigating the crops at critical stages can also be used for water management during dry season.

The most important measure for harvesting of rainwater will be dug out ponds for supplementary irrigation coupled with fish farming and preparation of series of check dams in seasonal *nullah.* Till now ponds alone created irrigation potential for about 2000 ha. The Hydroelectric Power Station at Diglipur also created good irrigation potential. As per Central Water Commission Survey in 1977, 26 *nullahs* have been identified as potential irrigation sources with a potential to cover 6020 ha. of land area. Micro-irrigation development like sprinkler, drip irrigation and other indigenous methods will cover the hillocks; undulating terrain using rainwater storage during rainy month will form a good network to support multifaceted activities.

Soil Amelioration

Soil erosion of 8-20 tonne per ha per year due to heavy rainfall, increasing salinity/acidity due to seepage of brackish water is a serious problem. Neutralising acidity is costly in ANI owing to high cost of lime. Therefore, strategic bunds, sluice gates, good drainage, putting fodder grasses/other vegetation to reduce run off loss may be a better substitute as being done in Dashrathpur area. This measure itself can rotate 2000 ha land under multiple cropping.

Soil reclamation should be taken up with integrated soil-tillage-crop. Organic practices such as green manuring, green leaf manuring, *in situ* farmyard manure (FYM), incorporation of crop residues, etc. should be applied regularly.

Organic Farming

Use of pesticides and chemical fertilisers is low and continuously declining. Therefore, islands can be converted into organic farming, using biodynamic practices, *agnihotra, rishikheti* and *panchakavya* practices to vitalise soil and microbial damage.

Integrated Pest Management

Integrated pest management using predators, biocontrol measures, crop rotation, and other practices should be developed and adopted.

Post-Harvest Measures

In view of huge losses owing to lack of post-harvest facilities, development of these facilities needs immediate attention. For instance, post-harvest loss in banana is reported to be over 40 per cent in the islands.

Investment Requirements

Estimates of funds that would be required for implementation of the above suggested measures are

TABLE 7.3

Investment Requirements

(Rs. Lakhs)

Components	*Five Year Plans*					*Expected Manpower Generated*					*Socio-economic Benefits*
	Xth	*XIth*	*XIIth*	*XIIIth*	*XIVth*	*Xth*	*XIth*	*XIIth*	*XIIIth*	*XIVth*	
Grain/planting material, storage and processing	15	15	10	10	10	10	20	30	30	35	Quality, disease free seed and seedlings for export support to land agriculture.
Farm mechanisation	70	60	50	50	50	-	-	-	-	-	Intensive cropping, more returns.
Multiple cropping	15	20	20	25	20	60	80	85	90	90	Self-sufficiency in many areas, higher advantageous export.
Watershed/Irrigation	80	100	50	40	20	5	7	3	2	2	Water crisis during dry spell will not occur.
Soil reclamation	200	300	150	100	100	20	30	20	10	10	More area under intensive cultivation, higher productivity lands.

Source: Estimate by author.

provided in Table 7.3. The suggested investment is expected to lead to direct and indirect benefits to people in rural areas, such as, increased crop yield, employment generation, intensive cropping, and increase in cultivable area.

Low Input—Low Volume—high Value Organic Agriculture

ANI has significant potential for high value agriculture. In ANI, of the 50,000 hectares available for cultivation, 38,000 hectares are under horticultural crops. The horticultural crops in the islands include coconut (25,000 ha is under coconut), fruits, vegetables, spices, cashew nut and oil palm. A wide range of medicinal and aromatic plants are also found in ANI. The productivity of crops is low mainly due to primitive methods of cultivation. Though some efforts have been made for the development of horticulture in ANI, there has been no visible impact in terms of increase in yield/production or income of the farmers. Therefore, there is a need for focused efforts. The following general measures are suggested for development of high value agriculture in ANI:

- cultivation of micro propagated plants;
- hi-tech nursery;
- high–density plantation;
- fertigation;
- hi-tech greenhouses;
- *in-situ* moisture conservation through mulching;
- mechanisation in horticulture;
- recycling of horticultural waste for environment quality improvement;
- biological control;
- organic farming.

Specific Suggestions for Identified Crops

Coconut

Coconut is an important remunerative crop of ANI. The plantations in the islands belong to individual holdings, co-operative societies and leased-out plantations to private parties and co-operative societies. The crop is cultivated in an area of 24,700 ha producing 87.2 million nuts annually. Of the total production, 74 per cent is contributed by the Nicobar group of islands. Per ha productivity is 3,530 nuts, which is very low when compared to the all-India productivity level of 6,847 nuts per ha. This implies an urgent need to take measures to improve the productivity of coconut. The following measures are suggested in this context:

- planting of quality seedlings from the seed nuts collected from selected palms;
- replanting in old and low yield areas;
- multi-tier cropping rather than mono cropping;[2]
- better soil and water management through cover cropping, mulching, recycling of crop wastes and water conservation measures, etc.;
- integrated nutrient management with both organic and inorganic fertiliser, however emphasis should be on organic cultivation;
- integrated pest management: rhinoceros beetle is a serious problem. This can be controlled by releasing baculovirus once in two years. This is estimated to cost Rs. 1,625 per ha per year;
- processing of copra at commercial level and marketing with "Organic tag" to meet the national and international demands;
- production of furniture using coconut trunk, and coir products;
- coconut based biomass gassifier for power generation;
- production of 'Organic Virgin Coconut oil';
- developing 'Coconut estates';
- strengthening national and international market linkages.

Areca nut

At present, about 4000 ha area is under areca nut plantation with the yield ranging from 2.6 to 4.0 tonnes per hectare under rain-fed conditions. In majority of plantations, farmers raise areca nut at 1.5 x 1.5 m spacing resulting in low production. Farmers' training in modern techniques of cultivation is thus important. Further, multi-tier cropping is recommended for areca nut. Processing of areca nut needs to be promoted.[3]

Cashew

Cashew is well suited for the agro-climatic conditions of ANI especially the middle-Andaman area.

2. The value of multi-tear crop (coconut + clove + black pepper) is estimated to be Rs. 1,24,815 as compared to Rs. 12,000 of mono crop of coconut.
3. The value of multi-tear crop (arecanut + clove + black pepper + nutmeg + cinnamon) is estimated to be Rs. 3,53,100 as compared to Rs. 97,500 of mono crop of areca nut.

Presently about 800 ha area is under cashew plantation with the annual production of 262 MT. Majority of plantations are poorly managed resulting in low yield. Planting of quality grafts from elite palms of local plantations may improve the yield.

Oil Palm

Presently about 1593 ha area is under oil palm plantation in these islands with the annual production of 1544 MT. Some processing support may provide requisite boost to this crop. However, allocation of more area for this crop is not recommended.

Spices

Studies have shown that the filtered light available in the coconut and areca nut plantation can sustain crops of spices like pepper, clove and nutmeg. Multi-tier cropping also increases the value of produce per unit area. In this context, plantation of cinnamon, black pepper, and clove are suggested. However, there is a need to develop technologies to minimise the cost of extraction of quills and harvesting of clove. Similarly, management of slow wilt disease in black pepper and development of white pepper making technology with organic cultivation need immediate attention. Developing 'organic spice estates' is recommended.

TABLE 7.4

Infrastructure Requirement for Spices

Items	*Unit (No.)*	*Budget (Rs. Lakh)*
Godown	1	10
Distillation Unit	1	5
Total		15

Source: As in Table 7.3.

TABLE 7.5

Infrastructure Requirement for Medicinal and Aromatic Plants

Items	*Unit (No.)*	*Budget (in Lakh)*
Tissue culture lab	1	25
Distillation plant with packaging centre	1	10
Total		35

Source: As in Table 7.3.

Ginger is already a well-established cash crop in Andaman group of islands. The major bottlenecks in cultivation of ginger are: bacterial wilt caused by *P. solanacearum; and* soft rot by *Pythium*. However, there is a good scope for improving the productivity of ginger. The requisite infrastructure is enumerated in Table 7.4.

Medicinal and Aromatic Plants

The unique agro-climatic conditions of ANI support a number of medicinal and aromatic plants. The species suitable for commercial exploitation are: *pippali*; *anola*; *patchouli*; *stevia*; *kalihari*; *neem*; lemon grass; and citronella. Requisite infrastructure for medicinal and aromatic plants is given in Table 7.5. Organic medicinal plant estates should be established along the lines of Small Farmers Agri-business Consortium (SFAC).

Fruits

Current production of fruits is 17,500 MT. Main crops are banana, papaya, citrus fruits and guava. Other fruits such as mango, pineapple and sapota are also grown. Productivity of all the fruit crops is poor owing to lack of proper management practices. At present, India imports tropical fruits like durian, rambutan, mangosteen, avocado from Southeast Asian countries,

TABLE 7.6

Exotic Tropical Fruit Crops with Export Potential

Fruit	*Adoption*	*Uses*
Durian	Needs deep fertile soils	Fruit has pulpy aril. Roasted seeds are eaten.
West Indian cherry	Can be grown in poor and stony soil	Fruit rich in vitamin C (300-400 mg/100 g) used to prepare source, juice and jelly.
Carambola	Adapted to seasonal dry period, different soil types and tolerant to light frosts	Fruits eaten fresh, fruit slices are used as fruit salad or processed into drinks and jams.
Rambutan	Can not tolerate frost and soils having high ph	Fruits have white, juicy aril which is consumed fresh, stewed or canned.
Mangosteen	Tolerant to heavy, poorly drained soils	Delicious fruits are consumed fresh and can also be cooked or preserved.
Bilimbi	Tolerant to different soils	Fruits are processed into pickles, sauces, preserve, etc.

Source: As in Table 7.3.

TABLE 7.7

Infrastructure Requirement for Fruits

Sl. No.	Infrastructure	Unit (Nos.)	Amount
1.	Tissue culture laboratory	1	50
2.	Poly house , greenhouse, net house	5	20
3.	Mist chamber	5	20
4.	Micro irrigation network	50	50
5.	Refrigerated van	2	30
Total			170

Source: As in Table 7.3.

which can be successfully grown in these islands. Since these crops also have export potential, there is a need to put policies in place so that their production and productivity is improved (Table 7.6).

Also, West Indian cherry, which is rich in vitamin C, should be grown to meet the nutritional requirement of local people. Infrastructure requirement for fruits is given in Table 7.7

Exotic Tropical under Utilised Fruits

There is good scope for careful introduction, evaluation and exploitation of several other exotic underutilised minor fruits/spices from other tropical iso-climatic region of the world. Most of them besides being tolerant to inclement weather and capable of establishing in different soils can be raised at low cost.

Vegetables

Vegetables are mainly grown during the post-rainy season. Vegetable production needs to be brought to semi-commercial level through technological interventions. Forty per cent of the rice area can be brought under vegetable production during peak rainy season through Broad Bed and Furrow (BBF) technology wherein rice and fish can be grown in furrows and vegetables on the raised beds. 'Vegetable Estates' and 'Organic vegetable hubs' should be formed along the lines of SFAC. Emphasis should be on improving the productivity using biological interventions.

TABLE 7.8

Infrastructure Requirement for Protected Cultivation of Vegetables

Sl. No.	Infrastructure	Unit (Nos.)	Amount(Rs. Lakh)
1.	Hi-tech greenhouse	3	75
Total			75

Source: As in Table 7.3.

Tuber Crops

Tuber crops are grown in small farms and homesteads. The crop is generally grown as a pure though it is adaptable to inter-cropping and rotation with other crops. To increase productivity of tuber crops introduction of improved varieties is necessary (Table 7.8)

Floriculture

Cut flowers, like tuberose, gerbera, crossandra, marigold and tropical orchids should be considered for commercial production as these have good demand in Southeast Asian countries markets (Tables 7.9 and 7.10). Orchids have high potential in Andaman & Nicobar Islands. Species like *Eulophia andamanensis, Dendrobium crumenatum,* etc. can be advocated for large-scale multiplication in these islands.

Post-Harvest Management

In ANI, post harvest loss is more than 20 to 25 per cent because of its geographic position and climatic conditions. In order to minimise the post-harvest loss, and increase potential for exports, efforts should be made for increasing shelf life of the produce by creating internationally approved storage, treatment, handling, packaging, and transport facilities. These facilities should be set up at nodal points such as Diglipur, Mayabandar, Port Blair, Neil island, Hevlock, Hut Bay, and Campbell Bay (Tables 7.11 and 7.12).

Organic Farming

Andaman & Nicobar Islands are blessed with a rich vegetation of tropical rain forests, coral reef ecosystem and a rich biodiversity. These have to be conserved and preserved. To this end organic farming should be promoted. Organic produce will fetch higher prices in the national and international markets. Generally the plantation crops produce lot of biomass like leaves,

TABLE 7.9

Infrastructure Requirement for Floriculture

Sl. No.	Infrastructure	Unit (Nos.)	Amount(Rs. in Lakh)
1.	Poly house, greenhouse	5	5
2.	Nursery for supply of planning materials	1	25
3. 5	Irrigation facility with wells	17	50
4.	Cool room with controlled humidity and temperature	1	50
Total			130

Source: As in Table 7.3.

TABLE 7.10

Infrastructure Requirement for Green Orchid

Sl. No.	*Particulars*	*Unit Size*	*Rate (Rs.)*	*Total (Rs. in Lakh)*
1.	Land development(land requirement is 1.0 ha)	1.0 ha	Rs. 2.50 lakhs/ha	2.50
2.	Land development (levelling)	1.0 ha	Rs. 15,000/ha.	0.15
3.	Fencing	400 rm	Rs. 100/rm	0.40
4.	Irrigation (well and pump set)	1 no.	Rs. 1 lakh/unit	1.00
5.	Civil structure (construction of shade house)	11,000 m^2	Rs. 330/m^2.	36.30
6.	Planting material:Cost of blooming size plant	Rs. one lakh.	Rs. 65/plant	65.00
Total				105.35

Source: Estimated by Author.

TABLE 7.11

Infrastructure Status for the Hi-tech Post-Harvest Handling in A&N Islands

Items	*Available*	*Units to be Created(Nos.)*	*Amount (Rs. in Lakh)*
Establishment of packaging station	Nil	7 (@ Rs 10 lakhs/unit)	70
Vapour heat Treatment (VHT)	Nil	7 (@ Rs 2 lakhs/unit)	14
Food irradiation technology	Nil	7 (@ Rs 4 lakhs/unit)	28
Pre-packaging	Nil	7 (@ Rs 2 lakhs/unit)	14
Packaging	Nil	7 (@ Rs 2 lakhs/unit)	14
Palletisation	Nil	7 (@ Rs 2 lakhs/unit)	14
Pre-cooling	Nil	7 (@ Rs 2 lakhs/unit)	14
Storage	Nil	1 (@ Rs 10 lakhs/unit)	10
Containerisation	Nil	7 (@ Rs 2 lakhs/unit)	14
Total	Nil		192

Source: Compiled by Author.

TABLE 7.12

Infrastructure for Value-added Coconut

Sl. No	*Infrastructure*	*Unit (nos.)*	*Amount (Rs. lakh)*
1.	Copra dryer	250	50
2.	Godown, grading and packaging centre (200 MT capacity)	4	100
3.	Desiccated coconut processing unit (10000 nuts per day)	1	25
4.	Vinegar processing unit (30 kilo litre per year)	1	15
5.	Curled coir and coir fibre unit (16000 husks/8hrs).	1	50
6.	Coir pith briquette (900 MT/year)	1	25
7.	Coconut oil mill to process (1500 MT copra per year)	1	35
8.	Activated carbon processing unit (300 MT/year)	1	90
9.	Quality testing lab.	1	50
Total			440

Source: As in Table 7.10.

fronds, empty fruit bunches, husk, etc. These can be converted in organic manure by hot fermentation, cold aerobic method and by vermi-composting. The vermi-composting is best done by using *Eudrilus eugnieae* and the cattle manure as starter. Biocontrol agents like *Metarrhizium anisopliae, Trichoderma* and organic waste should also be brought into the system. Fruits and vegetables produced by organic farming will also have better nutritive value, taste, flavour, and shelf life.

Human Resource Development

In ANI, horticultural research needs to be strengthened. There is also a need for skill development through short training courses in specialised areas like:

- nursery production of healthy planting materials;
- planting techniques in hill slopes in contour, soil conservation practice, *in-situ* water harvesting, moisture conservation technique;

TABLE 7.13

Estimated Production Potential of Horticultural Crops

Product	Potential Area (ha)	Production Potential
Plantation Crops		
Desicated coconut	25000	300 MT
Virgin coconut oil		900MT
Arecanut drying and supari making	4000	20000 MT
Spices		
White pepper processing	1000	100 MT
Dry ginger and ginger powder	10000	10000 MT
Clove	150	100 MT
Nutmeg	100	75 lakh tonnes
Cinnnamon	200	150 MT
Fruit crops		
Banana chips	4000	500MT
Less known fruits		5000 MT
Floriculture		
Orchids	10	15.0 MT
Foliages/cutflowers	10	30.00 MT
Anthurium	2	1.5 MT
Medicinal plants		
Neem	100	100 MT
Aonla	100	300 MT
Brahmi	150	100 MT
Bixa sp.	150	50 MT
Lemon grass	250	90 MT
Citronella grass	250	60 MT

Source: As in Table 7.10.

- plant protection measures for fruits and vegetable; and.
- on-farm storage, handling and preservation techniques.

Employment Potential of Horticulture

Horticultural crops offer a great potential for employment generation. Some projections of production potential of horticulture crops are presented in Table 7.13.

Post-Tsunami Scenario

Tsunami has caused extensive damage to agricultural crops and land in ANI. It is estimated that 2,178 ha of cropped area (paddy and other field crops) has been affected. Loss of crop has been estimated at Rs. 6.53 crore. Damage to plantation crops has been estimated at 5891 ha in terms of area and Rs. 515.46 crore in terms of value of crop.[4] The following suggestions are made in this context.

Saline Affected Areas of South Andaman

a. No crop can be cultivated in the seawater ingression areas due to salinity, which can cause root injury to crops. In such areas, either BBF based farming system with maricultur in the furrows or large-scale transplanting of saline/ brackish water resistant *Morinda citrifolia* can be taken up.

b. Preparation and re-strengthening of bunds to check the ingression of seawater with proper sluice gate arrangements and drainage system.

c. Alternative farming systems such as agroforestry, using mangrove species, sylvi aquaculture and agro aquaculture is recommended.

Bio Fencing

Fencing of thick mangroves wherever location permits followed by a layer of salt resistant timber, dual purpose trees, *Morinda citrifolia* (Noni), *Pongamia, Gliricidia,* etc. In the third layer, coconut based cropping system may be advocated.

Community Programmes

1. Food grain production at subsistence level; vegetables, oilseeds and perishables (excluding fish) should be at semi-commercial level; and processed *copra*, areca nut, medicinal plants, orchids should be at commercial level catering to the needs of national and international markets.
2. Nutritional kitchen garden programme at the household level.
3. Organic farming
4. Seed, grain, and fodder banks for meeting the supply during the disaster.

ANIMAL HUSBANDRY AND DAIRY

Development of animal husbandry and dairy is important as it plays a major role in assuring food security in the islands and has enormous potential for employment generation thereby contributing to

4. Source: ANI administration.

Measures of Reclamation of Agricultural Land

The following measures are recommended.

Situation	*Condition*	*Suggested measures*
I	Low-lying coastal areas where seawater has intruded only during tsunami and then receded permanently.	• At present there is salt encrustation on the surface layer, which should be scraped and removed from the field. • Growing of salt tolerant crops like sunflower, maize, watermelon, chili, gourds. • Surface mulching of all crops. • Addition of sufficient quantity of FYM and additional dose of 25 per cent N to all crops. • Raised bed method of planting with sowing/planting on slopes. • Localised irrigation either through drip or pitcher system. • Sowing of *dhaincha* (*S. aculeata* and *S. rostrata*) after harvest of dry season crops. • Raising bund all around the plots for impounding fresh rainwater. • Growing salt tolerant paddy varieties during monsoon season. • Aged seedlings (7 days more than normal).
II	Low-lying coastal areas where seawater reaches during high tide and recedes during low tide.	• Intercropping *dhaincha* in rice and its *in situ* incorporation. • Application of rock phosphate in place of SSP. • Repair of embankment all along the seacoast. • Provision and/or repair of one way sluice gate. • Raising of another dykes/ embankment in the low-lying areas to prevent intrusion of seawater in the good paddy field. • Provision of drainage as per the slope situation. • Alternate land use by adopting plantation cum brackish water fish culture in trench model. • Coconut and salt tolerant grasses on the embankment; and brackish water fish like milkfish, mullet, crab, shrimp on the trenches.
III	Low-lying coastal areas where there is permanent stagnation of seawater and the depth of impounding increases with high tide.	• Raised and sunken bed method of cultivation involving paddy cum fish cum vegetables cum fodder cum livestock. • Layer 1: Mangroves all along the seacoast. • Layer 2: Dykes all along. The height of dykes to be 6-8 inches more than the height of tide. • Layer 3: These dykes may be protected by a layer of sea *mahua*, casurina and other salt tolerant trees. • Layer 4: Series of low-lying brackish water pond may be constructed all along as the next layer. • Layer 5: A dyke of 1inch taller than the high tide as the next layer. • Layer 6: Low lying pond along with plantation crops on the dykes. • Layer 7: Rest of the area can be cultivated under salt tolerant paddy with all agronomic reclamation measures. • Layer 8: The paddy–vegetable sequence can be followed on the medium upland situation in the next layer. • Layer 9: Drainage *nullah* along the slopes may be constructed which will drain out in sea directly. The entire pond to be connected to *nullah*.

Source: Basic Statistics, ANI.

FIGURE 7.2

Reclamation of Agriculture Land

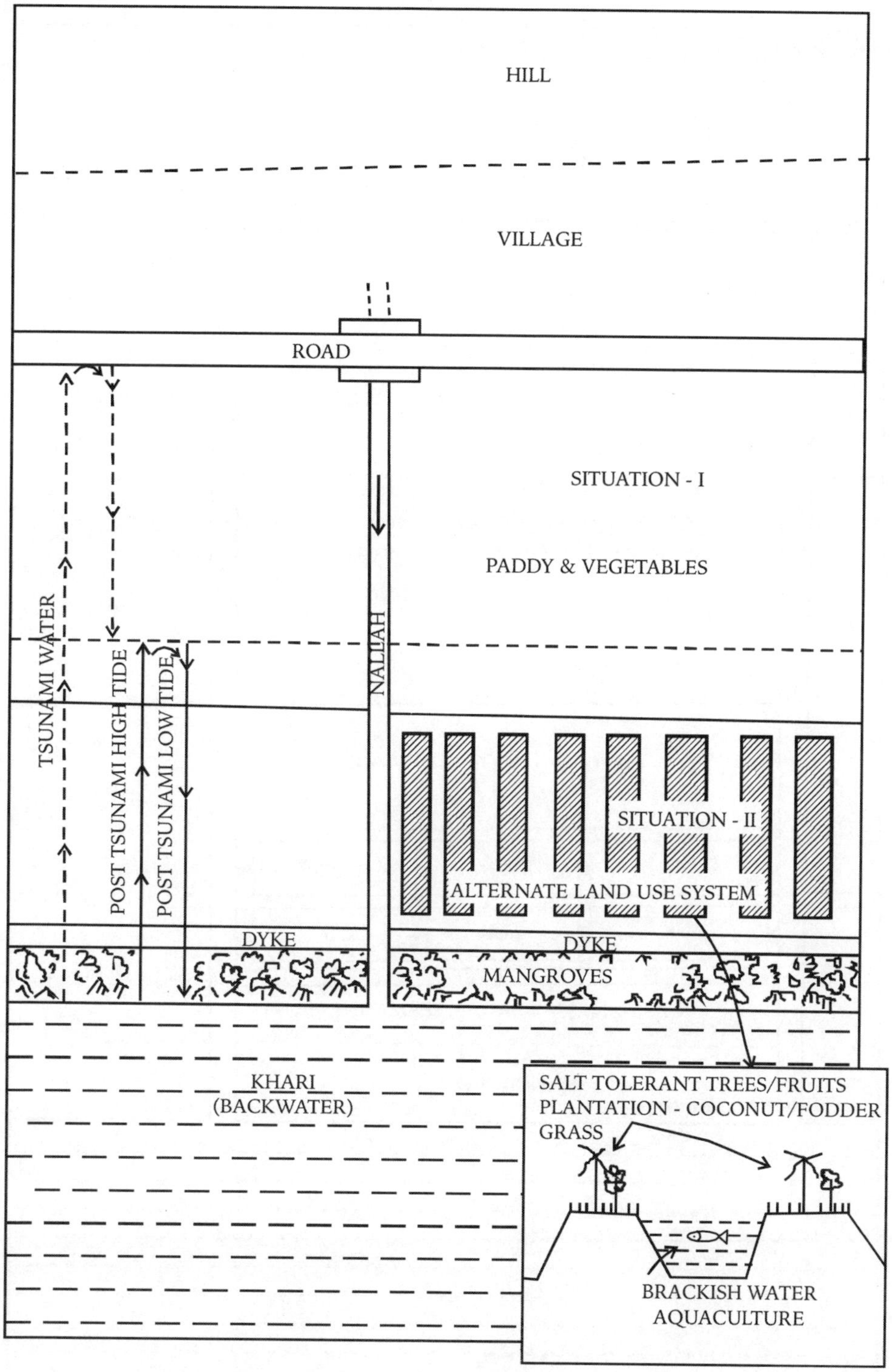

SITUATION I & II

FIGURE 7.3

Reclamation of Agriculture Land

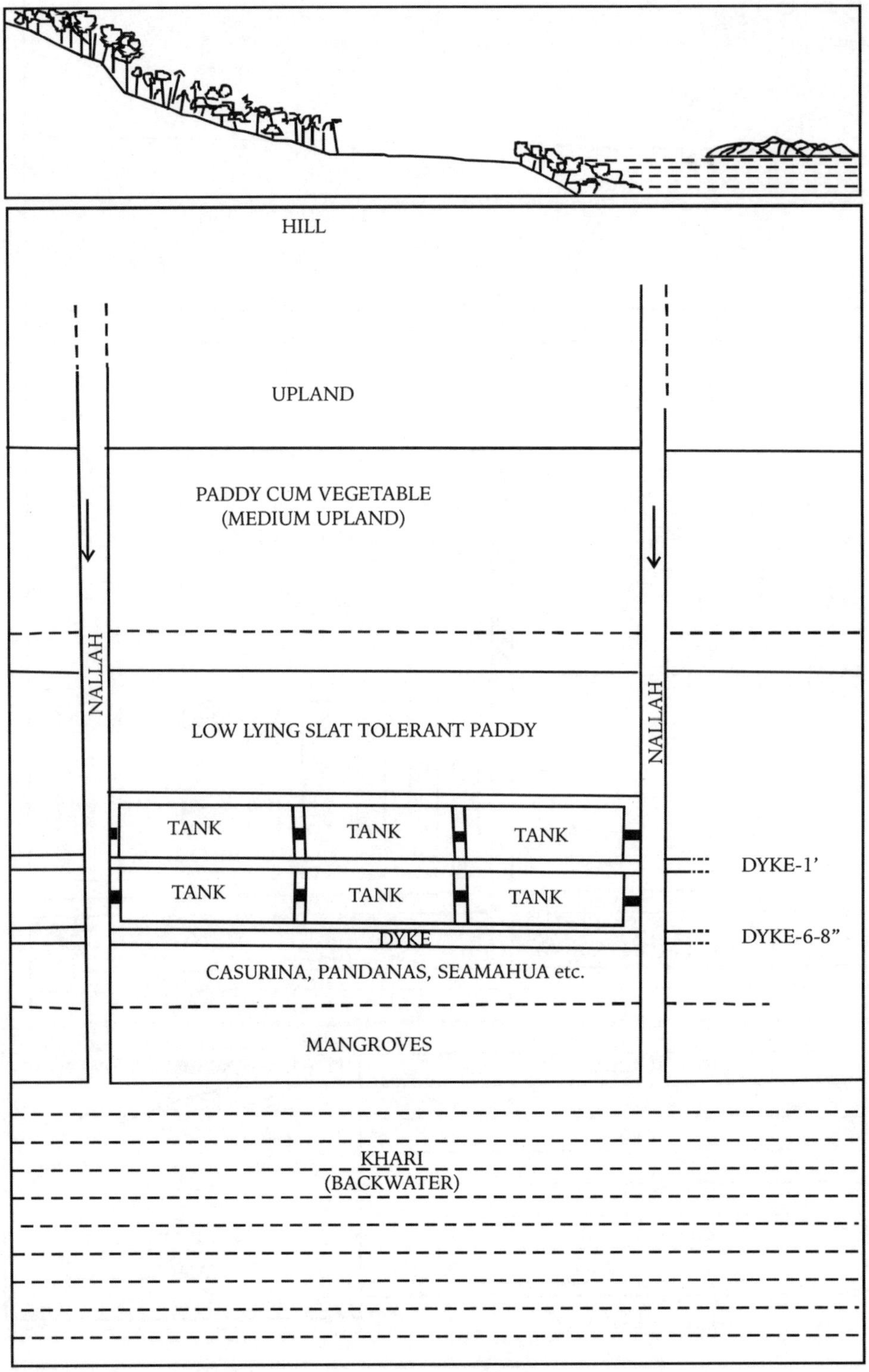

SITUATION III

improvement in the socioeconomic status of people in rural areas. The species available in the islands are cattle, buffalo, goat, pigs, fowls, and ducks. The main hurdles in the growth of this sector are low producing germ-plasm, unscientific rearing practices, poor marketing network and overall climatic factors.

Livestock: Status

The main livestock is pig followed by poultry and goat. A large proportion of the livestock population is in Andaman district except the pig which is more in Nicobar district (Table 7.14). Rearing practices mainly comprise open range systems. In South Andaman, however, all the systems (intensive, semi-intensive and open range) are practised. Intensive system of rearing for poultry is practised only at South Andaman. In Nicobar district, Great Nicobar is the only island where dairy animals are reared. Nicobares consider the pig as a family asset, just as coconut plantation is a village asset.

Due to sudden increase in human population starting in eighties, crossbreeding programme and co-operative dairy movement were launched. However, owing to various reasons it failed. Crossbreeds witnessed exorbitant mortality rates (both calves and adults), infertility/anoestrus and poor production. The research support of the ICAR Institute with integration made the crossbred a successful venture and laid the foundation stone of successful co-operative dairy movement in 1997-98. However, keeping in view the results of crossbreeding in Kerala, certain precaution is necessary. The cross population should not go beyond 40 per cent of total female population so that in subsequent generations hybrid vigour (essential for sustained production) is maintained in the population. A clear-cut breeding policy needs to be devised.

In early seventies modern poultry farming was initiated by the government and later a hatchery unit was also established. But it was not successful owing to various reasons. However, in eighties again integrated efforts were made which gradually became successful. Private sector entered into the foray initially by importing day-old layer and broiler chicks and supplying to farmers and later by establishing hatching units in the islands itself. The bulk of the demand comes from defence establishment. Up to 1997, dressed/undressed broilers in tonnes were imported from Chennai along with estimated 3.0 lakh day old chicks but from 1998, due to integrated approach in this sub-sector import was stopped. This phenomenon percolated to other islands also but needs to be stabilised. In the present scenario, role of government should be limited to remote islands only for promoting rural poultry production and disease control.

TABLE 7.14

Livestock Population in Andaman & Nicobar Islands

(in Thousand)

Category	*1982*	*1987*	*1992*	*1997*
Cattle	36.5	47.3	52.9	60.1
Buffalo	11.9	14.4	14.5	14.2
Goat	33.6	45.1	56.2	70.9
Pig	96.0	29.6	36.5	42.8
Poultry	319.9	442.8	614.2	800.9

Source: Basic Statistics, Andaman & Nicobar Islands.

The British opened first veterinary hospital at Port Blair (Goalghar) in 1940. Gradually, a very good network of veterinary hospitals (9), veterinary dispensary (11), sub-dispensaries (41), farms (6), hatchery units (4), polyclinic-cum-animal disease diagnosis laboratory, and liquid nitrogen plant to facilitate artificial insemination programme. These however, need to be equipped with modern facilities.

Strategy for Development

Small Dairies

Since the estimated carrying capacity of the islands in terms of present resources is around one lakh, rearing of genetically improved high yielding livestock should be encouraged. In this context, the Union Territory (UT) needs to devise a long-term breeding policy. The cluster villages around Port Blair and Rangat need to be promoted for small dairy unit holding. A strong village level dairy co-operative movement is essential. Also, system such as infertility control measures, calf rearing schemes, fodder cultivation schemes are needed. The total dry and green fodder production is far below the requirement.

The island specific technology developed at CARI, Port Blair using mass infertility control and synchronisation should be promoted. Integrated small dairies in rural areas comprising 5 to 15 animals either under coconut based cropping system or rice based cropping system seems appropriate. Perennial fodders like co-3, hybrid napier strain 21, 6 which give a yield of 130 to 250 tonnes/ha, paddy straw, and grasses should be promoted. The technology for integrated rural dairy development including crossbreeding is also available with the ICAR institute located on the islands.

Local Feed Resources and their Availability

The availability of local feed resources is uncertain, seasonal and location dependent. Due to this reason, a uniform feeding system cannot be suggested for all the islands. Other than grasses from the local grasslands, paddy straw constitute the bulk roughage source and potential availability of it is about 50,000 tonnes, followed by gliricedia leaves about 30,000, coconut meal 5,880, cashew apple waste about 200, fish waste about 3,000 and Banana fruit waste about 208 tonne per year. Fishing activity when done on a large scale using mechanised fishing gears and the catch being processed, it will provide large amounts of trash fishes, which could be used for fish oil production and fishmeal production. Since very little processing industry/facility are available most of the by-products are not utilised as feed resources. There is a need to have basic small to medium scale processing industry so that the activity could be done in an organised manner and available by- products could be harnessed as low cost feeds for livestock and poultry.

Rural Poultry Production System

The technologies developed at CARI, Port Blair using dual purpose breeds and strain cross which are not dependent on balanced feed and exploit locally available resources under semi range system may be a better substitute.

Meat Sector

In Nicobar district, piggery and goatery are family assets and rearing is a way of life. Incidentally, till now they are disease free, drug/chemical free also. Nicobar district has the potential of rearing about 20,000 breedable sows and over 20,000 ewes which can produce over 10,000 tonne pork and mutton annually without incurring any expenditure from outside. Private sector should be encouraged in processing, packaging, and marketing of meat which can fetch more than Rs. 100 crore in international markets at present prices.

Investment Requirements

Estimates of funds required for implementation of the above suggested measures are provided in Table 7.15.

Animal Health

The Islands have very good network of veterinary institutions but services are not up to mark. The islands owing to its inherent advantages are free from many dreaded diseases but lack of quarantine facilities may pose serious problem in future. The services and institutions need to be equipped and strengthened with systematic human resources development programme. Quarantine facilities at Elephant Point needs total revamping linked with disease diagnostic labs of ICAR and the department of Animal husbandry and veterinary services.

TABLE 7.15

Funds Requirements

(Rs. Lakh)

Components	*Five Year Plans*					*Expected Self Employment Generated (Nos.)*					*Socioeconomic Benefits*
	Xth	*XIth*	*XIIth*	*XIIIth*	*XIV*	*Xth*	*XIth*	*XIIth*	*XIIIth*	*XIVth*	
Dairy development (semen, co-operative set up marketing, product; germplasm)	300	300	300	250	200	2500	2500	2500	2500	2500	Villages will transform in economic/production hubs; womenfolk will get direct benefit.
Meat sector (pig/goat/chicken rearing, processing value addition, marketing)	400	500	200	150	100	3000	5000	3000	2000	2000	Tribals and women will get direct benefit. Nancowrie and Car Nicobar will become hub of production.
Rural poultry production (germplasm, housing and marketing support)	100	200	100	100	100	5000	5000	4000	4000	400	Rural poor and rural womenfolk will be major beneficiaries.
Animal health (medical, infrastructure, care)	250	250	300	350	200	200	200	200	200	200	Production will increase constantly.

Source: Estimated by Author.

Chapter 8

Fisheries and Sea Food Industry

With one-fourth of the total coastline of India and about 80 per cent of the total Exclusive Economic Zone (EEZ), ANI has significant potential in fisheries. However, this potential is yet to be tapped. Tsunami on December 26, 2004 has caused substantial damage to fisheries in ANI. Loss to the fishery sector due to tsunami is estimated at Rs. 34.37 crores (Table 8.1).

The present level of marine fish production in ANI is 30,000 tonnes, which is about 12 per cent of the estimated potential. Most of the produce is consumed locally. The exports are insignificant and have declined between 1996 and 2000 (Table 8.2). Marine fish production in ANI is faced with a complete lack of strategy to promote this activity.

In 1991, the Ministry of Agriculture constituted an expert committee to evolve a plan for deep-sea fishing, processing and export of fish in ANI. The committee after considering the existing infrastructure and the constraints in development of deep-sea fishing, processing and export of fish from ANI, made a number of recommendations which *inter alia* include the following:

- training of local people in fish handling and processing;

TABLE 8.1

Damage to Fishery due to Tsunami

Items	*Units (Nos.)*	*Average Rate of Loss (Rs.)*	*Total Loss (Rs. Lakhs)*
Houses			
a) Fully damaged	570	100000	570.00
b) Partially damaged	695	35000	243.25
Loss of Belongings	1265	15000	189.75
Fishing boats			
a) Local made dingies (traditional)			
Fully lost	744	65000	483.60
Partial loss	582	10000	582.00
b) Engine fitted			
Fully lost	391	200000	782.00
Partial loss	386	108000	416.88
Fishing Gears			
a) Gill net	1225	10000	122.50
b) Cast net	410	3000	12.30
c) Hook and Line	795	50	0.3975
d) Shore seine	24	50000	12.00
e) Long line	118	10000	11.80
Loss of fish in Freshwater ponds due to inundation	525	2000	10.50

Source: Department of Fisheries, ANI and CARI

TABLE 8.2

Year-wise Details of Export of Fish and Fish Products (kg.) from ANI

Items	*1996*	*1997*	*1998*	*1999*	*2000*
Live fish (Grouper)	-	-	5800	2000	7955
Frozen fish	9061	25400	26446	10499	14351
Dried fish	64632	52500	20117	33395	16416
Shark fins	1443	539	1432	2569	4530
Lobster (live)	232	860	2626	2145	10235
Crab (live)	11808	19424	11882	20815	18227
Prawn	20875	4523	1524	3441	11942
Total	108051	103246	69827	74864	83656

Source: Same as Table 8.1.

- establishment of cold storages, ice plants, chilled storages, processing plants, ice crusher, blast freezer;
- exploitation of the tuna and tuna-like fishes and the establishment of tuna canning plant on the basis of the tuna catch; and
- introduction of fishing vessels capable of judiciously exploiting the deep-sea resources, with equity participation from the private and public sector.

While some progress has been made,[1] it is far from being adequate to make any significant impact especially

TABLE 8.3

Post-Harvest Infrastructure Facilities Available in ANI

Sl. No.	*Items*	*Location*	*Year of Commission*	*Capacity*	*Ownership*
1.	Ice plant	Port Blair	5 tonne in 1968 10 tonne in 1996	15 tonne	Fisheries dept.
2.	Cold storage	Port Blair	15 tonne in 1968	25 tonne	Fisheries dept.
3.	Cold storage	Garacharama, South Andaman	1995	5 tonne	Andaman Fisheries Ltd.
4.	Chilled freezer	-do-	1995	5 tonne	-do-
5.	Blast freezer	-do-	1995	5 tonne	-do-
6.	Block Ice plant	-do-	1995	5 tonne	-do-
7.	Cold storage	Lamba Line, Port Blair	1987	30 tonne	Private sector

Ice Plants, cold storage and other infrastructure under construction

Sl. No.	*Items*	*Location*	*Capacity*	*Ownership*
1.	Ice plant	Hut bay, Little Andaman	10 tonne	Fisheries dept.
2.	Ice plant	Campbell bay (Great Nicobar)	10 tonne	-do-
3.	Cold storage	Hut bay, Little Andaman	15 tonne	-do-
4.	Cold storage	Campbell bay (Great Nicobar)	15 tonne	-do-
5.	Chilled fish storage	Sandoor, S. Andaman	5 tonne	ANIIDCO
6.	Cold storage	Diglipur, N. Andaman	50 tonne	-do-
7.	Block ice plant	-do-	5 tonne	-do-
8.	Blast freezer	-do-	5 tonne	-do-
9.	Plate freezer	-do-	1 tonne	-do-
10.	Chilled fish storage	-do-	10 tonne	-do-
11.	Shell ice plant	-do-	5 tonne	-do-
12.	Ice storage	-do-	5 tonne	-do-
13.	Ice plant	Rangat	10 tonne	Fisheries dept.
14.	Cold storage	Rangat	15 tonne	-do-

Source: MPEDA, 2001

1. At present a 25 tonne capacity cold storage and a 15 tonne ice plant is in operation at Port Blair. Another ice plant of 15 tonne capacity and cold storage with a capacity of 10 tonne has been commissioned at Hut Bay. A number of ice plants and cold storages are under various stages of construction. Fish markets with deep freezers for storage of excess catch have also been constructed at various places to facilitate marketing of fish and other marine products by the fish vendors (Table 8.3).

in view of the perspective plan of the ANI, drawn up for a period up to 2012, which aims to exploit at least 40 per cent of the estimated potential of fishery.

This chapter examines the present status of fishery and sea food industry in ANI, identifies the bottlenecks, and suggests strategies for the development of these sectors. The chapter is divided into two main sections. While section I addresses fisheries, section II discusses the sea food industry.

FISHERIES

More than 1.48 lakh tonnes of pelagic, demersal and oceanic fishery resources are estimated to be available in EEZ around the islands but, at present, only about 20 per cent of the estimated potential is being harvested. This indicates that there is substantial scope for developing fishery as one of the leading sectors for boosting the socio-economic status of ANI. Among the potential fishery resources, coastal tuna, oceanic tuna and tuna like-fishes are estimated to be around 0.673 lakh tonne and hence special attention should be given to these resources.

Strength, Weaknesses, Opportunities and Threats

Strength

- an EEZ encompassing 0.6 million sq. km. which is nearly 30 per cent of Indian ocean;
- the aggregate coastline is 1,912 km. which is nearly 25 per cent of Indian total coastline;
- vast magnitude of fishery resources including coastal pelagic, demersal and offshore and deep-sea fishes to the tune of 1.48 lakh tonne;
- relatively unpolluted coastal waters for developing coastal aquaculture; and
- availability of high value marine seafood such as shrimps, lobsters, crabs and fishes such as tuna, groupers, and snappers for export.

Weaknesses

- remoteness of the islands—more than 1000 km. from Indian mainland;
- many coastal areas are inaccessible especially on the western side of the islands, in the process restricting the development mainly to eastern sides of the islands' coasts;
- lack of indigenous expertise/technology, and trained personnel;
- lack of local capacity for capital investment on high cost activities;
- lack of infrastructure for large-scale fishing and coastal/offshore aquaculture;
- lack of reliable data base on the magnitude and dynamics of exploitable and cultivable aquatic resources;
- inadequate infrastructure for fish processing and marketing; and
- lack of comprehensive policy for fishing promotion and regulation for sustainability.

Moreover, due to the tsunami in 2004 more than half of the fishing boats (both traditional and motorised) and fishing gears have been lost. Nearly half of the dwellings of the fishers are either fully or partially damaged. The fear psychosis among fishers caused by the tsunami has also affected fishing though this could be a temporary phenomenon.

Opportunities

- enormous scope for commercial exploitation of fishery resources;
- availability of pollution free areas suitable for cage culture, hitherto unexplored even in the mainland India;
- scope for producing high-value black pearl and production of artefacts from important gastropod molluscs;
- scope for export of tuna and marine ornamental fishes;
- employment opportunities in the fisheries and related sectors; and
- scope for development of tourism due to the availability of a wide variety of sea foods and sport fishing.

Threats

- poaching of marine resources;
- possibility of overexploitation of specific species;
- salinisation of ground water resources due to coastal aquaculture activities; and
- impacts due to certain government policies like banning of exploitation of certain species.

Potential and Current Exploitation

Marine Fishery Resources

Capture Fisheries

The Fishery Survey of India (FSI) estimates of marine fishery potential in the EEZ of ANI have been widely accepted and are used as a baseline in this chapter. Of the estimated 1.48 lakh tonne of marine resources, pelagic, demersal, and oceanic resources are 0.56, 0.32, and 0.60 tonnes, respectively.

It has been reported by the Department of Fisheries that there are about 3,448 active and full-time fishermen and the present level of exploitation is around 30,000 tonne (due to the effect of December 2004 tsunami, there was a temporary reduction in total catch in 2005. Only 8,635 tonnes of fishes were landed in 2005, mainly due to extensive damage to fishing crafts and gears and the unwillingness of fishers to venture into the sea during the first half of the year). Almost all catches come from near shore waters. Tables 8.4a, b and c provide the estimated potential and present level of exploitation. The fish stock of A&N islands is regularly monitored by Fishery Survey of India, the fish catch is stagnating mainly due to the over dependence on traditional gears.

Pelagic

From Table 8.4a, it would be seen that on an average only about 25 per cent of the pelagic resources have been exploited and there is vast scope to increase the exploitation of mackerel, sardines, clupeids, seer fish and coastal tunas. However, anchovies and carangids are overexploited. This point towards the need for a clear policy for sustainable exploitation of fishery resources.

TABLE 8.4A

Fishery Potential and Exploitation (Demersal)

Sl. No.	*Name of Fishes*	*Potential (Tonnes)*	*Exploitation (Tonnes)*						*Remarks*
			2000	*2001*	*2002*	*2003*	*2004*	*2005**	
1.	Elasmobranchs	4200	1523	467	217	395	250	71	Underexploited
2.	Silver bellies	5000	1557	1467	965	662	1129	217	Underexploited
3.	Perches	8000	5636	7029	5330	9065	9303	3019	Underexploited
4.	Pomfrets	1900	1856	192	107	181	319	196	Underexploited
5.	Catfish	1000	510	321	170	126	454	32	Underexploited
6.	Threadfins	400	62	17	20	30	12	07	Underexploited
7.	Croakers	1200	86	41	64	63	40	30	Underexploited
8.	Gerrides	1400	-	-	-	-	-	—	Underexploited
9.	Goat fishes (Upenoids)	900	-	-	-	-	-	—	Underexploited
10.	Silver grunt (Pomadasyds)	100	-	-	-	-	-	—	Underexploited
11.	Drift fish (Airouma indica)	300	-	-	-	-	-	—	Underexploited
12.	Threadfins breams (Nemipaterids)	500	-	-	-	-	-	—	Underexploited
13.	Lizard fish	150	-	-	-	-	-	—	Underexploited
14.	Flat fish	50	-	-	-	-	-	—	Underexploited
15.	Bulls eye (Pricanthids)	100	-	-	-	-	-	—	Underexploited
16.	Cephalopods	100	-	-	-	-	-	—	Underexploited
17.	Penaied Shrimps	800	351	534	489	661	273	108	Underexploited
18.	Crab	1000	738	542	352	460	386	163	Underexploited
19.	Deep sea Lobster	120	-	-	-	27	35	37	Underexploited
20.	Deep sea Shrimps	110	-	-	-	-	-	—	Underexploited
21.	Deep sea Fishes	1970	-	-	-	-	-	—	Underexploited
22.	Others	2700	537	2185	2164	2978	1285	695	Underexploited
	Total	32000	9672	12795	9878	14648	13486	4575	

Note: * The drastic reduction in fish catch during 2005 was due to the impact of tsunami. Tsunami damaged many boats and fishers did not venture in to the sea during the first half of the year.

Source: Department of Fisheries, Andaman & Nicobar Administration.

Demersal

Only 38 per cent of the demersal resources are being exploited (Table 8.4b). This may be attributed to non-availability of suitable craft and gear for the exploitation of these valuable resources. Further, traditional boats operate in the in-shore and part of near-shore waters only. Fishing has to be done beyond the present fishing areas in order to augment the catch of demersal fishes. The bulk of the catch of A&N islands is from pelagic and demersal fishes such as sardine, mackerel, mullets, silver bellies, etc. Reef fishes, shark, etc. form catch of secondary importance and it is not a top-down model of exploitation.

Deep Sea/oceanic Fisheries

The potential of oceanic tuna and tuna-like fishes has been estimated at about 67,300 tonnes by FSI (Table 8.4c). This resource has not been utilised at all in the Bay islands. Apart from tunas, other groups like oceanic sharks, cephalopods (squids), deep-sea lobsters, prawns also offer scope for exploitation.

No separate estimate for resources like reef fishes, groupers, snappers, rabbit fish, lobsters, shrimps, bivalves, sharks, sea cucumbers, seaweeds is available at present.

Brackish Water Fishery Resources:Capture fisheries

The brackish water areas in ANI are estimated to be around 33,000 ha. However, capture fishery is very limited and mainly pertains to catching of prawns, crabs and fishes like mullets from creeks and bays. Central Agricultural Research Institute, Port Blair have developed eco-friendly brackish water aquaculture of mullets (*Liza tade*), milkfish (*Chanos chanos*), Seabass (*Lates calcarifer*), Prawn (*Penaeus monodon, P. merguiensi*) as well as mud crab culture. Majority of the area is under mangroves and reserved forests. The crab fishery is expanding at present. The mollusc resources like green mussels are very limited and cannot sustain any fishery. Other resources like clams and edible oysters are not used much except by some tribes and settlers.

Freshwater Fishery Resources

The sources of freshwater are rivers and *nullahs* in the Bay Islands that are 37 km. and 78.8 km. in length, respectively. In addition there are two rivers Galathea in Great Nicobar, and Kalpong in North Andaman. Further, there are about 800 ponds, each having a water spread area between 0.04 and 0.06 ha.

TABLE 8.4B

Fishery Potential and Exploitation (Pelagic)

Sl. No.	*Name of Fishes*	*Potential (Tonnes)*	*Exploitation (Tonnes)*						*Remarks*
			2000	*2001*	*2002*	*2003*	*2004*	*2005***	
1.	Anchovies*	6200	1954	1590	1718	976	1558	450	Under exploited
2.	Sardines	8000	3823	2389	3048	3696	2906	539	Under exploited
3.	Hilsha shard	2500	416	159	228	180	292	74	Under exploited
4.	Wolf herring (ChironCentrids)	600	237	129	15	47	-	—	Under exploited
5.	Mackerel	4500	1939	1512	2843	1128	1363	314	Under exploited
6.	Rounds Seads (Decapterids)	1300	-	-	-	-	-	—	Under exploited
7.	Other Carengids	6000	1007	2144	3750	4725	3038	1154	Under exploited
8.	Ribbon Fish	1000	424	253	97	62	64	44	Under exploited
9.	Half beaks and Full beaks (Belonids)	600	364	242	43	70	87	16	Under exploited
10.	Barracuda	2200	617	1489	946	1277	870	376	Under exploited
11.	Mullets	2500	1417	1682	1043	1196	1147	290	Under exploited
12.	Seer Fish	1800	1210	1019	1007	1842	915	374	Under exploited
13.	Naratic Tinas	18000	364	625	169	419	630	133	Under exploited
14.	Others	800	653	653	646	-	384	189	Under exploited
	Total	56000	14425	13886	15553	15616	13252	3953	

Notes: * Including *Thryssa species.*

** The drastic reduction in fish catch during 2005 was due to the impact of tsunami. Tsunami damaged many boats and fishers did not venture in to the sea during the first half of the year.

Source: Department of Fisheries, Andaman & Nicobar Administration.

TABLE 8.4C

Fishery Potential and Exploitation (Oceanic)

Sl. No.	*Name of Fishes*	*Potential (Tonnes)*	*Exploitation (Tonnes)*						*Remarks*
			2000	*2001*	*2002*	*2003*	*2004*	*2005**	
1.	Yellow fin Tuna	24000	54	92	25	61	07	20	Underexploited
2.	Skip jack Tuna	22000	48	83	23	55	06	17	Underexploited
3.	Big eye tuna	500	01	01	-	01	-	01	Underexploited
4.	Bill fishes (Marine sailfish, sword Fish)	2800	1307	316	82	253	169	69	Underexploited
5.	Wahoo (Acanthium solandra)	200	-	-	-	-	-	—	Underexploited
6.	Pelagic sharks	7000	-	-	-	-	-	—	Underexploited
7.	Doll fin fish	200	-	-	-	-	-	—	Underexploited
8.	Barracuda (Sphyreena bineua)	200	-	-	-	-	-	—	Underexploited
9.	Flying fish	300	-	-	-	-	-	—	Underexploited
10.	Oceanic Squids	2000	-	-	-	-	-	—	Underexploited
11.	Others	800	-	-	-	-	-	—	Underexploited
	Total	60000	1410	492	130	370	182	107	

Note: * The drastic reduction in fish catch during 2005 was due to the impact of tsunami. Tsunami damaged many boats and fishers did not venture in to the sea during the first half of the year.

Source: Department of Fisheries, Andaman & Nicobar Administration.

Demonstrations by Central Agricultural Research Institute (CARI) and others reveal that by adopting composite fish culture with fishes like, *catla*, *rohu*, *mrigal*, silver carp, grass carp and common carp in suitable ratios depending on the available feeding niches, an annual production of over 5 tonne per ha can be obtained. Introduction of carps will not affect the endemic population as the carps are already being cultured in irrigation ponds and backyard ponds. Moreover, there are no substantial freshwater endemic fishes recorded in A&N Islands.

There is no major freshwater capture fishery in the islands. The subsistence fishery is very marginal, amounting to less than 50 tonne a year, mostly comprising air-breathing fishers like catfishes (*singhi*, *magur*), *anabas*, and *tilapia*. Many Indian carps have been introduced in the islands for culture in irrigation ponds. Similarly, there is no systematic culture fishery activity, worth mentioning. Freshwater fish culture is reported to be picking up slowly in North and Middle Andaman.

Strategy for Development

Considering the existing status of fishery exploitation and the information collected through extensive stakeholder consultation, the following strategies are suggested for fishery development in the islands.

Increasing Fish Production

Coastal Fisheries

The fishermen community in ANI consists of migrants form West Bengal, Andhra Pradesh, Kerala, and Tamil Nadu either under settlement scheme or on their own. Presently, a majority of local fishermen use non-motorised wooden dinghies for fishing in which they go up to 7 to 8 nautical mile and, on an average, get a catch of 100-150 kg. The fishing gears used are: gill nets, hooks and lines, cast nets, shore seines, anchor nets, long lines, trawl nets, etc. However, in exceptional cases they go for multi-day fishing for reef fishes and shark, etc. up to a distance of 20-30 km. more.

In order to increase the catch, changes should be made in the design of the craft and the gears used. In the case of tuna fishing, the experience of Lakshadweep fishers would be desirable to emulate. In Lakshadweep, tuna are caught by pole and line and gill net. In Andamans, the feasibility of operating pole and line is yet to be assessed considering the uncertainty on the availability of adequate baitfish resources. However, upgraded gill nets can be used for catching the coastal tuna.

Upgradation/Replacement of Traditional Crafts with Motorised Boats

Fishing craft having 10m OAL, 3.1 m breadth and 1.1 m draft powered by 18 to 20 hp engine should be introduced. The design of the boat is readily available with the Central Institute of Fisheries Technology (CIFT). The boat which can hold about 500 kg fish would cost around Rs. 3.25 lakh. Use of this boat would allow fishermen to go into deep waters, beyond 10 nautical miles, resulting in increase in fish catch. In view of the ban on felling of trees in ANI, a combination of FRP and wooden boats may be considered.

Construction of Mechanised Boats

At present, there are only 6 mechanised boats. This can be raised to 50-90 in a phased manner for exploitation of fishery resources from the waters between 10 and 24 nautical miles. For exploiting demersal and midwater fish resources, medium sized boats (10-13 m OAL) would be useful to employ trawl net, long line, etc. The existing framework of assistance for the acquisition of mechanised boats may be improved to attract private entrepreneurs. Pelagic and midwater trawling or small purse seines should be introduced for exploitation of pelagic and mesopelagic resources, especially coastal tunas.

Deep-Sea/oceanic Fisheries

The oceanic fishery is primarily composed of yellowfin tuna, sailfish, bigeye tuna, swordfish and sharks. Against the estimated potential of 67, 3000 tonnes, at present only 1,000 tonne of tuna and tuna-like fishes are caught. This loss could be attributed to non-availability of suitable vessels and lack of clear policy of fishing in the EEZ of Bay islands.

In order to exploit marine resources at a sustainable level, the following action plan is recommended:

Promotion of Private Long Liners/Purse Seiners

Deep-sea water resources, particularly tuna and tuna-like fishes need to be focused upon through joint ventures on appropriate share basis. For this purpose, promotion policies and incentives will be required to attract capital investment from private industrial sector, non-resident Indians (NRIs) and multi-national companies (MNCs).

A medium size tuna long liner of 22-25m OAL for endurance fishing for 20 days, with a fish hold capacity of 70 MT can catch around 50 tonne per voyage. With a minimum of 10 voyages per year each vessel can bring a total of about 500 tonne per year. At least 80–100 such vessels can be introduced to harness the full potential of the tuna resources. Introduction of 45 such vessels is envisaged in a phased manner during Tenth and Eleventh Five-year Plans. The introduction of resource specific vessels like tuna long liners, purse seiners for pelagic fishes and squid jigging will substantially enhance fish production from deep sea/oceanic regions of the EEZ. Since the acquisition and development of such vessels is capital intensive joint ventures may be encouraged. However, appropriate policy guidelines should be developed in this context.

Oceanic Fish Aggregating Devices (FAD) are successfully used for catching big pelagic fishes, especially yellowfin tuna, in Southeast Asian countries and are being employed in the Caribbean's too. NIOT has deployed 26 oceanic FADs around the islands of Lakshadweep and encouraging results are forthcoming on the catch of oceanic fish around these FADs. Similar devices can be deployed in ANI also to augment exploitation of coastal and oceanic pelagic fishes. This might require up gradation of the fleet, craft and gear, and training for FAD fishing.

Commissioning of Collector Vessels

These would be required to transport fish from distant islands to Campbell Bay, and also to collect fish from offshore vessels. Cold storage facility in these vessels to keep the catch in good condition is necessary.

Ecolabelling

Marine fishery exploitation is carried out using traditional methods in many parts of ANI. This is an ideal situation for getting the fishery ecolabelled. Ecomark will fetch high value to the fishery products from the region. Initially, ecolabelling may be implemented in selected regions like the Nicobar group of islands.

Fisheries Regulation

Many coastal states and union territories have introduced the Marine Fishing Regulation Act (MFRA), which stipulates marketing of fishing areas for different categories of fishing crafts and gears. ANI is in the process of formalising such Acts for fishing in the territorial waters. However, there should be clear co-operative management for the development of coastal and deep sea fisheries in tune with the national policy and the norms/regulation in force from time to time in ANI.

For sustainable utilisation of resources, continuous monitoring and enforcement of relevant policies is a requisite. Therefore, it would be important that various concerned agencies such as Directorate of Fisheries, Department of Wild life, Coastal Aquaculture Authority of India and specialised institutions such as the ICAR, FSI, Zoological Survey of India (ZSI), and Ministry of Ocean Development (MoOD) work in close co-ordination.

Infrastructure

In order to increase the fish catch to about 30 per cent of the resource potential by 2012, numerous infrastructure facilities need to be created and the present fishing fleet should be upgraded. Tables 8.5 and 8.6 provide a list of infrastructure that would be required for the development of fishery.

Construction of Landing Centres

Landing centres, with facilities like auction hall, ramp, net mending shed, and engine repair shed need to be constructed in order to facilitate easy and hygienic handling of fish. The 2004 tsunami has damaged most of the existing fish landing centres and these need renovation. In the first phase, 11 landing centres at Junglighat, Dignabad, Guptapara, Uttara, Rangat, Mayabunder, Diglipur, Hut Bay, Neil Island, Havelock and Campbell Bay could be constructed. In the second phase, few more centres like Betapur, Panighat, Hope Town, and Swarajgram can be covered.

TABLE 8.6

Infrastructure Requirement for Development of Deep-Sea/Oceanic Fisheries

Particulars		*Existing*	*To be Created*		*Total by 2012*
			2002-07	*2007-12*	
Crafts	Ocean going vessels	0	15	30	45
	Minor fishing harbour	0	0	1	1
	Major fishing harbour	0	0	1	1
Transport	Collector vessels	0	0	2	2
Others	Processing/ canning plant	0	0	1+1	1+1

Source: Estimated by Author.

Construction of Major (Deep-sea Fishing) Harbours

The facilities in a harbour should include berthing and bunkering, landing and repair of long liners, handling, processing, storage, marketing, and transportation of fish and fishery products and other ancillary requirements. As per the recommendations of the FSI a major fishing harbour at Campbell Bay may be constructed to facilitate handling of deep-sea tuna resources. In addition, a minor harbour may be constructed in North Andaman to support fishing operations.

TABLE 8.5

Infrastructure Requirement for Development of Coastal Fishery

Particulars		*Existing*	*To be Created*		*Total by 2012*
			2002-07	*2007-12*	
Crafts	Traditional Craft	1738	-100	-500	1138
	Motorised	356	100	400	856
	Mechanised vessels	6	10	50	66
	Boat building yards	0	0	1	1
Landing centres/ Harbours	Fish landing centre	12+45	14	8	22+(35)
	Minor fishing harbour	0	0	1	1
Processing facility	Ice plant and cold storage	8	3	6	17
	Frozen storage	2	1	2	5
	Ice storage	3	1	6	10
	Chilled storage	1	1	3	5
	Plate freezer	2	2	2	6
	Blast freezer	1	2	2	5
	Processing plant	2	0	1	3
	Drying units	0	8	6	14
Transport	Insulated van	0	0	4	4
	Refrigerated trucks	0	0	2	2

Source: Estimated by Author.

The existing minor harbour in South Andaman can accommodate 70-75 purse seiners/long liners of 10-13m OAL. The proposed major harbour at Campbell Bay (Great Nicobar) may be constructed with adequate berthing and bunkering facilities for more than 100 deep sea going vessels of 11-75 m OAL and also for the two collector vessels.

Capacity Building

Human resource development is an integral part of economic development. The fishermen, unemployed youth and self-help groups need to be trained in the following areas of fishery development:

- operation of motorised/mechanised boats and improved gears;
- distant/endurance fishing to increase the fish harvest;
- scientific fish handling from the fishing ground to landing centre;
- net fabrication/mending, boat construction and repair, motor services and maintenance, fabrication of indigenous gadgets as fishing aids, etc.;
- deep-sea/oceanic fishing and operation of navigational aids;
- post-harvest processing and preservation of fish;
- marketing and export management;
- environment impact assessment, resource assessment and conservation; and
- GIS and remote sensing.

In order to facilitate development of fishery, adequate financial support has to be provided to the Department of Fisheries

Improving the Socioeconomic Status of Fishermen and Strengthening Fishermen Co-operatives

Furthermore, in order to improve the socioeconomic status of the fishermen, their participation in the progressive activities for fisheries development is crucial. Their education and living standard needs to be upgraded by organising adult education campaigns and providing financial aid/credit facility, living quarters in colonies near major fish landing centres, health/risk coverage, credit cards similar to *kisan* cards, common facilities for ice/fish storage and fish drying, etc. During the Tenth and Eleventh FYP, financial assistance may be necessary to assist the fishermen for construction of their dwelling and creation of common amenities.

Concerted efforts are required to activate and strengthen the co-operatives of fishermen. At present, even though fishermen co-operatives exist, majority of them do not function effectively. The NCUI and Fisheries Directorate should actively promote the beneficial activities of co-operatives through awareness campaigns and participatory training. Similarly, self-help groups can be promoted to take up vocations like fishery input supply, fabrication of fishery related materials, repair of boats and motors, value addition to fish harvest for which adequate funding should be provided through financial institutions.

SEA FOOD INDUSTRY

The action plan for the development of seafood industry in ANI must encompass development of viable technologies for commercial mariculture of a spectrum of fin-fish and shellfish species, seaweed culture and the development of deep-sea fishing for ground fishes, tuna and tuna-like fishes, squid, cuttlefish, deep-sea lobsters, deep-sea shrimps, and pelagic shark. Equally important would be development of infrastructure for post-harvest support including establishment of processing facilities, transportation, marketing, promotion of scientific methods of fish preservation, fish drying, and training of people in deep-sea fishing, fish handling, and processing.

Potential for Mariculture in ANI

The sea-locked Andaman & Nicobar Islands are subject to swift winds and gales of cyclonic weather commonly prevalent during the change of monsoon. Some of the islands are also subject to sea erosion. The islands are mostly grouped and are also moderately indented. As a result there are numerous bays, lagoons, creeks, and inlets with varying depths and different substrata, which are optimal for several types of mariculture operations. Ideal situations exist for raft culture and cage culture in the bays. Shallow lagoons are suited for pen culture. Water bodies in the creeks and inlets with the adjoining land area can be used for development of shrimp/fish farms.

It has been estimated that ANI has about 37,916 ha of marshy low-lying area and mangrove swamps,[2] which under tidal influence can offer suitable site for large-

2. CMFRI, 1975.

scale cage culture operation. The low-lying areas adjacent to the numerous creeks in the islands offer excellent sites for pen culture operations. The shallow protected bays such as Ariel Bay, Blair Bay, Sawai Bay, Hut Bay, and Campbell Bay are some of the areas where cage culture of fishes can be tried.

The protected bays and mangrove-lined creeks provide the right environment for the sea-ranching programmes that could be taken up in the islands. Production of juveniles on land-based hatcheries and their release into the sea for enhancing the natural population is possible in ANI for selected high demand/value species such as *Penaeus merguiensis, Haliotis sp.*, etc.

The realisation of the mariculture potential of the islands would require creating necessary infrastructure facilities. These would include land and farm development, shore establishments, energy and water supply, transport and communication, processing, storage, and trade facilities and human resource development.

Tsunami in 2004 has opened up another challenge for the development of coastal aquaculture in Andamans. It has resulted in tidal inundation of large areas of low lying agricultural fields. There has been a northeast-southeast tilt. The northern most inhabited region in north Andamans has risen between 0.5 and 0.8 metre, whereas the South Andamans has experienced subduction of similar intensity. CARI and MPEDA had identified 600 ha of tidal marshy areas for brackish water aquaculture before the tsunami. CARI has reported that after the earthquake, more areas have been affected by increased tidal ingress of above 1 mt. rendering the low-lying fields either permanently inundated or inundated for a period of 5-6 days during spring high tides because of land subduction. This has thrown challenges as well as opportunity to develop alternative farming systems in these areas. In addition, about 1000 ha of affected agricultural fields can be brought under brackish water aquaculture. Several freshwater fish ponds were also inundated with sea-water. Some areas ideally suited for mud crab fattening like the tidal mangrove areas in North Andamans (Diglipur) have dried up as the land has been elevated making it unsuitable for aquaculture activity.

Strategy for Development of Sea Food Industry

Coastal/Brackish Water Aquaculture

Even though 600 ha of tidal marshy areas were identified for brackish water aquaculture of shrimps and fishes before the tsunami, no culture activity was initiated. This was mainly because most of the identified area was under *patta* lands. The landholders did not show interest in shrimp farming because of the acid sulphate soil which could make it uneconomical. The land subduction subsequent to tsunami has made 1,600 ha area suitable for aquaculture. In post-tsunami scenario, there is permanent inundation of coastal lands including paddy fields, which are no more suitable for agricultural purposes as they are saline affected. Hence, only eco-friendly brackish water aquaculture can be practiced in such areas.

The Action plan for fostering a post-tsunami "New Andaman Movement" submitted by M.S. Swaminathan Research Foundation to the Lt. Governor of ANI has suggested developing ANI as organic island as it has about 85 per cent forest coverage and very little human interference. Chemical fertilisers and pesticides are also used in a limited way. Organic agriculture products have higher values and the islanders are to be educated in organic farming. The report also suggested Low External Input Sustainable Aquaculture (LEISA) and integrated farming system with saline tolerant field/ plantation crops, livestock and poultry. Just as organic agriculture, organic brackish water aquaculture could be developed by educating the prospective aqua- culturists and strictly enforcing the norms of organic farming. Organic agriculture is already in practice in A&N Islands, i.e., application of cow dung is more prevalent than application of chemical fertilisers.

Hatcheries for producing shrimp seed are required to be commissioned to facilitate shrimp farming. The Rajiv Gandhi Centre for Aquaculture (RGCA) has initiated a project on production of high health shrimp and specific disease free shrimps in Andamans. This facility could provide specific disease free broodstock and *nauplii* for hatcheries.

Cage Culture of Marine Fishes

ANI has excellent credentials for introducing true mariculture of fishes in cages due to the availability of enclosed bays and creeks. Cage culture of grouper, snappers, and sea bass is the only mariculture practices that can be suitably adopted in A&N Islands. Marine fish hatcheries have to be developed for producing quality fish seeds if cage culture is to be taken up. These will generate revenue and employment. Coastal fishers can be involved in cage culture in bays, creeks and nearshore areas, while state/corporate agencies can be involved in offshore cage farming.

Lobster Fattening

The increasing demand for Indian spiny lobsters in the world market and high price for lobsters have led to overexploitation of the lobster resources in the seas around India. About one-fourth of our commercial lobster catches comprise juveniles (< 100 g. size), which fetch hardly Rs. 20-25/piece as against Rs. 140-165/ piece for well grown (200 gm. and above). India loses a substantial amount of foreign exchange by supplying juveniles to overseas countries for farming. Export earnings can be increased by promoting lobster fattening.

The Ministry of Ocean Development has developed a technology for lobster fattening in indoor tanks, and open sea cages.[3] This could be modified to suit the island conditions. Projection of profit by lobster fattening programme sea cage culture for four sq. m area is given in Tables 8.7.

Mud-Crab Fattening

Scylla serrata (red crab) and *Scylla tranquebarica* (green crab) are the common mud crabs found in ANI, which have a good demand in the international market. The fishermen in ANI sell small crabs and commercial sized post-moult stage crabs ('water crabs') at very low prices to the exporters, who transport them live to foreign countries, where they are cultured or fattened for selling at a much higher price. Central Agricultural Research Institute, Port Blair has standardised the technology of culture of mud crab in tide fed brackish water ponds in Andamans. The Ministry of Ocean Development has also developed methods for crab fattening. Promotion of crab fattening is desirable in view of its potential for value addition. Estimates of profits from mud crab fattening are provided in Table 8.8.

Mussel Culture

Amongst the gourmet seafood, the mussels, green and blue, rank high along with the oysters and lobsters in terms of market demand. In the estuarine and marine biotopes of the Indian coast, the green mussel, *Perna viridis* is found commonly in the inter-tidal region.

Taking advantage of the above biological attributes, the green mussels can profitably be grown on mass scale under partially controlled environmental conditions. In tropical waters like India, rope and raft culture techniques are the best suited considering the high yield rate of this three-dimensional culture

TABLE 8.7

Projection of Profit from Lobster Fattening Programme through Sea Cage Culture for Four sq. m. Area

1.	I. Capital cost:Construction of MS cage (1.2 m x 1.5 m x 1.5 m)	10000	—
2.	II Working cost:Cost of juvenile (200 pieces) Rs.-25/piece*	5000	—
	II Working cost:		
3.	Feed cost (1200 kg clam with shell @ Rs. 5/kg)	6000	-
4.	Maintenance cost (Rs.-150/moth)	750	-
	Total Investment for fist crop (I + II)	21750	-
5.	III Projected sale price: Projected sale price per crop (180 No. x 250 g) @ Rs. 700/kg.	31500	
6.	Projected profit for first crop (5 months)		11750
7.	Second crop		21750
8.	Third crop		21750
9.	Fourth crop		21750
10.	Fifth crop		21750
	Overall profit in 2 years (subjected to factors mentioned below).		98750

Stocking are	:	8 sq. m	Stocking density	:	25/ sq. m
Stocking number	:	200	Harvesting size	:	> 250 gm
Stocking size	:	100 g	Fattening period	:	5 months
Survival	:	90 per cent	Life of cage	:	24 years
No. of crops	:	4 crops	(if maintained properly)		

Note: * Depending upon the effort made by beneficiary, the profit will vary. From the second crop onwards cost of cage can be added to the profit. If the beneficiary is able to arrange the juveniles and feed from wild, relevant cost can be added to the profit.

Source: Projected by Author.

3. The cage design, erection of cage, selection of suitable site for open sea cage culture and dissemination of technology for lobster fattening under captive conditions have been successfully carried out by MoOD/NIOT by involving the fishermen in farming and maintenance of cages.

TABLE 8.8

Economics of Mud Crab Fattening

SYSTEM- I	
Nature of crab:	Commercial sized water crabs (freshly moulted)
No. of cages	9 nos.
Total no. of crabs in ten cages:	90 nos.
No. of crabs stocked per cage:	10 nos.
Total fattening period:	one month
Average harvesting size:	500 gm
Production from the ten cages with 90 % survival	44.5 kg
Non-Recurring:	
Making of cages (total 10 nos.) @ Rs. 1300/cage	Rs. 13000.00
Sub-total (A)	Rs. 13000.00
Recurring:	
1. Cost of water crabs of commercial size @ 500 grams/crab @ Rs. 60/ kg	Rs. 2700.00
2. Feed cost @ FCR 1:1.5 Rs. 20 / kg for 70 kg	Rs. 1400.00
3. Miscellaneous	Rs. 50.00
Sub-total (B)	Rs. 4150.00
Total production (@ 90 % survival)	44.5 kg
Gross-income (@ Rs. 250/kg)	Rs. 11125.00
Net-income (Gross income – (B + 10%A)	Rs. 5675.00
SYSTEM- II	
Nature of crab:	Mud crab juveniles of 300-350 grams in cages
No. of cages	10 nos.
Total no. of crabs in ten cages	90 nos.
No. of crabs stocked per cage:	9 nos.
Total fattening period:	three months
Average harvesting size:	500 gm
Production from the ten cages with 90 % survival	40.5 kg
Non-Recurring Cost:	
Making of cages (total 10 nos.) @ Rs. 1300/cage	Rs. 13000.00
Sub-total (A)	Rs. 13000.00
Recurring Cost:	
1. Cost of crabs juveniles @ Rs. 50/ kg	Rs. 1350.00
2. Feed cost @ FCR 1:1.8 Rs. 20 / kg	Rs. 1456.00
3. Miscellaneous	Rs. 50.00
Sub-total (B)	Rs. 4970.00
Total production (@ 90 % Survival)	40.5 kg
Gross-Income (@ Rs. 250/Kg)	Rs. 10125.00
Net-Income (Gross income – (B + 10%A)	Rs. 5989.00

Notes: (i) The life of the cage is 10 months and 6 crops in a year could easily be obtained in the first system of fattening; and a minimum of 2 crops in the second system mentioned above, if farmers maintain the cages properly. The total net income in a year through 6 crops, in the first system, after allowing for depreciation for the cage will be Rs. 34050.00.

(ii) If the fishermen are fabricating the cages using indigenously available materials, namely cane, bamboo, arica nut logs, short-length wood from sawmills, etc. the cost indicated under the heading 'Non-Recurring' will be much less and hence will help the fishermen to get better returns.

(iii) If the fishermen are catching the crab juveniles/water crabs on their own, there will not be any expenditure on the stocking material, which will again add to the net returns.

(iv) If the fishermen are feeding the crabs with trash fish, clam, mussel, etc., which they themselves fish or collect, then there will not be any expenditure on the feed, which will further add to the net returns.

Source: Estimated by Author.

system. CARI has developed mussel culture technology in Bay Islands.

The mussel grows at an average rate of 8-10 mm per month under the rope culture technique as against 3-5 mm per month in natural bed. The mussels attain marketable size of 60-70 mm within a period of 18-20 weeks and are harvested by hand-picking. This technology could be introduced in ANI at selected locations particularly in the semi-enclosed bays.

The estimated production per hectare per year is 480 tonne with shell-on (168 tonne of meat) and on a rope the mussel production is up to 23 kg. per metre. A cost benefit analysis shows 181 per cent return on investment.

Marine Ornamental Fish Breeding and Export

Tropical ornamental fishes can be bred successfully only if a tropical climate is provided with a low cost hatchery. It would be cheaper to set up fish farms and hatcheries at places where there are no extreme climatic conditions. Breeding centres can have earthen grow out ponds, cemented cisterns/tanks and glass aquaria where breeding operations could be undertaken. Efficient packaging of ornamental fishes plays a key role in the success of the export trade. Breeding of marine ornamental fishes have got excellent scope in A&N Islands and may be a trade to reckon with. The advent of jet cargo services has brought new markets for ornamental fishes within selling distance while packing methods have been developed which ensure protection of high quality and internationally acceptable product. Healthy, well-fed fish, starved for at least 24 hours before packing can often withstand a 48 -56 hours journey.

Farming and Pearl Production in Black Lip Pearl Oyster

Surveys conducted in India have shown that black-lip pearl oyster (*P. margaritifera)* is available around ANI in low densities. During the Tenth FYP period, a project for culture of black-lip pearl has been initiated by the Centre for Marine Living Resources and Ecology (CMLRE), Kochi, in ANI involving an estimated outlay of Rs. 1 crore. Under this project, a detailed survey will be conducted to estimate the natural stock of the oyster in the island. Commercial scale production of cultured black pearls will be carried out. A suitable technology for black-lip pearl oyster farming will be developed and through hatchery systems the stock will be replenished. Central Marine Fisheries Research Institute, Kochi shall carry out the project in collaboration with CARI. Production of black pearl from black-lip pearl oysters is also a promising avenue in these islands.

Trochus and Turbo Culture

Because of the increasing value and demand for the shell, overexploitation of these species from many of the islands around mainland and ANI is very much evident.

The breeding and rearing of *Trochus* and *Turbo* are technically possible. The mass culture and transplantation practices of these species have been developed in Thailand, Indonesia, and Malaysia. Sea farming and resource management of these species are generally combined to protect the populations, either by limiting the size or amount of catch, restricting seasons or establishing sanctuaries. However, in India, the culture technology is yet to be developed.

The Ministry of Environment and Forests vide notification dated 5th December 2001, brought these species under Schedule IV of the Wildlife (Protection) Act 1972. Therefore, concerted efforts have to be put in for undertaking an in-depth study of the resources, their conservation and enhancement. Sea ranching would also be helpful for conserving these species in ANI.

With the above-mentioned problems and prospects, the project envisaged for implementation by the Ministry of Ocean Development during the Tenth FYP has the following objectives:

- To develop state-of-the-art technology for *Turbo* and *Trochus* seed production and reseeding and transplantation of the island waters to prevent the depletion of these economically important and endangered species through conservation and management of the stock in depleted areas around islands.
- To enhance the *Trochus* and *Turbo* resources in Andaman Islands through mass breeding, rearing, culture, and sea ranching.

Under this project a general survey will be made on the distribution, abundance and overexploited areas of *Trochus niloticus* and *Turbo marmoratus* around Andaman group of islands and mapped using remote sensing and GIS and a resource map will be prepared for identifying the biotypes suitable for trochus and turbo resources. The survey will also include selection of suitable sites for sea ranching considering the movement of juveniles after release, possible predators, and relationship between types of bottom on the survival rates.

A hatchery will be established for spawning, larval rearing and mass culture of juveniles, at Port Blair in a suitable location by the Andaman & Nicobar Centre for

Ocean Science and Technology (ANCOST) of MOOD/ NIOT for ranching in the Andaman seas in order to enhance the natural stock. In the hatchery, mass production of algae (for example, *Navicula* species) for feeding the larval stages has to be carried out. Production and mass culture of larvae and juveniles will be carried out. The juveniles produced have to be tagged and released in overexploited areas and new areas in Andaman islands for assessing the impact of ranching on population increase.

For conservation of the resources and technology, demonstration and training programmes will be conducted to transfer the technology to the user community. The island community will be involved in the management of these resources.

Seaweed Culture

Sea weeds or marine algae grow abundantly in the shallow seas, estuaries and back waters.[4] About 700 species of marine algae have been recorded from different parts of Indian coast including ANI and Lakshadweep. Of these, nearly 60 species are commercially important seaweeds. It is estimated that the total standing crop of all seaweeds in Indian waters is more than one lakh tonne (net weight) consisting of 6,000 tonne (net weight) of *agar* yielding seaweeds, 16,000 tonne (net weight) of algin yielding seaweeds and the remaining quantity of edible and other seaweeds.

Although there is some scope for seaweed culture in ANI caution needs to be exercised in view of its adverse implications for coral reef. Seaweed culture poses a threat to the balance of coral reef ecosystems. In coral reef ecosystems, there is big competition for hard substratum. The algae (seaweed) grow more quickly than the corals and smother them, especially the young corals looking to get a foothold on the reef. After the tsunami, corals have suffered heavily and regeneration of corals will take decades. In view of this sea weed culture in nearshore water is not advisable in the post-tsunami scenario.

Deep Ocean Water Aquaculture

Tropical oceanic islands like ANI have good scope for utilisation of Deep Ocean Water (DOW) for energy production, refrigeration, desalination, aquaculture, cold agriculture, neutraceutical and DOW beverages production. An excellent example of DOW water use is demonstrated by the Natural Energy Laboratory of Hawaii Authority (NELHA) at Hawaii. Similar technology development using DOW should be explored and established in ANI by the end of the Eleventh Plan. The NIOT is going ahead with this plan. It has successfully commissioned Low Temperature Thermal Desalination (LTTD) plant at Kavaratti in Lakshadweep and many more such plants are planned in other islands of Lakshadweep. Similar plants can be commissioned in ANI. LTTD plants draw large quantity of deep seawater from about 350 m deep which can be utilised for DOW aquaculture. The DOW can be extracted from still deeper waters if necessary.

Seafood Processing

Around 70 per cent of the fish catch in ANI is consumed fresh. The details of cold storage and other processing facilities now available/under construction in various centres (Marine Products Export Development Authority (MPEDA, 2001) is given in Table 8.3. Existing markets lack necessary facilities[4] and remain under-utilised/ unutilised. There are around 57 landing centres in the UT of which 12 have been identified for setting up infrastructures such as ramp, auction hall, net repairing hall, drying platform, boat repairing facility, ice plant, and chill fish storage.[5]

At present the fish landings from distant places like Diglipur, Mayabundar, to Port Blair is transported by motorised crafts. It is essential to provide better transportation facilities for fish catches, so as to reach the end-users in prime condition. Mobile refrigerated containers may be ideal for island conditions especially for the transport of fish from North Andaman to Port Blair.

The administration has already taken up construction of cold storage at various places as per the recommendations of the earlier committees. Further, cold storage and other post-harvest facilities should be developed only after careful examination of the utilisation and viability of the existing facilities. There is scope for construction of a chilling plant at Campbell Bay when the tuna vessels are introduced and commence operation. The construction of such facilities under private sector should be encouraged.

In view of the low investment and high returns, the possibility of entrepreneurs investing in projects for live fish export seems quite high. Live fish is a high value product and thus may be given priority over chilled fish and frozen fish when investment decisions are made.

4. Proper ventilation, drainage, availability of fresh water, space for dumping or clearing fish waste.

5. Some suggestions on processing and packaging of marine products are given in Annexure 8.1.

In order to encourage fish processing in ANI, the Administration may consider providing finance by way of grant over and above such assistance offered by the central government. Andaman & Nicobar Islands Development Corporation (ANIIDCO) may consider extending term loan for investment in fish processing at 4 per cent interest rate up to 50 per cent of the cost of technical civil work and machinery. The rest of the term loan may be at an interest rate not more than 9 per cent.

In order to meet the requirement of personnel in fish processing units, it is essential to train the local youth in institutions such as CIFT. The cost of such training should be met by the administration.

Summing Up

The development of seafood industry in Andaman & Nicobar Islands depends mainly on the policies framed by the ANI administration. While some progress has been made, it is far from being adequate to make any significant impact. The new policy should provide for augmenting the supply of the raw material such as finfish, shellfish, and seaweed through capture and culture fisheries. In the case of mud crab fattening, lobster fattening, seaweed farming, etc. technology could be provided by the various institutions located in ANI, such as Andaman & Nicobar Centre for Ocean Science and Technology (ANCOST) of Ministry of Ocean Development (MoOD)/National Institute of Ocean Technology (NIOT), Central Agricultural Research Institute (CARI) and the Fisheries Department. The funding support for such activities could come either from the lead/commercial banks, National Bank for Agricultural and Rural Development (NABARD) and the Fisheries Department of Andaman & Nicobar Administration from the budgetary allocations made for fisheries related activities.

To develop the seafood industry, the ANI Administration should promote the private sector involvement by providing funding support, tax holidays and augmenting infrastructure and communication support. With the upgradation of the airport at Port Blair and introduction of chartered flights to and from the countries of Southeast Asia, it will be possible to directly export live, fresh and value added marine products. This will reduce the cost of transportation. An appropriate branding and quality certification, such as 'A' quality produce from pollution free environs of ANI will provide an edge and additional value to the islands' marine products.

Rational exploitation of marine fishery resources and expansion of tourism are the two sectors that can contribute substantially to the economic development of ANI. The islands are endowed with rich biodiversity niches that need to be protected. But there are many sites in the bays, creeks and near shore areas in the islands, faraway from the biodiversity hotspots, that are ideally suited for introduction of sea farming of marine fish and shellfish. Such areas have to be identified and appropriate technology packages should be developed for introducing near shore mariculture involving coastal fishers and more capital intensive offshore farming involving state/corporate agencies. Similarly, introduction of Oceanic Fish Aggregating Devices (FADs) to exploit hither- to untapped oceanic fishes and artificial reefs in near shore areas for catching high value target fishes will enhance the marine fish productivity and export revenue. A planned introduction of such activities with rigorous safeguards to protect the biodiversity would generate employment and enhance the livelihood security of the islanders. Protection of environment and development should complement each other and should be judiciously harmonised to enhance the economic development of ANI. In addition, introduction of eco-labelling in ANI would bring its own safeguards against use of destructive gears and fishing practices. Proper implementation of such a policy would take care of the environmental concerns raised by some organisations regarding the development of marine fisheries in ANI.

Recommendations

- Make changes in fishing craft and gear to suit the exploitation of coastal and oceanic pelagics like tunas.
- Introduce fishing craft having 10 m LOA designed by CIFT.
- Fleet of mechanised boats should be increased to 50-90 by the end of Eleventh FYP.
- Engage private long liners/purse seiners for exploitation of oceanic tunas.
- Deploy oceanic FADs and educate the fishermen in FAD fishing.
- Initiate measures to get ecomark for marine fisheries produce from A&N islands.
- Introduce Marine Fisheries Regulation Act.
- Improve infrastructure for fish landings by constructing landing centres and a major fishing harbour in Campbell Bay.

- Educate fishermen in modern methods of fishing.
- Strengthen and activate fishermen co-operatives.
- Introduce integrated brackish water farming in tidal inundated areas and introduce the concept of organic farming.
- Introduce cage culture of marine fishes and hatcheries for production of fish seeds.
- Introduce lobster fattening in sea cages in selected areas.
- Expand mud crab fattening in mangrove pens.
- Introduce/develop technology for breeding and farming of black-lip pearl oyster.
- Introduce/develop technology for breeding and rearing of marine ornamental fishes.
- Develop technology for breeding, sea ranching and farming Trochus and Turbo for shell craft export.
- Introduce seaweed culture in selected areas.
- Introduce/develop technology for DOW aquaculture.
- Improve infrastructure for fish storage, processing and transport.

ANNEXURE 8.1

Processed Products

Frozen Prawns (Shrimp)

Type of Products: whole, headless, fantail round, fantail deveined, butterfly, raw peeled or peeled undeveined, peeled and deveined, cooked and peeled, peeled and cooked, deveined and cooked and whole cooked.

Frozen Lobster

Type of Products: Lobster tail (as shatter pack or individually as individual quick frozen (IQF]), lobster whole (individual pieces in polythene and frozen immediately), lobster meat (as blocks, shatter pack or as IQF), cooked lobster whole (frozen individually), cooked lobster tails (wrap individually in polythene and freeze as IQF).

Frozen mud crab (*Scylla serrata*) meat

Frozen cuttlefish

Type of Products: Cuttlefish is frozen in the following ways; whole (can be individually quick frozen or frozen as shatter pack.), fillets/flat pack (pack in polythene line waxed duplex cartons and add glaze water), rolled pack (pack as blocks, shatter pack or IQF), fillets with/without tentacles (pack as blocks, shatter pack or IQF).

Frozen squid

Squid is frozen in the following ways; squid whole, whole cleaned (pack as blocks, shatter pack or IQF), rolled pack, tube (pack as shatter pack or IQF), cylinder, tentacles squid fillets (pack as blocks), wings/fins (pack as blocks), rings (pack as blocks or IQF), headless/tube skin (pack as shatter pack or IQF).

Dried squid

Dried mussel meat

Fish Maws and icinglass

Air bladder of a number of species like eel (*Uraena sp.*), ghol (*Protonibea diacanthus*), catfish (*Tachysurus sp.*), kalawa (*Seramus sp.*), constitute the raw material for fish maws and icinglass. These products are useful as clarifying agent for wine, beer and vinegar. They can also be used as an adhesive base for glass and pottery and sizing agents in textiles, Indian ink and confectionery.

Canned crab meat (in brine)

Canned Sardines (natural pack)

Canned tuna

Shark fin rays

Fish wafers

Fish fingers

Shark liver oil

Squalene used in cosmetics, pharmaceuticals, medicines, lubricants and as bactericide

Fishmeal

High gel strength agar from seaweeds

Chapter 9

Small-scale, Village and Forest Based Industries

There is little industrial activity in the UT. The recent years have, in fact, seen a decline in industrial output owing to closure of wood based industrial units. There is no large-scale industry in Andaman & Nicobar Islands. As on March 2003, there was only one medium scale industry and 1531 small-scale and village industrial units.

This chapter is organised as follows: The next section provides an overview of the organisational set-up, industrial policy, and the number and type of industries in ANI. Section 9.3 assesses the status of industrial development in ANI in terms of its contribution to GSDP and employment followed by Section 9.4, which identifies factors inhibiting industrial development in the UT. Section 9.5 discusses the challenges facing the village and tiny industry and identifies potential areas for tiny units.

Organisational Set-up, Industrial Policy and Infrastructure in ANI

Small scale industries[1] (SSIs) are an important segment of the Indian economy that constitutes around 95 per cent of the industrial units, 40 per cent output of the manufacturing sector, 36 per cent of the exports, and provides direct employment to around 18 million people (SIDBI, 2000). The Government of India, through its industrial policies prevalent from time to time has evolved a set of supportive measures for promotion of SSIs. The main elements of India's supportive policy measures are reservation for SSIs, fiscal concessions by way of lower excise duties, preferential allocation and subsidisation of bank credit, extension of business services, and preferential procurement by the government from small-scale enterprises.[2]

In ANI, several steps have been taken to encourage industrial development. The entire territory of ANI has been declared as an industrially backward area, category-A, by the Government of India and hence it enjoys special facilities for the promotion of industries. The government set up Andaman & Nicobar Industrial Development Corporation (ANIDCO) to accelerate industrial development. The incentives and other supportive measures extended by the industries department in ANI (Annexure 9.1) can be categorised into nine groups. These are: financial assistance to the entrepreneurs, training and skill upgradation, extension of marketing support, transport subsidy, infrastructure subsidy, interest subsidy under the Prime Minister Rojgar Yojna (PMRY), infrastructure development, budgetary support as grant-in-aid to Khadi and Village Industries Board (KVIB), and other services. Details of these schemes are presented in Annexure 9.2.

In addition, credit is extended under the PMRY and by the KVIB. The KVIB has identified 15 village industries for providing financial, technical, and marketing support. Other organisations namely, Andaman & Nicobar Islands Integrated Development Corporation, A&N Consultancy Centre, Small Industries Services Institute, Coconut Development Board also work for promotion of small-scale and village industries in this

1. Different agencies define SSI differently. The Planning Commission for instance considers the entire village and small-scale industries sector as SSI sector. The National Sample Survey Organisation defines the entire industrial sector in terms of organised and unorganised segments, as well as in terms of industrial enterprises run by households and non-households. The Central Excise Department identifies SSIs on the basis of their annual turnover.

2. In spite of many natural advantages such as high labour intensity, positive income distribution effect, ability to export, scope to use local resources, potential for balanced regional development, capacity to promote entrepreneurship, flexibility in operation, lower startup costs, it is believed that it is difficult for SSIs to survive under normal market conditions due to imperfections in the markets. Therefore, government intervention through various incentives and other support is viewed as desirable and essential for the development of SSIs.

union territory. However, there appears to be little coordination between these agencies.

A Directorate of Industries headed by the Director of Industries looks into the design and implementation of schemes for promotion of industrial development, training and skill upgradation, extension of marketing support, consultancy services to entrepreneurs, etc. There are 8 functional Industrial Estates (IE), and 16 industrial training centres for imparting training on various activities like carpentry, tailoring, coir processing, food processing, cane, bamboo and sea shell handicrafts (Annexure 9.3 and 9.4). In addition, the ANI administration organises entrepreneurship development programme and provides other consultancy services to encourage unemployed youth and prospective entrepreneurs to set up their own units.

The new industrial policy of ANI emphasises on industries that are based on locally available resources. The policy aims at promoting industries like fishery, tourism, cane and bamboo based industry, rubber, coir and coconut based industries, agro-based and food processing industry. It proposes to also promote other industry like boat building and repairing, automobile bodybuilding, packaging and other service-oriented industries. The policy also lays emphasis on development of electronic industry, as A&N Islands offer a dust free climatic condition considered ideal for electronic industry. However, no clear strategy seems to have been identified to move towards achieving these policy goals.

Number, Type and Location of Industries

As noted earlier, there is no large-scale industry in Andaman & Nicobar Islands. As on March 2003, there was only one medium scale industry and 1,531 industrial units in small-scale and tiny sector (Table 9.1a to 9.1b). Of these, engineering based industries were the largest category comprising 21.16 per cent of the total small-scale industries followed by wood-based industry (15.74). Agro-based, food-based and textile-based industries constituted 8.68, 7.18 and 7.05 per cent, respectively. Besides, there are 64 marine-based industries and 2 coir-based industries though raw material for such industry is available in abundance. The regional distribution of industry shows that 78 per cent of the total number of units is located in South Andaman (Table 9.2a). This is partly explained by its proximity to Port Blair urban area and availability of infrastructural facilities around the city. Nicobar group of islands has only 49 industries (Table 9.2b).

Contribution of Secondary Sector to GSDP

The contribution of secondary sector to GSDP has shown a declining trend in the recent years. The contribution of this sector to GSDP at 1993-94 prices although increased from 19.87 per cent in 1993-94 to 27.53 per cent in 1997-98, it has declined to 22 per cent in 1999-00 and has stagnated thereafter. While the share of primary sector has also declined, the share of tertiary sector has shown a steady increase during this period. Contribution of secondary sector to the growth of GSDP, in ANI, at constant 1993-94 prices grew at impressive 11.84 per cent per annum between 1993-94 and 1997-98 when compared with the performance of the primary sector of the economy. However, contribution of this sector to GSDP in absolute terms sharply declined from Rs. 176.8 crore in 1997-98 to Rs. 119.5 crore in 1998-99 (at 1993-94 prices), showed recovery in 1999-2000 but has stagnated thereafter (Tables 9.3 and 9.4). This suggests relatively low exploitation of growth potential of the secondary sector.

Within the secondary sector both manufacturing and construction sectors grew at 8.5 per cent and 13.3 per year, respectively, during 1993-94 to 1997-98. Registered manufacturing grew at a relatively higher rate (9.2 per cent) than that of unregistered manufacturing (7.4 per cent) (Table 9.4). Due to lack of data, the growth trend in industrial sub-sectors could not be analysed for more recent years. However, our hunch is that the decline in contribution of secondary sector to GSDP after 1997-98 is largely due to the poor

TABLE 9.1A

Medium Scale Industries in A&N Islands 1996-2003

Category	*1996-97*	*1997-98*	*1998-99*	*1999-00*	*2000-01*	*2001-02*	*2002-03*
Wood based	4	4	4	4	4	closed	Closed
Chemical based	1	1	1	1	1	1	1
Total	5	5	5	5	5	1	1

Source: Directorate of Industries, Andaman & Nicobar Islands

TABLE 9.1B

Small Scale Industries in A&N Islands 1996-2003

Category	*1996-97*	*1997-98*	*1998-99*	*1999-00*	*2000-01*	*2001-02*	*2002-03*
Wood based	200	201	201	202	236	238	241
Agro based	118	120	121	123	123	127	133
Marine Based	56	57	58	60	60	62	64
Food based	90	91	96	99	101	103	110
Mineral Based	64	64	67	70	72	74	78
Chemical Based	38	38	39	39	39	39	39
Engineering based	259	267	280	281	283	300	324
Leather based	6	6	7	6	6	9	9
Textile Based	80	86	89	94	95	97	108
Coir based	2	2	2	2	2	2	2
Rubber based	1	2	2	2	2	2	2
Miscellaneous	232	262	284	318	342	368	421
Total	1146	1196	1246	1296	1361	1421	1531

Source: Directorate of Industries, Andaman & Nicobar Islands

TABLE 9.2A

Region-wise Small-Scale Industries in A&N Island as on 31.03.2003

Category	*South Andaman*	*Middle Andaman*	*North Andaman*	*Nicobar Ialands*	*Total*
Wood based	182	23	31	05	241
Agro based	91	17	09	16	133
Marine based	54	03	04	03	64
Food based	72	16	12	10	110
Mineral based	63	06	09	0	78
Chemical based	39	0	0	0	39
Engineering based	290	19	11	04	324
Leather based	93	08	03	04	108
Textile based	93	08	03	04	108
Coir based	02	-	-	-	02
Miscellaneous	299	74	43	07	423
Total	1278	174	125	53	1630

Source: Directorate of Industries, Andaman & Nicobar Islands.

TABLE 9.2B

District-wise Distribution of Small-Scale and Village Industries 2002-2003

District	*No. of Units*	*Employment (Number)*	*Investment (Rs. Lakh)*	*Production (Rs. Lakh)*
Andaman	1482	7109	927.93	6914.09
Nicobar	49	196	37.88	228.6
Total	1531	7305	965.81	7142.69

Source: Directorate of Industries, Andaman & Nicobar Islands.

performance of manufacturing sector. Invariably, the growth of an economy is accompanied by relatively higher contribution from the secondary sector, particularly manufacturing and construction. To give boost to secondary sector it would be prudent to focus on production of goods that would result in reduction of imports and increase in exports. In achieving this, a conducive environment is necessary. In this context, the government has an important role of a facilitator.

Employment in Industrial Sector

As per the 1991 census, the secondary sector in ANI employed over 23 per cent of the total workforce. In more recent years, while employment in manufacturing sector has increased marginally from 7.1 per cent of the total workforce in 1993-94 to 7.9 per cent in 1999-2000,[3] the share of construction has declined from 12.2 per cent of the total workforce in 1993-94 to 10 per cent in 1999-2000. The secondary sector as a whole employed 23.2 per cent of the total workforce during 1993-94, which declined to 19.4 per cent in 1999-2000. While it is true that the closure of wood-based industries have contributed to this trend, it needs to be recognised that new employment opportunities have not been created. Incidence of unemployment in ANI is significantly higher than for the country as a whole (for details see Chapter 12). What is more worrying is that

3. NSSO Surveys, 50th and 55th round.

TABLE 9.3

Contribution of Industrial Sector to GSDP at Constant (1993-94) Prices

(Rs. Lakh)

Industry of Origin	*1993-94*	*1994-95*	*1995-96*	*1996-97*	*1997-98*	*1998-99*	*1999-00*	*2000-01*	*2001-02*
Manufacturing	4146	4944	4772	6033	6241				
Registered	2619	3376	2956	4121	4060				
Unregistered	1527	1568	1816	1912	2181				
Construction	5847	8986	8429	8653	10928				
Electricity, gas and water supply	114.24	-174.71	-24.68	1049.42	515.44				
Total secondary sector	10107.24	13755.29	13176.32	15735.42	17684.44	11951.04	14597.41	13843.42	14117.23
Total GSDP	50868.63	56070.94	55728.91	59628.95	64223.2	59815	64791	61801	62911
Contribution of secondary sector to GSDP(%)	19.87	24.53	23.64	26.39	27.53	19.98	22.53	22.40	22.44
Contribution of primary sector to GSDP(%)	42.34	38.47	38.76	35.06	30.20	32.60	28.94	30.22	30.08
Contribution of tertiary sector to GSDP(%)	37.8	37	37.59	38.55	42.26	47.43	48.53	47.38	47.48

Source: *A&N Islands Basic Statistics*—1996-97 to 1998-99. DE&S. ANI.

TABLE 9.4

Growth of Secondary Sector (1993-94 to 1997-98)

(Percentage)

Industry of Origin	*Compound Annual Growth Rate (CAGR)*
Manufacturing	8.5
I) Registered	9.2
ii) Unregistered	7.4
Construction	13.3
Electricity, gas & water	35.17
Total secondary	11.8
Primary sector	-6.5
Tertiary sector	6.69
Total GSDP	4.8

Source: Estimated by Author.

the high unemployment is coupled with declining labour productivity.

Employment, Investment and Production in SSIs

Table 9.5 presents data on production, investment, employment, and number of firms in respect of small-scale industries in Andaman & Nicobar Islands. By cumulating this data we have computed the growth rate of average production, average investment, and average employment per firm (see Figure 9.1). It would be seen from the figure that between 1982-83 and 1995-96 there was stagnation in average production, investment and employment with the exception of the year 1988-89. After 1995-96, while the investment and production show some recovery the employment shows no change. We derive two more variables namely; marginal productivity of capital (MPK) and marginal productivity of labour (MPL) from Table 9.6. MPK is increment in production/increment in investment, and MPL is increment in production/increment in employment.

It is seen from Figure 9.2 that while MPK has increased, MPL has declined, which suggests that there has been technological progress. This technological improvement has been a capital augmenting one. As a result, the growth rate of average labour intake of the

FIGURE 9.1

Behaviour of Marginal Productivity of Capital and Labour

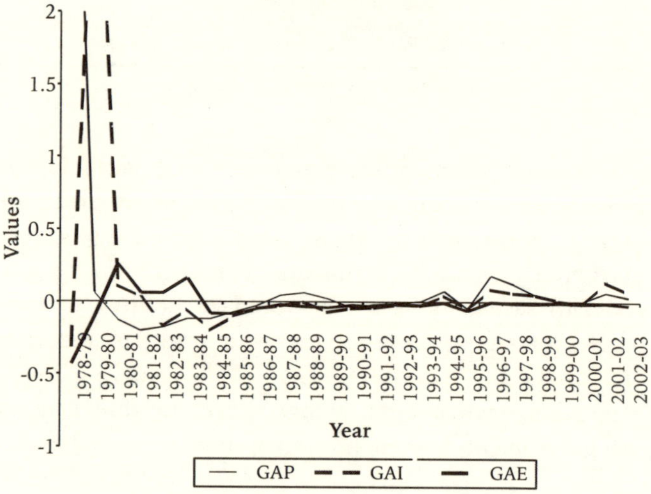

Source: Estimated by Author.

TABLE 9.5

Employment, Investment and Production in Small-Scale Sector in ANI

Year	No. of Unit	Employment (in Number)	Investment (Rs. Lakh)	Production (Rs. Lakh)
1978	10	97	2.84	12.72
1978-79	61	296	11.13	442.61
1979-80	27	93	73.85	211.29
1980-81	21	257	30.25	41.05
1981-82	36	284	40.21	29.98
1982-83	47	393	13.49	54.53
1983-84	39	549	21.71	41.92
1984-85	86	491	17.33	164.50
1985-86	82	361	27.30	163.95
1986-87	67	307	26.17	157.30
1987-88	66	371	28.77	251.41
1988-89	66	298	35.28	300.34
1989-90	78	323	15.44	284.81
1990-91	73	338	19.14	137.85
1991-92	70	252	17.27	171.50
1992-93	61	269	20.35	156.55
1993-94	57	198	13.93	179.74
1994-95	53	253	42.64	376.44
1995-96	102	197	21.84	163.19
1996-97	44	217	62.84	757.87
1997-98	50	190	57.07	698.61
1998-99	50	193	55.07	418.81
1999-00	50	202	29.88	227.47
2000-01	65	255	24.07	307.71
2001-02	60	239	133.51	661.57
2002-03	110	382	124.43	728.97
Total	1531	7305	965.81	7142.69

Source: Directorate of Industries, Andaman & Nicobar Islands

FIGURE 9.2

Behaviour of Marginal Productivity of Capital and Labour

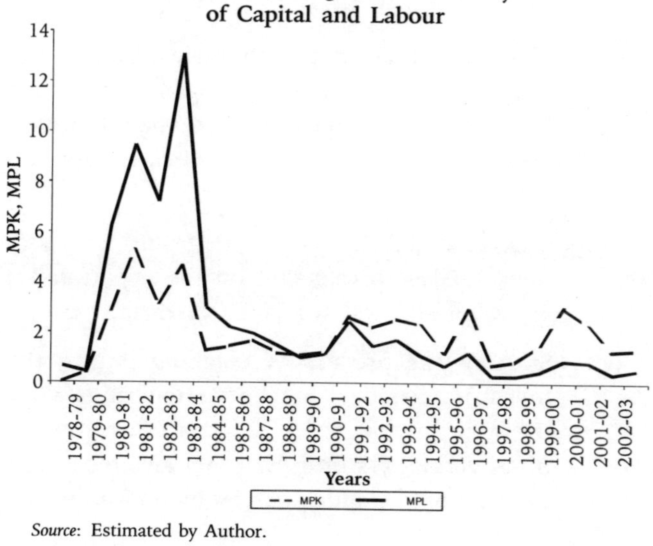

Source: Estimated by Author.

firms has gone down and at the same time the growth rate of average capital usage has gone up.

9.3.3 Performance of Registered Factory Sector

An analysis of the ASI data in respect of registered factory sector shows that the number of registered factories has increased from 52 in 1990-91 to 79 in 1997-98. The fixed capital and working capital also grew at 27.4 per cent and 20.42 per cent per annum, respectively, during 1990-91 to 1995-96. However, during the period 1996-97 to 1997-98 while growth in fixed capital has stagnated, working capital has declined sharply in absolute terms from Rs. 53.53 crore in 1995-96 to Rs. 21.08 crore in 1997-98. Further, although growth in value of output, between 1990-91 and 1995-96 was 20.9 per cent, which was comparable to performance in a number of states and at all-India level, the value of output has declined from Rs. 167.9 crore in 1995-96 to Rs. 158.83 crore in 1997-98. The growth in employment was also negative during the period (Table 9.6).

Among the registered factories, 39.24 per cent industries manufacture wood products and 36.71 per cent industries produce electricity. Other industries in this union territory are: food products, paper and paper products, leather and leather products, transport equipment, scientific equipment, watches and clocks, photographic and cinematographic equipment, etc. There are also some units in printing, publishing, and repair of goods.

Issues

Industries grow when the demand for their products grows. If the local market is small and does not provide enough demand then external markets are needed. Moreover, the output has to be sold competitively. Markets in ANI are small and access to outside markets is constrained owing to various factors including transport disadvantage. Other inherent inhibiting factors are physical remoteness, difficult terrain, and high marketing and transport costs. Further, local motivation to initiate business enterprises seems low; transport, water and power conditions are still poor, leasing land by investors from outside the UT is a tenuous process and access to ANI is expensive and cumbersome. The industrial policies so far in ANI, have not been able to overcome these and thus have failed to attract any noticeable amount of private investment in industry either locally or from outside.

TABLE 9.6

CAGR of Registered Factories during 1990-91 to 1995-96

(Percentage)

Items	*A&N Islands*	*Chandigarh*	*Delhi*	*Pondicherry*	*Punjab*	*Tamil Nadu*	*Maharashtra*	*West Bengal*	*All-India*
1. Number of factories	4.83	3.13	0.84	3.23	1.68	5.27	4.69	2.45	3.39
2. Fixed capital	27.49	20.85	25.50	35.66	15.67	17.78	17.78	18.38	17.31
3. Working capital	20.42	16.25	10.29	27.84	13.93	15.71	19.86	13.04	16.75
4. Number of workers	6.49	1.26	2.77	3.46	2.19	4.40	2.79	1.99	3.23
5. Number of employees	7.68	1.99	2.88	3.44	2.78	4.27	3.44	1.81	3.52
6. Value of output	20.92	14.25	17.64	19.85	13.70	16.86	15.91	11.57	16.33

Note: Computed from Annual Survey of Industries data.

The Way Ahead

There are at least three striking areas of strength:

- relatively high literacy rates and good health status as compared to most other states of the country;
- an abundant natural resources endowment; and
- potential for exports of seafood, agro-based products, medicinal plants, and horticulture products.

Given the abundant natural resource endowment in ANI, it would be prudent that its development strategy is based on sustainable exploitation of natural resources. The following sectors will play important roles in this context: fishery, agro-based fresh and processed products, medicinal plants and horticultural products, cane and bamboo and related industries, and handicrafts. While the first three industrial sectors are dealt with in specific chapters devoted to them, this chapter explores what has constrained the growth of these sectors, and what needs to be done to promote industrial growth in ANI?

(i) Industrial promotion strategy should be based on encouraging private investment not through subsidies but by improvements in infrastructural facilities and easing the process of various approvals. In promoting the growth of exports of fresh horticulture, marine, and agro products, and processed food (both agro-based and seafood), the first step would be identification of a few items keeping in mind their commercial value and the comparative advantage of the island.

(ii) The second step would be to focus on commercialisation of identified products. This would imply establishing effective forward and backward linkages so as to sustain a symbiosis between industry and agriculture,[4] encouragement to the use of modern technology and scientific techniques, investment in irrigation, development of fast means of intra-island transportation, and strengthening of farmers' training and extension services. Organic production largely prevails in ANI. It should be promoted further. A sound certification system of organic products will help in fetching higher prices for these products.

(iii) The third step would be to ensure availability of storage, processing, marketing, and transport facilities. In this context, export promotion groups have an important role to play. Such groups should be strengthened. In the initial phases however, the UT may need to consider setting up joint ventures where the UT entrusts management responsibility and project risk largely to the private investor.

(iv) The UT will need to introduce relevant and quality vocational training programmes in line with industry needs. Private participation should be encouraged in this area as well.

(v) Up-gradation of existing industrial estates with essential services to help entrepreneurs from outside to capitalise on the opportunities for value addition would be essential.

(vi) Starting the process of reaching out to the investors besides convening meetings with them directly in order to attract investments in a viable fashion will be an important element of the industrial promotion strategy.

4. If farmers/fishermen are assured of having outlets to market their produce, they will be encouraged to increase the production of these.

(vii) Prospective for investment is not productive if done on a general basis. Such prospecting should be purposive after the identification of specific viable projects. It is here that besides the relevant departments of administration the ANIDCO can make an important contribution to the development of the UT through the ongoing techno-economic studies followed by financing viable projects. It can also act as a catalyst in bringing other financing sources.

(viii) An international airport in the region will provide greater confidence to financiers and investors. With the ongoing efforts of conducting trade pacts with neighbouring countries there would be much greater probability of full export potential and tourism potential being realised.

Bamboo based Industry

In India, there is lack of a focused approach to promote bamboo growing/processing to meet the domestic requirements, and to explore the export potential. In India, about 10 million ha is under bamboo with an average annual productivity of 0.33 tonnes/ha. Bamboo production in the country is estimated to be around 4.5 million tonnes. There seems high potential for development of bamboo products and thus, there is a need to harness this potential through result oriented and coordinated strategy for development of bamboo.

Large quantities of bamboo are generally used locally in housing, fishing rods, as props in orchards, and vegetable gardens and in handicraft sectors. Technologies have been developed to produce the following new generation products:

(i) Bamboo Mat based Technologies: In India, several cost-effective technologies have been developed at IPIRTI, Bangalore for manufacturing sheet materials having properties similar or even better than plywood made from fast growing plantation wood. These technologies are not only environment friendly but also people friendly as they have immense employment generation potential, particularly for women in bamboo growing areas. Technologies now available for industrial adoption are:

- *Bamboo Mat Boards (BMB):* A cost-effective technology has been developed for manufacture of thin BMB sheets up to 6 mm thick as alternate to plywood sheet. BMBs are waterproof, resistant to insect and fire, dimensionally stable, and possess excellent physical-mechanical strength properties. At present four units are manufacturing BMB and IPIRTI has signed MOU for transfer of technology to one unit in Maharashtra.
- *Bamboo Mat Veneer Composite (BMVC)*: BMVC is a variant of BMB and makes use of veneers from fast growing plantation wood for manufacture of high strength structural panels.
- *Bamboo Mat Corrugated Sheet*: It is a roofing material and a substitute for Asbestos Cement Corrugated Sheets (ACCS), which are considered to be carcinogenic and have been banned in many countries. It promises to revolutionise roofing system in the country as also in several other counties.
- *Bamboo Mat overlaid particleboard*: Techniques have been developed for overlaying wood/rice husk particleboard with bamboo mat that enhances their application potential.

(ii) Potential Applications of Bamboo Mat Boards

- Construction
- For grain storage bins and packaging
- Housing
- Furniture

(iii) Reconstituted Wood from Bamboo: FRI, Dehradun has developed a laboratory technology for manufacturing restructured reconstituted wood from *Dendrocalamus Strictus*. This product offers possibilities for use as substitute of solid wood where directional strength properties are main requirements as in case of structural timbers used as doors, window frame, beams, and other load bearing structures.

(iv) Activated Carbon from Bamboo: The National Mission on Bamboo Applications (NMBA), in association with the Department of Chemical Engineering of IIT-Bombay, has carried out an investigative study on converting waste Bamboo (for three commonly occurring species) to produce activated Carbon.[5] The study finds that the activated carbon

5. Activated Carbon is a black solid substance resembling granular or powdered charcoal. It is extremely porous with a large surface area, and typically produced from organic precursors such as Bamboo, coconut shells, palm-kernel shells, wood chips, sawdust, corncob and seeds. Activated Carbon adsorption is an effective means for reducing organic chemicals, chlorine, lead, and unpleasant tastes and odours in effluent or coloured substances from gas or liquid streams.

prepared from bamboo was better than the activated carbon prepared from coconut shells in terms of surface area and adsorption capacity. It may also be noted that bamboo during its process of conversion into mat boards, laminated boards, flooring tiles, etc. generates a lot of waste material in dust and chip forms. Also about 30 per cent of the culm length (top portion for reduced diameter and wall thickness and bottom part for semi-rigid construction with too many knots) cannot be converted into the previously mentioned value-added products. Certain species of bamboo with small diameter such as *Melocanna baccifera* are as such not suitable for such conversion. Bamboo wastes are thus best converted into activated carbon for a high value addition.

With a view to exploring the potential of Bamboo based activated carbon on a commercial scale, the NMBA is preparing a 'business opportunity' report. The report will provide techno-economic evaluation, assessment of market demand, and the necessary investment for entrepreneurial actions. The report would provide the road map for a viable project on the production of activated carbon on a commercial scale. The Mission also supports such projects in partnership with the industries. This would go a long way in truly evolving value-added application avenues for Bamboo for catering to domestic and overseas markets using indigenous technology.

Handicrafts and Village Industries

In India, millions of people possessing traditional skills and knowledge of traditional techniques still make a living by producing handcrafted goods. In policy documents, support for the crafts is often sought on the basis that in relation to large-scale mechanised manufacturing, crafts are mainly rural, provide greater scope for women's employment, and enable family firms and household industry to survive.

The success and survival of crafts can be linked to the survival of a traditional lifestyle for their consumer, well-developed tourism and government support for upgradation of skills of craftsperson, marketing, and export.

To survive, old skills need to study, target and adapt to the needs of new buyers. The average artisan neither has adequate access to information about markets, buyers, tastes and technologies nor does he have adequate capital to implement this change successfully.

Another constraint faced by artisans is shortage of raw materials. This is both real and artificially created by the middlemen, cartels, and traders. Government sponsored co-operative societies which are often controlled by a small coterie, based either on a master craftsman, or one particular interest and/or caste group, often provide little service to the general membership.

In general, credit flow from financial institutions to the crafts sector has been negligible. As a result, craftsmen continue to depend largely on advances from intermediaries/moneylenders/traders. The problem is more serious in crafts supplying the domestic market, and those located in rural areas. More commercialised and export-oriented regions are better served by formal sector funding.

Handicrafts sector has been constrained by a number of problems. Their dispersed nature and the generally poor level of education and access to information have created a host of distortions. These problems not only affect the returns to craftsmanship negatively, but also restrict access to means of value additions such as training in skill upgradation, new designs inputs, and technical advancement. Administrative inefficiency and the play of interest groups further raise costs of transactions in these markets for artisans and buyers.

Given this, the first thing for the government to do is to support infrastructure around clusters and to upgrade technology. Simultaneously, the government should promote links with external agents such as buyers and export traders. Such agents can provide management know-how, good quality raw material, good design, and new technologies. Government should also facilitate interaction between designers, NGOs, and craft producers.

Potential Areas for Tiny Units

(i) Andaman & Nicobar Islands have rich supply of agricultural and forest products such as areca plants, banana and other broad leaf plants. Currently, with emphasis on eco-friendly materials and shift from plastic and synthetic materials, there is immense scope for making disposable cups and plates out of leaves that are available in abundance. Traditional banana leaf cups and stitched flat plates are being used to the extent of more than 50 million numbers in several states. These products made by rural craftsmen have poor physical strength and are far from being clean and hygienic as they also have splinters.

CFTRI has developed technology to convert abundant forest raw materials into food containers with improved dimensional stability, appearance, shapes, finish and hygienic quality. The Department of Industries may consider inviting CFTRI for demonstration. Information dissemination and training of people in this craft has the potential of generating employment and creating value addition to the raw materials otherwise wasted.

(ii) At present the surplus production of coconut after meeting local consumption is exported as *copra* without utilising the water, the shell or the husk. A NDB assisted entrepreneur has started marketing coconut water as *cocojal;* another is making husk briquettes for the Australian market. The shell yields high quality charcoal, which can be utilised either for growing orchids or for converting into activated carbon. Coconut water may be used for the preparation of vinegar or can be bottled and sold fresh.

(iii) Tiny units particularly cane and bamboo-based furniture and handicrafts units have an important role in the economic development of these islands. A number of these units are family based. These units should be encouraged to exploit export potential of their products. Access to good quality raw materials and credit, modern techniques and designs, and support in marketing of their products will help these units to become competitive. Administration may need to consider associating design and marketing experts in these products.

(iv) ANI is reported to have some rare varieties of orchids, mushrooms, and ornamental plants that are high value products. These can be produced in large quantities using scientific methods. Since these are perishable products, good marketing and transport network will be essential.

(v) Extracts and produce of medicinal plants too have large potential for generating employment and income. Kerala would be an example to follow in this regard.

ANNEXURE 9.1

Incentives and Supportive Measures Extended by Directorate of Industries, ANI

Financial Assistance to Entrepreneurs (1)	*Training and skill Upgradation* (2)	*Extension of Marking Support* (3)	*Transport Subsidy* (4)	*Infrastructure Subsidy* (5)	*Interest Subsidy to PMRY Beneficiaries* (6)	*Infrastructure Development* (7)	*Budgetary Support* (8)	*Others* (9)
Under loan to tiny cottage industrial project programme, term loan and working capital at a reduced rate of interest is provided. Term loan limit has been increased to Rs. 25 lakh under loan to tiny cottage industrial project programme. There is no working capital limit.	Organising trainings, workshops with revised curriculum and updated technology.	Marketing assistance through *Sagarika* Emporium: Credit Card facilities, Forex counter for foreign tourists, basic amenities for visitors, training for emporium staff, packaging facilities, arrangement of home delivery, fixation of price, advertisement, evening counter and a counter at Port Blair Port for *Sagarika* Emporium.	The Island Transport subsidy scheme had been extended for three more years till 31.03.2003 and the subsidy rate was 85 per cent, 80 per cent and 75 per cent for the three consecutive years starting 2000-01.	Fifty per cent subsidy on installation of genset, water harvesting and land equipments.	Seventy five per cent interest subsidy to PMRY beneficiaries. This has been raised from 50 per cent to 75 per cent in view of poor repayment.	Preparation for all the existing industrial estate and future requirement as per felt need.	Under this scheme the department provide budgetary support to District Industries Centre and Grant in Aid to A&N KVIB.	Computerisation simplification of procedure.
Activity such as tourism will be included in the entire programme of financial assistance.	Advanced training on mainland and at Port Blair.	Marketing assistance to all the products in SSI and handicrafts sector.	Inter-island Transport Subsidy.	Twenty five per cent capital investment subsidy.		Creation of infrastructure for IT enabled services.		Creation/down-sizing and upgradation of posts.
Interest free composite loan of up to Rs. 50 lakh for infrastructure development in IT, tourism, coir, fishing and handicraft related activities.	Conducting motivational and entrepreneurship development programme and study tour programmes.	Marketing assistance through exhibitions, participation in various fairs and in craft *bazaar* in mainland.	Hundred per cent transport subsidy on export of handicrafts (excluding sea-shell items).	Seventy five subsidy and installation of pollution control equipment.		Establishment of STP.		Review the operation of the department with changing economic scenario.
Interest free loan for procurement of DG set, water harvesting equipment, and land development. The loan amount be to enhanced from Rs. 2.75 lakh to 20 lakh.	Study on growth of cane and bamboo clusters of of ANI through UNDP.	Awards for development of new designs in handicrafts sector.	Mainland Island transport subsidy.	Fifty per cent capital subsidy on establishment of tourism, IT, handicrafts and eco-friendly industrial activities in rural areas.		Creation of infrastructure for cane and coir.		Improving work-culture and efficiency.

...*Contd.* ...

...Contd. ...

Financial Assistance to Entrepreneurs	*Training and skill Upgradation*	*Extension of Marking Support*	*Transport Subsidy*	*Infrastructure Subsidy*	*Interest Subsidy to PMRY Beneficiaries*	*Infrastructure Development*	*Budgetary Support*	*Others*
(1)	*(2)*	*(3)*	*(4)*	*(5)*	*(6)*	*(7)*	*(8)*	*(9)*
.Interest free loan for procurement of pollution control equipment.	Development of designs and establishment of R&D cell.			Seventy five per cent cost subsidy on acquiring ISO.		Providing basic facilities like water, sewage, electricity, internal road in all the industrial estates.		Construction , repair and renovation of office buildings.
				Hundred per cent reimbursement of training fee for entrepreneurs attending training in IT, fisheries and tourism disciplines in mainland India.				Engagement of professionals for consultancy purposes for working out employment avenues for the next 10 years.
				Seventy five per cent capital subsidy on establishment of cyber café and other IT enabled services in rural areas.				
				Fifty per cent subsidy on power tariff to IT, fisheries, tourism, coir and other marine based activities in rural areas.				
				Fifty per cent subsidy on procurement of copra drying kilns.				
				Hundred per cent subsidy on development of website or e-commerce under tourism, IT, fisheries, coir and handicraft sector.				

Source: Compiled from various sources.

ANNEXURE 9.2

Registered Factory Sector in Andaman & Nicobar Islands

Year	*A&N*	*Chandigarh Islands*	*D&N*	*Daman Haveli*	*Delhi & Diu*	*Pondicherry*	*Punjab*	*Tamil Nadu*	*Maharashtra*	*West Bengal*	*Total*
Number of factories											
1985-86	41	271			3186	125	5710	12429	14970	5619	101016
1990-91	52	295	127	53	3453	233	6255	14617	15595	5606	110179
1995-96	69	355	166	252	3631	282	6913	19895	20536	6482	134571
1996-97	64	353	308	454	3715	362	7178	19203	20186	6727	134556
1997-98	79	339	360	531	3561	380	6576	19746	20542	6903	135551
Fixed capital (Rs. in lakh)											
1985-86	794	2219			46159	3860	275000	515457	939020	468834	6008522
1990-91	2316	4544	11583	2702	87881	20380	566733	1138526	1138526	848988	13364759
1995-96	9943	14155	47316	49698	343367	127036	1357081	3039583	3039583	2336457	34846773
1996-97	10061	24133	154843	77272	366006	92311	1497604	3423659	3423659	2637594	38456016
1997-98	12911	26824	214287	84755	232544	112699	1577678	3482159	3482159	2618771	42152201
Working capital (Rs. lakh)											
1985-86	456	2399			70370	5194	73838	298679	659934	144121	2379864
1990-91	1755	6478	10608	923	180760	8342	203911	398630	801066	203859	4252040
1995-96	5353	15985	31796	31148	325330	36408	445945	956619	2374855	425301	10766313
1996-97	3256	15817	90423	64293	599284	42692	415647	936502	2181447	539678	11312174
1997-98	2108	17923	12051	74779	672734	60296	504346	1336389	3407076	920120	16500854
Number of workers											
1985-86	4740	9419			99181	5264	248200	688129	882587	639257	5819169
1990-91	4589	8871	4297	2205	102701	17325	311670	766377	908457	578651	6307143
1995-96	6694	9562	4860	7700	121029	21252	354941	992220	1071327	651206	7632297
1996-97	5170	10011	10590	13293	115318	25422	363391	991629	1034122	592861	7405858
1997-98	5440	17971	13069	14755	92017	29377	339024	1015420	1041091	661785	7604904
Number of employees											
1985-86	5537	12295			133068	6783	312523	856217	1200490	806434	7471515
1990-91	5511	12185	5680	2642	144554	21661	400960	962589	1239152	740980	8162504
1995-96	8590	13711	6831	10612	171396	26540	472798	1237400	1518013	825154	10044697
1996-97	6598	14439	14527	17925	167390	31761	482453	1238882	1455506	767822	9706895
1997-98	6875	25340	17986	19864	135402	36988	454186	1271838	1465980	832057	9925810
Value of output (Rs. lakh)											
1985-86	2416	15360			267493	5418	515473	1297331	2708899	954209	12015540
1990-91	5374	45749	90331	9820	564360	56711	1248100	2765359	6141791	1628735	27056354
1995-96	16797	101746	239430	221153	1231415	168107	2697112	7042912	14893747	3140868	67051425
1996-97	11727	92663	393566	318409	1322926	295004	2868247	7416348	14353064	3456292	69251963
1997-98	15883	126154	643386	343211	1532293	380136	3201909	8261186	17329894	4189466	82542261

Source: *Annual Survey of Industries.*

ANNEXURE 9.3

Status of Industrial Estates in 1999

Name of the Industrial Estate	Area	Number of Sheds	Number of Plots	Number of Sheds Allotted	Number of Plots Allotted	Proposed Sheds & Plots	Year Started
1. IE Garacharama	2.00 ha	10	31	10	31		1976
2. IE Dollygunj	17.88 ha	23	44	19	38		1993
3. IE Bakultala	11.50 ha	5	nil	5	nil	total 25 sheds and 50 plots	1995
4. IE Campbell Bay	3.42 ha	Under the process of development				25 sheds and 25 plots	1994
5. IE Wimberly Gunj	13.00 ha	Under the process of development				10 shed and 10 plots	1996
6. IE Mitha Khari	5.00 ha	Under the process of development				Exclusively for coir industries	1996
7. IE Little Andaman	2.00 ha	Estimates awaited from APWD					
8. IE Katchal	2.00 ha	Required land yet to be acquired					1996
9. IE Hutbay	2.00 ha	Estimates awaited from APWD				25 sheds and 25 plots	1999

Source: Status Paper on Directorate of Industries A&N Administration, 1999.

ANNEXURE 9.4

Industrial Training Centres in A&N Island in the Year 1999

Sl. No.	Name of the Training centre and Location	Trade	Year of establishment	Capacity to Impart training per batch	Duration of the course
1	Wood Working Centre, Port Blair	Carpentry	1959	10	18 months
2	Design Centre, Port Blair	Handicrafts in sea shell and wood	1959	12	12 months
3	Smithy Sheet Metal and Electroplating, Port Blair	Blacksmith, welding, electroplating, sheet metal works	1959	25	12 months
4	Women's Tailoring Centre, Garacharama	Tailoring and garment making (only for women)	1959	20	12 months
5	Coir Training Centre, Dollygunj	Coir processing and coir products manufacturing	1996	10	12 months
6	Women's Tailoring Centre, Diglipur	Tailoring and garment making (only for women)	1975	10	12 months
7	Carpentry and Blacksmithy, Diglipur	Carpentry, blacksmithy	1986	55	18 months 12 months
8	Extension Centre in Food Processing, Diglipur	Short-term courses in food processing	1985		
9	Carpentry Training Centre, Ranhgat	Carpentry	1975	5	18 months
10	Cane and Bamboo Training Centre, Rangat	Cane and bamboo handicrafts	1975	5	12 months
11	Carpentry Training Centre, Car Nicobar	Carpentry works	1963	10	18 months
12	Coir Training Centre, Car Nicobar	Coir processing and coir products manufacturing	1982	20	12 months
13	Women's Tailoring Centre, Car Nicobar	Tailoring and garment making (only for women)	1963	10	12 months
14	Carpentry Training Centre, Hut Bay	Handicrafts and furniture on wood	1999	10	18 months
15	Cane and Bamboo Training Centre, Campbell Bay	Cane and bamboo handicrafts	1999	10	12 months

Source: Status Paper on Directorate of Industries A&N Administration. 1999.

Chapter 10

Biodiversity Conservation and Forest Management

Introduction

The Andaman & Nicobar Islands are endowed with rich biodiversity both in terrestrial and marine ecosystems. According to the *State of Forest Report*, the forest cover in ANI is 6,964 sq. km. which is 84.42 per cent of its geographical area. Of this, 3,475 sq. km. (42 per cent) is under very dense forest, 2,809 sq. km. (34 per cent) is under moderately dense forest, and 680 sq. km. (8 per cent) is under open forest (FSI, 2005). The marine life is very rich. The islands are fringed by the most pristine of the coral reefs in the Indian Ocean region, which support thousands of species of fish, coelenterates, mollusks, crustaceans and sea snakes.

The coral reefs are of the fringing type on the eastern side, whereas they form barrier reefs on the western side of the islands. The fringing reefs are several hundred metres wide and spread over 11,939 km^2 including lagoons, banks, reef slopes and reefs. Barrier reef located west of the islands is 320 km. long. Limited surveys conducted so far have identified 198 species of corals of 58 genera (Turner *et al.*, 2001).

The islands offer important nesting beaches for four species of marine turtles, namely, Leatherback sea turtle (*Dermochelys coriacea*)—the largest of the marine reptiles, Hawksbill (*Eretmochelys imbricata*), Olive Ridley (*Lepidochelys olivacea*), and Green Turtle (*Chelonia mydas*). The Dugong is seen frequently in these islands. Estuarine crocodiles are found in areas less frequented by men. Besides these, seashells of different sizes, and fishes like sardines, tuna, barracuda, mullets, mackerels and flying fishes are in abundance. Marine algae (118 species) and marine angiosperms (sea- grasses) are found along the seashores of these islands.

The forests of these islands contain a mix of elements from the Indian subcontinent and Southeast Asia, and are recognised as a part of the distinct eco-region in the WWF Global 200 List of priority biodiversity hotspots with high endemism and distinctiveness. Existing literature indicates that plant species of more than 700 genera and 140 families are found in the forests of these islands. Forests can be broadly classified into tropical evergreen, semi evergreen, moist deciduous and mangrove forests. Wherever the forest is intact the canopy is stratified and dense allowing little light to come in. Tallest trees sometimes reach 50 metres and the ground vegetation is often negligible. The islands remain largely unexplored.

Andaman & Nicobar Islands encompass a broad range of ecological habitats and highly diverse ecosystems varying from sandy beaches to evergreen forests, disturbed secondary formations to virgin forest. Littoral plains on the coastal areas, muddy creeks, and island hills support micro habitats of thousands of species of plants and animals. 3,552 plant species have been recorded from these islands so far, and a large area still remains unexplored. Of the flowering plants, about 14 per cent are endemic to the islands and about 40 per cent are not found in mainland India. The uniqueness in species composition is reflected from the fact that 60 per cent of the endemic trees are endangered because of their scattered distribution in the islands. Of the 1,454 taxa of angiosperms, 221 are endemic, 60 of which are known only from type specimens and 22 only from type localities (Rao, 1996). Of the 5,357 species of fauna recorded, 487 (9 per cent) are endemic. If marine species are excluded (none of which are endemic), 13 per cent (487 of 3,704) are endemic. Endemism is very high in birds where 39 per cent of the 270 species and subspecies recorded from the islands are endemic. Other groups also show high degrees of endemism: over 50 per cent of butterflies, 60 per cent of 58 species of mammals, 32 per cent of 83 species of reptiles and 20 per cent of 10 species of amphibians recorded are endemic (Vijayan *et al.*, 2000; Khatri, 1993; and Sankaran, 2005).

The mangroves occupy 644 km^2 in the Andaman Islands and 27 km^2 in the Nicobar Islands (FSI, 2005). Mangrove area wise, the Andaman & Nicobar Islands are third in the country after West Bengal and Gujarat, but as far as density and growth are concerned mangroves of these islands are probably the best in the country. High growth of mangroves vegetation with healthy and giant size mangrove trees in India can be seen only in these islands. Due to remoteness of these islands and non-settlement of human beings in many parts virgin mangrove forests are available. The mangroves of Andaman & Nicobar Islands are different from those found in mainland because of the absence of perennial rivers in the islands and consequently no delta like structure is formed. All the mangrove forests are situated either as fringe on flat littoral zone, or along creeks as a narrow belt between the tropical rain forests and the sea. Along the creeks, the width of the mangrove forest ranges between 0.5 to 1.0 km (Dam Roy and Krishnan, 2005). However, a large part has been damaged due to tsunami and subsequent inundation.

Due to their physical isolation from the mainland, the islands show high endemism, rarity and distinct flora and fauna. These islands are also home to four of the last aboriginal tribes of humans, who are totally dependent on forests. Therefore, forest management and biodiversity conservation are of paramount importance in these islands. Loss of even small habitats may have serious consequences for sustainability of biological diversity.

Forest Management: An Overview

Forest management in ANI requires a unique strategy which has to be developed keeping in view the extensive forest cover, high degree of endemism, uniqueness of the insular flora and fauna and the fragile environment. Before Independence, the forestry operations were confined mainly to provision of timber and fuel required by the penal settlement, the Public Works and Marine departments of the Administration and export of timber to foreign timber markets mainly in London and New York.

After Independence, in order to promote the industrial activity, the new National Forest Policy 1952 emphasised that there is a need for generation of income from forests. The forests of these islands contributed substantial quantity of timber to the Indian Railways for expansion of its network after the Independence. When the Government of India decided to settle the refugees from East Pakistan in these islands and to colonise these areas with persons from various states, the Forest Department cleared large tracts of forest over flat land for the purpose of settlement and agriculture. In the initial years, lumbering and natural regeneration of forests were the main activities in the islands which provided employment to a large number of labour force. Till late 1980s, the Forest Department contributed 70-90 per cent of state revenue, provided the raw material required for the industries of the islands, met the requirements of Indian Railways and markets in mainland, and simultaneously met the requirements of sawn timber and non-timber forest produce of the local population. Thus, human settlement in these islands and socioeconomic growth of the region revolved around the forests and forestry operations.

With the increasing understanding of the importance of biodiversity and the intangible benefits of forests, policies and programmes of the forest department underwent major changes. For instance, the monoculture plantation of commercial species has been discontinued since 1985. The extraction of mangroves for poles and fuel wood was discontinued from 1988. The industrial coupes were discontinued from 1989 and the forestry working was completely departmentalised. In 1989, the Island Development Authority decided to phase out major industries and reduce timber extraction to meet local needs only. Consequently, there was a gradual reduction in the quantum of timber extraction over the years. From 1990 onwards, the harvestable yield was reduced by 50 per cent at the time of preparation of working plans itself, subsequently the girdling of non-commercial species was discontinued for ecological reasons.

The 'National Forest Policy 1988' laid emphasis on preservation of ecology and natural resources. At present, out of about 87 per cent of geographical area notified as forests, 35 per cent area is under tribal reserves which are home to the six aboriginal tribes. In order to conserve the nature and biodiversity, the islands have 96 wildlife sanctuaries, 9 national parks and a biosphere reserve which occupy an area of about 1969 sq. km. The mangrove vegetation which is unique in itself occupies an area of about 671 sq. km. and is totally protected. Thus, 70 per cent of the forest area is under complete protection from all kinds of biotic interference, and preserved for tribal welfare and for wildlife and biodiversity conservation.

The current forest management practices in ANI have been influenced by factors such as demographic pressure on the biological resources, the National Forest Policy 1988, various local initiatives for conservation of nature and promotion of local industries, and the recent orders of the Hon'ble Supreme Court. Priority areas include: protection of wildlife and coral reefs; provision of infrastructure for environmental protection; improvement in communication network; habitat improvement; creation of awareness among people including children; and building up of database for scientific management of forests and protected areas. Corals and mangroves are being given the highest priority in the conservation programme. The forest department has initiated many collaborative projects with institutions of repute for biodiversity characterisation, inventorisation of medicinal plants, protection of coral reefs, etc. (Jayaraj, 2003).

Management Units in the Current Working Plans

For the purpose of administration of forests, the forest areas of these islands are divided into 7 Forest Divisions. These are further divided into 44 Ranges—territorial as well as functional. The Ranges are organised into administrative units called camps on the basis of function such as, timber extraction, regeneration. For the purpose of protection, the ranges are subdivided into units called beats.

As per the directions of the Hon'ble Supreme Court in a public interest litigation filed by the Society for Andaman & Nicobar Ecology (SANE), Bombay Natural History Society (BNHS) and *Kalpavriksh*, the working plans are being revised. One of the recommendations of *Shekhar Singh Commission Report*, accepted by the Supreme Court was that timber extraction should be confined only to the forest areas which have already been worked. Such areas occupy just 15 per cent of the forest area and only these areas shall be reserved for meeting the local timber requirements in future. The rest of the forest area shall be totally protected. The court order also directed to bring the composition of the forests back to their original state by appropriate silviculture intervention. Accordingly, the areas which were earlier included in the conversion working circle have all been brought under eco-restoration working circle. The fellings which were concentrated under the shelter wood system have now been made dispersed, making the system akin to 'selection' system. Further, in order to meet the changed requirements, new working circles have been constituted (Jayaraj, 2003; Singh, 2002, 2003). In all the new plans, which have been prepared or under preparation, the working circles constituted are as follows:

(*a*) *Eco-restoration Working Circle*: The objective of management in this working circle is to bring back the forests to their natural profile and simultaneously carry out timber extraction for meeting the requirements of local people only. The system of regeneration will be the selection system, in which approximately three trees shall be removed per hectare and the gap shall be regenerated naturally.

(*b*) *Protection Working Circle:* This includes all catchments, ecologically sensitive areas and the tribal reserves. No forestry activity shall be undertaken in this working circle. These areas shall be subject to intensive patrolling.

(*c*) *Non-timber Forest Produce overlapping Working Circle:* This is a working circle constituted for the purpose of meeting the requirements of local public for non-timber forest produce such as, bamboo, *ballies*, posts, firewood, thatching leaves and also to meet the requirements of small-scale units utilising these products.

(*d*) *Canes overlapping Working Circle*: This working circle is constituted for the purpose of scientific management augmenting production of canes and its collection on sustained basis, besides catering to needs of local cane-based small-scale industries, handicraft units, local inhabitants and the forest department.

(*e*) *Mangrove and Littoral Swamp Coastal Belt Conservation Working Circle:* This is constituted with the objective of checking the reclamation, encroachment, and destruction of mangroves and also for eco-restoration of degraded mangrove areas, besides monitoring the changes in mangrove areas, inventorising its flora and fauna, and creating awareness about the mangroves.

(*f*) *Wildlife Protection Working Circle:* This includes all the protected areas such as wildlife sanctuaries and national parks and no forestry operation is undertaken in this circle. Various measures aimed at conserving wildlife and their habitats are taken up.

(*g*) *Eco-tourism overlapping Working Circle:* This working circle aims at promoting forest based tourism with the objective of creating awareness about environment among the tourists and also to generate income for the local community adjoining the forest areas. Representative forest ecosystems, coral reef areas, scenic beaches, turtle nesting sites, nature trails, bird watching sites, elephant ride, and the like are organised in this working circle without creation of any permanent infrastructure.

All recent plans, which are prepared or are under preparation, have miscellaneous objectives such as, Joint Forest Management/ Protection, reforestation of encroached forestland, social forestry, and consolidation of boundaries through survey and demarcation.

Future Strategies of Forest Management

Keeping in view the National Forest Policy, 1988 and management strategies detailed above, suggestions for future management of the environment and forests of ANI are presented below:

Forest Protection

The emphasis of the environment and forests sector being biodiversity and wildlife conservation, there is an urgent need to improve the protection network. The present protection machinery is not adequate to meet the challenges posed by the smugglers. Access to most of the islands including many of the wildlife sanctuaries and national parks is only by sea. However, lack of good sea worthy vessels poses a big constraint. In order to combat the increased activities of encroachments, illicit cuttings and poaching, effective communication network, adequate transport system, and arms may be provided to the staff in all the strategic areas including the tribal areas. Based on the recommendations of the *Shekhar Singh Commission Report*, a draft regulation to amend the Indian Forest Act 1927 in its application to the Andaman & Nicobar Islands has been submitted to the Ministry of Environment and Forests. The suggested amendment has provisions for eviction of encroachments, power to confiscate property involved in forest offences, immunity from prosecution in case of *bona fide* discharge of duties under the Act, enhancement of penalties, etc. The expeditious promulgation of the regulation is necessary. The Regulation for regulating the felling in non-forest areas proposed by the Administration also needs expeditious promulgation.

In an island ecosystem it is important to study the issues in conservation of endangered marine mammals such as dugong, dolphin, whale, whale shark found in these islands. This can be carried out under a Marine Conservation Cell which can function under the Chief Wildlife Warden with the Department of Environment and Forests. There is also a need to prepare Management Plans for marine protected areas and the linked habitats like coral reefs and beaches apart from mangroves.

Environmental Conservation

In ANI, ecological systems are very closely interlinked. For instance, destruction of forest cover can lead to increased erosion that could choke coral reefs, affecting the fish population in the specific area. Similarly, sand mining from the beach or destruction of mangroves will increase erosion by the sea waves leading to an increased vulnerability of the landmass. Thus, caution needs to be exercised in planning the developmental activities in ANI. These issues are being discussed and debated in the *State of Environment Report*, which is in the final stages of preparation. The Report is commissioned by the Ministry of Environment and Forests.

Biodiversity Conservation Measures

The Biodiversity Strategy and Action Plan (BSAP) for the Andaman & Nicobar Islands has been recently finalised after extensive consultations with the relevant government agencies, research organisations and NGOs (Jayaraj and Andrews, 2005). The strategies suggested for the conservation of biodiversity are as follows:

- Protected area management (*in situ* conservation): Demarcation of all protected areas, their reorganisation to make them ecologically sound, mapping of vegetation and coral reefs, and preparation of management plans is an urgent necessity. The Wildlife Institute of India (WII) is currently preparing a plan for consolidation of protected areas, at the request of the ANI administration and this needs to be implemented early.
- *Ex situ* conservation: Establishment of biological park, zoo, botanical garden, arboretum, seed banks, and gene banks can help in the conservation of rare, endangered and threatened species outside their natural habitat.
- Enumeration of biodiversity: Ecosystem/habitat survey, species enumeration and studies on genetic diversity within species will help in better

documentation and understanding of the biodiversity of the flora and fauna in these islands.

- Containment of threats to particular taxa: Several species are having restricted distribution and are endemic/endangered. Such species require special intervention, wherever they are threatened due to anthropogenic pressures (e.g., Nicobar Megapode, Narcondum hornbill, saltwater crocodiles, sea turtles, *Euphorbia epiphylloides,* etc.).
- Elimination of threats due to introduced species: There are over 600 introduced species reported from the islands. Wherever they are invasive or threatening the local flora and fauna, they are required to be eliminated urgently. Special attention would be required in the case of spotted deer and the feral elephants that are reportedly damaging the regeneration of forests. The WII has been requested by the ANI administration to suggest the action required in this direction, and this needs to be expedited.
- Introduction of alternative renewables: Alternative energy resources, alternative construction materials, water conservation and rainwater harvesting, bio-pesticides, cash crops in place of paddy, and development of ecotourism are to be adopted for sustainable management of environment.
- Social forestry and joint forest management: Joint Forest Management Resolution has already been notified for implementation. Social forestry is to be promoted on non-forest land, to the extent possible, for meeting the requirement of non-timber forest produce, so that the pressure on natural forest is reduced.
- Awareness generation: The local public, students and government employees are to be made aware of the rich biodiversity of the islands and the need for its protection.

The BSAP has also suggested action plans for various sectors of the government dealing with biological resources. The agriculture sector will concentrate on increasing the productivity so that the area under agriculture need not expand and encroach into the forest area. *In-situ* and *ex situ* conservation of the wild varieties of cultivated plants—which have application in crop improvement and breeding establishment of cooperatives for transport and marketing of the agricultural produce, introduction of organic farming, orchid cultivation and floriculture, water management for agriculture and household use, establishment of quarantine facilities, study on avifaunal changes with pesticide use and development of agroforestry. The tourism sector will involve the local residents in the tourism development, create awareness around the Protected Areas to avoid degradation of habitats, eliminate subsidies, study the environmental impact of tourism in the existing sites, and establish carrying capacity for each of the ecotourism sites, so that the adverse effects of tourism on biodiversity can be eliminated.

The animal husbandry and veterinary science sector will evolve ways and means to keep the livestock out of forests by introducing stall feeding with fodder crop, study the livestock carrying capacity of the islands, reduce the quantity of livestock by improving their quality and use of the local domesticated species in breeding. The population of the introduced species such as spotted deer, cats and dogs will be controlled as they have adverse effect on the native flora and fauna.

In order to understand the biodiversity better research and documentation is required of the ethnobotany of the native communities, little known taxa, medicinal plants, orchids, and mangrove epiphytes. While the biodiversity at landscape level has been studied by remote sensing (IIRS, 2003), the specific diversity of flora and fauna and the genetic diversity within the species are yet to be fully documented. Studies are required urgently on these lines. There is a need for strengthening the pollution monitoring, control, and enforcement mechanism as pollution is likely to increase with the increase in the population and developmental activities. A separate Directorate of Environment within the Department of Environment and Forests would help in this context.

The commercial orientation of the Department of Environment and Forests has changed with more emphasis on biodiversity and wildlife conservation. Also, the area of operation of the department has extended into marine ecosystem consequent to the inclusion of various marine fauna in Schedule I of the Wild Life Protection Act 1972. The forestry and wildlife research activities must be strengthened with collaborative projects on biodiversity characterisation, enumeration of medicinal plants, *ex-situ* conservation of edible nest swiftlet, coral reef monitoring, mangrove conservation, and planting stock improvement. Environmental education needs to be given importance through the establishment of arboretums, nature interpretation centres in public places and eco-clubs in schools, creation of green brigades and honorary wildlife warden posts. Various locale specific and general recommendations have been made by the recent studies such as the Biodiversity Prioritisation Project, Important Bird Area Project, Sustainable Management of Protected Areas, and National Biodiversity Strategy and Action Plan. These recommendations may be considered for implementation. The following studies may also be conducted:

- Studies on the geographical distribution, habitat, and propagation of rare and endangered species of plants.
- Studies on the various aspects of ecology of the different types of forests in the islands including studies on nutrient cycling and hydrology.
- Detailed socioeconomic studies on the use of different kinds of forest produce to identify the critical stakeholder groups who can in turn be targeted for development activities.
- Enumerations need to be carried out at sites all over the islands to compare the composition of logged sites of various ages with adjacent unlogged ones to quantify the extent of change. Which will enable areas to be identified for future logging operations that may be necessary to supply local needs.
- Exclosure experiments to exclude herbivores in both unlogged forest and natural regeneration areas to assess accurately the damage caused by these herbivores and to evolve control measures to be taken against them.

Ecotourism

The landscape of ANI has good potential for promoting eco-tourism. Interpretation centres, camping facilities, bird watching cruise in the creeks, and trekking programmes should be provided under the eco-tourism development. Rich flora and faunal value sites, turtle nesting and coral sighting sites could be added attraction for tourists in the islands. The potential for low volume, high value, eco-tourism aimed at promoting education and appreciation of nature should be exploited (Pictures 10.1 and 10.2). It is also important to check the growing commercialisation of ecotourism through the introduction of environmental audit systems.

Meeting the Needs of the Local People

Logging for commercial requirements has been stopped and logging to meet the local needs alone is being carried out. The introduction of 'reduced impact logging' is necessary, as the mechanised logging operations cause considerable damage to the biodiversity. The joint forest management programme has to be launched for meeting the requirement of the local people for non-timber forest produce in exchange for their role in protection of forests. Initially, JFM can be tried on an experimental basis at a few sites adjacent to settlements. Social forestry schemes can be taken up on revenue land which have been cleared of encroachments. In addition, other areas need to be earmarked for carrying out social forestry plantations with the sole objective of meeting the local needs in a sustainable way.

The cultivation of bamboo is gaining importance in view of its employment potential and its ability to replace the *ballies* and posts extracted from natural forests. There is an urgent need to establish afforestation plots on experimental basis with solid and thick-walled bamboo from mainland, as the local bamboo is hollow and thin-walled, which is not suitable for structural purposes. The cultivation of cane and bamboo on private and revenue lands needs to be encouraged. The degraded areas and areas where agricultural production is so low as to make farming unremunerative, needs to be brought under tree cover. For this purpose, demonstration plots need to be set up where local residents can perceive the benefits of planting tree species in their land. Cane processing should be recognised as a small-scale industry to boost its prospects. The concept of agroforestry has to be encouraged by the forest department, agriculture department and research organisations like CARI at Port Blair. Raising of high value horticultural crops as part of agroforestry system will increase the incomes of the farmers. Beekeeping needs to be encouraged as an income generating activity in such multi-tier agroforestry system. The small timber obtained as a result of logging operations can be utilised as flooring material. Technology transfer in the field of agroforestry, utilisation of small timber, timber seasoning and treatment, etc. should be obtained from ICAR and ICFRE.

Database Development for Efficient Forest Management

A sound database in forestry sector is a must to facilitate planning and execution of development and conservation plans. Planning and monitoring as well as project formulation wing needs to be strengthened in the department. The data on forestry such as forest area, forest flora and fauna, administrative units, personnel, offences detected, timber availability, wood based industries, non-timber forest produce are required to be incorporated on a GIS platform for quick and effective decision making. The forestry department has already prepared an Information Technology (IT) Plan which needs to be put in place at the earliest. The salient components of the IT Plan are:

(a) Forest Management Information System (FMIS)

It is an integrated system which can be used in monitoring the forest management activities across administrative units and levels of organisational hierarchy. FMIS can be developed with assistance of institutions such as WII, which has developed FMIS for the forest departments in some states.

(b) Environmental Information System

Information System (ENVIS) Centre located in the Department of Environment and Forests in ANI, is funded by the Ministry of Environment and Forests. ENVIS should be used for collection of information on various environmental parameters, such as, demography, urban concentration and slums, forest resources, pollution, industries, waste generation and disposal, livestock population, fisheries, occupation profile, development infrastructure.

(c) E-governance

Under the IT Plan the department has proposed to computerise the following activities: issue of permits, sale of sawn timber, allocation of sand, grant of permit for import of forest produce and booking of accommodation in forest rest houses/eco-huts. In addition, the entire process of saw-milling right from receipt of logs to disposal of sawn timber is to be monitored through a computerised programme. The stores will have computerised inventory of stores. All records of personnel are to be computerised for better human resource management. The preparation of all the bills are to be computerised to avoid delay in payments. The receipt, distribution and despatch of papers are to be computerised for timely processing of papers. The public grievances, staff grievances and the disposal of queries under the Right to Information Act will be monitored through a computerised system for timely disposal of the matter.

(d) Forest Education

The Forest Training School must have a Computer Training Cell to improve the computer literacy of the executive staff. They must also be trained in the use of Global Positioning System (GPS) in order to expedite forest survey and settlement operations.

(e) Forest and Wildlife Research

The enormous amount of data that are being collected by the Silviculture and Wildlife divisions needs to be systematically and scientifically analysed for efficient management of forest and wildlife. Use of statistical software needs to be promoted in this context.

Management of Mangroves

ANI is one of the richest mangrove areas in the world in terms of quality of vegetation and biodiversity of the 36 species of mangroves of which 7 species are found exclusively in ANI. Andaman district is richer in mangrove biodiversity compared to Nicobar district. With the increase in population in these islands, degradation of mangroves has become visible in the areas close to habitation. Degradation of mangroves is maximum in South Andaman followed by Middle Andaman and North Andaman.

Socioeconomic Dependence on Mangroves

Mangroves are important for coastal communities as they protect coastal areas from soil erosion and fury of sea waves. The mangroves provide breeding ground for the shrimps and are therefore important for sustained catch of shrimps, which are now being exported out of the islands. They also provide potential grounds for mud crab fattening and aquaculture. These activities have to be carried out after extensive environmental impact assessment. In this direction, the forest and fisheries departments should launch extension training activities among the villagers including awareness generation on the need to protect the mangrove resources for sustainable fishing operations.

Training of Mangrove Managers

Forest officers involved in mangrove management should be given specialised training in mangrove area management because of the unique nature of these forests and the different management approach they require. Besides, senior officers of the forest department should be sensitised about the importance of conservation and management of mangrove ecosystem in order to garner their active support towards achieving this goal.

Mangrove Conservation and Management in ANI

Though the mangroves in ANI are relatively safe, the following require attention: non-restoration of the areas previously felled, poor regeneration in the natural ecosystem, sand collection from the beaches, and consequences of uplift or submergence of land (Pictures 10.3-10.6). The strategy adopted in ANI for conservation and management of mangrove forests is quite comprehensive. The following suggestions may be considered for further strengthening the policy:

- full protection to the mangrove flora and fauna by imposing a ban on mangrove extraction;
- identification of potential mangrove areas for declaration as national parks and sanctuaries;
- eco-restoration of degraded and critical mangrove areas by afforestation of suitable mangrove species;
- identification of endangered mangrove species and providing full protection for their rehabilitation;
- checking of encroachment, destruction and reclamation of mangrove areas by effective measures;
- monitoring the changes in mangrove areas, namely its floristic and faunal composition and physiographic changes;
- creating awareness amongst the public on the importance of mangroves and the need for its preservation by education of the village folk; and
- protection measures to keep vigil on possible destruction of mangroves.

Management of Mangroves in Post-Tsunami Scenario

The tsunami has caused widespread destruction on the Andaman & Nicobar Islands.

The geological and geomorphologic changes in the islands are continuing as the seismic oscillations and tectonic plate tremors are still occurring and will last till equilibrium is achieved. The forests, especially the mangrove forests, have faced the brunt of tsunami.

The Action Plan for development of post-tsunami "New Andamans" prepared by the M. S. Swaminathan Research Foundation has attempted to quantify the changes in land cover and also the adverse impact of tsunami on the agricultural land and the mangrove forests (MSSRF, 2005). It is evident from the report that damage to mangroves in Katchal, Camorta, Nancowry and Trinket islands is extensive. The damage to mangroves in these islands is due to saltwater ingression and seepage of saltwater into the roots through the loose soil around the roots, deposition of sand on pneumatophores and also due to clearing of littoral forests adjoining mangroves.

Due to rising of the landmass the mangrove forests are drying up in Middle and North Andaman. The degradation of mangrove forests will continue to occur over a period of time as there are no green leaves to produce the required detritus and the dark atmosphere is lost due to drying of vegetation bringing in more sunlight. Consequently, this will have a long-term impact on the future potential of fisheries in and around Andaman & Nicobar Islands. The food security of tribals in Nicobar, during the months of February and March which depends heavily on Pandanus fruits has been affected severely due to the damage to littoral forests.

The Report (MSSRF, 2005) recommended action plans for the rehabilitation of mangroves. In mangrove areas where land is elevated to 0.6 to 0.8 m and water has withdrawn, tidal inundation by digging trapezoidal canals was recommended, to bring back the lost water and replenish the exposed and drying mangroves. Fresh water loving mangrove species such as *Excocaria agallocha, Heritiera* can also be planted after leaching of salts by monsoon rains. In the case of mangrove areas that are completely submerged, it was suggested that if the level of submergence is shallow, mangroves such as *Rhizophora, Ceriops, Bruguiera* could be planted, after trials in smaller areas. In case of deep and permanent submergence, nothing was possible. In the non-mangrove areas that are inundated by tidal water or submerged with seawater (mainly paddy fields), bioshield programme with planting of tree species like, casuarinas, areca nut, Pandanus, sea *mahua*, coconut, pineapple, cashew nut, kudsu vine and vetiver grass, cinchona, ficus and littoral forest species was recommended.

However, recent surveys show that any major interventions may not be necessary. Allowing the nature to take its own course has been recommended. Planting of casuarina is recommended only in those areas that are part of human habitations, and where large stands occurred earlier. Since each and every island is unique, with species and subspecies endemic to it, use of seed material collected from within an island or a group of islands has been recommended (Sankaran, 2005). Natural regeneration has been observed in the mangrove areas, and it is recommended that this needs to be protected and watched. Planting of *Pandanus nicobarensis* and *Nypa fruticans*, used by the tribals (Andrews and Vaughan, 2005) has already been initiated. The establishment of mangroves, depending on the hydrology of the area, should be allowed and

PICTURE 10.1

Ecotourism in Andaman & Nicobar Islands

PICTURE 10.2

Coral Reef based Tourism at Jolly Buoy, Mahatma Gandhi Marine National Park

PICTURE 10.3

View of Mangrove Vegetation at Mahatma Gandhi Marine National Park

PICTURE 10.4

View of Degraded Mangrove Vegetation due to Biotic Interference

PICTURE 10.5

Artificial Regeneration of Mangrove Species in Andaman & Nicobar Islands

PICTURE 10.6

Natural Regeneration of Mangrove Species in Andaman & Nicobar Islands

protected. Natural regeneration can be supplemented at a later stage, using nursery grown seedlings.

The Institute of Forest Genetics and Tree Breeding (IFGTB), Coimbatore is closely working with the Department of Environment and Forests in ANI in a project on raising bio-shield plantations using casuarina. It is providing technical inputs for raising plantations as well as producing quality planting stock.

Cane and Bamboo Development

Scope for Development of Cane

ANI has tremendous potential for development of cane. A comprehensive cane management plan is required for development and utilisation of this resource. A total of 19 species of cane have been reported in ANI, of which 6 are commercially used by the local industries. The average collection of cane is about 3 lakh metres per year and the collections are regulated as per the Working Plan for non-timber forest produce. Export of raw cane from ANI has been banned since 1995. However, the potential for export should be explored, as it can generate employment opportunities as well as revenue for the UT.

Protection and scientific harvesting of cane is important for promotion of its natural regeneration and to avoid wastage. Special vigil is necessary during fruiting period to prevent large-scale illegal collection and export of cane seeds from these islands. It has been observed that the cane permit holders have a tendency to overexploit the easily accessible areas, which hampers regeneration. Further, the permit holders do not collect full-length cane. Generally, mature cane is 20 metres or more in length, which is tightly entangled with other vegetation, mainly trees on which it climbs. Permit holders generally cut the base of the cane and pull it out, leaving the remaining upper part hanging on the tree. According to an estimate, this results in wastage upto 50 per cent. If the cane is cut at the base and pulled out after 15 days when it dries up partly, the entire length of cane can be brought down. Departmental extraction of cane can ensure proper and scientific harvesting of cane.

Scope for Raising Bamboo in ANI

One of the recommendations of the *Shekhar Singh Commission Report* is that the construction in the islands should be timber and bamboo based, and this has been accepted by the Supreme Court. Implementation of this recommendation would require use of solid/thick-walled bamboo, which are not native to the ANI, and will have to be introduced from the mainland. Raising of bamboo and cane in homesteads and other agroforestry models as component of multi-tier cropping system is an option. Technology Information Forecasting and Assessment Council (TIFAC) may be consulted in popularising the use of bamboo in construction of ANI. In what follows the role of bamboo in meeting the local needs of ANI is discussed. This however, draws heavily from Jayaraj and Bhatt, (1999).

Bamboo Resources

Six species of bamboo have been reported in ANI namely; *Dinochloa andamanica, Dinochloa nicobarica Schizostachyum flavescens, Schizostachyum kurzii, Schizostachyum rogersii,* and *Gigantochloa andamanica.* While *Gigantochloa andamanica* is very common and gregarious in semi-evergreen and deciduous forests, others are relatively scarce.

The bamboo brakes occur sporadically throughout the evergreen and semi-evergreen tracts, usually along the streams and wet hollows. They are usually seen forming an understorey in forests, where the soil is humus rich fine clay and permanently wet. Though a systematic survey is yet to be done, bamboo rich areas have been identified in various Forest Divisions and reported as follows:

Forest Divisions	*Potential Bamboo Areas*
1. Diglipur	Kalipur, Kalara, Kalighat, Nischintapur, Nabagram, Radhanagar, Gandhinagar, Sitanagar, Kishorinagar.
2. Mayabunder	Tugapur, Karmatang, Austin, Bajota, Pathertikry.
3. Middle Andaman	Rampur, Thoratang, Bakultala, Kalsi, Kadamtala.
4. Baratang	Lorojig, Adajig, Jarawa creek, Wrafter's creek
5. South Andaman	Jirkatang, Potatang, Pyinmanallah, Shoal Bay, Rutland.

Utilisation of Bamboo

At the time of settlement and colonisation operations in these islands, large quantity of bamboo were used in the construction of houses. In outlying areas of the islands, they are still the only available walling material. The main species used is *Gigantochloa andamanica* which is very common, and used in the construction of mats used for walling purposes. Since this is a thin walled bamboo it is broken into three or four pieces longitudinally using wooden mallets and then woven in the form of a mat. No preservative treatment is given to these and they last for about 2-3 years. Besides this major use, bamboo is used in fencing, for making fishing stakes, baskets, and mats.

Small-scale industries engaged in the manufacture of walling mats, baskets, etc. are collecting considerable quantity of bamboo. Though there is no demand for these products from industries, the domestic consumption is increasing steadily due to an increase in population.

Management of Bamboo Stands

The management of bamboo is prescribed only in the recent working plans under the minor forest produce working circle/non-timber forest produce overlapping working circle. Constant decline in bamboo resources over the years has been reported in all the working plans due to unsystematic exploitation. These plans recommend an annual yield of about 700 bamboo per ha, wherever the bamboo brakes exist. Collection of only one-third of culms per clump in a cutting cycle of six years has been recommended. The area under bamboo brakes has been estimated to be about 25,000 ha. Thus, the annual yield is around 175 lakh culms from all over the islands.

Bamboo Plantations

In order to augment the bamboo resources, plantation of bamboo using the rhizomes is being carried out from 1967–68, in certain blank patches of degraded forest areas and as under planting in teak plantations. The total area planted with bamboo till 2003-2004 is 2,710 ha in the UT. From 1999-2000 onwards seeds of thick-walled/solid bamboo, mainly *Bambusa bambos* and *Dendrocalamus strictus* are being procured from the mainland and plantations raised in the watershed areas, vacant non-forest lands and *panchayat* lands. For future it is proposed to increase the area under the thick-walled/solid bamboo in the non-forest areas, as they are more useful than the native Bamboo and can meet the needs of the public in construction activities, thus reducing the pressure on the natural forests for posts and *ballies*.

Research in Bamboo

Introduction of *Melocanna bambusoides* from West Bengal was tried in 1959 and again in 1973. However, this was not successful. Eleven species of bamboo from West Bengal were introduced at Jirkatang in South Andaman in 1970, but only two species, *viz*., *Bambusa tulda* and *B. nutans* survived. Definite conclusions could not be drawn from these trials as they were made with very less number of rhizomes after long transportation by ship from West Bengal. In 1989, introduction trials were made with *Dendrocalamus strictus*, *Bambusa bambos* and *Bambusa tulda* and all of them were found to grow well with the growth and survival of *Bambusa tulda* being the best. Trials with more species, especially the solid and thick-walled bamboo will be required, to meet the future requirement for structural purposes. The National Mission on Bamboo Applications should pay attention to this, through the Department of Environment and Forests or the IFGTB.

For the conservation of genetic resources of bamboo, preservation plots of *Gigantochloa andamanica* were established in 1979 at Austin-I (North Andaman) and Tugapur-I (Middle Andaman). Preservation plots for *Schizostachyum kurzii* at Rutland Island and for *Dinochloa andamanica* at Nayashar (South Andaman) were established in 1999. Bambuseta are available with the forest department as well as with the Botanical Survey of India at Nayashar. The following species are available in the collection: *Bambusa vulgaris*, *B. bambos*, *B. tulda*, *Dendrocalamus brandisii* and *D. strictus*, *B. vulgaris var. striata*, *B. vulgaris var. wamin* and *B. nana*. In certain private lands *Thyrsostachys oliveri* and *Dendrocalamus callostychus* exist. More species are required to be added for phenological and growth observations in the climatic and edaphic conditions of ANI.

Since 1999-2000 vegetative propagation of *Bambusa bambos* and *Dendrocalamus strictus* is being carried out by macro-proliferation by the Silviculture division. Attempts are required to be made for the vegetative propagation of native bamboo by culm cuttings or any other method instead of propagation by rhizomes, which is laborious.

In order to systematise the collection of *Gigantochloa andamanica*, which is getting depleted over the years, the cutting techniques and cutting cycles, have to be standardised. A large number of solid/thick-walled bamboo are required to be evaluated for their growth and yield in these islands in order to raise their plantations over large areas to meet the needs of the rural population as well as small-scale industries.

Future Potential

The current demand for *ballies*, poles, and posts for construction purposes is being met by extraction of non-commercial timber. Many a times the commercial species also get extracted owing to lack of supervision or the inability of the villagers to distinguish between commercial and other species. This leads to the degradation of forests around the settlements. The solid/thick-walled bamboo can substitute the requirement of *ballies* and poles/posts to a large extent and thus can reduce the pressure on the forests to some extent and can simultaneously help in reclamation of degraded areas in the villages. The present level of extraction is about two lakhs *ballies*, and about 50,000 posts per annum in ANI. *Dendrocalamus strictus* can substitute the *ballies* and *Bambusa bambos, B. balooca* or *B. tulda* can substitute the posts. The extent of plantation of these species required to substitute the current and future needs should be worked out division-wise/ village-wise.

The Department of Environment and Forests along with IFGTB can establish model plantations of various species of bamboo, both local and introduced species. In addition, agroforestry models involving bamboo should also be established to encourage farmers to take up commercial plantations of bamboo. In order to supply good quality planting stock of bamboo, the department should establish modern nurseries apart from establishing bambusetum containing the local and introduced bamboo species as well as the elite plus materials of the introduced bamboo species. ANI administration should encourage cultivation of bamboo by providing loan, and facilitating the marketing of produce. Assistance from the Department of Biotechnology as well as the Ministry of Rural Development apart from the financial institutions such as the NABARD should be tapped for taking up large-scale cultivation of bamboo in ANI. Value addition in bamboo is a key component for the development of forest-based industries in the islands. Technologies developed by TIFAC should be made available to people through demonstration projects. IFGTB, Coimbatore, can provide help in extension-cum-training programmes.

Application of GIS in Forestry Sector

The Department of Environment and Forests has established a GIS cell under the Tenth FYP. In addition, the Department of Space has funded the establishment of Andaman & Nicobar Space Establishment Cell (AN-SC). All these facilities are being used by various departments of the Administration. However, existing facilities for GIS applications in the department should be strengthened. A comprehensive exercise to map all existing forest areas and other land uses, using a combination of satellite imagery and ground truthing is a must.

The Department of Space, Government of India and the Department of Environment & Forests, Andaman & Nicobar Administration have assessed the biodiversity at landscape level using GIS, in a project funded by the Department of Biotechnology (IIRS, 2003). For the first time vegetation type and density map of major vegetation types have been prepared using satellite remote sensing data and intensive field observation to provide a comprehensive baseline data on the landscape pattern of the fragile island ecosystem. The spatial information along with detailed field sample observations have been used to determine the disturbance regimes and the biological richness at landscape level which provides information on the habitat quality and potential species and genetic variability. The results of the study on biodiversity at landscape level can be used for bio-prospecting and conservation. Further studies on species diversity and genetic diversity within the species are required.

The facilities of the GIS Cell are being used at present by the Department of Environment and Forests for forest mapping, identification of non-forest land under forest cover and settlement of revenue-forest boundary disputes. The existing facilities can also be used for the following purposes:

Monitoring Forest Degradation

Population growth, industrial development, bio-climatic changes and scarcity of land resources are the main reasons for forest degradation. To control forest degradation, the governments need to know where, when, how soon, and why such degradation happens. On the basis of such knowledge, a general and sustainable management of these resources is possible. GIS and remote sensing are an appropriate tool in doing this. The GIS adopts the numerical methods and spatial analysis tools to delineate the land use. This information can be used in analysing the types, location, and rates of changes in land use and the consequent forest degradation.

Preparation of Working Plans

Due to the rapid changes in the natural ecosystems in recent times, the conventional methods of forest vegetation monitoring have become obsolete. For better management of this dynamic ecosystem, use of a more realistic method is necessary. The GIS and vegetation mapping through satellite imagery provides an opportunity for the monitoring of ecosystem. Rapid appraisal of the forest inventory will help in identification of the correct strategy to achieve the desired goal of conservation of forests and biodiversity.

Forest Inventory

In any resource management exercise, continuous flow and updating of the inventory is one of the important components. Ever increasing population in a land-scarce situation is putting the natural forests and the ecosystem under increased pressure and threat and thus needs to be dynamically managed.

Forest stock maps constitute the basis of the working plan for the territorial forest divisions. They contain detailed spatial information about the recorded forest lands including the administrative jurisdiction at various levels, infrastructure, communications facilities, water resources, and the status of forest vegetation. Maps also include categorisation of forest into density classes, species distribution, assessment of growing stock, growth data for various species and age distribution. This information is vital in presenting the management options like afforestation of blank areas, reforestation of degraded forests, harvesting of mature crop (plantation) followed by regeneration, restoration of biodiversity in monoculture areas, and management of protected areas for biodiversity conservation.

Digital Databases

Managers for land-based systems have to invariably deal with a multitude of maps. Conventional maps are very difficult to synthesise and comprehend. Integration of remote sensing data with GIS related decision support systems could make the job of land managers easy.

Logging

Harvesting of forests produce is an important activity. While extracting the forest produce the economic viability of the extraction has to be looked into to maximise the profits. Transportation of forest produce from the extraction points to the selected depots takes a major share of extraction costs. In identifying the least cost paths, remote sensing and GIS can be very helpful.

Biodiversity Assessment

Assessment of biodiversity has been done at landscape level using the remote sensing and GIS tools. However, certain forest types reported earlier have not been distinguished by the spectral signatures, such as Andaman Secondary Moist Deciduous forests, Brackish water mixed forests, Sub-montane hill valley swamp forests and Cane brakes. These are required to be identified by field survey and their digital signatures have to be differentiated. This will help in further refining the forest type map. The present mapping has been done by a low level of sampling (0.004 per cent) and further refinement is possible by intensive sampling.

Biomass and Productivity Modelling

By conducting field surveys in different types of forests, the standing biomass as well as productivity should be estimated and applied to the areas which are set aside for timber extraction. This shall give a rapid estimate of the quantity that can be sustainably extracted from these areas.

Eco-development Planning

Digital Elevation Models will help in identifying sites that are suitable for check dams, soil and water conservation structures, raising plantations of cane, bamboo, fuel wood, etc. as a part of eco-development programmes in forest areas adjoining the villages.

Preparation of Micro-management Plans for Coral Reefs

Keeping in view the varying density of coral reef and other marine resources in different protected areas, there is a need to develop micro-management plans for each protected area. This will include time series analysis of coral density *vis-à-vis* quality of water in the habitat.

Water Resource Management

Mapping of the drainage basins, streams, etc. to develop hydraulic/ hydrologic modelling to address the issues related to water resource use is essential. The qualitative and quantitative data related to water sources and sinks are required to be incorporated on a GIS platform.

Identification of Important Habitats for Wildlife, especially Birds

The use of GIS and spatial analysis will help in identifying important bird areas and wildlife habitats in an unbiased manner. The large and the least fragmented patches of forests supporting high biological richness are to be identified for long-term protection.

Forest Development Agency and Joint Forest Management

The National Forest Policy 1988 has laid emphasis on natural regeneration, and biodiversity, preservation, and management practices that help the local people.

To translate this policy into action, the Ministry of Environment & Forests issued an enabling JFM Resolution on June 1, 1990, for the involvement of village community living close to the forest. It paved the way for voluntary agencies and NGOs to associate as an interface between the State Forest Departments and the Forest User Groups (FUG) for the revival, restoration, and development of degraded forests.

The 1990 Resolution focused on developing partnership between communities and forest departments. However, the programme suffered due to various factors like traditional law enforcing attitude and ethos of the bureaucracy, lack of understanding of socioeconomic and cultural value system of the locals, insufficient female representation, inter- and intra-village conflicts, lack of statutory authority to local institutions, coverage of only degraded forests under JFM, donor-driven rather than need-driven programme, and target-oriented rather than people-oriented approach.

Subsequently, in 1995, the Resolution was modified to incorporate women and landless households in the scheme. It was further revised in the year 2000, to provide for legal backup to the JFM committees, and extension of JFM in good forests areas.

JFM could not be implemented in ANI as it was not found practical. However, recently the ANI administration after consultations with the local bodies and in technical collaboration with the regional centre of the National Afforestation and Eco-development Board, Jadhavpur University, Kolkata has notified a resolution on JFM. This is now required to be implemented on an experimental basis in selected villages.

Action Plan for Implementation of Suggested Activities

	Activities / Year	*2006*	*2007*	*2008*	*2009*	*2010*	*2011*	*2012*	*2013*	*2014*
i.	Strengthening of Forest Protection machinery: Procurement of seaworthy vessel, vehicles, fast boats, arms and ammunition. Developing communication network. Establishment of Marine Conservation Cell.	■	■	■	■	■	■	■	■	■
ii.	Developing a sound database of forestry sector to facilitate planning & execution/ Implementation of the Information Technology Plan by the Department of Environment and Forests.	■	■	■	■					
iii.	Consolidation of protected areas into viable units. Preparation of management plans.	■	■	■						
iv.	*Ex-situ* conservation. Completion of the biological park. Establishment of gene banks/seed banks, etc.	■	■							
v.	Amendment to the Indian Forest Act in its application to the Andaman & Nicobar Islands through a Regulation/Introduction of Regulation to regulate felling in non-forest areas.	■								
vi.	Collaborative Projects with research institutes on: (a) biodiversity characterisation (species and genetic diversity); (b) *ex situ* conservation of edible nest swiftlet; (c) coral reef monitoring; (d) mangrove conservation; and (e) ecological studies on nutrient cycling and hydrology, etc.		■	■	■	■	■	■		
vii.	Creation of environment awareness through (a) establishment of Eco-clubs in schools; (b) establishment of interpretation centres; (c) publications, etc.	■	■	■	■	■	■	■	■	■
viii.	Introduction of Reduced Impact logging to meet local requirements of timber, strengthening of timber treatment and seasoning facilities.	■	■	■	■	■				
ix.	Launching of Joint Forest Management in selected localities on an experimental basis.	■	■							
x.	Carrying out social forestry/agroforestry schemes on non-forest lands including cultivation of cane and bamboo.	■	■	■	■	■	■	■	■	■
xi.	Introduction trials of more solid/thick-walled bamboo to meet local construction needs and establishing demonstration plots of bamboo.	■	■	■	■	■	■			
xii.	Strengthening of the GIS Cell.	■	■							
xiii.	Eco-restoration of degraded and critical mangrove areas by afforestation with suitable species, monitoring changes in mangroves and protection.	■	■	■	■	■	■	■	■	■

TABLE 10.1

Cane Species in the Middle Andamans

Sl. No.	*Species*	*Flowering Period*	*Fruiting Period*	*Major Uses*
1.	*Calamus andamanicus*	Nov-Dec	March-May	For furniture making.
2.	*Calamus longisetus*	Nov-Dec	March-May	For furniture making but less preferred.
3.	*Calamus palustris*	Oct-Nov	April-May	Fruits are edible.
4.	*Calamus pseudorivalis*	Oct-Nov	March-April	For furniture making and rafting purpose.
5.	*Calamus viminalis*	Nov-Dec	April-May	Fruits are edible.
6.	*Daemonorops kurzianus*	Nov-Dec	April-June	Leaves are used for thatching purpose.
7.	*Korthalsia laciniosa*	Oct-Nov	April-May	For making walking sticks.
8.	*Khortalsia rogersii*	Nov-Dec	March-April	For making stool.

Source: Office of the Divisional Forest Officer, Middle Andaman.

TABLE 10.2

Estimation of Growing Stock of Cane in Middle Andaman Forest Division

Name of Forest Range	*Total Area of the Forest Range(hectares)*	*Estimated Cane Growing Area (hectares)* *		*GrowingStock of Cane in Non-degraded Areas*							
				Calamus andamanicus (Mota Cane)		*Calamus pseudorivalis (Malai Cane)*		*Calamus longisetus (Jungli Cane)*		*Korthalsia laciniosa (Red Cane)*	
		Degraded	*Non-degraded*	*Average (Rmt/Ha)*	*Total Growing Stock(Rmt)*	*Average (Rmt/Ha)*	*Total Growing Stock(Rmt.)*	*Average (Rmt/Ha)*	*Total Growing Stock(Rmt.)*	*Average (Rmt. /Ha.)*	*Total Growing Stock(Rmt.)*
Rangat	12,150	3600	1500	192	2,88,000	160	2,40,000	207	3,10,500	168	2,52,000
Bakultala	10,865	2000	2000	216	4,32000	200	4,00,000	184	3,68,000	189	3,78,000
Bajalungta	34,906	9000	13,500	264	35,64000	280	37,80,000	207	27,94,500	231	31,18,500
Betapur	33,805	12500	13300	216	28,72,800	220	29,26,000	230	30,59,000	147	19,55,100
Long Island	8,118	1000	1500	168	2,52,000	240	3,60,000	161	2,41,500	105	1,57,500
Total	998,44	28,100	31,800		74,08,800		77,06,000		67,73,500		58,61,100

Note: * Estimated cane growing area excludes an area of 142.20 sq. km. declared as Tribal (*Jarawa*) Reserve which is well stocked with different varieties of cane and under profuse natural regeneration due to least biotic interference.

Source: Office of the Divisional Forest Officer, Middle Andaman.

TABLE 10.3

Supply of Cane to Small-scale Industries (SSIs) and Settlers from Middle Andaman Forest

Name of Range	*Calamus andamanicus /Mota Cane(Rmts.)*		*Calamus pseudorivalis /Malai Cane(Rmts.)*		*Calamus longisetus /Jungli Cane(Rmts.)*		*Korthalsia laciniosa /Red Cane(Rmts.)*	
	SSI	*Settlers*	*SSI*	*Settlers*	*SSI*	*Settlers*	*SSI*	*Settlers*
				1995-1996				
Rangat	2700		8000	11835			11000	
Bakultala	1900		2450			9835	4700	
Bajalungta	18000		4500		16000		1500	3004
Betapur	15400		23200		2000	4450	58300	
Long Island						126		
Total	38000		38150	11835	18000	14411	75500	3004
				1996-1997				
Rangat	4000		7000	4269			9500	
Bakultala	7000		10000				14500	
Bajalungta	26600	7764	4800		40000		13000	
Betapur	31300		41800			44000	79800	
Long Island								
Total	68900	7764	63600	4269	40000	44000	116800	
				1997-1998				
Rangat	4400		4300	4355			8700	
Bakultala						1895		
Bajalungta	2000		8500				5000	
Betapur	10400		25000			29530	46200	
Long Island						800		
Total	16800		37800	4355		32225	59900	
1998-1999								
Rangat	3200		2200	3705			3600	
Bakultala		1300		1150				
Bajalungta			600		1200	33200		4786
Betapur	85800		22700		12000		46000	
Long Island						800		
Total	89000	1300	25500	4855	13200	34000	49600	4786

...Contd. ...

...Contd. ...

SSI	*Settlers*	*SSI*	*Settlers*	*SSI*	*Settlers*	*SSI*	*Settlers*
				1999-2000			
Rangat	700		2000	2730			3000
Bakultala	2100		3000	3460			3500
Bajalungta	4500		6000	200		5185	10000
Betapur	17300		32800			29800	52700
Long Island						200	
Total	24600		43800	6390		35185	69200

Source: Office of the Divisional Forest Officer, Middle Andaman

TABLE 10.4

Cost Factors for Departmental Extraction of Cane

Sl. No.	*Species*	*Average Length of Mature Culm Rounded off to nearest Full Number (Metres)*	*Average Cost of Collection of per Piece 7 metres in Length (Rs.)*	*Royalty Rates per Piece 7 metres Rates in Length (Rs.)*
1.	*Calamus andamanicus*	24	6.00	2.45
2.	*Calamus pseudorivalis*	20	3.50	0.98
3.	*Calamus longisetus*	23	2.75	1.47
4.	*Korthalsia laciniosa*	21	2.50	0.56

Source: Office of the Divisional Forest Officer, Middle Andaman.

TABLE 10.5

Quantity of Bamboo Collected

Decade	*Quantity (in '000s)*	*Remarks*
1952-62	24700	The large quantity of collection is due to the colonisation scheme started in 1952 under which bamboo was extracted for construction of huts for settlers.
1962-72	15688	
1972-82	15184	
1982-92	16001	

Source: Jayaraj, R.S.C and P.M. Bhatt (1999). Bamboos in the Andaman and Nicobar Islands. (Unpublished). Prepared for the Seminar on Bamboos held at Bangalore.

TABLE 10.6

Trend in the Collection of Bamboo and its Correlation with the Population Increase

Year	*Quantity (in '000s)*	*Population (in '000s)*
1952-53	88	30.90
1960-61	370	63.54
1970-71	1595	115.13
1980-81	1003	188.74
1990-91	1454	279.11
Correlation between population and bamboo collection		
	Bamboo	Population
Bamboo	1	
Population	0.735202	1

Source: Jayaraj, R.S.C and P.M. Bhatt (1999). Bamboos in the Andaman and Nicobar Islands. (Unpublished). Prepared for the Seminar on Bamboos held at Bangalore.

ANNEXURE 10.1

Biodiversity Conservation and Forest Management

Training Module
for
Committee Members and Forest Frontline Workers
on JFM, FDA, Watershed, Micro-planning and Monitoring Issues

Introduction

This two day Training Module is aimed at developing a perspective for Joint Forest Management (JFM) Programme, Forest Development Agency (FDA) set up, Watershed Management and how to do Micro-planning besides Monitoring and Evaluation. Each of the above-mentioned themes are interlinked and complimentary to each other, leading to holistic development through Participatory Management. It is proposed to impart this Training Module through the Spear Head Team, which can work at the micro level in the field.

It is envisaged that this Training Module will have two days schedule. On the first day besides 'ice breaking', the Session–1 will give details of JFM, FDA and Watershed Management. The Session–2 will focus on Micro-planning and how to implement various works. The Session–3 will focus on Monitoring and Evaluation and how to assess the changes through simple indicators. On the second day the Session–4 is planned for practical training in nearby areas for understanding the concepts through demonstration based on the theoretical inputs.

Constitution of Spear Head Team

Under JFM Programme and FDA, the village community will have to take new responsibilities. For achieving the objectives of the programme they have to be motivated and organised into sustainable institutions. It is envisaged that the FDA will constitute a Spear Head Team (SHT) that will be responsible for promoting village institutions and their federations and also to assist them in discharge of the responsibilities.

A Spear Head Team at the District level will be a multidisciplinary team and shall consist of 5 persons (preferably two women members)–trained in social skills; forestry; watershed management; gender sensitisation; and conflict resolution. The multidisciplinary team shall have representatives from forestry, animal husbandry and social discipline headed by an Assistant Conservator of Forests besides a Range Officer and other members.

The other SHT members shall be graduates in their disciplines. SHT may appoint community organisers who may be diploma holders in social/technical disciplines. They would be general-purpose organisers and motivators to be located in different parts of the District, depending upon the scope for promoting JFM. It would be a great advantage, if FDA and SHT can identify NGOs in the District who would be willing to support participatory management. They could be given assistance for deploying their staff to work as community organisers and for undertaking community organising and capacity building activities at promotion stage as well as during implementation.

The members of the SHT will be drawn from Government Department as well as from outside. For the Government officials to join SHT, there will be need to provide incentives. The SHT will be appointed by FDA and will be responsible to the Member Secretary of the FDA. The leader of the SHT should be given autonomy in functioning with responsibility for reporting the progress against the programme decided in their consultation with FDA.

The FDA will have to invite applications from various Government Departments as also by public notice. The selection will be made by a Committee on which officers as well as NGO representatives shall be placed. The SHT shall be responsible for imparting training to the JFMCs in the FDA.

DAY – 1:
SESSION – 1 (1 HOUR)

Joint Forest Management

The Joint Forest Management Programme (JFM) in India represents a major effort in the last decade and a quarter to conserve the natural resources taking into consideration the needs of the people living in and around the forests who are partially or wholly dependent on forest resources for their livelihood. This has resulted in a paradigm shift in the National Forest Policy 1988; State Forest Departments and today in 27 states, there are 72,760 JFM Committees (JFMCs) covering 16.6 mha. of forestland benefiting around 46.37 lakh families.

The Ministry of Environment & Forests has issued guidelines in June 1990 followed by February 2000 circular through which JFM was extended to good forest areas; thrust was given for more representation to women and preparation of micro-plans. In the December, 2002 circular emphasis has been laid on Memorandum of Understanding between the State Forest Departments and JFM Committees; Coordination with *Panchayats* and to develop linkages for marketing of Non-Timber Forest Products.

This is one national programme, which is based on the Gandhian principle of *Gram Rajya*. By organising the villagers through the JFM Committees the motivated human resource is available for covering the scarce natural resource and their sustainable management. Out of 6 lakh villages in the country around 1.75 lakh villages with a population of about 350 million people are dependent on the forests either completely or in a substantial manner.

However, the success of the JFM Programme is now dependent on the fact that JFM Committees plan and manage the resources and the frontline staff in the State Forest Departments which includes the foresters and forest guards, facilitate the implementation of the various schemes and works.

The land available for development through JFM can be categorised into following categories:

(i) Farmlands

(ii) Community lands–including permanent pastures and village common land

(iii) Wastelands

(iv) Forestlands.

In order to develop the land through JFM, integration of technological inputs shall include the following:

(i) Agroforestry on Private agriculture land.

(ii) Pasture development on village Commons and Community lands.

(iii) Rehabilitation of degraded forests and wastelands by:

- Pasture development.
- Silvi-pasture development.
- Intensive Plantations.

(v) Silviculture management of good forests.

Forest Development Agency

The Forest Development Agency (FDA) set up has been established at the Territorial Forest Division level and it is aimed that through the FDAs, delay in flow of funds and multiplicity of schemes shall be avoided. FDA is the instrument to implement the National Afforestation Programme (NAP).

The 'objectives' of the FDA are:

- Direct involvement of people in afforestation and management of forests.
- Empowerment at the grass-roots level.
- Accounting of funds spent by the JFMCs.
- Transparency through micro-plan for all activities including entry point activities through PRA.
- Greater role of people in decision making.

The JFMC at the village level with FDA provide an organic link between the Forest Department and the grass-roots level communities. The FDAs are also required to act as conduit for channelisation of funds from other sources. It is proposed to constitute 800 FDAs in the country during the Tenth Five-year Plan.

Mechanism

FDA is required to sign MoU with JFMCs indicating mutual obligation, rights and role.

The FDA Project proposals are forwarded to the Ministry of Environment & Forests (NAEB) through the Principal Chief Conservator of Forests (PCCF) of the state. On approval funds are directly released to FDAs by the NAEB in installments. FDA is required to retain overhead component and transfer funds to the JFMC account. The account of JFMC is to be operated jointly by Member Secretary and Treasurer from the village. The state government through the PCCF has to monitor the implementation of the FDA Projects.

Composition of FDA

General Body

The Conservator of Forests is the Chairman. Members include 50 Presidents of JFMCs of which 20 have to be women, one non-official representative from the apex institutional framework of *panchayats*, DFO, Sub DFO/ACF and Range Officer concerned.

Executive Body

The Conservator of Forests is the Chairman. The Divisional Forest Officer is the Member Secretary cum Chief Executive. *Ex officio* members (without votary rights) include the District Development Officer, District level Officers of Agriculture, Animal Husbandry, Rural Development, Soil Conservation, Tribal Welfare, Industries, Public Health and Engineering and Education Departments. One Additional District Magistrate or Additional Collector has to be nominated by the Deputy Commissioner or District Collector. One non-official representative from the apex institutional framework of *panchayats* and fifteen nominees from the JFMCs in which minimum seven should be women are also members.

Watershed Management

The Watershed Management (WSM) has evolved and passed through several development stages. At the initial stages, WSM was a subject of forestry and related hydrology. Involvement of people was not an issue. It was solely an affair of the government Forest Department. Activities were targeted mainly at symptoms. During the second stage, it became a land resources management related activities with eye on economic benefits as well as Integrated Watershed Management (IWSM). At this stage beneficiary, rather involvement of the local people of the catchment areas was considered important. Finally, now it is a "Participatory, Integrated" WSM (PIWSM) with involvement and contribution from the people. Now, the PIWSM looks at symptoms as well as the causes. The entire village is a micro watershed hence any FDA Project has to take care of this issue.

The Watershed Management must focus on upstream and downstream linkages. For sustainability; local value addition, documenting best practices and lessons learned and establishment of Demonstration Centres is essential.

During watershed programmes plantations, soil and moisture conservation works, irrigation structures, roads, community halls, etc. are developed. The need is that village communities are able to manage these assets and carry further the developmental activities.

DAY – 1:
SESSION – 2 (5 HOURS – IN TWO PARTS)

Micro-planning

At the time of conducting the micro-planning exercise in a JFM Committee area above-mentioned category of lands have to be identified along with appropriate technologies.

Following heads should be considered while doing micro level planning:

(i) Rapport building and prioritising problems and solutions.

(ii) Priority setting and motivation exercises.

(iii) Socioeconomic and sociocultural survey.

(iv) Evaluation of forest dependency level.

(v) A study on traditions, cultural heritage and other rituals of villagers related to forests.

In Micro-planning, activities will have to be undertaken such as:

- Participatory planning, employing PRA techniques.
- Entry point activities to be undertaken like construction of school building, hand pump, meeting hall, approach road, etc.
- Raising of nurseries preferably by local women groups to fill up the blanks in the lands to be developed.
- Soil and water conservation works on watershed principles.
- Arrangement for protection of the assigned areas.
- Planting of saplings.
- Weeding and cut back operations.
- Soil work.
- Collection of non-timber forest produce and its equitable distribution.
- Harvesting of matured trees and its sharing between the JFMC and state Forest Departments (SFD).

While looking for the technological options we have to combine inputs of agriculture and forestry along with soil and moisture conservation works resulting in integrated land use. The wastelands can be forestlands or revenue wastelands. The land category wise technological options for land development are given below where various development measures for different types of land in a JFM Committee area have to be undertaken.

Agroforestry on Private Agriculture Lands

The area under agroforestry on agricultural land has to be location specific and dependant upon the needs of the landowner. However, areas, which are unsuitable for cultivation, should preferably be taken under farm forestry giving preference to local species of economic importance.

Linked with agroforestry is also the need for use of bio-fertiliser in increasing crop productivity. Growing *Prosopis juliflora* on the field boundaries for vegetative fence and cutting every two or three years helps in supplementing the fuel wood requirement and provides natural boundary of the farmland. jatropha and bamboo provide ample income opportunities to the villagers; hence they have to be promoted.

Standing quality silviculture crop in the farmer's field shall encourage the villagers to take active interest in plantation activities along the field bunds for socioeconomic upliftment.

Rehabilitation of Degraded Forests and Wastelands

The status of degraded forests (0.4 density and below) has to be found out from the field survey and a suitable site specific silvi-pastoral model has to be evolved that should encompass the following:

(i) Site-specific model.

(ii) Pre–treatment of soil/Pre–treatment of seed (Figure 1).

(iii) Choice of species.

In India the population is ever increasing leading to the insufficient resources. The people living near the forest or inside the forest, called as 'forest dwellers' depend solely on this natural resource for fulfilment of the basic needs and the degradation of forests is partly due to overexploitation of forests in terms of shifting cultivation, encroachment, illicit felling of trees and cattle grazing, etc.

In order to augment technology for land development the advancement made in the field of silviculture are essential to achieve the desired results and the efforts of Research and Development (R&D) are required to be replicated in the field to demonstrate to the local people. Some of the measures are listed below:

(i) Suitable silvicultural practices especially raising of nurseries, use of mulches, use of fertilisers (Figure 2) and Clonal propagation, etc.

(ii) Quick growing species to be evolved.

(iii) Suitable Model of 'multi-tier' plantation to be evolved and demonstrated.

(iv) The high yielding varieties of NTFPs and medicinal plants to be evolved and demonstrated.

(v) Multiple use and high yielding varieties of fuel, fodder, fruit bearing species are to be planted for improving economic condition of the people.

(vi) Wildlife habitat improvement for providing shelter, food and water and to work for wildlife conservation.

Figure 1

Seed Treatment

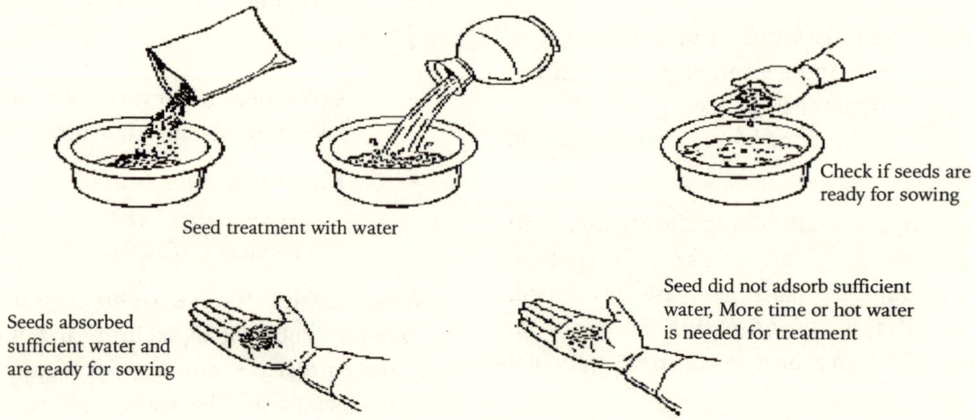

Figure 2

Proper Use of Fertiliser-Preferably Bio-fertiliser

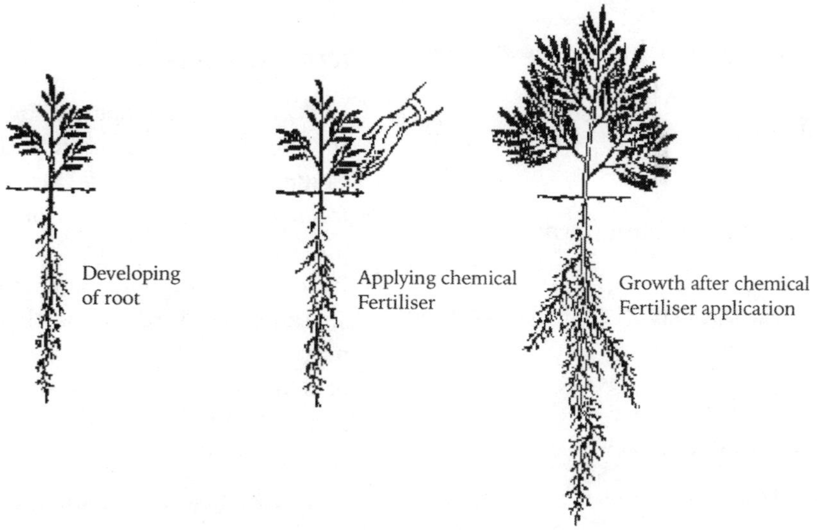

Once the programme provides the local people 'alternate solutions' as per the above listed measures, response of the local communities to the programme will be positive and they will be convinced not to overexploit the available forest resources in the vicinity of villages. The keenness to work in collaboration with the Forest Department will also be more and all activities that are detrimental to forests will be reduced.

The technological inputs should stress on strengthening the existing forests by:

(i) Enrichment planting.

(ii) Soil and moisture conservation works.

(iii) Multiple shoot cutting in coppice species for clean boles and availability of fuel wood.

(iv) Fodder production linked to increased milk production.

(v) Returning livestock manure to the farmland increases production, i.e., nutrient cycling (Figure 3).

Figure 3

Nutrient Cycle

In the frame work of the technological package the stress shall be on the principle of 'Care and Share' through 'socio–silviculture'.

Proposed Framework is applicable for following types of forest areas:

(i) **For Degraded Forests:**

- Multi-tier forestry.

  (Same area will have pasture/medicinal plants; tall trees).

- Rooted Stocks Management/Natural Regeneration/ Cut Back Operation.
- Watershed Development.
- Soil Conservation Works.

(ii) **Good Forest Area:**

- For Management and Protection.
- Seed collection/processing/value addition/ marketing of NTFP.
- Cultivation of Medicinal Plants.
- Raising of nursery stock–decentralised, at women's Self-Help Group level.

(iii) **For Both Areas:** Following items are important and are must:

- 5 per cent of the total budget amount should be for entry point activity.
- 5 per cent of the total budget amount should be for the capacity building.
- 5 per cent of the total budget amount should be for public awareness campaign.

The following points have to be given additional consideration:

(i) Area protected/managed and developed should be around 50 ha and more each year.

(ii) 10 per cent of the total budgeted outlay should be in terms of voluntary contribution of labour/money, etc.

(iii) Revolving fund shall be created from the income for sustaining the activity.

(iv) Maintenance and protection shall be from the revolving fund/voluntary labour.

(v) Village level/watershed wise plan shall be used after mapping of different types of area.

In hills, conifers like fir should be mixed with broad leaved species to avoid accumulation of undecomposed litter.

NTFP Management

Any land development option or technological input in the JFMC area can only be easily adopted by Committees if they are assured of 'quick returns'. Since forests have long gestation period the only option is 'intermediate yield' in the form of Non-Timber Forest Products (NTFPs) and fodder production which sustains the interest of the local community till the major harvest of timber and beyond. The annual income of a household near forest area is dependent on NTFP; hence NTFP management is an important part of any technological package.

Conservation, production, extraction and value addition (i.e., processing) of NTFP is required for better income generation to the JFM Committee members. This will also rehabilitate the degraded forests. An assessment of NTFP potential in the JFM area can be done by vegetation survey. After that, harvesting limits have to be decided to prevent overexploitation and unscientific harvesting.

Vegetation Survey

The Vegetation survey in the forest area has to be carried out under three groupings:

- To know the 'availability of NTFP species' collected in the area under JFM Committee along with description of its availability, parts used, season, uses, and value.
- 'Quantitative data collection'—preference ranking, using quantitative ranking method to find the local significance and economic value of the given species. In preference ranking and direct matrix testing, data can be cross-verified using paired or triad testing.
- A detailed 'grid sampling' of 0.1 ha each sample plot; as explained below in the Figure 4 in the JFM forest area after 1 year to find out the difference in NTFP availability between conserved and un-conserved areas.

Sample Plots can be systematically laid out. The size of the sample Plot is 31.7 m x 31.7 m. All NTFP species in the quadrate are identified and counted. Regeneration survey is done in 2 m x 2 m in the centre.

Figure 4

Formation of a Grid

A. Methodology for Vegetation Survey

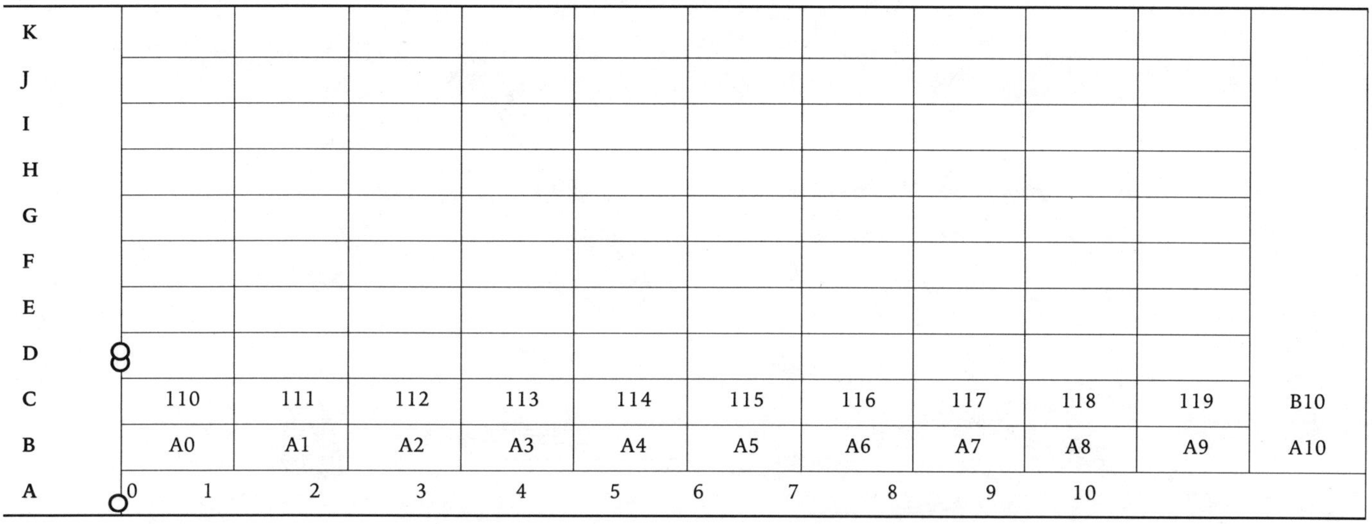

= Two selected grid points in each grid plan (area) is used

B. Example of Grid Serial

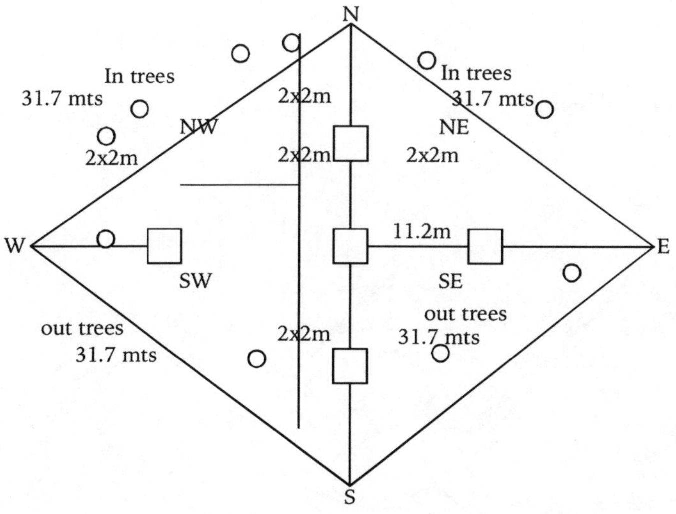

The Growing Stock enumeration and Regeneration Survey form an integral part of this sampling and with this assessment it is possible to quantify the extent of potential the area has, for further augmentation of NTFP resource. The survey also takes into account the regeneration of weeds like *Cassia tora* which are very important in the current environmental conditions for expanding the NTFP base.

Cultivation of these NTFPs on wastelands will not only develop the land but also lead to higher production of NTFPs. The Committee members can get higher income through integration of NTFP/ Agroforestry with 'micro-credit' linkages and organised market network. This can be done by establishing a 'federation' of JFM Committees, which can oversee such new advancements.

Forest Regeneration

The wastelands, which are totally barren, have to be taken under pasture development. The 'primary succession' has to be first ensured. The hill contours can evidently regenerate through improved protection, rotational grazing and the construction of simple engineering structures like boulder check dams, boulder contour bunds, Gully Plugging and Continuous Contour Trenches (CCT) laid out by 'A–Level' (Figures 5. A, B, C, D, E and F) at a contour interval of 5 m with 45 cm x 45 cm x 45 cm dug up and its loose soil spread 1 m wide in which grass seed is sown in the pre-monsoon season. Pebbles are arranged in front to prevent soil erosion.

Figure 5 A

Different Types of A–Frame

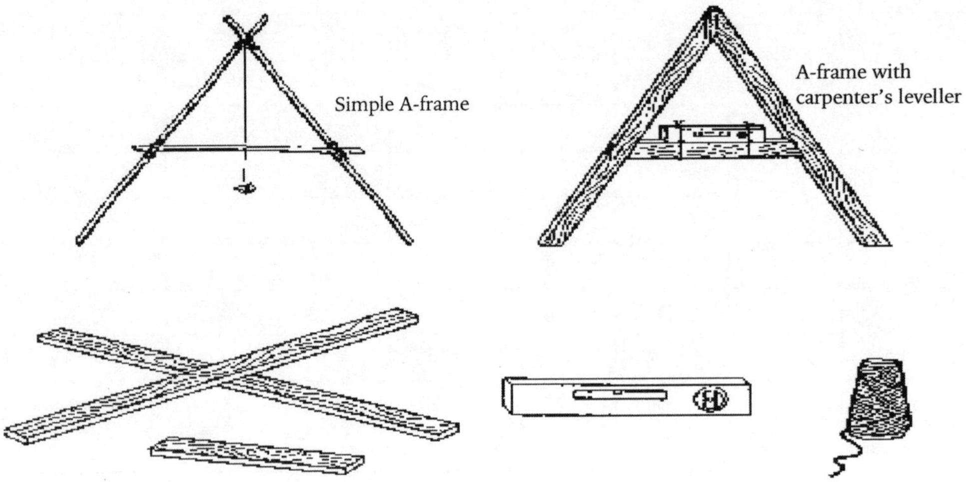

Figure 5 B

How to Make an A–Frame

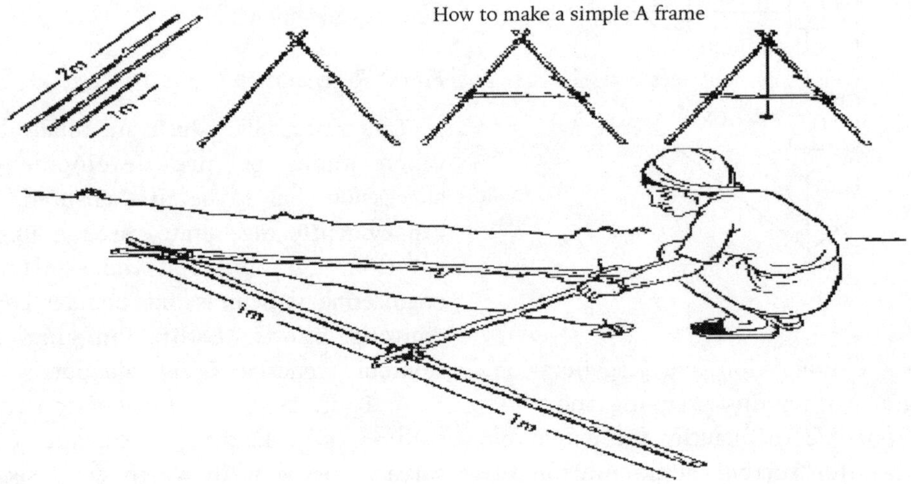

Figure 5 C

Calibration to Find the Centre of the Frame

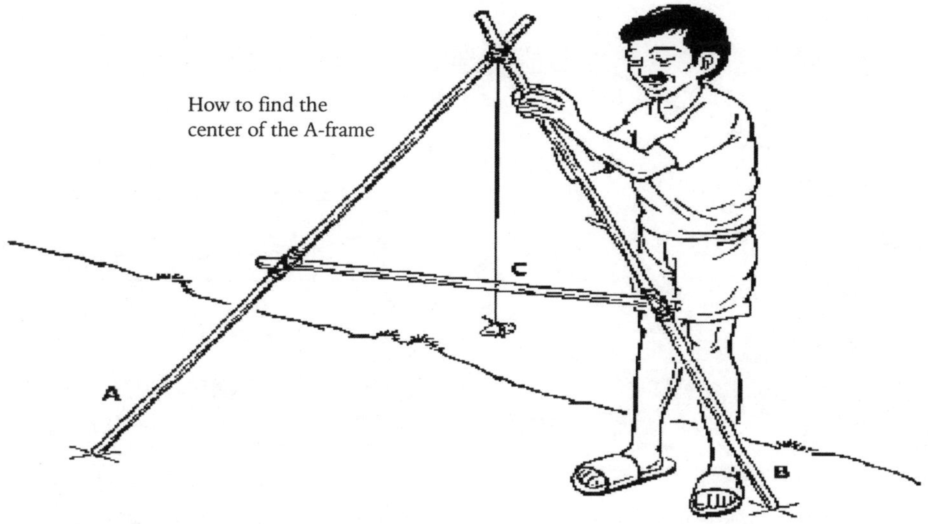

Figure 5 D

Calibration Continued

Figure 5 E

Locating Contour Lines

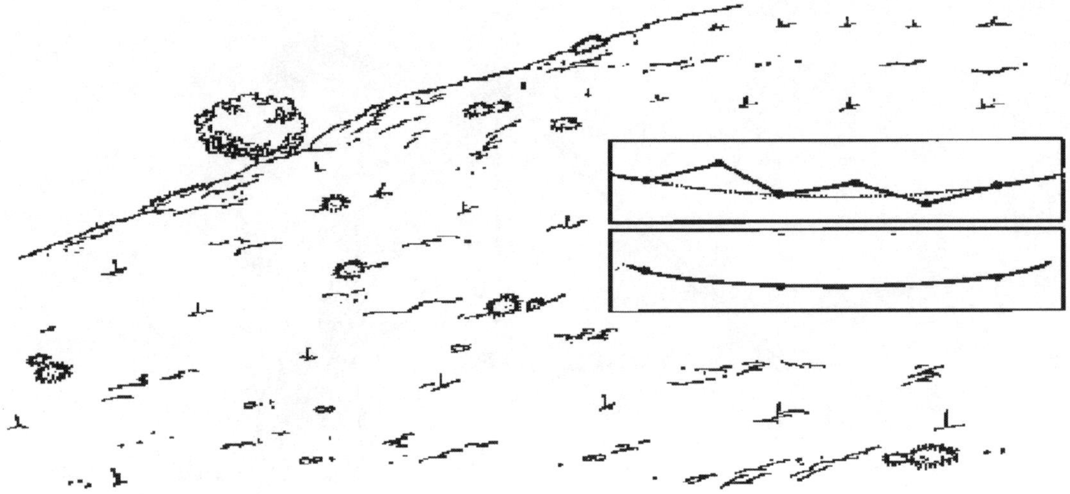

Figure 5 F

Adjust Contour Lines–Consider Only those Points which form a Smooth Contour

The use of low cost technologies like 'dykes' and 'percolation tanks' can catch the imagination of the people and can retain moisture for longer period. Growing grass on contours is an excellent example of blending technology with socioeconomic development. The fodder grasses such as *Heteropogan contortus, Cenchrus ciliaris, C. setigerus, Themeda quadrivalvis, Cynodon dactylon, Pennicitum pedicillatum* and *legumes* like *Stylosanthes hamata* and *S. scabra* are seeded. The tree density is kept at 300 trees/hectare. This is a very cost-effective technology. The Figure 6 explains this concept in detail.

Figure 6

Benefits to the Land

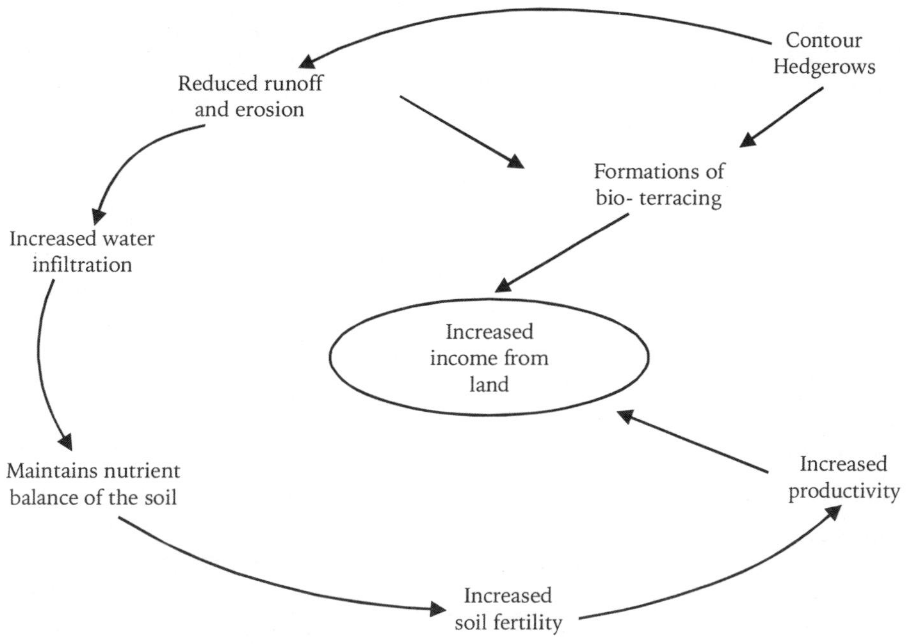

The ground situation of this technology as described above is depicted in Figure 7 below:

Figure 7

Schematic Depiction of Soil and Moisture Conservation Works

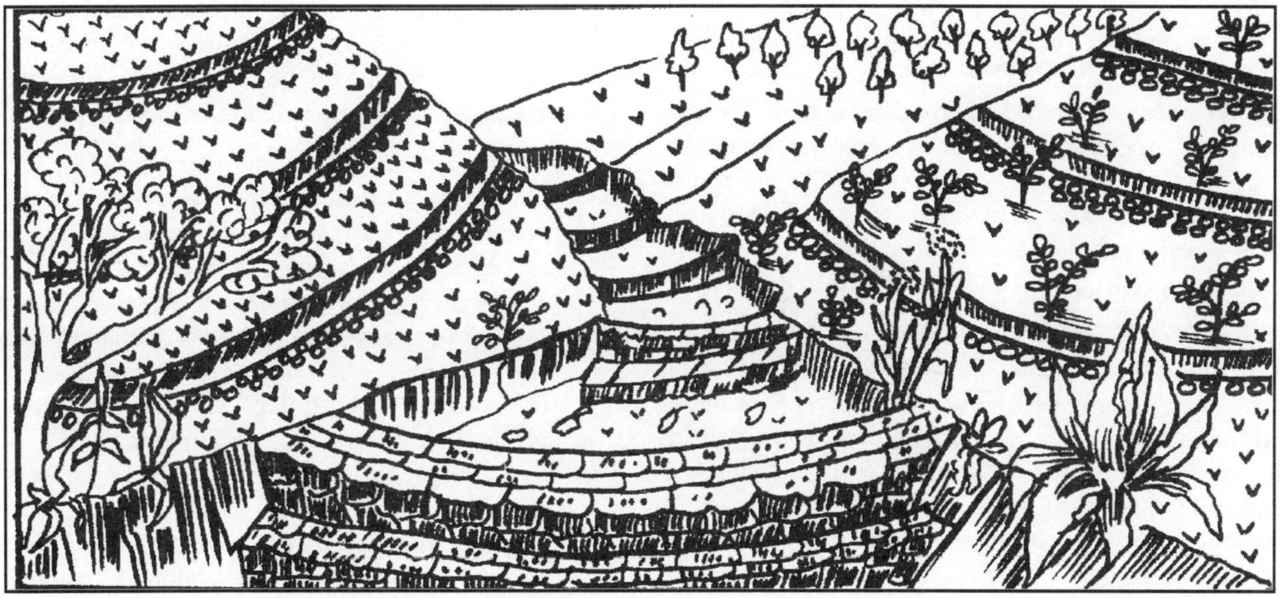

With CCT and series of check dams leading to soil deposition area under shifting cultivation has to be developed with separate technology choosing fast growing tree species and erosion control measures. Agroforestry Model combinations like Agri–silvi, Silvi–pastoral and Agri–horticultural with suitable inputs of soil and moisture conservation measures can be most effective. This should be done after discussion with village level Councils or Village *Panchayats*.

Provision has to be made for disposal of excess rainwater from the terraces whose shoulder bunds be planted with grass and other perennial shrubs to obtain the supply of fodder for domestic animals. Species selected may include *Albizzia stipulata, Grewia optiva, Celtis australis, Alnus nepalensis*, areca nut, coconut, bamboo and agriculture crops like beans, maize, coffee, chillies, ginger, yam, sweet potato, etc.

The degraded forest areas can be further divided into lightly degraded, moderately degraded and highly degraded depending upon the age and density of the rootstock.

In the 'lightly degraded forests', the density of roots is more than 2000 live root stumps per hectare and the age of the rootstock is not more than 40 years. Natural regeneration through coppice is the main stay of this treatment practice.

In the 'moderately degraded forests' degradation process starts normally 20-30 years back. The density in such category of forests is less as compared to lightly degraded forests, the age of the live rootstock is not more than 60 years and natural regeneration is completely absent. The gap planting is done with 500 trees per hectare. In such areas two types of treatments are required to be done. These include 'eco-restoration' using integrated watershed approach and multi-layered plantation of locally desired species in gaps and/or blocks at 3m x 3m or 4m x 4m with rehabilitation measures. The low cost and site specific mechanical and vegetative measures making full use of local available material is the most appropriate technology. *Ipomoea carnea* and *Agave americana* are good species for live hedge.

The silvicultural operations such as identification of stumps to be treated silviculturally, dressing of stumps, pollarding in first year, weeding in the second year, multiple shoot cutting in the third year and singling operation in the fourth year are required to be carried out simultaneously to promote natural regeneration from the rootstock. All cultural operations have to be carried out during October–December months to prevent damage to the growing stock during raining season.

The 'highly degraded forest areas' are devoid of existing rootstock but if it exists, its age is more than 100 years. Mere plantation of multiple species including 30 per cent fodder species is the major treatment with 750 trees per hectare along with intensive soil and moisture conservation works as mentioned above.

In areas where gullies have formed especially ravenous areas, species like *Dicanthium anulatum* can be planted in gully beds and live hedge with brushwood can be used for gully plugging. *Acacia nilotica, Prosopis juliflora* and bamboo (*Dendrocalamus strictus*) grow well in gully areas.

The 'major activities' in any category of land management and its development must include:

- **Grazing Management**—based on actual grazing requirement, carrying capacity of the land and as per the area voluntarily accepted by the JFM Committee members for closure. This has to be demarcated on a map and also on the site by laying out markings.
- **Fuel wood Extraction**—needs to be regulated by delimiting the area for closure, marking it over a map and in the field. The practice of adopting multiple shoot cutting technique in coppice species to tend the crop and at the same time regulate fuelwood supply to the users must be followed (Figure 8).
- **Fire Protection**—Prevention of fire by line cutting, which are traditional methods needs to be done at regular interval through commissioning of fire protection services from communities, gap planting with resilient species like *Acacia auriculiformis* and preparation of new fire lines.
- **Social Fencing**—The standard practice in the plantations and during closing areas for protection is to dig a Cattle Proof Trench (CPT) of 1.5 m top width by 1 m deep and 1.20 base in a trapezium form to close the area. This is a very costly operation (Rs. 1200 per hectares) though labour intensive. Recently, efforts have been made to involve community directly in voluntary protection, known as 'social fencing' by using live hedge for boundary demarcation of the area. The money thus, saved is used for eco-development activities in JFM Committee like constructing seed storage godowns, community

Figure 8

Fuelwood Production

halls, school building, stop dams, hand pumps and water conservation tanks, etc.

Gap Planting and Enrichment of the natural forests consists of '3 Models' based on local needs and multipurpose forestry management.

- **Fuelwood Model** with 50 per cent of the area to be planted with fuelwood species which will be removed from the canopy when cover is established.
- **Green manure and Fodder Model**—with 50 per cent of the area devoted to fodder and green manure.
- **Fruit/NTFP Model**—with 40 per cent area devoted to fruit and non-timber forest products.

DAY – 1:
SESSION – 3 (2 HOURS)

Monitoring and Evaluation

Every Programme has to be monitored and after a period of implementation, there should be an evaluation. For this purpose a Monitoring Committee/ Sub-Committee should be constituted by national, state and district fora to oversee the progress of various developmental works *vis-à-vis* financial sanctions, and physical verification of developmental works shall be carried out. The proforma for quarterly progress return and other ancillary reports are given in detail for submission by the executing agencies, i.e., the JFMCs.

The Central and State Advisory Committee should also regularly assign monitoring and evaluation to reputed independent agencies to provide their feedback to advisory committees. The advisory committees may also identify important issues, which may be studied by independent reputed institutions/experts to provide feedback that may lead to change in policy and procedures.

The implementing agencies through their state governments shall have to report periodically to the MoEF for any deviation from the proposed items of works well in advance. Annual physical verification (at the end of financial year) will be mandatory for reviewing the progress under this Programme. For local level monitoring, District/Divisional Forest Officer (DFO) will be responsible for reporting.

It is no exaggeration to assert that however desirable the purpose of a Project, formulated and crafted with utmost care, it is bound to carry within it the germs of inadequacies and gaps that would surface as the programme is implemented. Rather than to assume that the project design is near to perfection, it is far more realistic to assume the other way around that no project design can be without hidden malady and in fact would be carrying within its womb concealed problems, gaps, shortcomings and inadequacies that are bound to bare themselves as the implementation proceeds.

This can be corrected by adopting following approach:

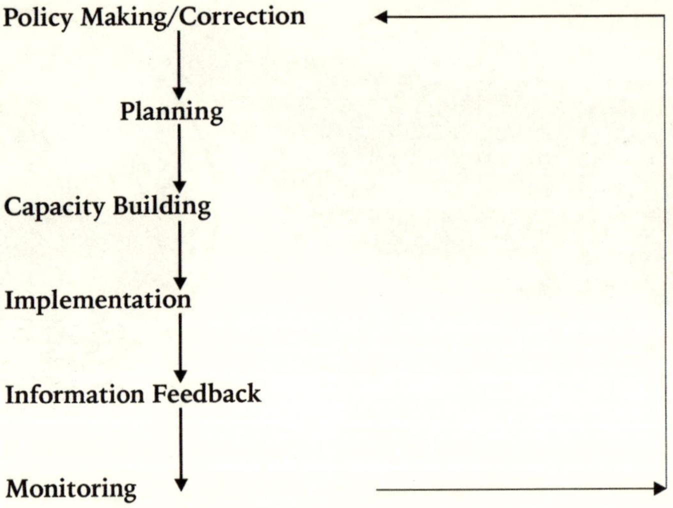

Criteria and Indicators

The following criteria for success are envisaged in this Scheme based on the performance indicators:

Sl. No.	*Criteria*	*Parameters for Success*		*Performance Indicators*
1.	Technical	Improved ecological condition	i.	Better availability of fodder, fuel wood and other NTFPs, etc.
			ii.	Status of regeneration by regeneration Survey (Figure 4).
			iii.	Increased availability of fodder, fuel wood and timber from non forestland.
2.	Institutional	Effectiveness of training and operationalising of principles of shared responsibility.	i.	Behavioural change in Forest Department Staff.
			ii.	Relationship between Forest Department and community.
3.	Institutional	Performance of villages and District level initiatives	i.	In terms of meeting, activities, articipation, and responsibilities.
4.	Sustainability	Cost-effective eco-development activities	i.	Employment generation and diversification.
			ii.	Value addition of goods.
5.	Equity	Empowerment of marginalised groups and women	i.	Economic empowerment.
			ii.	Social empowerment.
6.	Participatory	Voluntary contribution	i.	Increased development fund.
7.	Participatory	Better forest management	i.	Rotational grazing.
			ii.	Rotational patrolling.
			iii.	Decrease in forest offences.
			iv.	Control of forest fires.
			v.	Removal of encroachment from forestland.
8.	Financial	Expected returns on investment	i.	Intermediate returns.
			ii.	Expected final return.

Formats for Monitoring and Evaluation: I-VIII

Format–I: General Details

1. State:
2. JFM-Resolution/By Govt. Order:
3. Year of Implementation:
4. Area under JFM Programme:
5. District/Division:
6. Objectives/Aims:
7. Total No. of Villages in JFM Programme:

Format–II: Details of Joint Forest Management Committee

(As per GoI guidelines for strengthening of JFM Programme.)

Universal nomenclature should be adopted for the committees constituted under JFM programme. Accordingly each state shall have to notify by the corrigendum the name of committee (*viz.*, FPC, EDC, etc.) as JFMC for having a uniform pattern of Monitoring & Evaluation.

1. Notification & Constitution of Committee:
2. District/Division:
3. Number of JFMC:
4. Objective to be Achieved:
5. How JFMC Constituted:
6. a. Date of Formation of JFMC:
   b. JFMC Registered/Not registered under societies Registration Act 1860:
   c. Date of Functioning by JFMC:
7. a. Status of Land under JFMC:
   b. Area of Such Land:
   c. If Forestland, Name(s) of Compartment(s) Protected by JFMC:
8. Are Boundaries of JFMC Area Well Demarcated?
   a If Yes, Whether with the Consent of JFMC Member:
   b. No Prior Consent Obtained:
   c. How are the Boundaries Demarcated:

Format–III: Composition of JFMCs

1. State:
2. District/Division:
   a. Range/Beat:
   b. No. of Villages:
3. Village Community Type:
   a. Homogeneous/Heterogeneous
   b. SC/ST/OBC/Others:
   c. Total:
4. Number of Households in the Village:
5. Members in JFMCs per Family:
   (Husband/Wife)
   a. Husband Alone:
   b. Wife Alone:
   c. Husband/Wife as Joint members:
   d. No Representative from a Household (Reasons thereof):
6. Formation of Executive Committees:
7. Number of Members in JFMC and their landholding:
   a) <00.5 Ha, b) 0.5-1.0 Ha, c) 1-1.5 Ha, d) >2 Ha
8. Status of Land under JFMC:
   a. Forestland:
   b. Non-Forestland:
      (i) Private:
      (ii) Community Land:
      (iii) Fallow Wasteland, etc.:
   (The list could include all other categories of non-forestlands applicable to particular state).
9. If 8a:
   (i) Condition/Nature of Forest at the beginning of JFM Programme:
   (ii) Composition of Crop:

Format–IV: Implementation of JFM Programme

1. State: District: Division: FDA:
2. No. of JFMCs in the FDA:
3. Works and Activities Entrusted to JFMCs:
   a.
   b.
   c.
   etc.
4. Constraints in Execution of Works (if any):
5. Suggestions to Overcome 4:
6. Requirements of Villagers:
7. How Requirements Met before JFM Programme:
8. Mechanism of Benefit Sharing:
9. Revolving Fund/Community Fund
   If Any (Complete details):
   a. Who Maintains the Fund:
   b. What is the Role Assigned to Women Member:
   c. Auditing of Accounts, etc.:
   d. Whether External Funding Required:
10. Details of Works Done by JFMCs (Over a period of 1–3 yrs):

Sl. No.	*Physical Targets Financial Target*	*Achievements*	
		Physical	*Financial*

11. If a Major Activity is Afforestation of Land:
    a. Area of such Plantation:
    b. Choice of Species:
    c. (In Term of Survival, e.g. Age of Seedlings and the Status of Plantation based on the Data of Monitoring Done) Rating/Grading of Plantation:
12. Biotic Interference:
    a. Incidence of Cattle Grazing:
    b. Movement of Elephants, etc.:
    c. Poaching, etc.:
13. Incidence of Forest offences:
    a. Prior to Existence of JFMCs:
    b. After the Formation of JFMC:
    c. Whether Offenders Caught & Prosecuted:
14. Miscellaneous information:
    (Not included in 1-13)

Format–V: Strengthening of the JFMC through Training/Workshops/Seminar

1. State:
2. Training/Workshop/Seminar:
   Conducted So Far:
   If Yes
   a. To Whom Imparted Division/District-wise How Many JFMC Members Trained:
   b. Field Functionaries as Foresters/Forest Guards/Number of such Trained Officials:
3. Benefits of Such Training:
4. Constraints (As Non-availability of Fund, etc.):

Format–VI: Maintenance of Records by JFMCs

1. State:
2. District/Division:
3. Range/Beat:
4. JFMC/Registers/Record:
   a. Notifications Issued Regarding Constitution of Committees:
   b. Executive Committee Composition:
   c. Register of Revenue and Expenditure:
   d. Cash Book:
   e. Assets Created by JFMCs:
   f. All Other Records as Made Mandatory in Notification:
5. Inspection of the Records (By An Officer Not Below the Rank of RFO):

Format–VII: Socioeconomic Development in JFM Programme

1. State:
2. District/Division:
   a. No. of JFMC:
   b. No. of SC/ST/OBC/Others in JFMC:
   c. Total No. of Households:

   d. Total Area Under JFMC:
   e. Period of Formation of JFMC:
3. Nature of land:
   a. Before JFMC Constitution:
   b. After JFMC Constituted:
4. Biotic Interference:
   a. Encroachment:
   b. Grazing:
   c. Burning:
   d. Wildlife Menace:
5. Forest offence:
   a. No. of Offences Prior to Existence of JFMC:
   b. No. of Offences After JFMC Constituted:
   c. Offences Caught If Any:
   d. Offenders Presented: (Seizure Report/ Offence Report Drawn)
6. PRA based Micro Planning Done in the JFMC:
7. Conflicts in JFMC:
   Ways Devised to Reduce Conflicts:
8. Working of JFMC in Category: (a to d noting as)
   a. Very Good:
   b. Good:
   c. Average:
   d. Poor:
9. Identification of Activities to be Performed by JFMCs:
10. Achievements of JFMC Physical and Financial:
11. Distribution of Activities of Member:
   a. Men:
   b. Women:
   c. Are there Gender Biases: (Role of women)
12. Protection of Forests. One Activity If Area Chosen is Forest/Adjacent to Forest, How is this Achieved:
   a. By Voluntary Watchman:
   b. By Paid Watcher:
   c. By Allotting Duty to JFMC Members by Rotation:
   d. By Forest Staff Only:
   e. By Joint Patrolling:
13. Schedule of Patrolling:
   a. Periodic Intervals:
   b. No Such Period Fixed:
   c. Whether Assisted by Forest Staff: (Report if Any To Be Annexed)
14. Voluntary Services Rendered by Members of JFMC (Salient Ones):
15. AGM Held Every Year. If not, Reasons Thereof:
16. a. No. of Executive Committee Meetings Held During the Year:
   b. The Main Issues Discussed in it Protection of Forests:
   c. Conflict resolution, micro plan preparation, harvesting forestproduce and its distribution, raising nurseries and associatedplantation works:
17. The availability of Fund:
   a. Revolving/Community Development Fund:
   b. External funds/Grants-in-Aid:
18. Employment opportunities:
   a. Only villagers (no labour imported):
   b. For specific works skilled labourers from adjacent villages also given employment:
19. In JFM area:
   a. Activities of FD:
   b. Benefit to villagers:
   c. Quality of works:
   d. Suggestions if any:
20. Entry Point Activity undertaken:

Format-VIII: Socioeconomic Development in JFM Areas

1. Direct Benefits in terms of domestic requirement of villagers -
   a. Fuel wood:
   b. Fodder:

c. Fruit/Oilseed crops:

d. Thatching material for building houses:

e. Small timber:

f. Bamboo and canes:

g. Will vary in each state:

h. Other miscellaneous forest products/ NTFPs not entered earlier:

2. Indirect benefits:

a. Improvement in health standards of villagers: (incidence of diseases less, etc.)

b. Improvement in health of domestic animals of villagers/cattle protected from wildlife menace (in term of productivity, etc.):

c. List may include many other intangibles:

3. If plantation being one activity:

a. Are their intermediate returns. If yes, (income from it):

b. Final harvest income (if done):

4. Has JFMC involved people in other activities of handicrafts, etc. and income generation?

a. Basket making:

b. Brooms:

c. Others miscellaneous decorative items:

5. Interlinkages-Relationship of JFMC with:

a. Panchayat:

b. Forest Department:

c. NGOs:

d. New JFMC:

6. Innovative mechanisms adopted by a particular JFMC to boost economic return/income generation:

a. Agro-silvicultural Model:

b. Medicinal Plantation:

c. Agro-silvipastoral Model:

d. Apiculture:

e. Sericulture

7. Mechanism of sharing revenue:

(Each state has different mechanism-Is their any notification regarding sharing with JFMC)

8. Miscellaneous information:

DAY - 2:
SESSION - 4: FIELD DEMONSTRATION (FULL DAY)

Field work shall be carried out in the nearby JFM Committee area of FDA to help the members and forest frontline workers, understand the mechanism for effectively carrying out the above works. This will also clear their doubts and answer all the questions of the trainee group. The ideal methodology would be to identify an area in the FDA, which shall become the demonstration area.

The day should start at 8.00 AM with a meeting of committee members and forest frontline workers. The trainers have to guide as to how to conduct a JFMC meeting. After that, demonstration has to be given for constructing check dams, gully plugging, dykes, contour layout, multiple shoot cutting, etc. An example can be cited that while constructing a check dam care has to be taken that bottom of the upper check dam and top of the lower check dam has to be in one horizontal plane. Another example is that during stump dressing for coppice trees, it should be in a pyramid shape with a slope of 450 and the edges should not split. The villagers have to be explained the logic behind it that this will prevent water from entering the stump and arrest fungal attack. To achieve this objective the sickle or axe has to be very sharp edged.

Such details do bring a qualitative change in the working of an area and ensure sustainable improvement in the management of the forest resources.

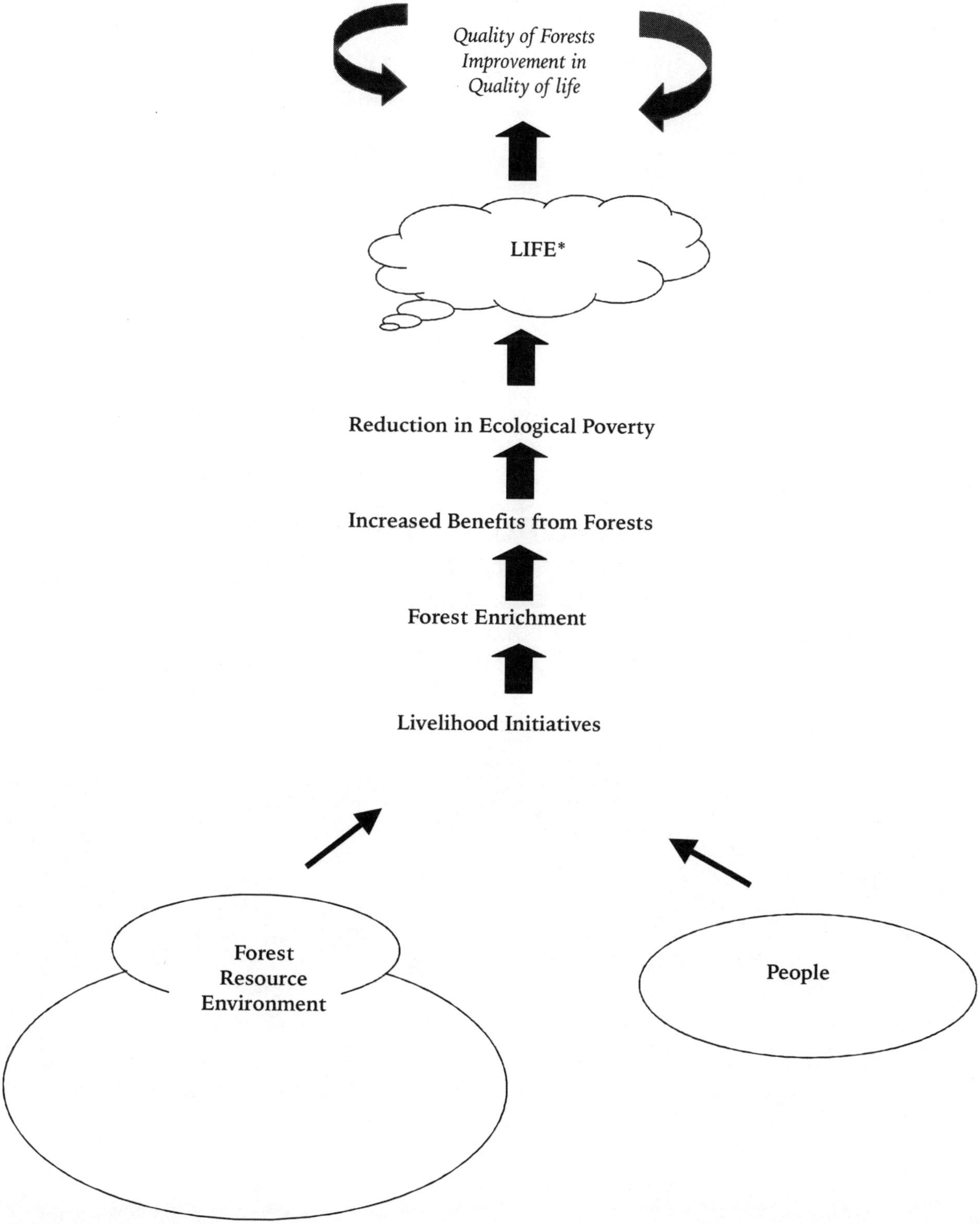

Note: * Livelihood Initiatives through Forest Enrichment.

Chapter 11

Tourism in Andaman and Nicobar Islands

Introduction

The Government of India has formulated a New Tourism Policy (NTP) to guide development of the tourism sector.[1] The key elements of the NTP 2002 are to:

- Position tourism as a major engine of economic growth.
- Harness the direct and multiplier effects of tourism for employment generation, economic development and providing impetus to rural tourism.
- Focus on both international and domestic tourism.
- Position India as a global brand to take advantage of the burgeoning global travel and trade and the vast untapped potential of India as a destination.
- Acknowledge the critical role of the private sector with the government acting as a proactive facilitator and catalyst.
- Create and develop integrated tourism circuits based on India's unique heritage in partnership with states, private sector and other agencies.
- Ensure that the tourist to India gets physically invigorated, mentally rejuvenated, culturally enriched and spiritually elevated.

Other than the declaration in the GoI policy on tourism, certain other developments on the policy front as also the limitations in the capacity of ANI bestow paramount importance on tourism for the future and development of these islands. Firstly, the recent imposition of a ban on felling of trees has adversely affected the predominant wood based industry. The low (existing) carrying capacity[2] of the islands is primarily due to the relative lack of naturally available agricultural land but the economic disability due to this 'natural' constraint gets accentuated due to the 'legal' constraint on utilisation of forest based resources.[3] Secondly, the fisheries sector though holds significant promise, is as yet severely underutilised both due to international restraints (on trawling and deep-water, large-scale fishing) as well as lack of sincere initiatives towards large-scale fishery development. Thirdly, although there are optimistic inferences on existence of significant reserves of petroleum and natural gas (P&NG), the sensitivity of the region to seismic/ seismological activity could be a major deterrent. Lastly, due to the tenuous/fragile environmental and ecological considerations, there is limited scope for either large-scale exploratory or other industrial activity.

The social and cultural concerns, relating to the protection of the rights of the aborigines and primitive tribes, have often been undermined by formalised planned development approach that does not address

1. It may be mentioned here that the draft tourism policy of 1997, Ministry of Tourism, GOI, recognised "development of tourism in the North-East, Himalayan region, Jammu & Kashmir, and the islands of *A&N* and Lakshadweep as part of overall strategy of economic development of the regions." For NTP see *http:/ /www.tourismofindia.com/misc/tourismpolicy.htm*.

2. Carrying capacity refers to the ability to sustain livelihood and human existence.

3. Note that nearly 92 per cent of the landmass on these islands is under forests with almost 86 per cent being reserved and protected. Fifty per cent of this area is tribal reserve, national park or wildlife sanctuary. Thus, a scientific approach towards forest management, collection and utilisation of forest produce (including timber) may significantly impact the development and growth of the economy of these islands.

the specific and precarious conditions prevailing on these islands, as distinguished from the problems faced by similarly underprivileged people on the mainland (some of these are discussed in chapter 6 of this report). The historical evidence on vulnerability of the islands and its indigenous inhabitants during periods of severe international conflict and the continued need to address the broader security concerns of the Republic of India also pose certain limitations on large-scale tourism development on ANI.

The chapter is organised as follows: In the next section we briefly outline the tourism policy of ANI followed by section which analyses the scope and reach of tourism and its benefits with special reference to India in the global context. Section begins with a discussion on tourism in island destinations and presents and expansive overview of tourism in ANI. The challenges facing the tourism sector in ANI are discussed in section while the section following details several concerns that should influence the development of tourism strategy of ANI. Last section summarises the issues in tourism on ANI.

Tourism Policy in ANI

The discussion of the socio-cultural, ecological and environmental and national security concerns, in the opening section, is not to eclipse the overarching need to consciously and carefully facilitate the larger human community to savour the bountiful natural beauty of ANI, if only to sensitise them towards the growing need to foster sustainable practices for human development through conservation and preservation of scarce resources.

The importance of tourism is borne out by the vision statement of ANI administration which states that, "the limited scope for industrial activity on the islands coupled with the decline in the wood-based industry pursuant to the Supreme Court judgement dated May 7, 2002 has led to tourism being identified as a thrust sector for economic development, revenue and employment generation on the islands. Keeping in view the fragile ecology and limited carrying capacity of the islands, the objective of A&N administration is to strive for sustainable tourism".

With the above broad vision, the objectives of tourism promotion and development (in ANI) are enunciated as follows:

- To address the growing unemployment problem by placing thrust on promotion of tourism.
- Total revenue generation being Rs. 84 crores only (2001-02), the future has to be planned with the objective of higher revenue generation.
- Promoting concepts of ecotourism
- To encourage private sector in tourism.
- To harmonise ecology and tourism for the benefit of the people of the islands.

The vision statement of the A&N administration is, "to develop ANI as an upmarket island destination for eco-tourists through environmentally sustainable development of infrastructure without disturbing the natural ecosystem with the objective of generating revenue, creating more employment opportunities and synergise socio-economic development of the islands."

In keeping with this vision the targets defined for tourism are as follows:

- To increase the earning from tourism sector.
- To achieve the goal of high value low volume eco-tourist inflow.
- To create employment opportunities for at least 1000 persons every year.[4]
- To improve the status/quality of existing hotels, tour operators and restaurants to the standards set by the Government of India and Union Territory (UT) administration.
- To discourage unapproved tourism business.
- To create awareness and tourism consciousness among the islanders especially stakeholders.
- To create adequate infrastructure in close coordination with concerned departments to ensure that tourism is sustained by an excellent foundation.
- To preserve the heritage and cultural traits of the islands and enable the development of rural societies.
- To promote sustainable development of different island destinations.
- To preserve the natural ecosystem as a treasure.

In line with the above tourism development targets a policy has been outlined, which incorporates the

4. This, however, seems to be a highly optimistic view of employment generating potential of the tourism economy. For example, Table 15 (pp.30-31) of Tourism Statistics published by the A&N Administration suggests that the manpower employed in the tourism industry of ANI (as on March 31, 2002) was 2781 (including those with GoI, UT administration, Govt. undertakings and the private sector).

policies and guidelines of GoI, to form the basis for promoting tourism in ANI. The administration is focusing on the following issues:

- Promotion of high value low volume eco-friendly and environmentally sustainable tourism.
- Undertaking tourism activities, which are not harmful to the ecosystem.
- To implement the master plan proposed by UNDP/WTO Report for sustainable development of tourism in Andamans.
- Playing the role of facilitator and encouraging private sector investment in development of tourism infrastructure.
- Gradual privatisation of management of existing tourism infrastructure.
- Development of new tourism activities/products.
- Marketing ANI as tourist destination at national and international level.

Tourism is widely considered to be the thrust sector with eco-tourism as the key investment area for long-term sustainable development, and accelerated private sector participation as the engine of growth for ANI economy. Although there is some loose evidence indicating that tourism and investment in tourism can be one of the principal drivers of economic growth and employment due to the strong backward and forward linkages of this activity, providing for large, direct and indirect employment opportunities (next section).[5] However, structured research (Harrison, 1992; Lundberg *et al.*, 1995) on tourism also presents serious concerns arising from the economic leakages in tourism activity (especially in case of island economies, see in section Tourisim in ANI), the distribution of gains from tourism related activities, the demonstration effects and the social consequences of tourism and the quality of employment generated in the host country or location of tourists. These and other relevant issues are briefly discussed and dispersed over the sections that follow.

Tourism Industry and Tourism Economy

The World Travel and Tourism Council (WTTC) defines travel and tourism (T&T) 'industry' as that which produces products and services for 'visitor' consumption. This is distinguished from T&T 'economy' that includes products and services that facilitate T&T industry demand (see GoI, 2002a). One can guess that the latter would include significant components from the hotels and restaurant, construction, banking and insurance, transport and communications sectors. To provide some estimate, T&T is considered as the worlds largest industry contributing approximately 4.2 per cent of global gross domestic product (GDP) while the T&T economy contributes about 10.7 per cent of global GDP.[6]

In some sense the T&T industry can be considered as the direct (or first round) contribution of the sector while the T&T economy would include the indirect and second (as well as later) round multiplier effect of the industry. This in turn implies that T&T industry is the driver sector and has a multiplier of 2.55 in the global economy context while providing for 8.2 per cent of global employment.[7] It however appears that in most places the discussion and analysis pertains to what is recognised as the T&T economy.

Generally, the large and more populated countries tend to have the highest tourist income multipliers (Harrison, 1992). Small island economies, lacking natural resources, are at the other end of the spectrum (Wilkinson, 1989) and are particularly vulnerable. For example, Fletcher (1989) reports the income multiplier for Turkey, Egypt, Bahamas and Western Samoa Polynesia to be respectively 1.96, 1.23, 0.79 and 0.39 (where the latter two are small island economies).

Tourism Traffic and Revenues

Much of the NTP design reflects the pre-occupation within the narrow domain of international travellers, however, this sub-section gives some indication of the importance of domestic (within country) tourism and

5. Incidentally, while it is possible to systematically measure the strength of backward and forward linkages of a particular sector in an Input-Output (I-O) framework, this exercise cannot be carried out unless tourism is presented as a separate sector. As yet, tourism is not reported as a separate sector in Central Statistical Organisation (CSO) publications. It is, however, conceded that organising such information is an onerous task, given the substantial lack of clarity in designating a tourist (see later for definition) especially in case of domestic travel. While in the case of foreign it is much easier to distinguish people as business and leisure tourists (or business cum leisure), it is much more difficult to classify domestic, who maybe on business, on pilgrimage, visiting relatives and not be a leisure tourist in the strict sense of the generally implied terminology.

6. By some measures tourism-related activities make up the world's largest economic sector accounting for over 4 per cent of global GDP and their combined (direct and indirect) contributions may well be over 11 per cent while providing over 200 million jobs (WTO, see *http://www.world-tourism.org* and Panigrahi (2003)).

7. One may need to readjust this multiplier for India and especially for ANI. The logic being that while products and services of direct consumption may actually be cheaper in India than the international average the associated products and services may be costlier (see later for comparison of transportation costs). This in turn would depress the size of the Indian T&T industry while relatively scaling up the size of the analogous T&T economy. Singh (1998), National Committee on Tourism (1986) reported a multiplier of 3.2 for India.

the special significance of the diversity in cultural and religious factors in stimulating tourism especially in India.

In 1951, India received 16,829 international tourists and the number has gone up to 2.36, 2.48 and 2.64 million in 1998, 1999 and 2000 respectively. Even outbound tourists from India are also growing at the rate of 15 per cent per annum over the last few years.[8] Contrast this with the approximately 320 million domestic tourists[9] in 2000 generating Rs. 912 billion in tourism revenues as compared to Rs. 250 billion from international tourists. Thus, the ratio of domestic to foreign tourists stands at 121:1 while, the ratio of domestic to foreign tourist revenues within India stands at 3.65:1.[10] This gives an indication of the vast difference in international to domestic revenue yield (GoI, 2002a). In per-tourist terms the yield from a domestic tourist is only around 3 per cent of the revenue from a foreign tourist.

International tourism receipts in India at US $ 3296 (3009) million in 2000 (1999) constitute just 0.69 per cent of world international tourism receipts putting India in the 29th position in world international tourism receipt rankings. However, due to the large proportion of domestic tourism India is placed 17th in the world rankings on the size of the T&T economy. In local currency terms, the foreign exchange earnings from tourism for India during 1999 was about Rs. 13042 crores. Moreover, the direct employment in this sector during 1998-99 was provisionally estimated at 14.8 million persons or about 2.4 per cent of the total labour force.

Of the 625 million world tourist arrivals in 1998, India however, received a meagre 2.36 million or 0.38 per cent and about 0.62 per cent of world tourist receipts. India's tourism industry earning of about US $ 1.8 billion[11] is yet significantly lower than that of substantially smaller (geographical area wise) countries like Singapore and Thailand at US $ 3.4 and 6.8 billion respectively.

Tourism Economy and Revenue Yields

Indian tourism exports in 2001 are estimated to constitute 9.5 per cent (approximately Rs. 308 billion) of its total exports as compared to the world average of 12.9 per cent pushing India down to the 31st position (from 29th in 2000).[12] International tourism on an average yielded US $ 682 (686) per tourist arrival in 2000 (1999). In contrast the per-international-tourist revenue of US $ 1248 (1213) in India comes to 1.83 (1.77) times the world average for the year 2000 (1999).[13] Thus, while India received approximately 0.38 per cent of international travellers it received a significantly higher world tourism revenue of 0.69 per cent.[14]

However, the contribution of tourism economy to India's GDP at 5.3 per cent is far below the world average at 10.7 per cent. Tourism provided direct employment to 14.79 million people in 1998-99 and enabled foreign exchange earnings of US $ 2917 million in 1999. According to WTTC, international tourists are likely to contribute Rs. 904.6 billion or up to US $ 20.5 billion and support up to 17.4 million jobs by the year 2010.[15]

As against 2.3 million tourists to India, China received 23.8 million tourists in 1997. India thus, descended to the 7th place from being 4th in 1985 in the Asian region as a destination for foreign tourists. These numbers however, need to be interpreted carefully. A significant role is played by business travellers among the tourists who are principally driven by the growing and potential business prospects of the country. While the overall economic growth and prosperity will on its own raise the inflow of international tourists (including business travellers) there is indeed a lot of

8. According to the AFF report (see A.F. Ferguson & Co., 2003), these can also be an important group to be targeted for diversion to visit ANI.

9. GoI (2002b) reports 176 million domestic tourists and an additional 150 million pilgrim tourists for 1999. The latter are distinguished on a specific attribute whereby they do not avail of paid accommodation. Note that this distinction is of immense importance while determining the demand for accommodations units and provisioning for hotel beds. It also has strong implications for forecasting the potential for income generation.

10. Utilising the 1999 figures the ratio for domestic to foreign tourists stands at 131:1 while excluding the pilgrim tourists it works out to 71:1. The ratio 67:1 in GoI (2002a) Report perhaps refers to the non-pilgrim tourists group.

11. The US $ 3009 million (in GoI, 2002b) perhaps refers to the tourism economy.

12. GoI, 2002b report suggests that tourism constitutes about 8 per cent of total world exports and up to 30 per cent of international trade in services.

13. Note that per-tourist yield is an incomplete indicator—one must also be able to estimate the per-tourist per day yield. We suspect that this would be much lower than the international average.

14. Note that while India's share in world tourist arrivals has remained unchanged at 0.38 per cent over 1998-2000, its receipts have grown substantially (as a proportion) from 0.62 to 0.69 per cent over the same period.

15. There is significant probability of a mismatch in the reported numbers due to the multiplicity of information sources. In part this contributes to the notoriety of tourism statistics.

scope to raise the number of leisure and amusement seekers by actively pursuing the objective of tourism development and these are the type of travellers who hold forth the largest prospect in the context of tourism in ANI. The Central Planning Commission of India, thus forecasts Indian tourism to grow at 7 per cent for the international tourists and at 9-10 per cent for the domestic tourists.

Spatial Distribution of Tourists in India

The comparative position (in 2000) of ANI on the map of tourism in India can be deciphered from ANI Tourism Statistics (refer Table 22: Estimated Domestic and Foreign Tourists Visiting India, p.40). It clearly indicates the miniscule flow of tourists to ANI out of the larger Indian tourism sector.[16] The ANI are ranked 27th and 22nd (out of 32) respectively in the number of domestic and foreign tourist arrivals. In percentage terms, the picture looks grimmer with domestic and foreign tourists to ANI respectively constituting about 0.04 and 0.08 per cent of the total tourists in the respective groups. However, tourism is increasingly considered to be the emerging lifeline of these islands.

Tourism in the Andaman & Nicobar Islands

The preceding sections in this chapter discussed some of evidences from the extant literature to elucidate and check the validity of some of the widely held notions about tourism and its potential to be an engine of growth and development including on the linkages of the sector and the multiplier effect to stimulate economic activity. In this sub-section we draw further lessons from experiences of other countries and regions, especially relating to the impact of tourism on stimulating growth of the host economy; and the sociocultural impacts that have significantly long-term repercussions especially for the less developed countries (LDCs) and the island economies.

Tourism on Island Destinations

While every tourist destination provides for something unique, international travel to islands is mostly governed by once-in-a-lifetime desire to experience the joy of virgin beaches, exclusivity, snorkelling, scuba-diving, camping, bird watching (local ornithology), limestone caves, game fishing, corals, etc. Beyond a certain degree however, the lure of natural environs plays a relatively minor part in deciding upon the destination. It is however the management and facilities that make the difference in attracting more tourists. These have been detailed in the recent reports on tourism in ANI (especially those by UNDP/WTO and AFF) along with an emphasis to upgrade tourist information facilities and some pre-requisites to boost private sector participation in guiding, providing quality boarding and lodging facilities, entertainment and leisure facilities including water sports (like scuba diving, snorkeling, kayaking, canoeing, parasailing, etc.) and spas and health resorts (to foster rejuvenation and revitalisation, etc.).

However, before one can formally make any constructive suggestions on the specific approaches to promote tourism on ANI there is also a need to take stock of relevant information collated by some of the neighbouring and competing island destinations, the financial costs incurred by a prospective tourist to ANI and other behavioural information that critically determine tourist responses. As mentioned earlier this Report does not make any attempt to present a precise action plan but rather tries to decipher the critical elements that circumscribe the boundaries for tourism activity and its ability to foster economic development through proactive policy and government intervention.

Tourism Activity in Neighbouring/Competing Island Nations

Among the countries neighbouring India, to populated countries and/or fast developing economies including China, Thailand, Malaysia, Singapore, Sri Lanka and Indonesia may have business interests in a significant number of cases but those travelling to Mauritius, Maldives, Seychelles are principally leisure seekers and to that extent these are comparable and competing destinations (with ANI) for both domestic and foreign. Improved business and economic environment would significantly enhance business and investment travel on its own but this would be limited to the mainland of India. For ANI the focus has to be significantly concentrated upon leisure and pleasure activities (see also *http://mauritius.voyaz.com*, and *www.visitmaldives.com*).

The number of Indian tourists to Sri Lanka in 2001 and 2002 were 46,000 and 69,970 respectively. In the first half of 2003, nearly 45,000 Indians have already travelled to Sri Lanka and the figure for the whole year

16. The number of tourists for all-India is a gross figures and thus higher than the number of tourists arriving at the frontiers. Due to the difference in sources for data generation an international tourist is counted as a fresh arrival every time he or she travels to a different state within the year.

is expected to cross 80,000.[17] Indian spend on an average US $ 60 to 100 per day in Sri Lanka and most of it on shopping. This has significant impact on the development of certain cottage industries. Again, while 13243 Indians travelled to Mauritius in 1999, this figure rose to 21,000 in 2002 and 14,001 Indians have already travelled to Mauritius in the first half of 2003 (see *Economic Times*, July 23, 2003).[18] The leisure tourists among these could be potentially diverted to ANI and similar expenditure (as in Sri Lanka) alone would increase tourism revenues by several folds.

Components of Costs for Tourists to ANI

Given the extant structure of transport operators,[19] the transportation costs (from mainland to islands) incurred by the tourists does not yield much revenue for ANI. On the contrary, the expenditure on the islands would presumably (and significantly) remain as income for the islanders. Given the average duration of stay, the present expenditure on transportation to the islands (from the mainland) constitutes upwards of 50 per cent of the total expenditure of an average tourist on the islands. Thus, there is urgent need to devise ways to reduce the costs of transportation to ANI, so as to release more discretionary expenditure with the tourists on these islands for consumption and purchase on the islands. This in turn would provide employment opportunities to the islanders and help in the development and growth of indigenous handicrafts and cottage industries.

Tourist Traffic on ANI

Tourist traffic to the islands has grown from a mere 9,500 in 1980 to more than 90,000 in 2001. Of these nearly 5,000 were foreign nationals.[20] Though the decadal (1990s) growth rate of tourist traffic to ANI is reportedly higher than the all-India average, it has actually dropped in the last five years. The AFF report also highlights that 95 per cent of tourist to ANI are domestic and largely from the leave travel concession (LTC) segment. Foreign tourists are largely from the back-packer category and both these groups contribute very little to the island revenues.

Domestic tourists generally originate from the east or south of the mainland of India.[21] These are mostly family tourists with 65 per cent of them travelling by air while 35 per cent travel by ship. Their average length of stay on the islands is between 4 to 5 days with an average expenditure of about Rs. 500 per day per person. The domestic tourist inflow peaks in the months of December and April that coincide with the holiday months in educational institutions.

However, as compared to the domestic tourists, the international tourists are more thinly spread throughout the year but even there a larger proportion prefer the sunny and mild winter months. On an average an international tourist stays on the islands for between 15 to 20 days. The normal per day per person expenditure is not very different from that by domestic tourists but the overall expenditure is between 4 to 5 times that of the domestic tourist largely on account of the longer duration of the visit.

Due to the shorter duration of their tour, the domestic tourists are often concentrated in the Port Blair area and do not spread out to other islands like the international tourists. The irregular and slow moving inter-island modes of transport further add to this inertia. The principal reason for a large concentration of population and tourists in Port Blair is that, for all practical purposes, it is the only point of connectivity with the mainland—although naval landing bases do exist in Diglipur and Car Nicobar. This and some other critical issues facing the development of tourism in ANI are further detailed in next section.

Profile of Tourists on ANI

Guess estimates of the number of tourists and their expenditures on the various islands of the A&N archipelago may be compiled from AFF report (pp.43, 51, 58, 65 and 71). Further, based on a primary survey with 130 domestic tourist respondents and 50

17. Indian travellers to Sri Lanka however may also include a significant number of meeting-up-with-the-family tourists influenced by the presence of strong familial relations between mainland Tamils and Tamils in Sri Lanka. But note that the number is comparable to the number of domestic to ANI.

18. On the other hand almost 37,000 Mauritians travelled to India in 2002, though a large proportion of them are students.

19. Mention must be made of the significant role of the national carriers in several island destinations which pitch-in with their efforts in promoting the destination. The ANI being a part of a larger nation are handicapped by the absence of such a service.

20. The relevant data may be sourced from Rajavel (1998), pp. 143 and 145 for the years 1978-1995, A. F. Ferguson report for 1996-2000 (p.32). See also, for data from 1987-88 to 1998-99, Directorate of Economic and Statistics, A&N Administration, ANI: Basic Statistics, various issues; and for data for 2001-2003, Tourism Statistics, DIPT.

21. Anecdotal discussions revealed that a change is taking place in the structure of the domestic tourists whereby a significant number now originate from the west of India.

foreigners, Rajavel (1998), concludes that a larger proportion of domestic tourists lie in the 20-40 age group, while among the foreigners the largest group is formed by those between 40-50 years of age.

The proportion of females among foreign tourists is almost equal to that of the males while in case of domestic tourists females constitute only about one-third of the total. It however appears that there could be some bias in the methodology adopted for eliciting response from the tourists. For example, while there is little issue with the timing of eliciting the responses, there is a possibility of some error especially when trying to correlate respondents with gender distribution in the context of domestic tourists and the relatively qualitative nature of responses, etc. However, the conclusions in the AFF report that very little is known about the islands as a tourist destination and the relative lack of promotional effort on the part of the tourist offices and bureaus, as also the inconvenience in getting precise information on transportation, accommodation and fooding, are also borne out from the survey of Rajavel (1998). The next section attempts to systematically present the challenges and issues for tourism development on ANI.

Challenges for Tourism Development in ANI

The options facing ANI with regard to development of tourism and the likely impact they may have on the overall economic development of the region have several dimensions. Some of these have been discussed and articulated along with various strategies to evolve a suitable action plan in the reports generated by United Nations Development Programme/World Tourism Organisation (UNDP / WTO (1996)), A.F. Ferguson & Co. (AFF (2003)), Foundation for Aviation and Sustainable Tourism (FAST (2002)) and a book authored by N. Rajavel (1998).[22] We undertake an analysis of some of the findings of these reports, to bring forth the various issues in the development of tourism in ANI. In particular, however, we compare the findings of the study by Rajavel with those in the AFF report. In several instances these appear to present strongly differing views. Even the report by FAST has adjudged that the UNDP/WTO report is founded on infeasible optimism and probably the same holds for some of the projections (especially related to tourist traffic and employment potential) presented in the AFF report.

The AFF Report came about 5 years later than the survey period by Rajavel, but some of the observations are particularly relevant. For example, Rajavel reports that almost two-thirds to three-fourths of the domestic tourists travelled by ship, while only 10 to 20 per cent of foreigners chose this mode. Conversely, while only between one-fourth and one-third of the domestic tourists chose to travel by air almost 80 to 90 per cent of foreigners chose this mode.[23] Compare this with the AFF report finding that more than 65 per cent of all chose to travel by air. In this context it is important to elucidate whether air capacity to the islands has increased sharply over the five-year gap between the two studies and whether the cost differentials forced domestic tourists to chose water transport over air or whether this was largely determined by the nature of entitlements in the LTC segment. The effort in the following sub-sections is to highlight the principal concerns and, a comparison of the differing findings of the reports is presented only when it appears to be critical in taking a policy or investment decision.

Transportation to and from Islands to Mainland

The foremost area of concern posing significant challenges to the promotion and sustainability of tourism to ANI pertains to the transportation of a visitor between the island and the mainland. All tourists to the islands (domestic or foreign) travelling by air or ships are routed from the mainland of India via Kolkata (West Bengal)/Vishakhapatnam (Andhra Pradesh)/ Chennai (Tamil Nadu) (except in the case of international cruises and chartered flights).[24]

Travel by Air

Port Blair can be reached by air only from Chennai and Kolkata and two domestic airlines namely, Alliance Air (a subsidiary of Indian Airlines) and Jet Airways are operating their flights on these sectors (AFF Report, p.82).[25]

22. Note that this is not an exhaustive listing of the reports on ANI tourism, but these are the ones which the present author had the privilege to delve into at some length.

23. The range is because tourists may choose to take different modes on their outward and inward trips.

24. Foreign (and Indian) tourist charter flights are also permitted to land at Port Blair subject to the fulfillment of guidelines of the Director General of Civil Aviation, but these are highly infrequent and in turn constrained by availability of supplementary tourism facilities.

25. The A&N website (*http://andaman.nic.in*) shows that flights from Kolkata to Port Balir operate only on 4 days in a week.

The only airport on ANI is at Port Blair with unidirectional access. The naval airstrips at Diglipur and Car Nicobar are currently not open for civilian use. Even at Port Blair only morning flights are in operation. While not much can be said about the fare charges (that vary from around Rs. 7000 to 8500, one way) there is some reason to believe that the high rate of sales tax on aviation turbine fuel (ATF) in the respective originating states of Tamil Nadu and West Bengal significantly contribute to high costs of travel by air. Although this holds true for almost all travel by air, in general, in India, what makes the problem acute in case of ANI is the prohibitive costs (given present technological limitations) of developing transportation infrastructure for alternative modes of fast transport.

Often the prospective report instances of inconvenience in booking seats. The problem is especially acute during the tourist season months. Anecdotal discussions also suggest that the availability of seats is substantially reduced due to the special quotas retained for use by government and defence personnel even on these commercial flights.

Travel by Sea

Passenger ship services are regularly available between Port Blair and Chennai/Kolkata/ Vishakhapatnam. There are 3-4 sailings every month from Kolkata and Chennai to Port Blair and *vice versa* while there is a single sailing per month from Vishakhapatnam.[26] The voyage from the mainland to the island takes about 50 to 60 hours and the ships normally berth at Port Blair for about two to four days.

The shipping schedule is normally available in advance for the next 30 days. However, booking a berth may yet be quite cumbersome as uncertainties in the schedule maybe forced due to weather conditions. Even the journey may also take almost twice the normal travel time under adverse and stormy weather conditions. The operating records however, suggest that the capacity is severely underutilised because of disruptions in service either due to maintenance works or due to poor weather conditions.[27]

The fares applicable (see, *www.andaman.nic.in*) to the islanders are considerably lower by about 32 to 65 per cent depending on the class and vessel, with higher reductions normally for the lower classes. However, given the existing costs of operations both the shipping and air services may appear to be subsidised even for tourists. This is not to suggest that the fares should be raised further, but rather there is a strong case to reduce the costs of these services by improving the efficiency of operations.

There are other reasons not to raise the travel costs any further as revealed in the survey by Rajavel. The responses collated revealed that almost 71 per cent of domestic tourists complained of serious discomfort in arranging for their travel needs while only 12 per cent of foreigners expressed a similar opinion.[28] Conversely, only 16 per cent of domestic tourists and 52 per cent of foreigners expressed trouble-free transit. The remaining 13 per cent domestic and 36 per cent foreigners expressed some average level of satisfaction.

Similar is the contrast between the domestic and foreign tourists regarding their view on the mode of transport itself. The level of satisfaction in travel between mainland and island was reported as excellent by almost 58 per cent of foreigners while less than 22 per cent of domestic tourists expressed such opinion. In contrast, almost 25 per cent of domestic and 4 per cent of foreigners expressed complete dissatisfaction. The remaining 48 per cent domestic and 38 per cent foreign tourists expressed average satisfaction with the transit arrangements.

It seems that the difference in the experience of the tourists may largely be due to the particular styles of international and domestic travel operators and agencies whereby the former have sufficiently long and evolved chain of operations while the latter may be working on relatively fewer and shorter branches of some networks. While, it is not clear as to the precise nature of discomfort, it does bear out that some capacity expansion in air and sea transportation is most desirable especially because the quotas (for security and administration personnel) become restrictive for the tourists.

Further, even under full capacity utilisation assumption, there remains a substantial demand-supply gap in case of marine transportation (see AFF Report, pp.83, 85 and 87). The Directorate of Shipping Services

26. One ship from Kolkata stops at Mayabunder, but entry to Mayabunder is mostly from Port Blair, as is true for all other islands.

27. The available shipping capacity for the mainland-island service can be seen from the AFF Report (p.83).

28. One may draw some encouraging conclusion regarding the strong lure of the natural beauty of the A&N islands that entices visitors to overcome substantial initial discomfitures.

thus proposes to introduce a 1000 passenger vessel, in the Tenth Plan, with an average speed of 20 knots per hour.[29]

As mentioned earlier, all travellers to ANI (except those on cruise ships and chartered flights) are routed from the mainland of India. Such an arrangement is particularly inconvenient and imposes significant time and transport costs for those intending to tour these islands from the east of the Indian mainland. Even for tourists travelling from countries to the west of India the stopover time may appear cumbersome. This in itself is a significant deterrent to international from the neighbouring countries. This might (and probably has already) significantly impact the profile of the international to the islands. Table 11.1 gives an idea of the relative proximity of ANI to some of the currently tourism boom locations in the South and Southeast Asian nations. This, however, is only by way of exposition, as the real concerns in allowing improved accessibility both by air and sea corridors including the provisioning of international airports and ports are strongly governed by security and environmental considerations that are discussed later.

While the mainland-island connectivity is the first hurdle that needs to be overcome to smoothen the passage of the tourists to ANI, this alone is unlikely to induce actual travel to the islands. The improvement in the quality of infrastructure on the islands needs to be pursued simultaneously. This covers not just the boarding and lodging facilities but also the inter-island transportation facility on the islands.

TABLE 11.1

Distances of Some Selected National and International Locations from ANI

Location on A&N Islands	*Country/City*	*Distance in Km.*
Port Blair	India/Chennai	1191
Port Blair	India/Kolkata	1225
Port Blair	India/Vizag	1200
Great Nicobar	Indonesia/Sumatra	146
Great Nicobar	Indonesia/Atjeh (Acin Head)	135
Car Nicobar	Thailand/Phuket	378
Port Blair	Burma/Rangoon	422
Port Blair	Thailand/Phuket	447
Port Blair	Thailand/Bangkok	544
Port Blair	Malaysia/Penang	655
Car Nicobar	Malaysia/Penang	558
Port Blair	Bangladesh/Cox's Bazaar	668
Port Blair	Malaysia/Kuala Lumpur	817
Port Blair	Singapore	1011
Car Nicobar	Singapore	897

According to the survey by Rajavel almost 87 per cent of the domestic tourists worked their way around to and on the islands on their own while less than 10 per cent of them utilised the service of a travel agent and less than 5 per cent used the services of the tourist office. However, in case of foreigners more than 60 per cent relied on tourist agents with another 24 per cent relying on the tourist office and only about 14 per cent trying to venture out on their own.

The discomfort level experienced by the domestic tourists may thus, be strongly correlated with their effort to work things out on their own, without seeking much assistance or service from dedicated tour operators and service providers. While, there may be cost considerations or some level of disbelief in their efficacy by the domestic tourist, the foreigners in general prefer a risk-avoidance strategy and may also be confirming their bookings sufficiently in advance.

Transport within ANI

The critical factors facilitating the dispersal and spreading out of tourists on the islands are (a) speed, and (b) costs of transit. There is likely to be a low upper bound on the time (number of days) available for touring the islands. Moreover, a large part of the budget for tourism may be pre-empted by the mainland-island transit costs. While it is not precisely quantified, travel on the islands and inter-island transit involves relatively long waiting time due to infrequent and irregular availability of modes of transport and lack of synchronisation between the alternative and (often) complementary modes. Moreover on a very broad assumption the speed of transit between the islands averages between 12-18 km. per hour.[30]

The survey by Rajavel does not report the perception of the local population about the foreshore-island services, but there is some reason to believe that probably tourists, given their frame of mind of visiting a new place, are more open to absorbing some level of uncertainty, delays and disruption than the local

29. 1 nautical mile equals 1.85 kilometres.

30. Tables 22.8 and 22.9 (p.320-31), in Basic Statistics: ANI, present the distance and fares for inter-island travel by waterways.

population. Rajavel's survey however yields that nearly 58 per cent of foreigners and almost 28 per cent of the domestic tourists did not go to any other island. Almost 32 per cent of domestic tourists and 10 per cent of foreigners used boats for inter-island transit, while about 5 and 18 per cent respectively utilised a taxi. Almost 22 and 6 per cent respectively used a bus and the remaining 13 and 8 per cent respectively used private van or car.

One reason for the relative low spreading of foreigners maybe on account of the relatively higher risk perception associated with certain (and probably the only in some instances) modes like *doongies* (country boats that appear to be very unsafe).[31] Of the 72 per cent domestic and 42 per cent foreigners who made inter-island visits only about 15 and 4 per cent respectively expressed excellent opinion about their modes of transport. Twenty eight per cent of domestic and 34 per cent of foreigners expressed opinion ranging between good and satisfactory while 30 per cent domestic and 4 per cent foreigners expressed dissatisfaction.

The greater level of dissatisfaction on the part of the domestic tourist may arise from her/his approach to pack-in relatively greater number of inter-island visits within a short span of time while relying more on slower and public modes of transit and the relatively lesser preparedness and allowances for uncertainties. Given the distances involved, the costs of transportation (in Rupees per km. as compared to travel on the mainland by similar modes) do not appear to be high, but the speed of transit probably is a major deterrent for the foreigners. This not only inhibits the effort in spreading-out of tourists but also imposes excessive burden on the existing facilities.

It is also suspected that the foreshore-island services may be badly disrupted unless speedy measures are implemented. The foreshore services that connect Port Blair to nearby islands are extremely critical for the islanders themselves. Along with the procurement of vessels there is an associated need to upgrade the port, anchoring, berthing, storage and processing facilities.[32] Specifically, in the case of inter-island transportation, there is clear backing up of the investment in the upgradation of infrastructure for tourism by the needs of the host population to absorb this enhanced capacity.

There are a total of 572 islands in this archipelago, however, 412 of these are in the form of isles and rocks. There are only 24 islands with some non-forest land of which 11 are exclusive tribal reserves. While the infrastructure needs must also be extended to the exclusive tribal reserves with continued efforts to bring them into the mainstream of development, there are only 13 islands available for tourism development. These are however spreadout over 700 km. latitudinally, and critically inhibit infrastructure development. Providing air connectivity to each of these islands may not be feasible by conventional means. One may need to understand the viability of short distance chopper services, fixed-wing aircrafts, seaplanes or whether fast water-based modes (catamarans) can be provided. Alternatively, high quality and intensive tourism development can be concentrated in a smaller geographical region. The latter needs to carefully weigh the ecological and environmental impact of such activity.

Furthermore, there are strategic defence and security concerns relating to the positioning of the air and sea assets of the Indian nuclear command apart from the regulatory constraints on construction activity (namely, Forest Conservation Act, Wildlife Protection Act, Protection of Tribals, Coastal Regulation Zones, etc.). These probably have moulded the infrastructure provisioning as also any sincere moves towards strengthening the inter-island linkages even as a tourist destination.

Specifically for ANI, it appears that the irregularity rather than the infrequency of water-based transportation is a greater hindrance to tourist movement. This is true both for travel from the mainland to the islands and inter-island movement. Not only are the vessels old and slow but also cannot be utilised to their reported capacity due to frequent breakdown and repair and maintenance works. The inter-island services deploy 4 vessels, MV *Sentinel*, MV *Chowra*, MV *Derring* and TSS *Yerewa*. This service connects Port Blair up to Diglipur in the North and Campbell Bay in the South. MV *Sentinel* and TSS *Yerewa* were to be decommissioned in the year 2001 and MV *Chowra* is to be decommissioned in 2004. There is significant delay in ordering and receiving of vessels. For example, even the vessels proposed in the Eighth Plan have not been acquired yet.

31. This is in sharp contrast to the observations in the AFF Report where foreigners are reported to be spreading out to other islands while domestic tourists are reportedly concentrated in Port Blair itself.

32. One cannot however, easily infer on the desirable connections that would entail not merely upgradation of the present facilities but setting up of new infrastructure. The new connections and the corresponding infrastructure required are given in some details in the UNDP/WTO and the AFF Reports.

The Supreme Court ruling further constrains the development of land-based transport network leaving sea and air transport as the only legally available alternatives. The air transport alternative may face similar constraints as in the case of land-based transport in the availability of land for airport development. The sea transport alternative may also face some constraints because of the CRZ guidelines. However, the last of these appears to be the only viable long-term alternative and there is urgent need to expand the fleet of vessels.

As presented in the preceding section, several tourism boom areas are positioned significantly closer to ANI than the mainland of India. While the closest point of this archipelago to the mainland of India may be lesser than the current points of connectivity with it, it is probably more desirable to develop the infrastructure on the islands rather than opening up another point on the mainland. While the countries of the West may indeed be more prosperous with higher capacity to spend, there is no *a priori* reason to believe that those to the East may be less willing to spend, if only the cost disadvantages imposed upon them could be appropriately mitigated. There is thus an important case to consider the potential benefits of allowing direct access to from these countries to ANI, both by provisioning for international flight terminals and improving the anchoring, berthing and port facilities to promote water-based transportation. Although one needs to weight the benefits against the potential security and environmental costs such provisioning may significantly cut the time and resource cost for several international given the proximity of the islands to important Asian transit points like Singapore, Bangkok, Kuala Lumpur, etc.

The time and cost disadvantages are apparent even for the Indian high value travellers. For example, the return fare by air between New Delhi and Bangkok, Maldives, Mauritius and Seychelles maybe lower than that between New Delhi and ANI. Moreover, these destinations entail the additional 'pride' of travel to a foreign country. Similarly, one may look at transit from other important Indian cities.[33]

Although the location of the Indian traveller within the geographic bounds of the nation may also significantly impact the overall transportation costs, one must note that international are (in most cases) directly able to reach the above-mentioned competing destinations. For example, there are 3 flights per week to Mauritius from Mumbai and 2 per week from Delhi and a weekly flight from Chennai. There is a weekly flight from Mumbai to Seychelles, frequent flights to Thailand from Delhi, Kolkata, Mumbai, Chennai etc.

A table in the AFF Report (p.107) presents the costs of air transit faced by Indian mainland outbound tourists from selected Indian cities to ANI and certain neighbouring (and competing) international tourist destinations. The present routing of international tourists to ANI via the mainland of India imposes significant additional costs of transit for international inbound tourists varying between 30 to more than 100 per cent of the costs of travelling to any of the neighbouring or competing destinations (depending on the country of origin) apart from additional time required for the extended routing.

Problems and Limitations in Policy and Planning: The tourism policy of ANI proposes:

- Eco-friendly tourist resort at Goodwill Estate, Netaji Nagar, North Passage Island, Smith Island and Long Island.
- Camping facility at Barren Island.
- Management of existing guest houses and providing additional amenities.
- Privatisation of guest houses in a phased manner.

The above policy guidelines, however, do not address the broader issue of the transportation bottlenecks and thus fail to envisage how the provision of above facilities may attract more tourists. Planned development of tourism in ANI was started in the 1970s, but only in the eighties this was identified as a thrust area for sustainable development. The investment outlay on tourism related aspects in the Tenth Five-year Plan, proposed for ANI, maybe noted from the Tenth Five-year plan (2002-07), Vol-III, General Economic Services, Tourism (pp.Y1-Y18). However, even by any conservative estimates a planned allocation of merely Rs. 51 crore (over a 5 year horizon) appears to be highly unlikely to make any significant improvement in the infrastructure and tourism development needs.[34]

33. There is a presumption that a majority of high-value tourists actually reside in a major city or a metropolis.

34. The UNDP/WTO Report has identified 5 zones for tourism development (in the Andamans) while the AFF Report has proposed a hub and spoke approach also covering the Nicobar district. These reports also provide a roadmap for implementation of the tourism development programme but the investment-needs design of both these reports must be backedup with more rigorous inputs for commercial viability. Unfortunately, both the reports are either lacking or appear much less convincing on this aspect.

Given the geographical positioning of ANI, they pose severe limitations for integration into any of the identified domestic travel and tour circuit (GoI, 2002a). However, they continue to present a vast potential even for the domestic tourist looking for beach and coastal travel. The perspective plan (AFF Report) thus suggests that ANI maybe included in the international cruise circuit. The proximity of the islands to Thailand, an important point on the international cruise route, presents an opportunity to derive some benefit from this high value segment of international tourism activity. Alongside this, the possibility to include the islands into the international air-travel circuit by encouraging a stopover for the international flights (and tourists) to and from Southeast Asia may be explored.

Security, Environmental and Sociocultural Issues

The critical element impacting any perspective plan for tourism development and circumscribing the limits on development of tourism infrastructure on ANI calls for evolving of clear policy stance primarily addressing 3 concerns:

Security Considerations

There is a proposal to set up a strategic nuclear command that would take ANI into a critical security zone and impact both domestic and international tourist movements. This will also have significant impact on infrastructure possibilities, air and sea corridors and types of civilian vessels or crafts to be allowed for transportation of personnel and cargo.

Environmental Considerations

(a) The Coastal Regulation Zone (CRZ) guidelines; and (b) the Supreme Court ruling on the observations made in the *Shekhar Singh Committee Report*. The latter, targeted at the preservation of the forest cover would severely (and adversely) impact the timber and logging industry. Both the considerations severely limit the availability of agricultural land and/or availability of revenue land for infrastructure provisioning (including roads, buildings, modes of transport) and building of structures. Further, there is a ban on extraction of sand from the coastal areas and on commercial plantations in the reserved and protected areas with orders to evict encroachers while disallowing concrete or permanent structures on forestlands.

Sociocultural Considerations

These pertain to recognising the rights and needs of the autochthons, the protection of primitive and native tribes and curtailing the encroachment of settlers and resettlers.

The present set of regulatory controls applicable to the islands include:

- Indian Forests Act, 1927.
- Andaman & Nicobar (Protection of Aboriginal Tribals) Act, 1956.
- Wildlife Protection Act, 1972.
- Forest (Conservation) Act, 1972.
- (Prevention and Control of Pollution) Act, 1974, 1981.
- Environmental Protection Act, 1986.
- Coastal Regulation Zones, 1991.

While most of the acts in force are designed to protect the ecology and environment, the CRZ guidelines are generally perceived to be inhibiting. In case of CRZ I, no new construction is permitted upto 500 metres from the high tide line (HTL) while this is reduced to 200 meters in case of CRZ III. CRZ II and IV also restrict development up to 200 metres from the HTL. However, it is reported that internationally CRZ norms of 50 and 70 metres are commonly used and combined with stringent limits on land area covered, number of buildings, etc. There is thus a suggestion to look at the CRZ regulations on a case-to-case basis.[35]

Identifying the Right Pitch for Tourism Promotion and the Development Alternatives

Several important aspects need to be elucidated to present the right pitch for tourism. Not the least among these is to highlight the health and hygiene attributes. Significant emphasis must be laid on dispelling fears about diseases including malaria, filariasis, waterborne diseases, etc. Misapprehensions, if any, must be allayed, by detailing the healthcare and emergency facilities available alongside some certification from international agencies. Disspelling such misapprehensions there is some proposal to popularise and develop spas and health tourism on these islands.

Again, while growth in tourism is considered to be in large part propelled by the general improvement in

35. In this regard, the July 24, 2003 notification of the Ministry of Environment & Forests is a significant step forward whereby the 'no development zone' has been reduced to a minimum of 50 metres for CRZ III and IV zones.

the investment and industrial climate of the region, the current tourism boom areas of the Southeast Asian region have also experienced a significant decline in the social and cultural mores and ethics. Similar evidence is also reported in countries as diverse as Swaziland (Harrison, 1992) and Sri Lanka (Crick, 1992) other than the oft-repeated examples of Philippines and Thailand.

According to the AFF Report, tourist traffic is expected to grow to 134527, 168393 and 243342 by the years 2007, 2012 and 2022 respectively, but the bounds for the tourism development strategy for ANI are defined by:

- The socioeconomic benefits from promoting tourism.
- The core 'nature' offering.
- The compliance with the WTOs Bali declaration of:
  - Economic sustainability by providing economic returns/earning potential to local community/intermediaries.
  - Social sustainability of tourism whereby the society can absorb it without disharmony.
  - Ecological sustainability within natural and regenerational capacity.
  - Cultural sustainability whereby the tribals/ locals can maintain their distinct characteristics.
- Environmental and natural regulatory factors.
- Tourist preferences and expectations.
- Balancing stakeholder interest.

Sustainable tourism development envisages:

- Operating within natural capacities for regeneration and future productivity of natural resources.
- Recognising contribution that people, communities, customs and lifestyle make to tourism experience.
- Providing these resources with equitable share in the economic benefits of tourism.
- Guidance by the wishes of local people and communities.

The Hub and Spoke Approach

The proposed direction of development (in the AFF Report) is in the form of a hub and spoke approach—with 6 hubs and several spokes with single or multiple offerings mainly as excursion points for camping, jungle trails, trekking/rock climbing, snorkelling/scuba diving, kayaking/canoeing. Each set of hub and spokes is further proposed to be developed along a zoning concept whereby a core zone would be circumscribed in a buffer zone which in turn would be engulfed in the peripheral zone. Four phases are proposed to evolve over the next 20 years. The first of these is for the next 2 years, the second spread over the 3rd to 5th year, the third over the 6th to 10th year and the last beyond 10 years.

The positioning of ANI for tourism is broadly to capitalise on the core natural offering of pristine beaches and coral reefs combined with a strategy that promotes variety and spreading out by highlighting the uniqueness of experience by exploration and isolation enhancing the learning and contemporaneous eco-friendly wander-lust.

The hubs identified as principal excursion points for development are Diglipur (North Andaman), Mayabunder (North-Middle Andaman), Rangat (Middle Andaman), Port Blair, Havelock and Neil (South Andaman), Little Andaman (Little Andaman) and Car Nicobar, Katchal and Great Nicobar (Nicobar). All of them provide for natural beauty in beaches and forests. Man-made facilities can be potentially developed including adventure sports (water sports like, water skiing, parasailing, snorkelling, kayaking, canoeing and scuba diving; forest trekking, bird watching, camping, fishing).

In the near term (next 2 years or so), the AFF Report recommends that, the infrastructure and products at and near Port Blair need to be improved. In the short-term (in the next 3–5 years), a second entry point in Diglipur would greatly reduce the burden on Port Blair apart from expanding the available products, it would facilitate the spread of tourists by featuring exclusivity and higher yield of revenues, the medium term (in the next 6-10 years) may foster the development of cruises to the Nicobar Islands apart from the circuits (Diglipur–Mayabunder, Port Balir–Baratang–Rangat and Port Blair–Little Andaman) developed in the short-term. In the long-term (more than 10 years) one may consider introducing a third entry point in Great Nicobar and develop a circuit of Great Nicobar–Katchal–Car Nicobar).

This approach towards tourism development seems desirable, however there is little doubt that unless there is an improvement in the transportation sector there is little scope to actualise the subsequent tourism development strategy.

Additional Issues in Tourism Development

Promotional Expenditure

While the budget-tourist, whether domestic or international, would continue to provide for the critical mass (for base tourism activity), effort should be made to spread them out over the year while attracting significant high-value tourists by designing a concerted marketing and promotion strategy (advertising using mass media, maybe associating with the film and motion pictures associations,[36] special events, festivals and announcements, etc.) targeting tourists, tour operators, airlines, hotel-chains, etc. The likely effect of special promotional drives and expenditures can be gauged from Table 11.2.

TABLE 11.2

Promotional Expenditures in 1995

Country	*Tourist Arrival (Millions)*	*Promotional Expenditure (Million USD)*	*Promotional Expenditure per Tourist (USD)*
Australia	3.80	75.8	19.95
India	2.10	15.4	7.33
Malaysia	7.90	25.5	3.23
Republic of Korea	3.80	30.5	8.03
Singapore	6.40	44.7	6.98
Thailand	6.90	42.9	6.22

Source: *Action Plan Recommendations of the Task Force.*

While per international tourist promotional expenditure (column 4) in India is higher than several of the smaller and neighbouring nations, the total expenditure (column 3) is significantly lower and it is quite often advocated that the level of promotional expenditure significantly enhances its efficiency. One can see, from the table, that among the countries listed there, the level of promotional expenditure is lowest in India.

Projecting Tourist Traffic

The AFF Report envisages that the proportion of foreign tourists would be 8,25,40 and 50 per cent respectively in the years 2002, 2007, 2012 and 2022. This, however, appears to be highly optimistic and assumes a significantly higher growth rate for foreign tourists than domestic tourists. The break-up is assumed to be equally applicable to all the hubs proposed for development. The actual experience of tourist movement to the islands, however indicates that over the last two decades the number of domestic tourists has shown less volatility than the number of foreign tourists.

With the growth of intra-regional tourism the flow of foreign tourists is expected to gain greater stability, however, it remains true that fluctuations would be wider in respect of inflow of foreign tourists than for the domestic tourists. The FAST Report envisages that domestic tourist traffic would grow to 1,55,000 in 2012 and international arrivals to 15,000. The said Report criticises the highly optimistic tourist traffic growth rates earlier suggested by the UNDP/WTO Report (prepared in August 1996), when the realised tourist traffic proved to be less than one-third of the projections (international tourists were projected to grow at 31 per cent per annum).

A significant reason for non-realisation of estimated tourist growth also lies with the slow progress in requisite and commensurate infrastructure upgradation but there is little gain in expecting a sudden (and voluminous) surge in investments to absorb the highly optimistic projections. Evidence from erstwhile predominantly tourist economies of Philippines, Cuba and Colombo (Sri Lanka) does indicate that additional and huge investments in premium boarding and lodging arrangements may lie unutilised due to small changes in tourist perceptions about their security concerns (Richter, 1992; Harrison, 1992). Moreover, forceful seclusion of the host economy residents may further alienate the locals from the foreigners as well as from the local elite, who in most such cases corner the major chunk of any increase in income (Hall, 1992a).

The projections on tourist traffic as given in the AFF Report (pp.125, 127, 131, 135, 138, 142, 146, 149 and 152) instill some discomfort, whereby the number of domestic tourists in Port Blair is shown to decline while the number of foreign tourists continues to grow rapidly. In fact, given the present assumptions, both Diglipur and Port Blair, which experienced relatively larger tourist arrivals, show a decline in domestic tourists inflow in the year 2007 as compared to 2002. This contradicts their own view whereby they suggest that given the shorter duration of stay of an average domestic tourist on these islands they prefer to remain concentrated rather than spreading out to other neighbouring islands. The latter claim is however also contentious as Rajavel, concludes (from his primary survey) that almost 24, 60 and 14 per cent of the foreigners spend between 0-5, 5-10 and 10-15 days

36. This can probably has the highest impact factor as compared to other promotional measures.

respectively on the islands. While, amongst the domestic tourists about 19, 37 and 28 per cent fall in the respective categories with the remaining 16 per cent or so preferring to stay beyond 15 days. This is in sharp contrast to the profile presented in the AFF Report where a majority of the domestic tourists are reported to stay for less than 5 days while a majority of the foreigners are reported to stay for 15 days or more.

The limits to increasing tourist traffic to the islands are also fortified by the competing supply of the core products offered by ANI. The rich western (European and North American) countries are closer to similar destinations in the Caribbeans and Mauritius and a decline in long-haul travel (refer to increased intra-regional tourism as compared to long-haul tourism in section 11.2) certainly does not augur well to attract European and North-American tourists to these islands.

While there can be some dispute over the estimation and projection methodologies adopted by differing agencies, there is indeed little doubt that the number of tourists are likely to increase. However, given that the idea of projections is to guide investment decision making, especially to upgrade and expand infrastructure and boarding and lodging facilities, care must be taken so that precious resources do not get locked into forms of capital and assets that have little to contribute towards the betterment of the lives of the host population.

Social Concerns, Investment Needs, Economic Gains, Employment

There is indeed a large diversity in the natural beauty offering on the islands and those on the islands face relatively lower internal security and law and order problems. These islands are relatively much less polluted both socially and environmentally (than say the mainland of India or even other important tourist destinations like Thailand or Sri Lanka). However, it is precisely in this setting that one needs to be very cautious with adverse outcomes of the demonstration effect of foreigners. For the autochthons international and domestic tourists may appear to be equally foreign or alien. Given the relatively weak sense of ownership, it is likely that a tourist may not always behave in an ecologically/environmentally/socially desirable manner.

A variety of tourism products are however envisaged in the AFF Report, entailing an expenditure of Rs. 39,160 crore at current prices of which 760 lakh pertains to transport infrastructure, Rs. 23,190 lakh on accommodation infrastructure, Rs. 14,956 lakh on tourism products and Rs. 254 lakh on others. Note however that this does not include the costs and investments pertaining to basic infrastructure (power, water, sewerage, roads) or shipping (both mainland and inter-island), communication and air connectivity and related infrastructure. The AFF Report (pp.130, 134, 137, 141, 145, 148, 151 and 154) gives the island-wise break up of the proposed investment needs over the 20-year horizon.

The potential from tourism is estimated to yield increased contribution to SDP, resources for protection and conservation of natural resources, new employment opportunities, scope for redeploying local community, improvement in the state of infrastructure, improvement in the quality of life. The direct revenue from tourism with average stay of domestic tourists for 5 days and foreigners for 10 days with corresponding spending of Rs. 1000 and 2000 per person per day is expected to yield Rs. 300 crore at current prices. Moreover, every Rs. 1 million worth of investment in tourism is expected to result in 47.5 direct and 17 indirect jobs. The application of this norm would result in 1,85,725 direct and 66,740 indirect jobs in ANI with significant role for women.

While, there are likely costs due to pressure on available resources, increased inflation, economic leakages and adverse impact on culture, simple application of the above norm appears to yield highly optimistic employment potential (as seems to be the case with the AFF Report). The likely demand for employment must also bear some relationship with the number of applicants on live register of employment exchange (Basic Statistics, 1996-97 to 1998-99, A&N Islands Administration, Table 13.2, p.224). It appears that the present trend of demand for employment is unlikely to match the estimated supply of employment opportunities (as envisioned in the AFF report). Further, the AFF Report (p.24) also reveals that there has been some decline in the proportion of the employed population.

This only indicates that the rate of growth of employment opportunities has not kept pace with the rate of growth of population. Although the recent Supreme Court decisions may have resulted in some loss of employment and investment opportunities especially with respect to timber and other forest based activities, it is unlikely that even the existing trend rate of growth of population would supply the number of workers as maybe absorbed by the projected growth in employment opportunities (as estimated in the AFF Report) due to suggested investment in tourism.

Local Resource Constraints

While, the present weakness of this destination lies mainly in the costs (in terms of time, money and convenience) perceived by tourists. Relative lack of indigenous production also does not augur well for the upliftment of the island economy. Large-scale development of an economic activity not owned-up by the principal (targeted) beneficiaries may not be sustainable. This is especially true for development of tourism as the focal point. Unless tourism can take into its fold the economic and financial growth of the native population, it is unlikely to be welcome by the natives for long. In most countries with high tourist dependency, the actual benefit accruing to the natives is quite low. While the priced goods and services involving transportation, boarding and lodging are mainly in the control of large multinationals, the locally provided goods namely the natural environs are relatively freely accessible. Moreover, the demand generated by these corporations, in turn, is for low skill inputs (mainly casual labour, bell boys, chamber maids, etc.), banking on servitude from the native population. The dynamics of the tourism has an in-built incentive not to allow disruption of the basic ingredient of servitude by the natives. However, this process is doomed to be resisted by the natives sooner than later. Critics of tourism projects generally highlight the strong negative perception of the impact of tourism both on the tribes and on the environment.

This weakness is accentuated by the large propensity of dependence on imports from the mainland and significant scarcity of natural resources on the islands specifically for the requisite construction and infrastructure activities. With any growth in inflow of tourists, the dependence on the mainland is likely to rise further.

Short Duration of Tourist Season

The tourist amenable (sunny) season is short (due to long monsoon spells both southwest and northeast). This calls for cautious development of lodging infrastructure that may not be utilised for a large part of the year—or efforts can be made to spread the tourists throughout the year—in that case the islands need to be pitched differently than purely as beach destinations.[37] This further entails that significant man-made interventions have to be exercised. While acknowledging that there are natural limits on the carrying capacity of the islands due to its fragile ecosystem, there is sufficient reason to believe that even this capacity is severely underutilised. The stringent environmental, forest and CRZ regulations may inhibit any development purely as a policy inducement or policy constraint. There is thus a need to take a relook at these regulations based on widely accepted international practices.

Facilitating Investment Interest on ANI

The administrative machinery for development of tourism also needs to be restructured. There are 4 agencies involved in the promotion of tourism in A&N. These are:

- Directorate of Information, Publicity and Tourism (DIP&T) that formulates policy/strategy for tourism development, budgets for tourism development and publicity including preparation of brochures, etc.
- The Department of Forest is the custodian of vast natural resources of A&N.
- The Andaman & Nicobar Islands Forest Plantation Development Corporation Limited (ANIFPDCL).
- The Andaman & Nicobar Islands Integrated Development Corporation Limited (ANIIDCO). The ANIIDCO is also designed to extend incentives to encourage private sector investments by providing soft loans and capital investment subsidy.

However, the existing framework has certain limitations in that the tourism agencies have overlapping functions and suffer from a diffused vision. Multiplicity of regulatory agencies and that too at different levels and ministries in the central government also leaves a lot to be desired. The government should balance its role as a regulator, strategist, growth driver, marketer, facilitator, knowledge bank and stakeholder.

There is urgent need for public-private partnerships to infuse a burst of capital inflow. In most other island destinations, 100 per cent private investments are largely restricted to hotels/resorts/pure entertainment projects, while Joint ventures are preferred to run state owned assets. The current state of environmental and regulatory controls presents several road-blocks to private participation. The ANI Tourism Promotion Board (ANTPB) (as proposed in the AFF Report) could facilitate public-private partnerships. The FAST Report

37. There is some evidence in the last couple of years of an improvement in the room occupancy in the monsoon months.

also envisages the setting up of a plan implementation cell (PIC, analogous in its functions to the ANTPB as suggested in the AFF Report) to assist in speedy clearance of investment proposals by coordinating with the various ministries and agencies. In this context, it is worth mentioning that two major foreign collaborated projects to set up eco-friendly resorts are already under way.

Behavioural Considerations for Realistic Projections

Keeping in view the projected growth in tourist traffic the AFF report (pp.129, 133, 137, 140, 144, 148, 150, 154) has compiled the incremental demand for lodging facilities at the various locations. While, the numbers there appear to be consistent with their tourist traffic and demand projections, these appear to be highly optimistic projections. Effort should be made to introduce the *novelty* element in lodging by construction of tree-top *machaans* and eco-restlets with locally available, low cost construction material. There is some anecdotal evidence to believe that tourists are not necessarily looking for luxurious accommodation. This is especially borne out by the relatively faster growth of the informal paying-guest kind of arrangement experienced in several less developed countries especially in the island nations. Similar evidence is also found in Goa in India as also in Kandy (Sri Lanka).

It is quite likely that such a development in the informal sector probably sows the seeds of gradual erosion of ethics and cultural mores with strong and adverse demonstration effects. There is some reason to believe that a more proactive role of the government in regulating and legitimising such practices would substantially reduce the adverse effects. While this will definitely ease the additional lodging requirements (for tourists), it would also provide income-generating opportunities for the local population. But care needs to be exercised that such a move should be preceded by a large-scale educational campaign along with general acceptance from the local population to devise broad codes and ethics for the locals and the tourists.

Lodging

Rajavel's survey elucidates the responses of the tourists regarding the boarding and lodging facilities on the islands. The broad pattern which emerged reflects that almost 86 per cent of foreigners chose private accommodation with the rest lodging in government or municipal accommodation, while only 45 per cent of the domestic tourists chose private accommodation, 25 per cent preferred government or municipal accommodation and nearly 22 per cent put up in regional *samajams*.

Nearly 31 per cent of domestic tourists however declined to comment on the quality of accommodation, while 30 per cent expressed dissatisfaction and 21 per cent of foreigners concurred with this view. The proportion of foreigners expressing satisfaction was about 22 per cent with a similar proportion among the domestic respondents. 17 per cent of domestic and 78 per cent of foreign tourists expressed average opinion on the quality of accommodation.

It is not identified as to which category of accommodation did the non-responding group belong, but clearly the greater reliance on government/ municipal accommodation by the domestic tourists correlates to their higher level of dissatisfaction with the quality of lodging. Again, the design of the questionnaire to elicit responses relating to the problems in acquiring some service and the experience with the service may not be clearly decipherable. That is to say that the 'views' on accommodation and the 'level of satisfaction' with accommodation may not always be clearly segregated by the respondents. The same arguments can however be forwarded on queries relating to transport and fooding.

Fooding

Nearly 76 per cent of the foreigners chose to take meals in their place of stay while only about 36 per cent of the domestic tourists preferred this arrangement. Only 15 per cent of domestic and 8 per cent of the foreign tourists expressed indifference with their choice of eating outlets. However, only about 11 per cent of domestic and 18 per cent of foreign tourists expressed complete satisfaction with the quality of food and eating places. Almost 47 per cent of domestic and 34 per cent of foreign tourists expressed strong dissatisfaction on this criterion. The remaining 38 per cent of domestic and 48 per cent of foreign tourists expressed opinion ranging from satisfactory to good for the quality of food and hotels. Similar pattern of opinion is generated with regard to bar facilities. The predominant opinion about the level of prices for the various services, was that these were steep and on the higher side. This however corroborates that the quality of services and the prices being charged for them are not adequately matched. There is some possibility of this to be an outcome of the relative lack of fooding facility in several places of accommodation chosen by the domestic traveller.

Summary

The principal challenge, facing the growth of tourism in ANI, is connectivity and the commensurate infrastructure to facilitate faster, direct and regular accessibility. However, caution needs to be exercised in that, any large-scale investment in transportation infrastructure development should be essentially backed by the priorities, needs and demands of the resident population. In this regard, priority must be accorded to inter- and intra-island services that would also enable wider dispersal of tourists on the islands and reduce the burden on Port Blair.

The relative dearth of open land along with the need to conserve the green cover as well as the coastal zones of this fragile ecosystem, calls for greater stress on the development of water based transportation system. However, given that airstrips already exist in Diglipur and Campbell Bay, these can be utilised with greater efficiency for transporting tourists from mainland to the islands.

Special effort must be made towards realistic assessment and projection of tourist traffic. This should keep in view the limited carrying capacity and the sparse latitudinal distribution of the islands. The employment and income generating potential of tourism should also be cautiously analysed along both the quality and quantity dimensions.

The predominant class of tourists consists of nature lovers, while some of them are also interested in adventure activities (including, trekking, camping, scuba diving, etc.) there may be others with special interest in culture, heritage, bird-watching, ecology, etc. There is concurrence, both among the domestic and foreign tourists, on the excellent natural beauty of the islands. But as argued earlier, these are not priced although, in the eyes of the tourist they do have significant value. Thus, caution needs to be exercised in that an eco-conscious tourist is not necessarily the 'high value' tourist. Ecotourism essentially pertains to those who leave a relatively smaller environmental footprint. But it is quite likely that most high value tourists actually have much larger environmental footprints. The availability of trained guides is a prerequisite towards this endeavour and the existing perception on this aspect is not very encouraging.

Closely linked to the perception of pristine environmental conditions is the availability of health and hygiene facilities. However, the commonly expressed view is that the islands lack in quality health facilities. Special efforts may have to be initiated to dispel such perceptions (maybe through certification from some international health agencies).

There is need for greater macroeconomic consistency in planning and investment including scope for private-sector participation. In the present structure, there exist multiple agencies with overlapping functions. This leads to delays in decision making resulting in severe undermining of administrative capacity.

Special drives for tourism promotion, by affiliating with the media and motion pictures association (including ecological and environmental content based TV channels like, Discovery, National Geographic and History) can do wonders in inducing the desire to visit these islands. Such drives may firmly place ANI in the viewers mind-space.[38] Increase in the level of promotional expenditures may have a salubrious effect on the quality and quantity of tourists. The commensurate fooding, lodging and security needs should also be carefully assessed as these go a long way in leaving a lasting impression of a joyful experience.

38. For example, recently a movie named 'Kaho Na Pyar Hai' made a significant contribution in promoting New Zealand as a tourism destination among Indian travellers, prompting Ministerial acknowledgment from that nation.

Chapter 12

Manpower Planning and Employment

Formation and utilisation of manpower resources assumes critical importance in the manpower development process. The manpower formation process is partly natural, and largely dependent on demographic forces. In particular, the aggregate size of the labour force and its distribution by age and sex are determined on this basis. Further distribution of labour force, in terms of its productive capabilities, is determined by the facilities for education, training, healthcare, etc. Utilisation of manpower, *inter alia,* depends upon the economic base of the economy that includes the potential of the farm and non-farm based activities.

Earlier, in many countries attempts were made to plan their educational systems by means of formal models of manpower forecasting, based on a set of fixed relations between the anticipated growth in output and the educational or skill requirements to produce such output. However, in practice, forecasts and outcomes have differed enormously because technological change and its implications for the demand for skills have been too elusive to predict. Thus, the move is towards recognition of the fact that what matters is the individual demand for education/training/skill development by students/workforce and their families in response to wages, opportunities for self-employment and other market signals. This is not to imply that the necessary infrastructure for technical/vocational training and skill development should not be provided. Instead it suggests that the factors which suppress the demand for vocational/ technical training and skill development should be identified and removed.

This chapter is organised as follows: Next section briefly discusses the employment and population dynamics followed by an overview of trends in employment in the following section. Section discusses trends in labour productivity. The next section identifies main issues followed by section that discusses some concerns that should influence the strategy to improve the employment situation in ANI. Finally, last section suggests some measures to improve labour productivity.

Employment and Population Dynamics

In ANI, the decennial growth rate of population, after peaking in the decade of the 1970, decelerated to 48.7 per cent during the 1980s. A further decline in the decadal growth rate (26.94 per cent) is observed during the 1990s. While this sustained decline in the rate of growth of population is a good achievement for the UT, the age profile of the population (in 1991 more than 20 per cent and 10 per cent population was in 20-29 and 15-19 age groups, respectively) implies that a large number of young people will continue to enter the workforce for quite some time to come. Thus, the need to enhance employment opportunities in the UT will continue.

The 1991 Census showed significant dependence of the UT on the primary sector for employment with about 40 per cent of the workforce engaged in the primary sector (Table 12.1). The secondary sector accounted for only 23.1 per cent of the workforce. Dependence of workforce on the tertiary sector was little over 37 per cent with the bulk of employment in the sub-category of "other services". This distribution of the labour force, coupled with a decline in growth in agricultural yield, underlines the need for sustained government intervention for creation of jobs.

In the organised segment, the public sector continues to play a very dominant role, and accounts for more than 86 per cent of employment in the UT (Table 12.2). Between 1991 and 1998 there was complete stagnation in employment in both the public and private sectors. However, during 1998-2000 while public sector employment increased by 3.12 per cent,

TABLE 12.1

Distribution of Population (Workforce by Major Activities) as per 1991 Census

Major Activities	*Persons*	*Rural*	*Urban*	*Persons as % of Population*	*Persons as Per Cent of Workers*
Primary	39417	37131	2286	14.04	39.85
Secondary	22823	17360	5469	8.14	23.07
Tertiary	36653	18342	18311	13.06	37.08
Non-workers	181760	132873	48887	64.76	-
Workers	98901	72833	26068	-	100
Total Population	280661	205708	74955	100	-

Source: Basic Statistics, 1996-97 to 1998-99, Andaman & Nicobar Islands.

TABLE 12.2

Employment in Organised Sector by State/Union Territory

State/Union Territory	*Employment (Lakh)*											
	Public Sector						*Private Sector*					
	1981	*1991*	*1997*	*1998*	*1999@*	*2000*	*1981*	*1991*	*1997*	*1998*	*1999@*	*2000*
1. Andhra Pradesh	11.13	13.88	15.11	15.09	15.10	15.21	3.32	3.75	4.72	5.42	5.50	5.64
2. Assam	3.58	5.01	5.49	5.35	5.32	6.09	4.99	5.49	5.67	5.57	5.50	6.98
3. Bihar	12.35	14.06	14.42	13.79	13.61	14.35	3.11	2.57	2.59	2.55	2.54	2.30
4. Delhi	5.33	6.24	6.25	6.25	6.30	6.26	1.85	2.15	2.22	2.21	2.22	2.21
5. Goa	0.25*	0.66*	0.70	0.69	0.70	0.70	0.28*	0.33*	0.39	0.39	0.40	0.41
6. Gujarat	7.38	9.60	9.55	9.55	9.50	9.37	6.00	7.00	8.17	8.34	8.20	8.08
7. Haryana	3.21	3.96	4.29	4.24	4.28	4.09	1.85	2.06	2.41	2.33	2.34	2.32
8. Himachal Pradesh	2.28	2.36	2.46	2.50	2.54	2.55	0.12	0.30	0.42	0.43	0.44	0.40
9. Jammu & Kashmir	1.48	2.05	2.00	2.00	2.00	2.05	0.09	0.11	0.11	0.11	0.11	0.14
10. Karnataka	7.95	10.17	10.84	10.86	10.92	11.12	3.45	4.30	7.32	7.57	7.57	7.51
11. Kerala	4.99	8.31	6.25	6.30	6.45	6.44	5.18	5.12	5.52	5.60	5.65	5.85
12. Madhya Pradesh	11.39	14.24	14.19	14.05	13.76	12.03	2.10	2.45	2.60	2.48	2.39	2.15
13. Maharashtra	19.29	22.82	23.46	23.32	23.05	22.90	13.65	13.66	15.36	15.17	15.05	14.71
14. Manipur	0.36	0.55	0.78	0.78	0.80	0.64	0.01	0.01	0.02	0.02	0.02	0.02
15. Meghalaya	0.44	0.64	0.69	0.70	0.71	0.73	0.04	0.05	0.08	0.08	0.09	0.09
16. Mizoram	0.15	0.33	0.40	0.40	0.40	0.35	0.01	0.01	0.02	0.01	0.01	0.02
17. Nagaland	0.39	0.64	0.69	0.73	0.74	0.74	0.01	0.02	0.03	0.03	0.03	0.03
18. Orissa	4.71	6.64	7.09	7.07	7.23	7.15	0.01	1.10	0.93	0.94	0.95	0.91
19. Punjab	4.68	5.70	5.93	5.99	6.03	6.18	1.67	2.21	2.53	2.48	2.51	2.60
20. Rajasthan	7.06	9.53	10.24	10.09	10.15	10.14	1.76	2.31	2.70	2.64	2.64	2.59
21. Tamil Nadu	11.98	15.79	16.45	16.29	16.30	16.25	6.88	7.10	9.10	9.32	9.16	9.22
22. Tripura	0.62	0.88	1.00	1.00	1.00	1.10	0.06	0.10	0.11	0.11	0.10	0.13
23. Uttar Pradesh	17.94	21.41	21.12	20.88	20.58	20.04	5.63	5.36	5.42	5.36	5.29	5.10
24. West Bengal	15.00	15.75	14.93	14.87	15.31	14.94	10.68	8.90	7.99	7.98	8.11	7.82
Union Territories												
25. Andaman & Nicobar Islands	-	**0.32**	**0.32**	**0.32**	**0.32**	**0.33**	-	**0.04**	**0.04**	**0.04**	**0.04**	**0.05**
26. Chandigarh	0.42	0.60	0.63	0.64	0.64	0.64	0.15	0.16	0.18	0.19	0.24	0.25
27. Pondicherry	0.28	0.43	0.40	0.42	0.42	0.44	0.14	0.10	0.12	0.09	0.09	0.11
28. Daman & Diu	-	-	0.02	0.02	0.02	0.02	-	0.05	0.12	0.09	0.13	0.12
All-India	154.84	190.57	195.59	194.18	194.15	192.83	73.95	76.76	86.86	87.48	86.98	87.82

Notes: @ = Quick Estimate
* = includes Daman and Diu
Totals may not tally due to rounding off; Sikkim, Arunachal Pradesh, Dadra and Nagar Haveli and Lakshadweep are not covered under the EMI Programme

Source: Directorate of Employment and Training, *Employment Review* (various years).

the corresponding increase in private sector was over 25 per cent, which is a welcome trend.

Trends in Employment

Growth in Employment

Growth in employment is a much desirable outcome of development process, and captures the economic attainment and hence the level of well-being of the people. Between 1983 and 1993-94 employment in ANI grew at 6.1 per cent, which was third highest in the country and substantially higher than the national average of 2.1 per cent. Furthermore, during this period growth in female employment was more than three times than that of male employment; and growth in employment in rural areas was substantially higher than in urban areas (Table 12.3). During 1993-94 to 1999-2000, growth in employment decelerated sharply

TABLE 12.3

Growth in Employment in Urban and Rural Areas

(Per Cent Per Annum)

States/UTs	*Urban*						*Rural*					
	1983-1993-94			*1993-94 to 1999-2000*			*1983-1993-94*			*1993-94 to 1999-2000*		
	Male	*Female*	*Persons*	*Male*	*Female*	*Persons*	*Male*	*Female*	*Persons*	*Male*	*Female*	*Persons*
Andhra Pradesh	3.5	4.2	3.7	2.4	1.6	2.2	1.7	2.5	2.0	1.3	0.1	0.8
Arunachal Pradesh	-	-	-	4.7	10.7	5.6	-	-	-	-0.4	-1.4	-0.8
Assam	0.8	3.5	1.0	2.2	6.2	2.7	1.4	3.1	1.7	2.5	2.1	2.4
Bihar	1.3	-1.4	0.9	3.4	4.7	3.6	1.9	-1.8	0.9	2.1	2.9	2.3
Goa	4.3	1.4	3.5	3.1	-4.4	1.5	0.0	-4.7	-1.8	2.1	-4.0	0.4
Gujarat	3.2	3.6	3.3	2.6	0.7	2.3	2.0	1.3	1.7	1.8	2.4	2.0
Haryana	3.1	7.5	3.8	1.8	-3.7	0.8	2.2	4.3	2.8	2.0	-3.0	0.5
Himachal Pradesh	2.0	4.8	2.6	2.0	-3.1	0.8	2.9	3.0	2.9	1.4	1.6	1.5
Jammu & Kashmir	2.4	6.7	3.1	2.1	-9.8	0.3	1.5	5.8	2.9	2.3	-0.4	1.3
Karnataka	2.7	0.6	2.2	2.5	3.9	2.8	2.0	2.7	2.3	1.8	0.3	1.2
Kerala	4.9	3.3	4.4	3.2	3.3	3.2	1.1	-2.3	-0.1	1.0	0.8	0.9
Madhya Pradesh	3.2	3.7	3.3	3.5	2.3	3.3	2.2	1.6	1.9	1.4	1.4	1.4
Maharashtra	2.6	4.2	2.9	2.5	-0.5	1.9	1.8	1.9	1.9	1.3	-0.2	0.6
Manipur	4.5	3.0	3.9	5.6	5.0	5.4	3.2	2.8	3.1	2.1	-2.2	0.6
Meghalaya	3.9	4.6	4.0	-1.4	3.3	-0.1	3.0	3.9	3.4	3.1	2.9	3.0
Mizoram	9.8	12.7	10.6	5.0	6.8	5.6	-0.8	3.3	0.4	5.0	2.1	-
Nagaland	2.6	6.8	3.2	4.7	20.2	8.0	-	-	-	4.6	15.4	8.7
Orissa	2.6	6.7	3.3	3.3	4.0	3.4	1.6	2.7	2.0	1.2	0.7	1.0
Punjab	2.6	-0.4	2.1	2.1	6.5	2.6	1.5	-1.5	0.6	1.2	6.0	2.5
Rajasthan	3.1	1.6	2.8	2.8	0.8	2.4	2.4	2.5	2.5	2.0	0.4	1.4
Sikkim	-1.0	-1.7	-1.1	1.6	9.4	3.0	3.5	0.8	2.8	1.4	9.0	3.4
Tamil Nadu	2.2	2.9	2.4	1.8	1.1	1.6	1.4	1.8	1.6	1.1	-0.7	0.4
Tripura	5.7	9.4	6.3	2.5	-4.6	1.3	2.9	10.6	3.9	2.7	-5.7	1.4
Uttar Pradesh	2.7	4.1	2.9	3.5	2.3	3.3	2.2	0.8	1.8	1.4	1.3	1.4
West Bengal	1.8	3.1	2.0	1.3	-1.3	0.8	2.7	1.9	2.5	1.7	-0.6	1.2
Andaman & Nicobar Islands	**3.5**	**12.0**	**4.7**	**3.0**	**4.4**	**3.3**	**4.0**	**13.1**	**6.6**	**2.1**	**-11.1**	**-2.0**
Chandigarh	3.4	5.3	3.8	1.6	-2.1	0.9	6.2	0.0	5.3	8.6	10.9	8.9
Dadra & Nagar Haveli	-	-	-	2.0	-10.1	-0.6	3.3	2.9	3.1	3.7	-1.7	1.4
Daman and Diu	4.8	-2.9	2.6	5.8	9.5	6.5	3.7	-2.6	1.3	4.1	5.7	4.6
Delhi	3.7	3.7	3.7	2.2	5.5	2.6	8.1	0.1	6.6	6.7	-11.2	5.2
Lakshadweep	-	-	-	5.8	16.2	7.8	-		-	1.2	2.8	1.5
Pondicherry	6.1	1.4	5.6	4.7	4.4	4.6	-0.1	-1.2	-0.5	1.1	1.0	1.1
All-India	2.8	3.2	2.9	2.6	1.5	2.4	2.0	1.5	1.8	1.6	0.8	1.3

Source: Planning Commission (2002). *National Human Development Report 2001*, Government of India.

to -0.7 per cent against the all-India average of 1.6 per cent. This can be attributed mainly to the decline in growth of employment in rural areas for both males (from 4 per cent to 2.1 per cent) and females (from 13.1 per cent to -11.1 per cent), and for females (12 per cent to 4.4 per cent) in urban areas.

Growth rate in employment at the national level has declined in spite of acceleration in GDP growth during nineties implying a fall in employment elasticity of output growth. The question is: if employment elasticity of output growth declines, how will the country achieve its 10 million a year employment growth target of the Tenth Plan? Much of this new employment (9.47 million new jobs) is expected to be generated in the agricultural sector. Will the agricultural sector in ANI be able to fulfil the target at a time when it is faced with a declining share in GSDP, and over 40 per cent of the workforce already engaged in primary sector? Further, there seems little, if any, scope for shift towards labour-intensive technologies in primary sector.

Sectoral Distribution of Workforce and Shift in Structure of Employment

The sectoral distribution of urban workforce shows that there was a decline in the share of secondary sector from 25.9 per cent to 22 per cent between 1993-94 to 1999-2000, the consequent gain was shared by the tertiary sector by 3.3 percentage points and the primary sector by half a percentage point (Table 12.4a, and b). This can partly be attributed to closure of wood-based industries. At the all-India level, a decline was observed in the primary sector, while the secondary and tertiary sectors gained. Sectoral distribution of workforce in rural areas of ANI gained in favour of the primary and secondary sectors. In the tertiary sector, while the share of construction increased, there was a sharp decline in the share of trade and services.

The long-term shift in the structure of employment in rural areas shows that self-employment has eroded, share of regular employment has stagnated and casualisation of labour has increased. In urban areas, share of self-employed and casual labour increased by about 4 percentage points and over 7 percentage points, respectively, during 1993-94 to 1999-2000. The percentage of regular employees, however, declined sharply by over 10 percentage points during the same period (Tables 12.5 a, and b).

Mobility of Workers Across Sectors/Occupation

Over a period of time various features related to employment of a worker, such as his/her occupation, industry or status of work might undergo a change. Percentage of employed persons who changed nature of work has been highest among males employed in establishments in rural areas and both males and females in urban areas (Table 12.6a & b). Seven per cent urban males, 2.9 per cent urban females and 4.2 per cent males in rural areas have shifted from establishments during 1997-1999. Another significant change in the nature of work was observed for urban males employed in industry (2.4 per cent) and occupation (2.1 per cent).

Workforce and Labour Force Participation Rates

A striking feature observed is the sharp decline in workforce and labour force participation rates between 1993-94 and 1999-2000, in rural areas in ANI. This decline was more in the case of females than that of males. To some extent, the decline may be attributed to higher attendance of children in schools and also to withdrawal of elderly persons from the labour force (Table 12.7a & b). In urban areas, however, labour force participation rate grew by 8.85 per cent between 1993-94 to 1999-2000 for males, and by 15.28 for females. Growth in workforce participation rate was relatively higher for urban males (9.9 per cent) than for females (6.2 per cent) during the same period indicating relatively greater number of unemployed females *vis-à-vis* males waiting to join the workforce.

Incidence of Unemployment

Decline in growth of employment opportunities is reflected in the growing incidence of unemployment in the UT. An analysis of data presented in Table 12.8 reveals that the incidence of unemployment has been consistently higher than the national average during both eighties and nineties. It has increased in ANI during the nineties and has been more prevalent among females in urban areas in 1999-2000. Incidence of unemployment as per cent of labour force is also significantly higher (4.3 per cent) than for the country as a whole (2.3 per cent) during the same year. Unemployment rate among the youth (15-29 years) was higher in urban areas though it has sharply increased in both rural and urban areas for both males and females between 1993-94 and 1999-2000 (Table 12.9a & b).

Trends in Labour Productivity

The productivity of labour is an essential condition for the prosperity of enterprises as well as well-being of workers and their families. The production facilities at work-place and the remuneration are crucial

TABLE 12.4A

Per 1000 Distribution of Usually Working Persons in the Principal Status and Subsidiary Status Taken Together by Broad Industry Division for each State/Union Territory

Rural Persons

States/UnionTerritories	1993-94									1999-2000								
								Services									Services	
	Agri-culture etc.	Mining & Quarry-ing etc.	Manu-factur-ing	Electricity, Water, etc.	Construc-tion	Trade, Hotel & Restau-rant	Trans-port	Fin, Inter-national Busi., etc.	Pub. Admn. Edu., Comm. Serv., etc.	Agri-culture etc.	Mining & Quarry-ing etc.	Manu-factur-ing	Electricity, Water, etc.	Constru-ction	Trade, Hotel & Restau-rant	Trans-port	Fin, Inter-national Busi., etc.	Pub. Admn. Edu., Comm. Serv., etc.
Andhra Pradesh	793	7	69	-	17	45	10	2	56	788	8	56	1	22	46	17	2	60
Arunachal Pradesh	864	1	8	8	26	2	16	4	68	834	0	28	3	44	6	1	2	81
Assam	792	2	35	3	7	69	13	2	77	677	3	40	1	18	81	27	3	151
Bihar	843	5	34	3	13	45	10	1	46	806	5	61	1	22	45	14	2	44
Goa	454	5	112	28	50	92	63	52	143	287	58	114	3	125	190	117	8	98
Gujarat	787	5	92	2	24	29	15	3	43	798	4	69	2	27	39	24	2	35
Haryana	719	6	40	4	43	53	35	2	98	685	4	73	9	65	60	33	6	64
Himachal Pradesh	803	1	33	8	63	30	8	2	53	736	0	40	11	92	34	23	4	60
Jammu & Kashmir	758	1	36	11	60	25	27	6	75	763	0	42	4	66	36	17	2	69
Karnataka	812	7	67	2	15	37	7	2	50	821	8	54	0	15	45	15	4	38
Kerala	563	16	128	3	57	90	40	11	92	483	17	126	2	94	119	62	18	81
Madhya Pradesh	898	12	32	2	9	16	5	-	25	871	4	40	1	18	27	7	1	31
Maharashtra	826	4	50	2	24	33	11	4	48	826	1	49	2	23	38	18	3	39
Manipur	638	1	123	3	28	45	15	9	137	753	6	74	0	9	37	14	2	105
Meghalaya	860	6	10	3	16	38	11	-	58	865	7	7	0	16	42	11	2	50
Mizoram	889	-	5	1	12	19	1	1	71	855	3	10	0	11	30	1	1	90
Nagaland	749	8	2	2	18	45	6	-	171	797	1	6	7	8	28	13	1	139
Orissa	809	11	64	1	18	44	7	1	46	782	4	82	1	12	46	11	2	40
Punjab	747	-	49	12	35	49	26	4	79	726	0	59	8	53	58	38	3	55
Rajasthan	799	18	36	2	70	24	10	2	39	777	14	43	2	79	35	17	3	30
Sikkim	586	22	44	7	35	59	20	2	224	608	8	25	28	38	63	36	8	196
Tamil Nadu	705	4	129	2	23	48	20	8	62	679	5	139	2	40	56	26	6	47
Tripura	476	-	54	2	68	107	32	-	257	457	0	40	0	80	118	23	1	281
Uttar Pradesh	800	2	64	1	20	43	15	2	53	762	1	78	1	33	54	21	3	46
West Bengal	633	2	161	1	24	75	27	4	72	636	3	166	1	22	85	33	4	50
A & N Islands	**633**	**4**	**53**	**13**	**81**	**67**	**28**	**6**	**115**	**650**	**3**	**32**	**8**	**114**	**46**	**39**	**3**	**106**
Chandigarh	136	-	164	10	204	145	131	-	210	661	0	102	0	80	62	16	17	63
Dadra & N. Haveli	660	19	69	2	60	17	106	2	64	552	14	184	0	62	26	110	0	52
Daman & Diu	524	-	261	-	6	62	29	11	107	342	0	423	0	8	91	44	7	85
Delhi	103	-	514	-	8	105	71	9	191	75	0	260	4	100	304	84	6	166
Lakshadweep	399	-	56	26	96	52	72	-	297	536	0	34	7	84	65	72	0	202
Pondicherry	647	-	138	-	35	49	25	-	106	599	0	138	22	47	106	11	7	71
All-India	**784**	**6**	**70**	**2**	**24**	**43**	**14**	**3**	**54**	**763**	**5**	**74**	**2**	**33**	**51**	**21**	**3**	**49**

Source: Employment and Unemployment Situation in India: 1993-94 and 1999-2000.

TABLE 12.4B

Per 1000 Distribution of Usually Working Persons in the Principal Status and Subsidiary Status Taken Together by Broad Industry Division for each State/Union Territory

Urban Persons

States/UnionTerritories	*1993-94*									*1999-2000*								
								Services									*Services*	
	Agri-culture etc.	*Mining & Quarry-ing etc.*	*Manu-factur-ing*	*Electricity, Water, etc.*	*Construc-tion*	*Trade, Hotel & Restau-rant*	*Trans-port Storage, etc.*	*Fin, Inter-national Busi., etc.*	*Pub. Admn. Edu., Comm. Serv., etc.*	*Agri-culture etc.*	*Mining & Quarry-ing etc.*	*Manu-factur-ing*	*Electricity, Water, etc.*	*Constru-ction*	*Trade, Hotel & Restau-rant*	*Trans-port Storage, etc.*	*Fin, Inter-national Busi., etc.*	*Pub. Admn. Edu., Comm. Serv., etc.*
Andhra Pradesh	164	19	191	11	79	198	87	28	224	95	8	194	5	115	255	92	42	193
Arunachal Pradesh	79	-	133	36	93	150	53	29	425	87	0	4	18	112	335	10	9	425
Assam	30	61	104	6	28	290	75	20	386	60	5	72	6	52	300	83	56	366
Bihar	115	38	167	37	47	230	83	26	282	109	43	179	12	50	294	70	34	210
Goa	121	19	101	24	133	162	110	38	291	18	27	138	16	190	258	176	50	126
Gujarat	80	6	310	7	65	180	79	22	250	94	5	246	5	80	270	84	37	178
Haryana	111	2	249	6	82	189	76	22	263	91	18	207	5	60	366	69	26	158
Himachal Pradesh	175	6	35	34	75	168	23	33	452	110	0	80	37	98	219	50	48	358
Jammu & Kashmir	140	3	80	26	64	199	64	31	393	132	1	83	13	127	272	41	24	308
Karnataka	166	25	231	15	64	170	64	41	224	108	3	238	5	99	264	75	52	155
Kerala	253	5	188	6	80	167	78	30	193	95	3	202	5	107	305	87	44	152
Madhya Pradesh	163	24	170	13	54	183	85	28	279	154	18	182	4	79	263	82	24	194
Maharashtra	93	5	249	9	56	196	93	50	249	57	3	234	7	79	260	111	59	191
Manipur	293	-	144	11	26	137	31	22	333	283	9	105	0	42	199	36	12	312
Meghalaya	30	1	22	5	80	252	17	18	569	13	0	38	3	105	222	48	9	562
Mizoram	410	2	44	3	48	146	13	1	331	303	15	38	0	94	187	29	20	314
Nagaland	62	5	41	4	78	220	37	17	535	84	0	62	7	52	117	3	21	654
Orissa	157	21	166	20	57	163	100	21	293	130	15	195	9	101	234	72	31	213
Punjab	93	-	242	16	50	256	59	27	257	87	0	225	12	64	314	85	34	180
Rajasthan	161	9	194	16	83	178	83	35	243	129	24	210	6	107	215	78	37	.194
Sikkim	9	-	81	4	71	354	10	10	458	21	23	97	18	53	336	19	19	414
Tamil Nadu	122	3	299	7	75	186	76	30	202	89	4	282	7	73	253	88	41	163
Tripura	60	7	87	3	28	173	60	39	538	27	0	37	2	41	246	49	28	570
Uttar Pradesh	149	1	236	10	41	217	72	33	240	90	0	255	4	62	295	75	28	192
West Bengal	51	21	302	10	53	177	83	37	265	30	8	257	12	64	254	112	42	220
A & N Islands	**142**	**6**	**72**	**58**	**129**	**125**	**128**	**20**	**318**	**153**	**0**	**122**	**19**	**79**	**220**	**160**	**13**	**233**
Chandigarh	5	-	208	5	82	191	33	54	421	16	0	177	13	65	282	45	64	337
Dadra & N. Haveli	266	2	270	4	56	151	29	31	185	81	0	541	0	49	150	69	22	88
Daman & Diu	97	-	184	7	35	250	67	-	358	119	2	148	0	37	368	114	8	204
Delhi	12	1	143	7	106	225	68	51	286	17	0	244	3	54	285	67	52	279
Lakshadweep	444	-	28	29	97	38	61	9	289	245	0	46	16	91	300	49	6	246
Pondicherry	158	-	205	23	111	162	31	35	274	54	0	332	5	136	241	54	30	148
All-India	123	12	236	10	63	194	79	34	248	88	8	227	7	80	269	87	41	195

Source: NSSO (1997). Report No. 409, NSS-50th Round, *Employment and Unemployment in India, 1993-94; Employment and Unemployment in India, 1999-2000*, Part-I, NSS Report No. 458, 2001.

TABLE 12.5A

Per 1000 Distribution of Usually Employed by Category of Employment For Different States and Union Territories

Urban Persons

States/Union Territories	*Principal and Subs. Status**			*Principal and Subs. Status#*		
	Self-Employed	*Regular Employed*	*Casual Labour*	*Self-Employed*	*Regular Employed*	*Casual Labour*
Andhra Pradesh	403	341	256	367	387	246
Arunachal Pradesh	220	695	85	241	590	169
Assam	453	431	116	447	429	124
Bihar	478	356	166	537	302	161
Goa	350	445	205	263	514	223
Gujarat	383	409	208	410	341	249
Haryana	450	404	146	448	428	124
Himachal Pradesh	384	525	91	376	516	108
Jammu & Kashmir	450	503	47	481	404	113
Karnataka	413	369	218	388	396	216
Kerala	398	268	334	413	291	296
Madhya Pradesh	413	385	202	463	330	207
Maharashtra	366	496	138	338	515	147
Manipur	639	333	28	603	306	91
Meghalaya	341	558	101	263	564	173
Mizoram	610	331	59	495	338	167
Nagaland	391	544	65	242	717	41
Orissa	372	443	185	428	358	214
Punjab	489	400	111	477	409	114
Rajasthan	510	379	111	499	365	136
Sikkim	453	482	65	327	565	108
Tamil Nadu	361	373	265	347	441	212
Tripura	388	483	129	313	530	157
Uttar Pradesh	587	295	118	550	323	127
West Bengal	373	470	157	432	400	168
A & N Islands	**248**	**559**	**193**	**291**	**442**	**267**
Chandigarh	302	597	101	331	615	54
Dadra & N. Haveli	398	442	160	343	514	143
Daman & Diu	441	415	144	557	391	52
Delhi	421	468	111	411	548	41
Lakshadweep	421	451	128	457	383	160
Pondicherry	319	406	275	293	408	299
All-India	424	395	181	422	400	178

Source: *: NSS Report No. 409, *Employment and Unemployment in India, 1993-94.*
#: NSS Report No. 458, *Employment and Unemployment in India, 1999-2000.*

determinants of productivity of labour, besides other factors such as skills and attitudes towards work. Labour productivity is used as an indicator to measure the direct contribution of labour in economic development. One of the widely used measures of labour productivity is value of industrial output per worker. It is a matter of concern that in ANI the average annual productivity of an industrial worker was Rs. 1.28 lakh in 2001-02 which is lowest among all States and UTs in India[1] (Table 12.10). Even greater concern is decline in labour productivity in ANI from Rs. 1.87 lakh and 2.31 lakh respectively in 1996-97 and 1997-98 to Rs. 1.28 lakh in 2001-02. Average labour productivity at the national level increased from Rs. 7.78 lakh in 1996-97 to Rs 11.88 lakh in 2001-02 registering a 42.39 per cent rise.

1. Comparable figure for the country as a whole was Rs. 11.88 lakh, while highest labour productivity was Rs. 36.13 lakh in Dadra & Nagar Haveli.

TABLE 12.5B

Per 1000 Distribution of Usually Employed by Category of Employment for Different States and Union Territories

Rural Persons

States/Union Territories	*Principal and Subs. Status**			*Principal and Subs. Status#*		
	Self-Employed	*Regular Employed*	*Casual Labour*	*Self-Employed*	*Regular Employed*	*Casual Labour*
Andhra Pradesh	475	52	473	458	59	483
Arunachal Pradesh	854	123	23	793	126	81
Assam	578	144	278	582	166	252
Bihar	523	40	437	523	35	442
Goa	382	317	301	377	309	314
Gujarat	502	68	430	542	63	395
Haryana	677	94	229	664	124	212
Himachal Pradesh	856	71	73	787	101	112
Jammu & Kashmir	824	100	76	818	86	96
Karnataka	559	48	393	502	53	445
Kerala	454	115	431	429	137	434
Madhya Pradesh	619	40	341	566	35	399
Maharashtra	487	76	431	443	73	484
Manipur	830	121	49	800	100	100
Meghalaya	797	63	140	796	44	160
Mizoram	911	73	14	890	84	26
Nagaland	781	192	27	821	166	13
Orissa	564	45	391	487	42	471
Punjab	627	105	268	655	130	215
Rajasthan	790	46	164	799	49	152
Sikkim	570	270	160	620	261	119
Tamil Nadu	416	93	491	367	118	515
Tripura	569	128	303	472	111	417
Uttar Pradesh	743	45	212	727	56	217
West Bengal	557	95	348	522	70	408
A & N Islands	**626**	**253**	**121**	**603**	**257**	**140**
Chandigarh	317	258	425	364	563	73
Dadra & N. Haveli	389	91	520	501	161	338
Daman & Diu	438	260	302	258	532	210
Delhi	337	643	20	370	454	176
Lakshadweep	318	502	180	463	370	167
Pondicherry	329	204	467	220	162	618
All-India	**581**	**66**	**353**	**558**	**68**	**374**

Source: * NSS Report No. 409, *Employment and Unemployment in India, 1993-94.*

\# NSS Report No. 458, *Employment and Unemployment in India, 1999-2000.*

Issues

ANI is a non-industrial economy and has significant dependence on imports from outside. The high import intensity of the expenditure has restricted the potential for income and, therefore, employment generation within the UT. Public administration has become the propelling force behind income growth. However, this can not be sustained for long and this is becoming evident from the virtual stagnation of per capita incomes in the UT and thus narrowing of the gap between per capita GSDP in the UT and the average per capita GDP for the country as a whole.

Productivity of industrial workers in ANI is low and declining. In rural areas self-employment has eroded, share of regular employment has stagnated, and casualisation of labour has increased.

There has been relatively lesser exploitation of growth potential of primary and secondary sectors. A

TABLE 12.6A

Percentage of Employed Persons* who had Changed Nature of Work by State/UT, 1999-2000

(Urban India)

State/Union Territory	*Male*				*Female*			
	Establishment	*Status*	*Industry*	*Occupation*	*Establishment*	*Status*	*Industry*	*Occupation*
Andhra Pradesh	3.5	0.7	1.1	1.3	2.2	0.3	0.6	0.6
Arunachal Pradesh	1.1	0.0	0.5	0.5	6.2	0.0	0.0	0.0
Assam	1.8	0.3	0.5	1.0	5.1	0.0	3.3	3.3
Bihar	1.2	0.1	0.4	0.3	0.0	0.0	0.0	0.0
Delhi	1.4	0.4	0.6	1.0	1.1	0.2	0.2	0.7
Goa	10.4	0.9	4.7	3.7	11.4	3.8	0.7	5.2
Gujarat	4.9	0.8	1.6	1.4	3.9	0.4	0.7	0.4
Haryana	7.0	1.3	2.7	2.3	6.0	1.3	2.2	0.0
Himachal Pradesh	5.0	0.9	1.1	0.9	0.7	0.0	0.3	0.3
Jammu & Kashmir	1.6	0.7	1.1	1.0	0.0	0.0	0.0	0.0
Karnataka	3.5	0.9	1.1	1.2	2.6	0.2	0.6	0.6
Kerala	8.1	1.3	2.6	2.9	5.0	0.0	0.9	0.6
Madhya Pradesh	5.5	0.9	1.3	1.0	6.9	0.0	0.5	0.5
Maharashtra	6.5	1.4	2.1	1.9	7.4	0.6	1.0	1.0
Manipur	0.8	0.3	0.6	0.4	2.6	0.0	0.7	0.7
Meghalaya	0.6	0.0	0.7	0.0	0.5	0.0	0.0	0.6
Mizoram	5.8	1.1	1.1	1.4	7.3	0.5	0.7	1.2
Nagaland	3.9	0.0	0.0	0.0	5.0	0.8	0.4	0.4
Orissa	1.5	0.3	0.5	0.5	3.5	0.0	0.2	0.2
Punjab	3.1	1.2	1.9	1.8	3.6	0.0	0.1	0.1
Rajasthan	4.1	1.1	1.0	1.2	3.6	0.0	0.0	0.0
Sikkim	1.6	0.0	0.6	0.2	0.0	0.0	0.0	0.0
Tamil Nadu	7.3	0.9	1.8	1.6	6.0	0.6	1.1	0.8
Tripura	0.3	0.0	0.0	0.3	1.1	0.0	0.0	0.0
Uttar Pradesh	3.6	0.8	1.1	1.0	2.8	0.1	0.0	0.0
West Bengal	3.4	0.6	0.9	0.9	4.8	0.0	0.4	0.4
Union Territories								
Andaman & Nicobar Islands	**7.0**	**2.4**	**2.3**	**2.1**	**2.9**	**0.0**	**0.0**	**0.0**
Chandigarh	3.8	0.5	1.3	0.7	2.0	0.0	0.0	1.8
Dadra and Nagar Haveli	2.8	0.6	1.9	1.9	0.0	0.0	0.0	0.0
Daman & Diu	5.9	3.1	3.4	3.9	3.9	2.2	2.2	2.2
Lakshadweep	7.3	3.3	4.9	5.4	2.4	1.4	1.4	1.4
Pondicherry	13.8	1.1	3.1	3.0	18.1	0.5	4.2	4.2
All-India	4.5	0.9	1.4	1.3	4.5	0.3	0.7	0.6

Note: The Changes have been observed during the two years preceding the survey. * Figures relate to principal usual status of individuals of age 15 years and above.

Source: National and Sample Survey Organisation, Report No. 458, 56th Round, *Employment and Unemployment Situation in India, 1999-2000*. Establishment include all producing units covering household enterprises.

planned exploitation of agriculture, fishery, and bamboo could provide the necessary boost to manufacturing and self-employment. It would be prudent to focus on production of those products that would reduce dependence on import from outside the UT and/or provide competitive advantage in export out of the UT.

Measures to Improve Employment Situation

Government should assign top priority to tackling rising incidence of unemployment. While physical remoteness and inadequate markets locally are crucial factors that have stifled the growth of potential industries in ANI, it must be recognised that the

TABLE 12.6B

Percentage of Employed Persons* who had Changed Nature of Work by State/UT, 1999-2000

(Rural India)

State/Union Territory	*Male*				*Female*			
	Establishment	*Status*	*Industry*	*Occupation*	*Establishment*	*Status*	*Industry*	*Occupation*
Andhra Pradesh	3.1	0.5	0.5	0.6	2.9	0.3	0.3	0.4
Arunachal Pradesh	0.7	0.0	0.0	0.2	0.0	0.0	0.0	0.0
Assam	3.7	0.3	0.9	1.0	2.0	0.0	0.4	0.6
Bihar	2.0	0.1	0.3	0.3	2.7	0.1	0.2	0.2
Delhi	0.9	0.0	0.0	0.0	0.0	0.0	0.0	0.0
Goa	3.6	1.2	1.5	1.6	2.8	0.0	0.0	0.0
Gujarat	10.6	1.8	3.1	3.7	12.8	0.7	2.8	3.2
Haryana	7.0	0.6	1.2	0.5	15.5	0.0	0.0	0.0
Himachal Pradesh	3.5	0.7	0.7	0.7	0.1	0.1	0.0	0.1
Jammu & Kashmir	0.8	0.3	0.5	0.4	0.8	0.0	0.2	0.0
Karnataka	4.8	0.7	0.6	0.9	6.1	0.1	0.2	0.3
Kerala	9.8	1.8	3.0	3.1	7.0	0.1	0.6	0.6
Madhya Pradesh	8.5	0.3	0.6	0.4	11.2	0.1	0.5	0.5
Maharashtra	13.6	1.0	1.1	1.5	16.3	0.5	0.3	0.7
Manipur	0.5	0.1	0.5	0.6	0.7	0.0	0.0	0.0
Meghalaya	1.2	0.1	0.1	0.1	0.5	0.0	0.0	0.0
Mizoram	0.2	0.0	0.1	0.2	0.9	0.0	0.2	0.4
Nagaland	0.7	0.2	0.0	0.0	0.0	0.0	0.0	0.0
Orissa	2.1	0.3	0.5	0.5	2.6	0.0	0.1	0.3
Punjab	2.6	0.6	1.3	1.3	4.5	0.0	0.0	0.0
Rajasthan	4.7	0.5	0.5	0.7	1.9	0.2	0.1	0.4
Sikkim	1.1	0.3	0.6	0.3	1.0	0.0	0.5	0.2
Tamil Nadu	15.0	0.7	0.8	1.0	18.2	0.1	0.3	0.4
Tripura	3.6	0.4	0.9	0.6	6.9	0.0	0.7	0.7
Uttar Pradesh	2.5	0.6	0.7	0.7	2.7	0.1	0.0	0.2
West Bengal	4.2	0.4	0.7	0.8	4.1	0.1	0.4	0.3
Union Territories								
Andaman & Nicobar Islands	**4.2**	**1.0**	**0.9**	**0.7**	**0.0**	**2.8**	**0.0**	**0.0**
Chandigarh	7.9	1.5	2.3	1.5	3.3	0.0	0.0	0.0
Dadra and Nagar Haveli	4.4	1.0	2.0	1.5	1.1	0.9	0.9	0.9
Daman & Diu	15.2	4.8	9.8	9.7	3.4	2.5	1.4	2.5
Lakshadweep	3.7	0.0	0.0	0.7	0.0	0.0	0.0	0.0
Pondicherry	21.9	1.7	3.2	2.6	24.7	0.8	1.7	1.7
All-India	5.8	0.6	0.9	0.9	8.1	0.2	0.4	0.6

Note: The changes have been observed during the two years preceding the survey.

* Figures relate to principal usual status of individuals of age 15 years and above.

Source: National and Sample Survey Organisation, Report No. 458, 56th Round, *Employment and Unemployment Situation in India, 1999-2000.*

investment plans of the UT have not given desired attention to investment on developing/improving necessary infrastructure for the development and growth in potential sectors—agriculture, fishery, horticulture, medicinal plants, bamboo development, rural based non-farm sectors. Such infrastructure would include efficient transport facilities, energy, water supply, irrigation, crop (including seafood) storage, handling and processing, packaging, and marketing infrastructure.

A major part of the infrastructure can be provided through public employment schemes. At the same time government should make efforts to create a favourable environment for private investment to supplement its efforts.

TABLE 12.7A

Labour Force Participation Rates by State/Union Territory, 1999-2000

State/Union Territory	*Rural*		*Urban*	
	Male	*Female*	*Male*	*Female*
1. Andhra Pradesh	61.1	48	53.2	18.5
2. Arunachal Pradesh	42.5	31	40.6	11
3. Assam	54.6	16.2	56.6	13.8
4. Bihar	50.3	17.4	46.6	8.2
5. Delhi	54.1	3.7	54.6	10.9
6. Goa	57.9	21.5	58.4	15.9
7. Gujarat	58.8	41.3	54.7	13.8
8. Haryana	48	20.2	52	10.1
9. Himachal Pradesh	54.6	47.4	53.2	14
10. Jammu & Kashmir	55.4	33	50	6.8
11. Karnataka	60.1	38.1	56.2	18.6
12. Kerala	58.7	27.3	59.1	25.4
13. Madhya Pradesh	53.9	38.3	50.9	13.6
14. Maharashtra	54.1	43.7	56.3	14.7
15. Manipur	50.5	25.7	47.8	22.5
16. Meghalaya	56.9	41.9	40.7	21.1
17. Nagaland	53.2	45	43.3	21.8
18. Orissa	56.5	30.2	51.11	15.3
19. Punjab	54.2	26.3	56.5	12.8
20. Rajasthan	50.3	38.8	49.9	14.1
21. Sikkim	51.9	24.6	55.6	22.5
22. Tamil Nadu	61	43.4	58.4	22.6
23. Tripura	50.8	7.6	52.2	8.2
24. Uttar Pradesh	48.6	20.2	51.2	9.7
25. West Bengal	54.9	16.5	61.1	12.9
Union Territories				
26. Andaman & Nicobar Islands	**56 (62.9)**	**19.3 (42.9)**	**65.2 (59.9)**	**24.9 (21.6)**
27. Chandigarh	78.9	12.9	56.5	15.3
28. Dadra and Nagar Haveli	59.1	35.4	66.4	11.2
29. Daman & Diu	66.5	30	56	20.3
30. Lakshadweep	55.1	20	46	22
31. Mizoram	56.3	44.1	49	26.5
32. Pondicherry	58.8	29.4	57.4	18.1
All-India	**54 (56.1)**	**30.2 (33.1)**	**54.2 (54.2)**	**14.7 (16.4)**

Note: Figures relate to usual status of individuals. Labour force covers those involved in gainful activity regularly + those involves in gainful activity occasionally + those unemployed. The figures represent the size of labour force as per cent of population. Figures in brackets are for 1993-94.

Source: National Sample Survey Organisation, Report No. 458, *Employment and Unemployment Status in India, 1999-2000.*

TABLE 12.7B

Workforce Participation Rates by State/Union Territory, 1999-2000

State/Union Territory	*Rural*		*Urban*	
	Male	*Female*	*Male*	*Female*
1. Andhra Pradesh	60.5	47.8	51.1	17.8
2. Arunachal Pradesh	42.2	31.0	39.9	10
3. Assam	52.9	15.1	52.2	11.2
4. Bihar	49.2	17.3	43.2	7.5
5. Delhi	52.0	2.9	52.8	10.5
6. Goa	53.9	18.1	49.8	10.6
7. Gujarat	58.4	41.3	53.8	13.5
8. Haryana	47.5	20.2	50.8	9.8
9. Himachal Pradesh	53.6	47.1	49.9	13
10. Jammu & Kashmir	54.8	32.7	47.8	6.2
11. Karnataka	59.5	38.0	54.5	17.8
12. Kerala	55.3	23.8	55.8	20.3
13. Madhya Pradesh	53.8	38.2	48.8	13.4
14. Maharashtra	53.1	43.4	53.2	13.7
15. Manipur	49.5	25.3	44.5	21.1
16. Meghalaya	55.7	41.8	39.3	19.7
17. Nagaland	51.8	44.1	39.3	19.9
18. Orissa	55.1	29.9	47.5	14.5
19. Punjab	53.0	28.0	54.9	12.5
20. Rajasthan	50.0	38.8	48.6	13.8
21. Sikkim	50.2	24.1	51.9	20
22. Tamil Nadu	59.4	43.0	56.3	21.5
23. Tripura	50.4	7.3	49.4	7.5
24. Uttar Pradesh	48.1	20.1	49.0	9.4
25. West Bengal	53.4	16.0	56.7	11.7
Union Territories				
26. Andaman & Nicobar Islands	**54.7 (61.4)**	**18.0 (42.2)**	**63.2 (57.5)**	**20.6 (19.4)**
27. Chandigarh	78.4	12.8	54.7	13.6
28. Dadra and Nagar Haveli	58.2	35.4	65.6	11.2
29. Daman & Diu	65.5	30.0	54.9	18.6
30. Lakshadweep	49.7	11.5	43.2	17.9
31. Mizoram	55.5	44.0	47.1	25.9
32. Pondicherry	56.0	28.7	56.5	16.9
All-India	**53.1 (56.3)**	**29.9 (22.8)**	**51.8 (52.0)**	**13.9 (15.4)**

Note: Figures relate to usual status of individuals. Workforce covers those involved in gainful activity regularly + those involved in gainful activity occasionally. The figures represent size of workforce as per cent of population.

Source: *Employment and Unemployment in India, 1999-2000*, Key Results, Report No. 455, National Sample Survey Organisation.

Good infrastructure and advance crop handling, storage, packaging and marketing facilities would lead to growth in investment in farm-based and also non-farm industries thus improving the employment situation in the UT. Fisheries, food processing, horticulture and floriculture have great potential for generating rural non-farm employment. However, this would require a transition from subsistence to

TABLE 12.8

Incidence of Unemployment in Urban and Rural Areas

(As % of labour force)

States/UTs	Urban Incidence of Unemployment									Rural Incidence of Unemployment								
	1983			1993-94			1999-2000			1983			1993-94			1999-2000		
	Male	Female	Persons	Male	Female	Persons	Male	Female	Persons	Male	Female	Persons	Male	Female	Persons	Male	Female	Persons
Andhra Pradesh	4.5	3.4	4.2	2.9	3.8	3.2	4	3.9	4	1	0.2	0.6	0.8	0.1	0.5	0.9	0.5	0.7
Arunachal Pradesh	-	-	-	0.8	5.5	1.4	1.7	8.6	3	-	-	-	1.4	0.3	0.9	0.7	0.2	0.5
Assam	4.2	10.8	4.8	5.5	27.8	8.7	7.7	20.5	9.8	1.9	1.9	1.9	4.5	8.1	5.3	3.2	6.8	4
Bihar	4.8	1.5	4.4	6.9	10	7.3	7.3	8	7.4	1.3	0.2	0.9	2	0.7	1.7	2.2	0.3	1.8
Goa	5.4	8.5	6.4	8	15.9	10.1	14.6	33.3	18.6	0.1	2	0.9	6.9	13	9	6.9	15.8	9.3
Gujarat	4.4	3	4.1	3	4.6	3.3	2	2.2	7	0.6	0.2	0.4	1.2	0.3	0.9	0.6	0	0.3
Haryana	4.5	6.5	4.8	2.5	3.3	2.7	2.8	2.6	2.7	2.9	0.3	2.2	1.6	0.5	1.2	1	0	0.8
Himachal Pradesh	7.6	7.6	7.6	3.5	0.4	2.7	6.4	8.4	6.8	1.4	0.5	1	0.9	0.1	0.6	1.8	0.6	1.3
Jammu & Kashmir	3.2	7.6	3.8	8.2	9	8.4	4.4	9.2	4.9	0.6	0.2	0.5	0.9	0.5	0.8	1.2	1	1.1
Karnataka	4.2	4.4	4.2	3	6.5	3.7	2.9	4.8	3.4	0.8	0.5	0.7	0.9	0.3	0.7	0.9	0.4	0.7
Kerala	9.4	15.1	11.2	6.6	18.5	10.2	5.5	19.9	10	7	7.3	7.1	5.4	9.8	6.8	5.7	13.2	8.1
Madhya Pradesh	3.2	1.1	2.8	5.3	3.9	5	4.1	1.5	3.6	0.3	0.1	0.2	0.7	0.2	0.5	0.7	0.2	0.5
Maharashtra	5.3	3.7	5	4.2	4.7	4.3	5.5	6.3	5.7	1	0.1	0.6	1.2	0.3	0.8	1.9	0.8	1.4
Manipur	0.5	0.1	0.3	4.8	2.8	4.2	7	6	6.7	0.6	0	0.4	1.2	0.4	0.9	2.1	1.6	2
Meghalaya	8.4	9.2	8.6	1	3.6	1.7	3.4	6.9	4.5	0.4	0.1	0.3	0.4	0	0.2	0.4	0.3	0.4
Mizoram	1.1	1	1.1	0.4	0.5	0.4	3.3	2.3	2.9	0.1		0.1	1.5	0.4	1.1	1.4	0.3	0.9
Nagaland	0.4	0	0.3	6.9	5.9	6.7	9.3	8.9	9.2	-	-	-	2.2	0	1.5	2.6	2.1	2.4
Orissa	4.5	5.5	4.6	6.7	6.1	6.6	7.1	5	6.7	1.5	0.4	1.2	1.8	0.9	1.5	2.4	1.1	2
Punjab	3.5	4.7	3.7	3.1	5.4	3.4	2.8	2.3	2.8	2.1	1.5	2	1.3	1.2	1.3	2.2	1	1.8
Rajasthan	3.7	0.9	3	1.8	0.4	1.5	2.6	1.9	2.5	0.4	0.1	0.3	0.3	0.1	0.3	0.6	0.2	0.4
Sikkim	9.9	6.9	9.4	1.4	8.2	2.5	6.4	13.2	8	1	0.7	0.9	0.6	1.4	0.8	3.3	1.9	2.8
Tamil Nadu	6.5	6.2	6.4	4.1	6.8	4.9	3.4	5	3.8	2.3	1.1	1.8	1.8	0.6	1.3	2.7	1	2
Tripura	6.8	29	10.8	5.9	17.6	8.4	5.3	8.7	5.8	1.4	14.7	2.8	1.5	6.4	2.4	0.9	3.6	1.2
Uttar Pradesh	3.9	2.7	3.7	3.3	0.6	2.9	4.3	3.3	4.1	0.8	0.1	0.6	0.9	0	0.7	0.9	0.3	0.8
West Bengal	8.1	12.8	8.8	6.3	15.1	7.9	7.2	9.7	7.8	2.1	1.6	2	1.8	2.1	1.8	2.7	2.9	2.7
Andaman & Nicobar Islands	**6.1**	**26.5**	**8.8**	**4**	**10.1**	**5.4**	**3.2**	**17.3**	**6.7**	**3.3**	**2.6**	**3.2**	**2.5**	**1.8**	**2.2**	**2.2**	**6.9**	**3.3**
Chandigarh	6.2	12.1	7.4	3.3	20.5	7.5	3.3	11.3	4.8	3	0	2.5	2.7	4.5	2.9	0.6	0.5	0.6
Dadra & Nagar Haveli	-	-	-	0	1.4	0.4	1.2	0	1	1	0.3	0.7	0.8	0.8	0.8	1.6	0	1
Daman and Diu	5.4	8.5	6.5	4.5	11.2	5.9	1.4	8.6	3.2	0.1	2	1	1.4	0	1	1.5	0	1
Delhi	3	4.6	3.2	0.9	6.4	1.6	3.2	4.7	3.5	2.3	0	1.7	0	0	0	3.8	21.4	4.7
Lakshadweep	-	-	-	14.7	33.8	18.6	6.2	18.6	9.8	-	-	-	5.8	40.7	14.7	9.9	42.5	18.8
Pondicherry	9.8	6.8	9	5.7	9.7	6.7	3.3	6.5	4.1	2.1	3.1	2.5	3.4	0	2.3	4.7	2.4	4
All-India	5	5.2	5.1	4.1	6.6	4.6	4.5	5.9	4.8	1.4	0.7	1.1	1.5	0.8	1.2	1.7	1.1	1.5

Source: Planning Commission (2002). *National Human Development Report 2002*, Government of India.

TABLE 12.9A

Usual Principal Status Unemployment Rate among the Youth (15-29 years) for each State and Union Territory

Urban

States/Union Territories	*Unemployment Rate in 1993-94*												*Unemployment Rate in 1999-2000*											
	Male				*Female*				*Persons*				*Male*				*Female*				*Persons*			
	15-19	*20-24*	*25-29*	*15-29*	*15-19*	*20-24*	*25-29*	*15-29*	*15-19*	*20-24*	*25-29*	*15-29*	*15-19*	*20-24*	*25-29*	*15-29*	*15-19*	*20-24*	*25-29*	*15-29*	*15-19*	*20-24*	*25-29*	*15-29*
Andhra Pradesh	55	124	63	83	99	146	95	113	66	128	69	90	135	134	62	101	94	140	62	97	134	136	62	100
Arunachal Pradesh	110	75	-	30	254	250	-	129	173	112	-	53	0	142	89	91	541	316	26	185	118	216	71	119
Assam	49	285	127	170	440	613	364	498	168	379	163	246	205	344	155	222	8	705	557	450	127	390	228	266
Bihar	197	260	139	191	413	464	136	314	216	282	138	203	226	265	200	230	88	500	122	210	205	283	192	227
Goa	379	214	45	157	425	633	405	502	395	317	101	237	542	389	223	335	749	524	410	551	614	433	254	392
Gujarat	124	84	27	71	178	250	45	160	130	105	28	81	79	71	15	51	12	82	116	70	68	72	23	53
Haryana	88	89	20	60	222	429	81	208	99	109	25	71	157	54	24	61	0	182	0	89	150	67	22	63
Himachal Pradesh	95	150	100	121	-	67	-	16	68	141	85	106	161	110	185	156	0	510	302	391	123	204	197	193
Jammu & Kashmir	243	232	134	187	-	556	377	336	176	304	177	219	245	216	93	156	33	403	271	276	217	234	118	171
Karnataka	104	99	48	80	124	231	131	166	109	129	69	101	45	129	31	70	55	114	67	85	48	126	37	73
Kerala	335	212	101	190	437	477	421	452	368	297	184	268	414	212	67	184	551	607	385	508	453	353	164	288
Madhya Pradesh	206	182	82	143	131	251	55	143	193	193	78	143	101	128	80	103	16	84	31	48	90	121	71	94
Maharashtra	163	146	57	110	162	226	49	146	162	164	55	117	216	165	73	137	278	249	113	196	228	177	82	147
Manipur	97	126	227	180	86	-	147	80	94	90	210	154	86	214	239	226	611	69	291	242	308	173	254	231
Meghalaya	96	125	8	53	-	199	120	110	70	152	37	75	61	149	102	119	195	131	212	177	104	144	154	143
Mizoram	-	27	7	16	-	15	32	14	-	21	17	15	49	113	148	127	171	61	38	60	63	91	111	103
Nagaland	146	292	145	175	-	156	-	83	143	231	121	154	0	340	308	311	0	555	106	233	0	410	246	283
Orissa	193	232	150	187	177	232	167	191	186	231	153	188	120	303	182	223	61	310	88	164	105	304	163	211
Punjab	128	93	16	73	227	322	235	277	133	115	29	87	105	88	41	69	56	124	124	103	97	91	45	71
Rajasthan	70	65	21	50	-	41	24	23	60	63	22	46	123	59	41	67	253	93	27	122	143	64	39	74
Sikkim	-	81	-	30	-	362	-	132	-	138	-	74	221	132	154	156	0	495	167	299	167	234	156	190
Tamil Nadu	171	133	59	114	179	206	166	184	173	151	84	133	168	118	38	94	163	207	81	148	166	141	47	108
Tripura	45	321	152	184	-	580	444	423	34	384	237	251	11	352	234	221	0	353	69	173	9	351	212	214
Uttar Pradesh	91	117	58	89	49	87	17	81	88	115	54	86	102	86	105	97	162	228	37	144	109	97	101	102
West Bengal	213	252	156	199	180	576	288	403	210	334	178	240	262	250	126	201	143	383	181	238	241	270	136	207
A & N Islands	**166**	**227**	**132**	**174**	**1000**	**500**	**157**	**333**	**232**	**290**	**138**	**207**	**128**	**117**	**47**	**98**	**380**	**471**	**398**	**421**	**214**	**210**	**174**	**199**
Chandigarh	215	71	-	63	164	607	207	400	214	184	37	122	178	135	38	100	371	479	173	329	200	208	66	145
Dadra & N. Haveli	-	-	64	0	315	-	-	0	92	-	56	0	54	69	0	32	0	0	0	0	48	61	0	30
Daman & Diu	147	149	-	83	-	450	162	302	122	208	41	110	42	83	0	39	20	189	121	90	29	102	27	53
Delhi	-	50	-	18	-	204	43	104	-	68	5	26	159	89	37	79	135	109	130	120	157	93	49	85
Lakshadweep	505	347	219	340	842	530	397	564	638	400	265	408	357	384	122	288	418	676	455	535	373	471	245	362
Pondicherry	129	200	44	126	261	319	252	270	180	224	98	165	142	145	41	92	216	212	0	160	184	162	35	112
All-India	**134**	**139**	**67**	**108**	**168**	**277**	**129**	**194**	**141**	**165**	**78**	**124**	**154**	**139**	**75**	**115**	**155**	**226**	**115**	**166**	**154**	**154**	**82**	**124**

Source: Employment and Unemployment Situation in India, 1993-94 & 1999-2000, Report No. 409 & 458, National Sample Survey Organisation.

TABLE 12.9B

Usual Principal Status Unemployment Rate among the Youth (15-29 years) for each State and Union Territory

Rural

States/UnionTerritories	Unemployment Rate in 1993-94												Unemployment Rate in 1999-2000											
	Male				Female				Persons				Male				Female				Persons			
	15-19	20-24	25-29	15-29	15-19	20-24	25-29	15-29	15-19	20-24	25-29	15-29	15-19	20-24	25-29	15-29	15-19	20-24	25-29	15-29	15-19	20-24	25-29	15-29
Andhra Pradesh	55	124	63	83	99	146	95	113	66	128	69	90	135	134	62	101	94	140	62	97	134	136	62	100
Andhra Pradesh	14	25	10	17	4	1	1	2	11	14	6	10	21	48	19	29	6	30	9	15	15	40	15	23
Arunachal Pradesh	45	72	28	43	2	18	-	6	26	42	13	24	41	43	11	25	9	11	0	4	18	26	7	15
Assam	99	165	87	118	218	238	59	160	128	181	79	128	103	138	72	102	203	329	194	245	114	171	93	125
Bihar	43	63	45	50	48	27	-	12	42	54	34	43	91	68	40	63	54	11	10	19	85	58	33	55
Goa	321	208	89	163	427	368	226	329	372	269	131	224	278	248	102	178	589	321	338	431	444	260	158	247
Gujarat	27	34	10	27	10	10	5	8	26	24	9	19	26	15	9	18	18	0	0	0	29	10	7	14
Haryana	48	54	4	35	29	-	2	9	42	37	3	26	61	25	14	29	0	0	44	17	60	23	17	29
Himachal Pradesh	10	48	8	23	-	9	-	4	5	29	5	13	93	119	36	78	88	50	56	58	93	95	43	72
Jammu & Kashmir	45	27	-	25	10	14	9	11	30	22	4	19	57	111	46	73	125	111	126	117	61	112	54	79
Karnataka	13	39	10	22	-	25	3	10	8	33	6	17	26	34	7	22	8	13	2	7	21	28	5	17
Kerala	262	174	80	156	417	364	184	290	302	235	119	200	300	205	92	178	458	526	356	451	349	301	163	258
Madhya Pradesh	11	27	12	17	2	2	1	2	9	17	8	11	15	33	10	19	9	4	2	4	13	22	8	14
Maharashtra	29	52	15	32	8	10	3	6	19	31	9	20	74	95	36	66	53	26	15	28	64	69	27	50
Manipur	22	24	56	40	9	19	13	14	15	21	38	28	64	56	44	52	0	107	62	72	47	72	49	58
Meghalaya	13	18	-	10	-	-	-	-	8	8	-	5	22	15	0	11	0	16	4	7	12	16	2	10
Mizoram	-	53	43	36	-	23	-	8	-	42	31	25	2	26	103	49	0	0	41	14	0	16	80	34
Nagaland	30	41	76	54	-	2	-	-	18	26	51	34	29	153	83	99	92	145	53	100	53	150	76	100
Orissa	46	61	26	43	13	34	4	18	32	50	18	34	141	84	48	84	65	41	27	43	114	71	43	72
Punjab	46	33	6	29	51	58	6	37	47	39	6	31	103	61	17	56	56	333	45	133	99	76	18	61
Rajasthan	10	13	9	10	5	3	1	3	8	9	6	7	18	22	16	19	9	2	0	3	14	15	11	13
Sikkim	-	18	18	16	63	8	67	42	13	15	27	19	74	84	131	102	0	103	25	50	49	89	95	84
Tamil Nadu	38	73	34	49	14	28	9	17	27	54	23	35	108	80	51	76	38	40	11	28	78	65	35	57
Tripura	22	39	48	47	87	174	106	126	34	70	62	58	37	22	18	28	127	57	182	128	61	25	39	39
Uttar Pradesh	24	24	10	20	17	12	-	8	23	21	8	17	37	33	26	32	0	14	11	9	31	31	23	28
West Bengal	39	54	33	42	15	57	19	30	33	54	29	39	107	92	39	75	87	88	39	72	102	91	38	74
A & N Islands	**57**	**118**	**18**	**64**	**65**	**58**	**4**	**40**	**60**	**92**	**12**	**54**	**97**	**86**	**80**	**85**	**231**	**5**	**204**	**155**	**127**	**66**	**115**	**104**
Chandigarh	125	79	-	52	1000	52	-	42	142	72	-	50	23	21	21	21	36	0	0	35	24	21	22	22
Dadra & N. Haveli	66	6	-	22	-	39	-	17	39	24	-	20	230	0	0	41	0	0	0	0	122	0	0	25
Daman & Diu	72	33	-	35	-	-	-	-	59	29	-	29	21	61	0	29	0	0	0	0	17	53	0	25
Delhi	-	-	-	-	-	-	-	-	-	-	-	-	67	87	67	75	1000	539	0	548	86	121	65	92
Lakshadweep	92	303	-	185	1000	884	477	762	441	529	214	387	109	567	244	369	1000	456	1000	793	727	526	428	558
Pondicherry	193	86	43	81	-	-	-	-	118	59	35	60	240	121	48	107	82	0	82	61	171	89	58	92
All-India	**33**	**49**	**23**	**35**	**19**	**28**	**9**	**19**	**28**	**41**	**19**	**29**	**65**	**62**	**32**	**51**	**41**	**49**	**24**	**37**	**57**	**58**	**28**	**46**

Source: Employment and Unemployment Situation in India, 1993-94 and 1999-2000, Report No. 409 and 459, National Sample Survey Organisation.

TABLE 12.10

Labour Productivity among Indian States and Union Territories in 2001-02

State/Union Territories	*Per Worker Value of Output (Rs lakh)*						*Per Worker net value added (Rs lakh)*					
	2001-02	*00-01*	*99-00*	*98-99*	*97-88*	*96-97*	*2001-02*	*00-01*	*99-00*	*98-99*	*97-98*	*96-97*
Andhra Pradesh	6.86	6.76	6.43	5.68	4.30	4.79	1.19	0.98	1.00	0.92	0.83	1.04
Assam	7.08	7.77	6.83	7.18	4.79	4.70	1.10	1.14	1.49	1.35	0.92	0.97
Bihar	10.47	11.53	9.85	6.63	9.92	8.13	1.09	1.16	1.61	1.11	3.07	1.83
Chhattisgarh	13.77	13.22	12.75	12.33	-	-	2.41	2.59	2.32	3.25	-	-
Goa	23.44	26.02	24.03	20.05	15.66	16.56	4.68	4.73	4.40	4.58	3.34	4.69
Gujarat	20.43	17.02	14.41	13.87	12.63	10.68	2.43	2.24	2.34	2.32	2.19	1.90
Haryana	15.70	14.85	14.89	8.99	10.37	9.22	2.27	1.85	2.18	1.45	1.63	1.50
Himachal Pradesh	14.37	16.46	13.20	12.81	6.56	6.17	2.82	3.32	2.79	2.60	1.72	1.97
Jammu & Kashmir	6.17	5.78	0.81	-	2.89	4.47	0.73	0.69	0.10	-	0.48	0.86
Jharkhand	10.39	11.11	84.66	11.24	-	-	1.74	2.33	28.54	3.89	-	-
Karnataka	11.04	9.76	8.64	8.26	7.16	6.80	1.44	1.75	1.70	1.66	1.47	1.52
Kerala	7.30	8.52	8.20	7.33	5.64	5.54	1.13	1.13	1.20	1.45	0.97	1.02
Madhya Pradesh	16.43	14.49	16.47	9.48	9.64	9.44	2.56	2.45	2.11	1.47	2.11	2.29
Maharashtra	14.48	15.77	14.90	11.56	11.70	10.93	2.58	2.67	2.84	2.25	2.37	2.44
Manipur	1.52	-	-	-	3.31	1.86	0.25	-	-	-	1.90	0.89
Meghalaya	13.02	-	-	-	2.33	2.09	1.81	-	-	-	0.38	1.12
Nagaland	3.54	-	-	-	6.66	2.93	0.67	-	-	-	0.55	1.28
Orissa	11.20	10.29	8.96	7.63	8.31	7.55	1.30	1.83	2.03	1.46	2.13	1.87
Punjab	9.29	9.77	11.27	9.52	6.99	6.28	1.31	1.20	1.65	1.55	1.07	0.98
Rajasthan	13.74	13.26	12.77	10.03	9.94	8.61	1.94	2.26	2.26	1.50	2.11	1.91
Tamil nadu	8.56	9.11	8.57	6.82	6.50	6.38	1.37	1.46	1.30	1.21	1.13	1.28
Tripura	2.81	-	-	-	2.56	1.90	1.08	-	-	-	0.43	0.58
Uttaranchal	12.71	11.32	9.15	6.87	-	-	2.26	2.23	1.51	1.12	-	-
Uttar Pradesh	12.82	12.02	10.68	9.36	9.39	8.10	2.18	1.17	1.79	1.69	1.98	1.59
West Bengal	7.53	6.88	5.92	4.95	4.93	4.72	1.14	1.00	0.97	0.99	1.08	1.04
A & N Islands	**1.28**	-	-	-	**2.31**	**1.87**	**0.19**	-	-	-	**0.57**	**0.58**
Chandigarh	8.36	9.89	10.65	11.03	4.92	7.21	1.10	1.47	1.51	1.38	0.69	1.20
Dadra & Nagar Haveli	36.13	33.78	40.37	31.73	34.81	31.93	5.36	4.60	5.93	6.32	7.84	6.16
Daman & Diu	22.08	18.25	21.06	17.34	17.02	18.63	3.26	3.42	4.09	2.97	2.94	3.94
Delhi	11.65	11.87	13.03	11.77	11.40	9.30	1.70	1.67	2.21	1.86	2.29	1.60
Pondicherry	16.49	15.27	13.66	12.88	10.24	8.76	3.44	3.26	2.33	2.85	2.57	2.16
All States	**11.88**	**11.62**	**11.00**	**9.15**	**8.30**	**7.78**	**1.83**	**1.80**	**1.90**	**1.70**	**1.65**	**1.62**

Source: The Economic Times, September 1, 2003.

commercialised agriculture and fisheries. Tourism, handicrafts, ship repair and servicing also have good potential.

The government of India plans to go in for bamboo plantation over six million hectare during the next 10 years under its National Mission on Bamboo Technology and Trade Development, as this has been now regarded as a money and job spinner. According to Planning Commission estimates, altogether, 8.6 million jobs would be created, that is, 1.4 million jobs per million ha of plantation in the next 10 years. An important question however is will farmers be involved in bamboo cultivation? Will forest laws be changed which do not allow farmers to sell bamboo except in Northeast of India. In ANI, bamboo could be a major employer. An enabling framework is all that is required to realise this potential.

Further, opening up markets in the neighbouring countries by developing and opening waterways would provide the much needed thrust to growth in employment.

Measures to Improve Labour Productivity

Emphasis on Education

There is widespread evidence that education has a positive impact on labour productivity. Studies have shown that the spread of technology depends on the learning potentials and motivation that are linked to the development of formal schooling; implying the presence of a causal link from education to economic growth. Ensuring the provision of quality education is, therefore, a must.

Emphasis on General Skills at the Secondary Level

While there has been a temptation in many economies to vocationalise secondary schools in order to make them more relevant to the job market, a cautious approach is required in view of the empirical evidence that shows that many of those who studied vocational subjects took up jobs such as office clerk, which were unrelated to their training.[2] Such evidence coupled with high unit cost of vocationalising the curriculum (scale diseconomies), favours the more conservative policy of emphasising general skills—like science, social science, commerce and maths—in secondary education. This system would provide a lot of flexibility to fit into a variety of occupations or enrol for extensive vocational training or go for higher studies in a variety of fields. In an era when shifts in business and/or changes in outputs and services demanded are increasingly expected to happen over shorter periods of time, workers who can adapt to changing environment faster and have the capacity for quick learning of new skills will be valued more. Sound grounding in general skills at the secondary level is therefore, highly desirable. There is, however, scope for introducing selective vocational courses at the secondary level that do not require strong mathematical and scientific skills. Some of these training courses are for the purposes of: welder, fitter, surveyor, electrician, tailor, chef, house keeping, etc. In secondary schools introduction of lower level courses, say 'level B', in science and maths may be considered for those opting for above vocational courses.

Emphasis on Employment-based Vocational Training

Creation of technical and vocational skills in the labour force is crucial. Planning for vocational training in ANI should involve two steps. One, identification of training courses and their contents in line with the current and potential (in near future) demand in the market. Two, provision for quality training. Potential employers know more about the demand for labour as well as the demand for specific skills than the formal school system does, and they are better placed to follow technological developments in a variety of occupations. Government should support and encourage technical institutes in private sector with strong linkages with the industry. Renowned autonomous technical institutes in mainland should also be encouraged to open outreach centres in ANI. This does not mean that the public sector vocational institutions would be closed down. Private/autonomous institutes will only play a complementary role. People will enrol in them voluntarily, pay for their courses, and thereby help to ensure the relevance of what those schools offer. If students pay the cost of their education, they are more likely to make better choices on whether to enrol and what to study. For the talented poor, selective scholarships and loans can be provided. Public vocational institutions typically financed by the taxpayer generally provide inadequate alternative. Public institutions will compete with those in the private sector; some of them may close down eventually if their performance is poor in terms of poor enrolment, examination performance, and placement of students. Institutions such as Indian Institute of Technology and Manipal Foundation should be encouraged to set up training centres in ANI. Their presence will not only provide a healthy competition to the existing training centres but also an opportunity to learn from them in improving their teaching levels. While the suggestions on what training courses should be offered have been listed in chapters on specific sectors in the report, the UT administration may consider introducing/strengthening the following courses: training in shipping, fishery, information technology, conservation of natural resources, disaster mitigation and management, food processing, bio-fuel, handicrafts, software, plumbing, and electrical work.

Employment Generation: Some Projections

Agriculture

Components	*Expected Employment in Various Plan Periods (No.)*			
	X	*XI*	*XII*	*XIII*
a) Grain/planting Material, Storage and Processing	10	20	30	30
b) Multiple Cropping	60	80	85	90
c) Watershed/Irrigation	5	7	3	2
d) Soil Reclamation	20	30	20	10

Source: Chapter 7.

2. Placement profile of vocational schools in ANI provides some support to this.

Animal Husbandry

Self Employment

Components	*Expected Employment in Various Plan Periods (No.)*			
	X	*XI*	*XII*	*XIII*
a) Dairy Development	2500	2500	2500	2500
b) Meat Sector	3000	5000	3000	2000
c) Rural Poultry Production	5000	5000	4000	4000
d) Animal Health	200	200	200	200

Source: Chapter 7.

Chapter 13

Disaster Management

The ANI constitute nearly one-fourth of India's coastline. These islands are biodiversity hotspots, with a variety of endemic species of flora and fauna. They are home to ethnic communities. The islands are located in a region identified under the seismic zone V, corresponding to high incidence of seismic activity. The region has one of the largest identified fault lines in the tectonic arrangement causing severe turbulence in the 10-degree channel separating the two groups of islands. Between 1989 and 1998, earthquakes rocked the region every six days on an average. A tsunami, with an amplitude reaching 1.04 metres, was recorded way back in 1881.[1] Given these issues, preparedness (that is, knowing where and when the natural phenomenon will occur and relaying this information at maximum speed to those who are likely to be affected)[2] and mitigation measures (like, coastal zone regulation, construction of earthquake-resistant buildings) to reduce the impact[3] of these calamities, should have assumed top priority.

This chapter is organised as follows: the next section briefly describes the extant situation with regard to the financial and institutional arrangements for coping with natural disasters. These largely follow from the recommendations of the Planning Commission and the Finance Commissions. Section 3 discusses the various regulations that are intended to safeguard and reduce vulnerability of the populace while section 4 focuses on the recent disaster due to the tsunami—the loss of lives, the damage to property and infrastructure—and consequent efforts at relief and rehabilitation. Finally, section 5 concludes with broad suggestions to improve preparedness and strategies for enhancing resilience to cope with disasters.

Where Do We Stand?

After the super-cyclone in Orissa and the earthquake in Bhuj (Rajasthan), the central government reviewed the country's disaster preparedness. A high powered committee was set up in 1999 which submitted its report in 2001. This report acknowledged the importance of investment in mitigation measures. Important recommendations emerging from the report of the committee include:

- A national policy on disaster management: for prevention, preparedness and mitigation before and after disaster.
- Putting aside at least 10 per cent of plan funds at the national, state and district levels for schemes to address prevention, reduction, preparedness and mitigation of disasters.
- Microzonation of all urban areas to mitigate earthquake threat, to put in early warning systems for cyclones and strict enforcement of building codes set by the BIS.

In response to these recommendations, a draft national policy for disaster management has been put together but is yet to be finalised and implemented. In 2002, the Centre asked the State governments to

1. However, there is no recorded account of the damage caused.
2. The occurrence of natural phenomena like volcanic eruptions, tornadoes and cyclones, forest-fires, floods, earthquakes, etc. are quite common, but they do not always transform into what we term as disasters. Most often disasters are so named if they cause extensive damage to human life and property, but there are relatively fewer eponymous references when human life and property escapes this fury. To a large extent, this could be due to lack of preparedness for these calamities.
3. Inadequate planning, poverty, and a range of other underlying factors create conditions of vulnerability that result in insufficient capacity or measures to reduce the potential adverse consequences. Vulnerability may contribute as much to the magnitude of the disaster as the natural phenomenon itself. Thus, hazard-risk reduction should be integrated with sustainable development policies and programmes at all levels.

convert their departments of relief and rehabilitation into disaster management departments, with specific responsibilities for disaster mitigation and preparedness. This was to be followed by a separate ministry of disaster management at the Centre. However, the progress till date appears unsatisfactory.

To earmark funds for disaster prevention and preparedness, the Eleventh Finance Commission (EFC) also deliberated upon allocation for disaster prevention and mitigation under the Central Calamity Fund. This was a change from the earlier practice of budgeting for only relief and rehabilitation. It was intended to provide some momentum towards disaster prevention and mitigation. The following recommendations of the EFC have a direct bearing on the Plan:

- Expenditure on restoration of infrastructure and other capital assets, except those that are intrinsically connected with relief operations and connectivity with the affected area and population, should be met from the plan funds on priority basis.
- Medium and long-term measures be devised by the concerned ministries of the Government of India, the State Governments and the Planning Commission to reduce, if possible, eliminate the occurrences of these calamities by undertaking developmental works.
- The Planning Commission, in consultation with the state governments and concerned ministries should be able to identify works of a capital nature to prevent the recurrence of specific calamities. These works may be funded under the Plan.

However, in practice, again there is very little progress in this direction.

After the Gujarat earthquake (in the Kutch region), flow of information was identified as the single most important system that needed to be made effective in practice. But the procedure followed in the wake of the tsunami (December 26, 2004), despite having received some information to that effect within a minute of its appearance, shows that the system of dissemination of information is grossly inadequate.

Financial arrangement, for an emergency response to natural calamities, is available in the form of a National Calamity Contingency Fund (NCCF) and the States' Calamity Relief Fund (CRF). The CRF is used for meeting the expenditure for providing immediate relief to the victims of the calamity and for meeting expenditure on restoration of damaged capital works such as drinking water, housing, as part of providing immediate relief. State's CRF have a 75 per cent (of the total yearly allocation as indicated by the Finance Commission) non-plan grant contribution from the centre. The size of the CRF has been enhanced from Rs. 11,007.59 crore in the EFC period to Rs. 21,333.33 crore under the allocation of the Twelfth Finance Commission (TFC) period for the years 2005-06 to 2009-10. The contribution of Central government has been increased from Rs. 8,255.69 crore to Rs. 16,000 crore.

Funds from the NCCF are released for natural calamities of rare severity. The assistance from NCCF is however, available only for immediate relief and rehabilitation. The NCCF (initial corpus of 500 crore) is to be recouped by way of collection of National Calamity Contingent Duty and levy of special surcharge for a limited period on central taxes. A National Centre for Calamity Management (NCCM) under the Ministry of Home Affairs has also been established to monitor natural calamities. It is expected to monitor such occurrences on a regular basis and assess their impact on the area and the population.

The CRF was mandated to provide immediate succour and relief to victims of cyclones, drought, earthquake, fire, floods and hailstorms. The TFC has extended the scope of the term "calamity" to include landslides, avalanches, cloud-burst and pest attacks.

The Tenth Plan document envisages that the development projects should be sensitive towards disaster mitigation. It states that "it makes good economic sense to spend a little extra today in a planned way on steps and components that can help in prevention and mitigation of disasters, than be forced to spend many multiples more later on restoration and rehabilitation." This has been a significant step to provide disaster prevention and mitigation, the desired appreciation and thrust.

In the present scheme of things the role of the central government is mainly in financial and logistical support and that too in the post-disaster situation. The responsibility to cope with natural disasters is essentially that of the state government. The district administration is the focal point for implementation of all government plans.

The Tenth FYP suggests that the local bodies can be effective instruments in tackling disasters through early warning system, relief distribution, providing shelter to the victims, medical assistance. But the above design may not be effective in several cases. In the aftermath of any disaster, often it is the local administration which itself is in a state of extreme shock—with communication lines and other transport infrastructure in a shambles. The local administration in the immediate post-episode situation may be in disarray to make any significant headway. Thus, the immediate relief has to come from neighbouring areas.

Institutional understanding to enable the administration of the neighbouring areas to respond immediately and extend support needs to be forged. In several cases even the indications of an impending disaster may not be observed locally, when the point of impact of a disaster may be different from the point where the first signals are received. This envisages that the local administration should be constantly feeding-in and receiving inputs from a centralised system. The early warning system, in several cases, thus may be initiated outside the local area. While there must be in place an effective mechanism for propagation of a warning system at all levels, the principal responsibility, of developing and putting in place a synchronised and co-coordinated early warning system, should primarily rest with the central government. The additional need to avoid undue panic also warrants that the centralised system is most suited for this purpose so that it may corroborate the indicators along various parameters before triggering a warning signal.

The local level must however be equipped to conduct regular drills and mock exercises for propagation of the warning signals and conduct safe and quick evacuation. Disasters or rather the preparedness and mitigation (including relief and rehabilitation) may be looked upon as a broader 'security' concern and thus entail a greater coordination even in terms of international cooperation. Institutional arrangements for dealing with natural disasters, including at the United Nations level need to be strengthened. The roles and responsibilities of each level of the government must be carefully reviewed, especially when the local or district level administration in the affected areas, are probably in no shape to respond.

Several plan schemes appear to address the reduction and mitigation of natural calamities. Some schemes under the Tenth FYP that may be considered as developmental expenditures towards disaster preparedness and mitigation are given in Annexure 13.1. However, a detailed overview is needed to assess their achievements to restructure, reformulate and strengthen these schemes.

The Coastal Regulation Zones, 1991

The ecological sensitivity of the ANIs is delicately poised and this circumscribes the capacity of these islands to sustain human settlements. Various rules and regulatory legislations such as Indian Forests Act (1927), Andaman & Nicobar (Protection of Aboriginal Tribals) Act (1956), Wildlife Protection Act (1972), Forest Conservation Act (1972), Water Prevention and Control of Pollution Act (1974), Environmental Protection Act (1986), Coastal Regulation Zones, 1991(CRZ) influence the human settlement on these islands.

While most of the acts in force are designed to protect the ecology and environment, the CRZ guidelines are generally perceived to be inhibiting. In 1991, The MoEF notified the country's coastal stretches as coastal regulation zones.[4] The following features of CRZ are worth noting:

- Areas 200 metres from the shore, to be kept free for waves.
- 'No development zones' up to 500 metres.
- No new construction was permitted within 200 metres of high tide line.
- Sand from beaches and coastal waters could not be used for construction or other purposes.

Since its notification in 1991, the CRZ has been amended several times. The following three amendments are especially relevant in the case of ANI:

(i) The January 31, 1997 amendment permitted sand mining and ground water withdrawal in CRZ of ANI.

(ii) The October 19, 2002 amendment permitted non-conventional energy facilities, desalination plants and airstrips in ANI.

(iii) The July 24, 2003 amendment relaxed 'no development zone' to 50 m in ANI and Lakshadweep to promote tourism.

In the ANI most of the islands have a narrow width with settlements on coastal areas. A major part of the coastal stretches of ANI are under CRZ-I, a small portion under CRZ-IV and a very small portion is under CRZ-II. Restrictions under CRZ-I being most stringent,

4. India has a long coastline stretching over 5,700 km. The India Ocean is one of the six major cyclone prone regions of the world. The average coastal population density is 432 persons per sq. km. as against 256 persons per sq. km. for the entire country. Therefore, it is crucial that coastline areas have a specific, well managed system to combat disaster.

CRZ-IV areas, most of which are revenue land, are the only ones available for developmental projects. In this regard, the July 24, 2003 notification of the Ministry of Environment & Forests is a significant step. Although, it is reported that internationally CRZ norms of 50 and 70 metres are commonly used and combined with stringent limits on land area covered, number of buildings, etc. there is a need to look at the CRZ regulations on a case-to-case basis.

In the wake of the recent disaster, there perhaps is a need to evaluate whether the extant set of regulations is sufficient to enhance preparedness in navigating through episodes of natural calamities by institutionalising the need for a conservationist approach towards development of the ANIs. Needless to mention that there is also an urgent need to implement and enforce the existing regulations.

Simultaneously, one may also take up a detailed overview to see if there is some need to explicitly bring in certain legislation that would reinforce the present set of regulatory laws without jeopardising the opportunities for otherwise sustainable development. While no amount of preparedness may seem sufficient, given the high degree of uncertainty in the form and manner of an episode, the additional regulations (if at all) may be needed to institutionalise the mitigation aspect. The preparedness measures must include some mechanism to induce a wider appreciation and sensitisation about the natural environment and ecology of the ANIs. This can be achieved through existing institutional networks such as schools, and various literacy and health programmes.

The coastal management policies must emphasise the issue of livelihood security of poor fishing communities, as well as the developmental needs of the region. Good coastal management thus, needs the involvement of all stakeholders, from government organisations of coastal villages to industry and facilitators like conservators, environmental NGOs and scientists.

Disaster Management/Plan/Strategy/ Mechanism in ANI

Tsunami: Damage Assessment and Assistance[5]

ANI administration has prepared a memorandum on the damage caused by the tsunami in ANI. This report puts, as on January 2005, the number of loss of human lives, and the number of missing and injured persons at 1942, 5555 and 1514, respectively. The report highlights severe damage to the infrastructure. This included submergence of 20 MW power house, damage to 21 jetties, roads, bridges and 13,950 ha of plantation and field crop. As a result, the economy of these islands has been badly affected. Revival of agriculture, industry, tourism, and fishery will require special efforts in the islands.

The report estimated a total cost of Rs. 3,836.56 crore for addressing the damage. However, to meet the immediate needs for gratuitous and temporary relief, out of Rs. 139.46 crore requested by the ANI administration Rs. 120.45 crore was approved by the Central government. Subsequently, a High Level Committee—set up to facilitate assessment, development, implementation and monitoring of relief programmes and provide necessary guidance and approvals—approved assistance of Rs. 2,430.12 crore. With this the total approved assistance as on February 2005 was Rs. 2,550.57 crore. Sector-wise summary of assistance sought for reconstruction and rehabilitation is given in Annexure 13.2.

Action taken by ANI Administration

The memorandum prepared by the ANI administration acknowledges the importance of early warning of impending disaster and its effective and speedy dissemination to the people in successfully reducing the impact of the disaster. It further notes, that the strategic planning and quick thinking on the part of the administration resulted in implementation of a number of effective steps to reduce the impact of the disaster and prevent secondary disasters even though the primary disaster could not be prevented due to lack of any tsunami warning system in the country. A list of measures taken by the administration to provide immediate relief to people is in Annexure 13.3. The report emphasises the need to integrate disaster mitigation with developmental policy.

Due to lack of information on financial, administrative and institutional arrangements in ANI for prevention, and mitigation of the impact of natural occurrences, it was not possible to attempt an analysis of the preparedness and mitigation measures implemented in ANI. Thus, the next section makes

5. See the *Memorandum on Earthquake/tsunami Damages*, Andaman & Nicobar Islands, January 2005, and report on 'Proposed Rehabilitation Programme', prepared by the office of the Chief Coordinator of the Core Group on Tsunami Rehabilitation Programme.

some broad suggestions to improve preparedness and strategies for enhancing resilience to cope with disasters.

Suggestions

The states have the responsibility to provide security to its citizens, especially the poor and underprivileged—who are unlikely to have the capacity to protect themselves from unseen and uncertain natural hazards, simply because their present itself is at stake. There is, thus, a need for greater emphasis on reducing risk factors by preventing/reducing the negative impact in the event of a natural phenomenon. This can happen when disaster prevention and mitigation is considered a high-return investment with benefits in the form of long-term cumulative cost savings. Apportioning funds towards such long-term objectives however, requires enhanced social awareness and strong political determination.

Disaster management should be mainstreamed into development strategies/projects of all stakeholders—national, state and local governments, and international organisations, including the UN and international financial institutions—in order to prevent and mitigate the impact of natural disasters and thus save precious human lives, minimise other economic and ecological losses, and mobilise larger outlays on reconstruction and rehabilitation.

In developing policies to deal with natural hazards it is important to ensure that the management approach is focused, action oriented, and transparent with realistic targets and clear accountability. Measurable indicators should be developed to help governments assess their progress in implementation of the programmes. ANI administration needs to be better equipped to undertake techno-economic and environmental appraisal of developmental projects to ensure the suitability of such projects for the UT. Ecological monitoring of various natural assets is yet another necessity. A suitable administrative arrangement for this purpose needs to be created.

The provision for disaster preparedness and mitigation needs to be built into the state plans, and not as a part of calamity relief. Financial and institutional arrangement for calamity relief, though of paramount importance, should be such that these induce preparedness and mitigation measures. Additionally, the developmental efforts of the state plans should be adequately supplemented with rules and regulations that circumscribe exposure and vulnerability to disasters and calamities.

The preparedness measures must include some mechanism to induce a wider appreciation and sensitisation about the unique natural environment and ecology of the ANIs and the risks associated with the unsustainable use of natural resources.

Development and strengthening of institutions, mechanisms and capacities at all levels, in particular at the community levels that can contribute to building hazard resilience is extremely important. Community level institutions can play an important role in this context as they can be important referral point between community/people and the government. They can help in building a culture of safety and resilience among people. They can also spread awareness among people about various programmes of the government such as early warning system, and evacuation plans; and educate people about the importance of conservation and sustainable use of natural capital and the need to follow safety plans. At the same time they can help put together and institutionalise the widely dispersed traditional knowledge and customs to mitigate the risk of natural hazards. Government responses based on community's own priorities, knowledge, and resources are likely to be more acceptable to people and thus more effective in reducing risk factors.

Adequate provision and maintenance of physical infrastructure such as safe shelter in the event of a natural phenomenon can be very capital intensive and can divert limited resources towards reducing perceived but infrequent risks rather than addressing more urgent social needs. Lifeline infrastructure in at-risk areas, such as health centres/hospitals, offices, emergency headquarters, schools, must be disaster-proof—serving both a protective and symbolic function. People are more likely to respond positively to evacuation plans when protective shelters are familiar structures located in familiar places.

Trust of community/people in government machinery is an important factor determining cooperation/positive responses from people in governments' efforts towards reducing risk factors. Good governance in general would go a long way in winning people's trust and thus ensuring their cooperation.

Broader financial arrangement, in terms of social security and insurance can also be a significant institutional mechanism for relief and rehabilitation.

ANNEXURE 13.1

Tenth Plans Schemes Towards Disaster Preparedness and Mitigation

The following schemes under the Tenth Plan may be considered as developmental expenditures towards disaster preparedness and mitigation.

Volume I

Sector: Agriculture and Allied Activities

Sub-sector: Crop Husbandry

Scheme No. 4: Plant protection including surveillance and quarantine

Scheme No. 6: National agricultural insurance scheme

Sub-sector: Soil Conservation

Scheme No. 1: Conservation of soil in ANIs

Scheme No. 2: Reclamation of saline affected land, stream bank erosion, prevention of gravel deposition and drainage scheme

Sub-sector: Fisheries

Scheme No. 7: Welfare of fisherman families

Sub-sector: Forestry and Wildlife

Scheme No. 4: Natural regeneration and enrichment of forests

Scheme No. 11: Biodiversity and wildlife conservation, and eco-development

Scheme No. 13: Protection of forests and coastal ecosystems

Scheme No. 14: Conservation of mangroves

Scheme No. 15: Ecotourism

Volume II

Sector: Irrigation and Flood Control

Sub-sector: Minor Irrigation

Scheme No. 3: Flood control including anti sea-erosion in ANIs

Volume III

Sector: Transport

Sub-sector: Ports and Lighthouses

Scheme No. 5: Establishment and maintenance of local navigational aids at various ports in ANIs

Scheme No. 9: Fire and safety, health, welfare, quality management and training

Scheme No. 10: Port conservancy and pollution control

Sector: Communication

Sub-sector: Island Communication

Scheme No. 1: modernisation of island communication

...Contd. ...

...Contd. ...

Sector: Science and Technology

Sub-sector: Science and Technology

Scheme No. 2: Ecology and environment

Scheme No. 3: Establishment of pollution control committee

Volume IV

Sector: Social Services

Sub-sector: Social Security and Welfare

Scheme No. 1: Home for orphan girls

Scheme No. 3: Home for aged and infirm

Scheme No. 7: Home for neglected juveniles

Sub-sector: Relief on account of Natural Calamities

Scheme No. 3: Enhancing preparedness in managing disasters

ANNEXURE 13.2A

Summary of Reconstruction and Rehabilitation Assistance

State/Union Territory	*State/UT Damage Assessment Report*[1]	*Category*[5]	*Request Noted by Central Government*[2]	*IMG Recommen -dation*	*Approved by the HLC*[3]	*Balance Unallocated*[4]
1	*2*	*3*	*4*	*5*	*6*	*7*
Andaman &	3836.56	A	2261.73	313.19	313.19	
		B	157.92	215.65	215.65	
		(A + B)	(2419.65)	(528.84)	(528.84)	
		C	78.76	293.04	293.04	
		D	1338.15	1728.69	1728.69	
		Total	**3836.56**	**2550.57**	**2550.57**	**1285.99**

Notes: 1. The assistance request (column 4) noted by the Central government as on January 17, 2005 need to be reconciled with the final assistance requests submitted by the Union Territory as in column 2.

2. Based on HLC Meeting Agenda Papers Office Memorandum No. 32-2/2005-NDM-I, Ministry of Home Affairs (NDM Division) dated February 15, 2005 for Andaman & Nicobar Islands.

3. Based on Office Memorandum No. 32-2/2005-NDM-I, Ministry of Home Affairs (NDM Division) dated February 15, 2005 for Andaman & Nicobar Islands

4. Calculated as the difference of the estimate of assistance given by the UT damage assessment report and the amount approved by the HLC.

5. A. Assistance, which is as per the CRF/NCCF Norms

B. Assistance, which is covered under the norms but will require relaxation in regard to the scale of grants

C. Assistance, which is covered under the norms but will require a special package as mere relaxation in the scale would not suffice

D. Assistance, which is not covered under the norms and is to be covered under the special package.

IMG and HLC are Inter-Ministerial Group and high Level Committee, respectively.

Source: Report on 'Proposed Rehabilitation Programme', prepared by the office of the Chief Coordinator of the Core Group on Tsunami Rehabilitation Programme.

ANNEXURE 13.2B

Sector-wise Summary of Reconstruction and Rehabilitation Assistance Requested by ANI*

	Roads and Bridges	*Power/ ICT*	*Ports & Jetties*	*Fisheries/ Boats*	*Agriculture/ Forests/Animal Husbandry/Livelihood*	*Water & Sewerage*	*Social Infrastructure***	*Housing*	*Long-term Infrastructure Upgradation*	*Total*
Andaman & Nicobar Islands	178.20	483.18	302.08	37.02	1666.54[a]	29.01	283.62	302.80	414.65	3697.1

*Notes:** Does not include gratuitous relief of Rs. 139.46 crores requested by ANI.

** Social Infrastructure includes social security of victims, repairs, reconstruction and restoration of Government buildings, public distribution system, industries department, government polytechnic and college (JNRM), police department, social welfare (*Anganwadis*), labour department, education, health, panchayati raj institutions, municipal council, ANDICO and losses to co-operative societies.

a. Includes Rs. 898.34 crore for reclamation of plantation area and regeneration/rejuvenation and construction for revival of agricultural activities in paddy lands as well as loss of vegetable/paddy crops and plantation crop amounting to Rs. 598.35 crore.

Source: Report on 'Proposed Rehabilitation Programme', prepared by the office of the Chief Coordinator of the Core Group on Tsunami Rehabilitation Programme.

ANNEXURE 13.3

Measures taken by the ANI Administration to provide Immediate Relief after Tsunami

- 205 relief camps were set up, where about 45,811 people were staying.
- Medical teams were dispatched in sufficient numbers.
- The disposal of dead body was given priority.
- The help of Defense Forces was obtained to gain access to the remote islands.
- Special Relief Officers were posted in all the islands to coordinate the relief work.
- The Deputy Residents Commissioners of Kolkata and Chennai were designated as Special Relief Officer and assigned the task of coordinating procurement and dispatch of relief supplies from Kolkata and Chennai.
- An officer of the level of Joint Secretary to Government of India from Ministry of Home Affairs was always available at the islands to facilitate coordination with Government of India for relief operations.
- Government of India mobilised relief supplies from various sources to assist Andaman & Nicobar Administration for relief work.
- The only helicopter of Andaman & Nicobar Administration was put to its full use for air-lifting of doctors, engineers and other personnel engaged in relief work.
- The entire health delivery system was reactivated and medical relief was organised at a war footing. All steps were taken to ensure that there is no epidemic.
- Lt. Governor announced an *ex gratia* payment of Rs. 2000/- per family to all affected families from LG's relief fund.
- Immediate steps were taken to restore roads and bridges, power, water and inter-island water transport.

References

A.F. Ferguson & Company (2003). *Perspective Plan for Tourism Development in Andaman & Nicobar Islands*, Ministry of Tourism & Culture, Department of Tourism, Government of India, February.

Andaman & Nicobar Administration. *Vision Document of the State Development Report*, pp.158-63.

———. *Annual Tribal Sub-Plan (2003).*

———. *Annual Tribal Sub-Plan (2003-04).*

———. *Tenth Five Year Tribal Sub-Plan (2002-07).*

———. *Basic Statistics*, 1996-97 to 1998-99, Directorate of Economics and Statistics, The Manager, Government Press.

———. *Basic Statistics*, Directorate of Economic and Statistics, Andaman and Nicobar Administration, Port Blair.

———. (2002). *Tourism Statistics*, Planning and Statistical Unit, DIPT, Port Blair, October.

Andrews, H.V. and A. Vaughan (2005). "Ecological Impact Assessment in the Andaman Islands and Observations on the Nicobar Islands", in R. Kaul, and V. Menon (eds.), *The Ground Beneath the Waves: Post Tsunami Impact Assessment of Wildlife and their Habitats in India*, Vol. II, Wildlife Trust of India, New Delhi, pp. 78-104.

Awaradi, S.A. (1990). *Computerised Master Plan (1991-2021) for Welfare of Primitive Tribes of Andaman & Nicobar Islands*, Andaman and Nicobar Administration, Government of India, Port Blair, India.

Census of India (2001). *Provisional Population Tables*, CSO, Government of India.

Central Marine Fisheries Research Institute (CMFRI) (1975). *Assessment of Fishery Resource Characteristics of the Penacid Shrimps of the East Cost of India*, Study Report, Kochi.

Crick, Malcolm (1992). "Life in the Informal Sector: Street Guides in Kandy, Sri Lanka", in David Harrison (ed.), *Tourism and the Less Developed Countries*, Ch. 10, John Wiley & Sons, US, pp.135-147.

Dam Roy, S. and P. Krishnan (2005). "Mangrove Stands of Andamans vis-à-vis Tsunami", *Current Science*, Vol. 89(11), pp.1800-1804.

Fletcher, J.E (1989). "Input-Output Analysis and Tourism Impact Studies", *Annals of Tourism Research*, Vol. 16(4), pp.515-29.

Forest Survey of India (2005). *State of Forest Report 2005*, Dehradun, India.

Foundation for Aviation and Sustainable Tourism (2002). *Andaman and Nicobar Islands: Action Plan for Sustainable Development*, November, New Delhi.

Government of India (2004). *Report of the Twelfth Finance Commission.*

———. (2002). *10th Five Year Plan, 2002-2007*, Planning Commission.

———. (2002a). *Report of the Steering Committee on Tourism for the Tenth Five Year Plan (2002-2007)*, Planning Commission, TFYP, Steering Committee No. 12/2002.

———. (2002b). *Report of the Working Group on Tourism for the Tenth Five Year Plan (2002-2007)*, Planning Commission, TFYP Working Paper Sr. No. 85/2002.

———. (2001). *Provisional Population Tables*, Paper 1 of 2001, Series 36, Andaman and Nicobar Islands, Census of India, Dr. Sharat Chauhan, Director of Census Operations, A & N Islands.

———. (1996). *Development Strategy for Environmentally Sustainable Tourism in the Andamans* in 3 volumes, World Tourism Organisation and United Nations Development Programme, Ministry of Civil Aviation and Department of Tourism, Government of India, Shnakland Cox Entec, August 1996.

———. (1991a). *Census of India 1991*, Tables on Houses and Household Amenities, Census Abstract, Series 27, Part VIII, Andaman and Nicobar Islands, Directorate of Census Operations, A & N Islands.

———. (1991b). *General Population Tables and Primary Census Abstract*, Series 27, Part II A & Part II B, Andaman and Nicobar Islands, Directorate of Census Operations, A&N Islands.

———. (1990). *Report of the National Commission for Scheduled Castes and Scheduled Tribes, Atrocities on Scheduled Castes & Tribes: Causes and Remedies Commissioner for Scheduled Castes and Scheduled Tribes*, April 1990.

———. (1988). *Census of India 1981*, Series 24, Andaman & Nicobar Islands, Part IX, Special Tables for Scheduled Tribes.

———. (1988). *Report of the Commissioner for Scheduled Castes and Scheduled Tribes*, Twenty-Eighth Report, 1986-87.

———. (1983). *Report of the Commissioner for Scheduled Castes and Scheduled Tribes*, Fourth Report, April 1981–March 1982.

———. (1976). *Census of India 1971*, Series 23, Andaman & Nicobar Islands, Part V-A, Special Tables on Scheduled Tribes.

———. *Action Plan Recommended by the Task Force set up by the Ministry of Tourism*, GoI.

Hall, Michael C. (1992). "Sex-tourism in South-east Asia", in David Harrison (ed.), *Tourism and the Less Developed Countries*, Ch. 5, John Wiley & Sons, USA, pp.64-74.

Hall, Derek R. (1992a). "Tourism Development in Cuba", in David Harrison (ed.), *Tourism and the Less Developed Countries*, Ch. 8, John Wiley & Sons, USA, pp.102-120.

Harrison, David (ed.) (1992). *Tourism and the Less Developed Countries*, John Wiley & Sons, USA.

IIRS (2003). *Biodiversity Characterisation at Landscape Level in the Andaman and Nicobar Islands using Satellite Remote Sensing and Geographic Information System*. Indian Institute of Remote Sensing, Department of Space, Government of India.

Jayaraj, R.S.C. and H.V. Andrews (2005). *Andaman and Nicobar Islands Union Territory Biodiversity Strategy and Action Plan*, prepared under the National Biodiversity Strategy and Action Plan-India. GOI/ UNDP, Centre for Herpetology, Madras Crocodile Bank Trust, Mamallapuram- 603 104, Tamil Nadu.

Jayaraj, R.S.C. (2003). "Forest Management in the Andaman & Nicobar Islands with Special Reference to Ten Selected Islands", presented in the Workshop on *Integrated Coastal Zone Management Plan (ICZMP)*, Institute of Ocean Management, Anna University, Port Blair, March.

Jayaraj, R.S.C. and P.M. Bhatt (1999), *Bamboos in the Andaman and Nicobar Islands*, (Unpublished), prepared for the Seminar on Bamboos, Bangalore.

Khatri, T.C. (1993). "Butterflies of the Andaman and Nicobar Islands: Conservation Concerns", *J. Res. on the Lepidoptera*, Vol. 32, pp.170-184.

Lundberg, Donald E., Mink H. Stavenca and M. Krishnamoorthy (1995). *Tourism Economics*, John Wiley & Sons, USA.

The Marine Products Export Development Authority (MPEDA) (2001). *Report of the Expert Committee for the Preparation of Fisheries Policy for Andaman and Nicobar Islands*, p.55.

———. (2004). *Export from Andaman and Nicobar Islands during 2002-03*, p.3.

M.S. Swaminathan Research Foundation (MSSRF) (2005). *Action Plan for Development of post-tsunami "New Andamans"*, Chennai, p.97.

Naithani, H.B. (1999). "Nomenclature and Identity of Some Bamboo Species", *Indian Forester, Vol.* 125 (11), pp.1129-1140.

Panigrahi, Srikanta K. (2003). *"Eco-Tourism in India", Employment News*, June 21-27, New Delhi, India, p.1.

Planning Commission (2002). *National Human Development Report*, Oxford, New Delhi.

Rajavel, N. (1998). *Tourism in Andaman and Nicobar Islands*, Manas Publications, New Delhi, India.

Rao, P.S.N. (1996). "Phyto-Geography of the Andaman and Nicobar Islands", *Malayan Nat. J.*, Vol. 50, pp.57-79.

Richter, Linda K. (1992). "Political Instability and Tourism in the Third World", in David Harrison (ed.), *Tourism and the Less Developed Countries*, Ch. 3, John Wiley & Sons, USA, pp.35-46.

Sankaran, R. (2005). "Impact of the Earthquake and the Tsunami on the Nicobar Islands", in R. Kaul, and V. Menon (eds.), *The Ground Beneath the Waves: Post Tsunami Impact Assessment of Wildlife and their Habitats in India*, Vol. II, Wildlife Trust of India, New Delhi, pp.10-77.

Small Industries Development Bank of India (SIDBI) (2000). *Annual Report 1999-2000*.

Sinclair, M. Thea and Mike Stabler (1997). *The Economics of Tourism*, Routledge, USA.

Singh, Ratandeep (1998). *Dynamics of Modern Tourism*, Kanishka Publishers, Distributors, New Delhi.

Singh, M.P. (2003). *Working Plan of Middle Andaman Division (2003 - 2013)*.

———. (2002). *Working Plan of South Andaman Division (2002 - 2012)*.

The Economic Times (2003). "Mauritius, Lanka gain on Indian Arrivals", July 23, p.4.

Turner, J.R., D. Vousden, R. Klaus, C. Suryanarayana, D. Fenner, K. Venkataraman, P.T. Rajan and N.V. Subba Rao (2001). *Remote Sensing and Rapid Site Assessment Survey*, Report of Phase I: April 2001, GOI/UNDP GEF, Coral Reef Ecosystems of the Andaman Islands, New Delhi.

Vijayan, L., R. Sankaran, K. Sivakumar and V. Muruagan (2000). *A Study on the Ecology, Status and Conservation Perspectives of Certain Rare Endemic Avifauna of the Andaman and Nicobar Islands*, Salim Ali Centre for Ornithology and Natural History, Coimbatore.

Wilkinson, P.F. (1989). "Strategies for Tourism in Island Economies", *Annals of Tourism Research*, Vol. 16 (2), pp.153-77.

Web Sources:

http://andaman.nic.in

http://mauritius.voyaz.com/

http://www.mauritius.net

http://www.tourismofindia.com/misc/tourismpolicy.htm

http://www.visitmaldives.com

http://www.world-tourism.org

http://www.wttc.org

Others:

Communication with Mr. K. S. Siddhu, Chief Coordinator, Core Group, Tsunami Rehabilitation Programme, Planning Commission.

Detailed Note for Inclusion in the State Development Report of the Andaman and Nicobar Islands, Andaman and Nicobar Administration, Tourism Vision.